GRAHAM FRAZER AND
GEORGE LANCELLE

Zhirinovsky

THE LITTLE BLACK BOOK:
MAKING SENSE OF THE SENSELESS

PENGUIN BOOKS

PENGUIN BOOKS

Published by the Penguin Group
Penguin Books Ltd, 27 Wrights Lane, London w8 5TZ, England
Penguin Books USA Inc., 375 Hudson Street, New York, New York 10014, USA
Penguin Books Australia Ltd, Ringwood, Victoria, Australia
Penguin Books Canada Ltd, 10 Alcorn Avenue, Toronto, Ontario, Canada M4V 3B2
Penguin Books (NZ) Ltd, 182–190 Wairau Road, Auckland 10, New Zealand

Penguin Books Ltd, Registered Offices: Harmondsworth, Middlesex, England

First published 1994
1 3 5 7 9 10 8 6 4 2

Set by Datix International Limited, Bungay, Suffolk
Printed in England by Clays Ltd, St Ives plc

CONTENTS

PREFACE

The title *Little Black Book* is a clear reference to Mao Tse-Tung's *Little Red Book*, which contains sayings of the red tyrant of China. There are differences between the two, the most obvious being that Mao's book was compiled by himself and Zhirinovsky's by us. The colour black of fascism (or of national socialism, as Zhirinovsky calls it) replaces the red of Communism. Also Chairman Mao was in power when he wrote it, whereas Zhirinovsky has made his statements while aspiring to supreme power.

Mao Tse-Tung and Zhirinovsky have, however, one thing in common: neither of them seems to have been deterred by the destructive force of nuclear weapons or, more precisely, both have wanted to give the impression of not being afraid of it. Zhirinovsky has repeatedly threatened Japan and Germany, for instance, with nuclear attacks, which the rest of the world fondly hopes is mere posturing and exhibitionism, that is, a kind of hoax. Mao Tse-Tung, latter-day Chinese sage as he was, said in 1955: 'The atomic hoax of the United States cannot scare the Chinese people. We have a population of 600 million, and a territory of 9.6 million square kilometres. That little bit of atomic weaponry that the United States has cannot annihilate the Chinese people. Even if the United States had more powerful atom bombs and used them on China, blasted a hole in the Earth or blew it to pieces, [while] this might be a matter of great significance to the solar system, it would still be an insignificant matter as far as the universe as a whole is concerned.'[1] Mao did have original ideas.

1 V. Xuanji (*Mao's Selected Works*), pp. 136–7, 'A Conversation between Mao and Finland's First Ambassador to China'.

Zhirinovsky also has original ideas; not least is he prepared to threaten nuclear first strikes, but there is also, of course, his obsession of wishing Russian soldiers to wash their boots in the Indian Ocean. But these are firmly embedded in a confused jumble of present-day Russian 'views': banalities. The wild ideas have to be associated with the homely, the bellicose with the blander side. As a consummate demagogue or politician, if you like (according to him, the two concepts are more or less co-extensive), he has an unusually keen sense of what the prevalent prejudices, dreams, fears and aspirations are in Russia, and he tailors his pronouncements to what the audiences he addresses want to hear. As W. Lepukhin, a member of the Russian Duma, said: 'Vladimir Wolfovich has no ideology. His consciousness is the same as the rest of the confused Russian reality; so it is received by the masses as revelation.' (*Die Zeit*, 14.1.94.)

Russian banalities are to a large extent unknown in the West, and one man's banality is another man's novelty. One thing is certain: his ideas startle the West.[2] At the moment Zhirinovsky is interested only in Russian opinions and attitudes: he has, or wants to give the impression of having, a well-developed contempt for Western and other countries, for their preferences and current views of the commonplace.

What he says abroad, apart from Serbia perhaps, serves only two purposes: to get publicity for himself in the Western media and to demonstrate to his audience back home his scorn for Western countries in particular, which are supposed to be much admired at the moment by many reformist Russian leaders, and less and less by the population, thereby also defying the respect that the West expects from a country whose social, economic and political systems have

---

2 They also startle his own audience, for he has a knack of compounding banalities to produce an amalgam unheard of before – for instance, every Christian should love his neighbour and oppose barriers to nations' coming together; this is not quite what is implied, however, when he says: 'I love the Balts . . . We won't build any frontiers.'

proved unviable. His views also fly in the face of the current 'informed' opinion of the reformers in Russia, who are trying to find a way out of the quagmire in which the Soviet Union landed Russia.

But perhaps most of all he brings to the surface desires in his audience that they did not know they had, which, however, correspond to their deep longings: he is a virtuoso of a demagogue.

Russia's only claim to superpower status is its military might and, in particular, its nuclear arsenal. In the words of Andrei Kozyrev, Russian Foreign Minister: 'Russia is still a superpower, a nuclear superpower, a military superpower, which can probably destroy the world in thirty minutes.'[3] This is perhaps a crass simplification of what the reformers in the Russian leadership think of their country's present importance in the world, a reductionism and vulgarization worthy of Zhirinovsky.

But what is the status of the set of banalities of which Zhirinovsky is the mirror? And how does he relate his original ideas to banalities? Does he really express that body of opinion for the sole purpose of making himself popular because a large section, perhaps the majority, of the Russian population share it and like to hear it said out loud in public? How far does he take these views seriously and believe in them?

What Zhirinovsky voices in his speeches, statements and writings (when he does not happen to outline an original idea) are not so much opinions as 'mental tics', such as people would conjure up when daydreaming about their country, its identity, its standing and importance in the world, and about their own identity as defined by belonging to that country, as well as the troubles which may derive from all that. These underpin the utterances a man might make in a bar after a good many glasses of vodka when rational thought is not paramount.

Such 'views' are determined largely by a continuing tradition that is made up of myths and realities about past history as handed down

3 *Call Me Hitler*, BBC 1, *Panorama*, 28.3.94.

by generations up to the present time. They are complemented by individual experiences, but what really counts is the body of such shared traditions and experience, reduced to the lowest common denominator; that is, the 'matters of common knowledge' that thinking people may be ashamed to voice or think unnecessary to mention, and, for that very reason, these are precisely the things that foreigners are unlikely to know. The elements in such a body of 'knowledge' may vary from person to person but are sufficiently uniform to constitute a rudimentary national identity. Politicians, who share it, also take it for granted and inevitably formulate their programmes taking it into consideration. Their success or failure depends to a large extent on how well they manage to incorporate it and build upon it.

There is such a body of 'opinions' in every country; parts of it may be gradually covered up, shaped or eliminated as new shared knowledge and experience are absorbed by the population. When politicians are at a loss for a real opinion they may fall back upon this shared body of commonplaces, as we can see, for example, in Britain when questions of the European Union are discussed, or in Germany (problems of the *Gastarbeiter*), or in France (immigration).

We have compiled Zhirinovsky's imaginary book from his statements, speeches and writings, selecting representative views that belong to this body of 'matters of common knowledge', shared prejudices and aspirations on which any populist demagogue builds his career. If Zhirinovsky falters, somebody else is likely to step in his shoes and do much the same, perhaps less outspokenly, less frankly and with much less skill; but the body of opinion reflecting that lowest common denominator in Russia will remain the same for a good while.

For in Russia all political and social thought of the past two or three generations has remained frozen by the Utopian ideology of Communism, which has been resolutely maintained by the leadership, although such faith in it as there ever was has dwindled at an ever-quickening pace. Promises and hopes have gradually proved to be hollow and vain; most of the leadership and the population have become more and more disillusioned and cynical as the gulf between theory and practice has widened. Faith and hope had, in fact, been in fairly short supply since the Stalinist period. From 1990 onwards Russians have been reaching back to their pre-Communist past, dusting down many old attitudes and ideas, which, in some form or other, continued their subterranean existence under the permafrost of totalitarian Communism. As we shall see, Zhirinovsky is particularly careful to exclude the Communist tradition from his rhetoric, although neither could he help to preserve, nor did he want to discard, anything that his potential constituency has kept alive.

He also has a 'subtext' that may add up to giving some coherence to his practical suggestions, such as they are; there may, after all, be a 'figure in the carpet' – a matter that we shall examine further in the Postscript. In the Introduction we discuss all such traditions as live on in the mind of the 'common man', Zhirinovsky's 'little man', with whom he resolutely identifies himself. The main part of this little book contains his sayings, which are sometimes relevant in more than one context, with commentary where necessary.

INTRODUCTION

The prevalent mood of present-day Russian society is characterized by disillusionment, resentment and despair; these are feelings on which populist demagogues like Zhirinovsky construct their platforms. To what extent can such a mood be traced back to past experience as it lives on, perhaps in a distorted or exaggerated form in the mind, and what part of it is a reaction to the present situation?

IN THE CLUTCHES OF THE PAST

'The Russians idolize the past, hate the present and fear the future,' said Chekhov. Most nations do their best to make the most of their past, usually emphasizing its moments of glory or supposed happiness (the blurred outlines of distant events are the stuff that national myths are made of). Russians, however, differ from most other nations in one important respect: they seem to draw almost as much upon past misfortunes and suffering as upon past glory and happiness when they think about the present and the future. (A similar attitude can be found in Serbia: the battle of Kosovo in 1389, where the Serbs suffered a crushing defeat at the hand of the Ottoman Turkish army, resulting in four and a half centuries of Ottoman rule, is perhaps the most fêted event in Serbian history.)

Foreign invasions have for centuries weighed heavily on the Russian mind: the memory of the Tatar invasions of 1240, in particular, whose consequence, the rule of the Golden Horde, retarded the formation of a properly unified Russian state and the free development of society and culture by at least two hundred years and distorted it, perhaps for that reason, in the long run.

The Tatar invasion has, however, left another legacy: the feeling that Europe is indebted to Russia for having saved Christian Europe from the barbarian hordes, a debt, which – it is felt in Russia – has never been repaid or even acknowledged by appropriate gratitude. The Europeans have always assumed that what saved them was the sudden death of the Great Khan in Mongolia, which prompted the invading Batu Khan to abandon the European campaign and return to Asia, and that the Teutonic Knights also played a hand at Liegnitz.

Then there were the invasions from the west: the Lithuanians, the Poles, the Germans, the Swedes, Napoleon and, finally, the Germans again in the two world wars. Russians played an important role in defeating Napoleon alongside many European nations. They were on the side of the Entente powers in the First World War, and the Soviet Union as an ally was crucially important in saving Europe from Nazi Germany in the Second World War. Although this debt has always been duly acknowledged, the Russian sense of having been short-changed has persisted. Zhirinovsky also claims that Russia saved Europe from the Ottoman Turks, but, in fact, they chose the route across the Balkans to Hungary and Vienna. The only significant invasions from the east were the Japanese ones; most invasions in north Asia were undertaken by the Russians in conquering the whole of Siberia, and later Central Asia and, nearer home, the Caucasus.

Striving for security, Russia has acquired a vast empire, for no country can ever feel absolutely safe: expansionism has become a habit, almost a complex, to which Zhirinovsky panders in his political programme. But there is more to it than that.

A LAND IN SEARCH OF WARM SEAS

Zhirinovsky's expansionist programme perplexes foreigners far afield and frightens neighbours. The last thing Russia needs now is more land, a Swiss or a Japanese would think: making the most of what you have got is the hallmark of successful nations in history.

Russians look at the USA and Canada, on a resource-rich continent not dissimilar from their own territory, and ask themselves why they cannot be as rich. In a BBC TV *Panorama* programme (28.3.94) about Zhirinovsky the journalist asked a north Russian peasant couple why they supported Zhirinovsky. The woman said the following: 'Ideally, everything ought to be Russian, everything ours, home-produced. What a country this is, so much land, land, so much forest ... we ought to be the richest country in the world, but we're beggars, downright beggars.' Zhirinovsky thinks he has got the answer for her. Sea borders are the best borders, he contends, talking of England and of its empire: 'England was a sea power with the best sea borders! Mongolia has no sea borders: it is a shabby state. Today we have no colonies. The colonies provided England with the lion's share of its profit. Today we receive nothing from colonies and yet feed beggarly appendages. We should be thinking about colonies.' (Clearly, Switzerland is not uppermost in Zhirinovsky's mind, whereas reflecting on Swiss history might do him and modern Russians a lot of good, since it is the very opposite of a shabby state.)

If only Russia had access to a warm ocean – which for her would have to be the Indian Ocean, or the Mediterranean at least, instead of the frozen Arctic coastline and cold Baltic shore – then at last it could be a success, becoming almost a giant peninsula with other lesser peninsulas, China, India and Indo-China. Hence the logic of the 'Last Dash to the South'.

Zhirinovsky's solution is typical of Russian history. Russia possesses reasonably warm seas already: the Caspian and the Black Sea, which gives it access to the Mediterranean and, beyond it, to the world's oceans. This partly explains the long tsarist quest for Constantinople. It is typical of Russians to pose their problems in terms that require solutions in the shape of extending their borders. Dissatisfied with what they have got and unable to digest it properly (unlike the Swiss and the Japanese, for example), they are like peasants covetous of their neighbours' land. Not displaced persons, they are misplaced persons in their own eyes, because they live in the north and hanker after warm holiday resorts.

Zhirinovsky has a plan for combining 'business' with pleasure, 'business' being the occupation of new territories. He suggests that Russian troops should be issued with new and better automatic weapons, which would make it possible 'for any platoon of Russian soldiers to pacify any region. And what is more, that should not be an unpleasant affair. It is always necessary to bring order to these regions. So, on the shores of the Indian Ocean and of the Mediterranean there should be centres for resting, youth camps, sanatoria, dispensaries. A vast construction project should be initiated for the purpose of rest and relaxation. The whole of the south should be an unbroken series of sanatoria, resting homes for the industrial north, for people of any nationality, for all nationalities. A unified, uniform economic, legal and political space will create favourable conditions for the development of all arts and crafts, for culture, for education, life, in such a way as to satisfy the wishes of all.'[1]

Zhirinovsky does not suggest the execution of such a plan along, say, the shores of the Caspian Sea: that would not be any good; no one would believe that such a plan could be realized there. His audience prefers to hear about some impossible project so long as it is outside the area Russia already possesses, as if he were saying, 'There, away in far-off lands that we will occupy, everything will be possible.' So long as they do it at other people's expense. He also outlines plans for the local population of such occupied areas: where there is a dense concentration of people they can retain their customs, and part of the population will anyway live on the steppes, in the mountains, in the desert, in yurts, nomadic tents ... they will tend their cattle; that is quite normal, he says. This plan, however, would soon send shivers down the spines of Estonians, Latvians or Lithuanians, many thousands of whom were indeed made to live on the steppes of Central Asia, where they were deported after the occupation of the Baltic states by Stalin in 1940. But to Zhirinovsky's Russian

1 V. *Zhirinovsky, The Last Dash to the South*, Moscow, 1993, p. 66.

followers all that would seem reasonable. These things are due to the Russians; they have endured enough. 'We have suffered enough. We should make other people suffer,' said Zhirinovsky, clearly expecting, and probably getting, approval from his listeners.

It is a culture of self-pity, in which a vast capacity for warm, human sympathy towards others can turn into an individual's self-obsession if he is outraged by what he regards as a bad hand dealt to him or his people by cruel fate. The anger turns outwards: a man killing others while being sorry for himself. But the Russian people are 'full of mutually contradictory properties', says Berdyaev:[2] 'despotism, the hypertrophy of the state and, on the other hand, anarchism and licence; cruelty, a disposition to violence and, again, kindliness, humanity and gentleness; a belief in rites and ceremonies, but also a quest for truth; individualism, a heightened consciousness of personality, together with an impersonal collectivism; nationalism, laudation of the self and universalism, the ideal of the universal man; an eschatological messianic spirit of region, and a devotion that finds its expression in externals; a search for God and a militant godlessness; humility and arrogance; slavery and revolt. But never has Russia been bourgeois.'

Also, they can give many things to those peoples that come under their sway, who should be grateful for it all. Russians, probably more than most colonizers, expect to be loved. As Russian troops were withdrawn from Central European countries in the Warsaw Pact, on the day of their departure many soldiers had flowers in their hands, hoping for a warm 'adieu', and were hurt when hardly anybody turned up at the railway stations, and those that did come seemed to attest a different frame of mind. Russians are sincerely hurt that they are not wanted in the Baltic states, for instance. It may be unrequited love, in response to which Zhirinovsky has made many harsh

2 N. A. Berdyaev, *The Russian Idea* (reprint), Greenwood Press, Westport, 1979.

statements about the former republics (see Chapter 1). It is partly that, but also they feel that they spent, or rather wasted, a lot of money on these republics – helped them to Russia's own detriment. An important point of Zhirinovsky's programme for the rehabilitation of the Russian economy is to stop providing former republics with fuel and raw materials and, of course, all kinds of aid, so they will come crawling back (see Chapter 1 and Chapter 5). It is quite true that in Soviet times some western and Caucasian republics had a higher standard of living than the Russian Federation, and the same was true of some Central European countries under Russian occupation. The Soviets did not benefit all that much from their colonies, failing to turn expansion to their profit, but at the same time they greatly hampered the economic development of those countries and republics. To judge by the words of Zhirinovsky, that will and readiness to make sacrifices for the sake of expansion is still there; it has survived another break in Russian history. Perhaps he hopes that next time it will turn out differently – a novel application of Dr Johnson's 'triumph of hope over experience'.

In any case, Zhirinovsky feels that Russia can bring peace and order to turbulent areas. That was, in fact, the case in Soviet times, and it was recognized by some people in the West too. In 1957 Carew Hunt, an Oxford don, by no means a left-winger, remarked to an East European: 'After all, the part of the world you come from caused two world wars, and now the Russians have taken it out of circulation. Shouldn't we be grateful?' That opinion may be echoed nowadays, given the crisis in the former Yugoslavia. An opportunity for Russian peace-keeping forces in Bosnia has already opened up. Zhirinovsky has certainly anticipated such a role for some time: 'I have an idea for ... using armies abroad ... soldiers under contract for hard currency could serve and perform tasks assigned by the world community,' he said in an interview given to *Krasnaya Zvezda* in May 1991.

It can be argued that Russia's vastness and propinquity to every chief geopolitical zone of the world, Europe, the Middle East, the Far

East and North America, has been Russia's curse. Not on island continents, as are the USA and Australia, it has to be worried about attacks from all quarters. Expansion into its vast abode has been the guiding dynamic of Russian history. Whenever it has a 'Time of Troubles' (see introduction to Chapter 5), with a loss of land, its immediate reaction afterwards has been to take it back and expand even further. By extending its power across the globe, even into Africa and fatally into Afghanistan, the USSR came unstuck.

Zhirinovsky's irredentist call to expand is just the latest in Russia's history, in its new 'Time of Troubles'. What looks antiquated and nineteenth-century to the West or Japan seems normal, a matter of common sense, to Zhirinovsky and his followers.

The singular lack of success in making Russia 'the richest country in the world' instead of being 'downright beggars' has given rise to two attitudes in many Russians: self-pity, sometimes bordering on despair, and an ever-present suspicion that they are victims of evil plots hatched either inside Russia or abroad.

PLOTS GALORE

Xenophobia in General and Anti-Semitism in Particular

As for internal enemies, the first on the list are the Jews. Anti-Semitism is, of course, far from being a monopoly of Russians, but it is said to permeate particularly deeply present-day Russian society. It has straddled the 'interruptions' that are 'characteristic of Russian history'.[3] In the twentieth century, for example, tsarist Russia's problems have been blamed on the Jews, just as has Communism, which, according to prevalent opinion, was foisted on Russia by 'Marx and the Jewish Bolsheviks: Lenin(!), Trotsky, etc.'. The same applies to the current economic reforms ('the Jewish Gaidar'), which have been

3 Berdyaev, *The Russian Idea.*

causing so much misery. Anti-Semitic rhetoric is therefore an absolute necessity for a populist demagogue. It is poignant that Zhirinovsky himself is half-Jewish, which he resolutely, though rather ineffectually, denies. The question is, did so many people vote for him despite that fact, or in ignorance of it, in the December 1993 elections? That is a question we do not feel qualified to answer, but if they supported him despite his having a Jewish lineage on his father's side, could it be that they think, 'There is our chance. We have a clever Jew on our side; he will surely be able to sort out those Jewish plotters, and he will know how to get hold of the secret of becoming a rich country, which those Westerners discuss at their G7 meetings, to which no Russian can gain entry'? (It must, however, be said that Zhirinovsky condemns Hitler for marring National Socialism with racism (see Chapter 6).)

As for conspiracy theory – another widespread feeling in many countries – it gains special meaning through Russian military might. One hundred years ago the Russian philosopher Vladimir Solovev wrote the following:

Let us imagine a person healthy in body and strong, talented and not unkind – for such is, quite justly, the general view of the Russian people. We know that this person (or people) is now in a very sorry state. If we want to help him, we have first to understand what is wrong with him. Thus we learn that he is not really mad; his mind is merely afflicted to a considerable extent by false ideas approaching *folie de grandeur* and a hostility toward everyone and everything. Indifferent to his real advantage, indifferent to the damage likely to be caused, he imagines dangers that do not exist and builds upon this the most absurd propositions. It seems to him that all his neighbors offend him, that they insufficiently bow to his greatness and in every way want to harm him. He accuses everyone in his family of damaging and deserting him, of crossing over to the enemy camp. He imagines that his neighbors want to undermine his house and even to launch an armed attack. Therefore he will spend enormous sums on the purchase of guns, revolvers and iron locks. If he has any time left, he will turn against his family.[4]

Added to this is the Russian feeling that – like the Serbs – Russians win wars and lose the peace. Zhirinovsky's bellicose rhetoric can hardly come as a surprise. In fact, any nationalist politician is likely to be 'afflicted' by the same sentiment. And nationalism – a pendant of the xenophobic conspiracy theory – is hardly to be avoided in the difficult times Russia is now going through.

The Vote of the Dead

One of the arguments G. K. Chesterton advanced – half tongue-in-cheek, no doubt – in defence of conservatism was that a real democracy cannot rely exclusively on the opinion of the people who happen to be alive at any particular time; the vote of dead forebears must equally be taken into account. In the case of fanatical nationalism the dead are enfranchised to help form a mythical public opinion, and the democracy embracing the dead is trusted to flourish. Is that, perhaps, the role of the word 'democratic' in the name of Zhirinovsky's party?

The Latest Avatar

Zhirinovsky's racism and xenophobia are amply illustrated in Chapter 6; they are of the usual kind, so they need little explanation. The only aspect of his stance that jars is that he does not want even Jews to leave Russia on the grounds that Russia has always been a multi-national society and should remain so (see Chapter 6), although he adds that ideally a nation should consist of only one nationality.

The main external enemy for Zhirinovsky is the West because anti-Western feeling is quickly spreading in Russia (see Chapter 6). He has

---

4 Quoted in Walter Laqueur, *Black Hundred*, Harper Collins, New York, 1993.

to ride this wave and can also use it for demonstrating his opposition to the present government, even though its 'market romanticism' is quickly fading.

ANTI-WESTERN ATTITUDES

Hostility to the West has a long and venerable history in Russia, although it has been punctuated by sometimes quite long periods when at least some sections of the society have succumbed to the blandishments of well-organized and intellectually sophisticated Western countries.

The oldest objection is a religious one, the opposition of the Orthodox Church to Rome, which has weathered all historical changes and is periodically revived through its association with Russian nationalism or with the Orthodox brotherhood idea. An example of this is the present Russian–Serbian axis (see Chapter 3).

A different but also fairly consistent anti-Western theme is that many Russians recoil from Western rationalism; on the theological plane medieval scholasticism was always considered spiritually barren and antagonistic to Orthodoxy and, later, to the 'Russian idea'. Intellectualism is pernicious for the 'Russian soul'. As Tyuchev put it: 'Russia is not to be understood by intellectual processes. You cannot take her measurements with a common yardstick. She has a form and a stature of her own: you can only believe in Russia.'[5]

The periodic Westernizing tendencies of Russian rulers provided a rich source of anti-Western feeling. The reforms of Peter the Great, who had travelled extensively in Europe and saw the necessity of introducing fundamental changes in Russia, not least by modernizing the Russian army and navy, marked a century of Westernization. It was only skin-deep, but both he and, later, Catherine the Great were so resolute in that policy, their 'snobbery' towards the West was so profound, that it gave rise to a typically Russian phenomenon, which

5 Quoted by Berdyaev, *The Russian Idea*, p. 1.

was later very skilfully adapted by the Bolsheviks to their own scheme of things.

The Potemkin Village Effect

Potemkin villages were façade villages constructed out of stage décor, which passed, at a distance, for real villages; with them Catherine the Great wanted to impress her foreign visitors. Prince Gregory Potemkin, who was her lover and one of her ministers, invented the idea. He suggested to the Empress that its implementation would be appropriate for the occasion of the visit of Emperor Joseph II of Austria and the Polish king, Stanisław Poniatowski, to southern Russia in 1787.

Catherine attempted, and succeeded in, the creation of a court around herself in which German and French writers and philosophers gathered and raised the intellectual level of St Petersburg. Catherine was a German princess who knew exactly what Western courts were like. She also knew that St Petersburg, despite its architectural splendour, was not the result of organic evolution, as it would have been in a much more evenly developed European country, but an artificial implant by her predecessor in an essentially very backward country. The Empress wanted to use Potemkin villages in an extended, metaphorical sense as well, to suffuse her entire reign with an aura of enlightened despotism. Eminent foreign visitors and admirers like Diderot, Euler and Voltaire praised her rule and held her up as an example to be emulated. In fact, her reign saw the greatest peasant revolt of Russian history, that of Pugachev in 1773–4, which was a revolt against the harsher terms of serfdom imposed by Catherine herself.

The construction of Potemkin villages did not continue after Catherine the Great, but the concept of pretence systems had already taken root in the country and, in that conceptual sense, was used extensively at later times in Russian history, in particular that of the most ambitious, impossibly ambitious, project Moscow ever had – that of the Bolsheviks, who not only wanted to catch up with Western countries and equal them in both military strength and social and political eminence but also aimed at leading the world in the construction of an entirely new society, in which Western countries, mere acolytes, would sedulously imitate the Russian example.

Communist society turned out to be even more repressive than Russian society was under the tsars. Under Stalin the population was subjected to atrocious conditions, mentally as well as physically; the threat of arrest and deportation to Siberia loomed constantly.

In the countries of Western Europe, however, some people took seriously Stalin's and his successors' pretence that the Soviet Union was a completely new and model country. The Communist parties followed Moscow's lead, and one after another Western intellectuals, who visited the Soviet Union from the 1930s to as late as the 1970s, were taken in by the Potemkin façade created for their benefit by the Soviet authorities through carefully arranged tours of a few model cities and their shops, listened to the opinions of the 'ordinary people' stage-set for them by the KGB, then came back knowing nothing about the archipelago of labour camps all over the country and extolled the new Soviet regime. Among them in the 1930s was G. B. Shaw, who was not even a Communist, only an idealist. He also took the word for the deed, the façade for the real thing. Many other Western intellectuals were prepared to project the few model 'Potemkin' towns and industrial centres, shops and 'ordinary people' on to the whole country.[6] Even later, after Khrushchev's revelations about Stalin and the brutal repression of the Hungarian revolution in 1956, though some Western Communists were disillusioned, other left-wingers, anticipating Gorbachev, suggested that the Soviet Union might need some time to develop fully, but was on the right path and would eventually eliminate all shortcomings and establish 'Communism with a human face'.

The greatest success of the Potemkin effect, however, was yet to come – when some leaders of the Soviet Union, cocooned in their

6 See P. Hollander, *Political Pilgrims*, OUP, New York, 1981.

closed *nomenklatura* world, started to believe their own rhetoric and thought that they could reform the Soviet Union and create that 'Communism with a human face'; notably Mikhail Gorbachev who, overpowered by his own Western snobbery, in the end went through the door of a theoretical Potemkin façade, tried to sit down on a state-of-the-art Potemkin hologram-chair and fell to the real ground.

Another example of Bolshevik Potemkin construction was the creation of the republics, thereby sometimes fostering the separate national identity of, for instance, the Kazakhs, the Turkmens, the Kyrghyz. The Russians wanted to give the impression that Communism was already international and was going to include an ever-growing number of countries – the Communist messianic message made that necessary. Little did the Bolsheviks suspect that this pretence would one day come home to roost. But the majority of Russians, even if they are not very interested in the issue, are convinced that most of the former republics are integral parts of Russia and should remain so.

The Potemkin image lives on; at the end of the Brezhnev epoch a Russian woman, on her first trip to the West, walked along the Kurfürstendamm in West Berlin and exclaimed: 'But this is a Potemkin village! You can't all be this rich!'

How would Zhirinovsky's Potemkin world come about? Is it that he pretends to be the long-suffering little man who has endured so much humiliation and hardship behind the façade (see Chapter 6)? Or is his game to call the Potemkin bluff of some of the reformers?

AN IMPOSSIBLE-PROJECT SYNDROME

Russian history has been studded with a long series of impossible projects; enthused by their vast and rich land, the Russians have long believed that they should be the natural rulers of the world. This view is aptly reflected in a deduction made by the English geopolitician Sir Halford Mackinder, of which Zhirinovsky would approve: 'He who commands the marches commands the heartland. He who commands the heartland commands the world island. He who commands the world island commands the world.'[7]

In the sixteenth century Ivan the Terrible aimed to set up a totalitarian state *avant la lettre* with a secret police force, the *Oprichnina* or 6,000 black horsemen, the elimination of opposed forces and the total control of society, including the restriction of the population to one place. Lacking the means of surveillance to succeed, his rule led to the Time of Troubles (1603–14), when anarchy arose and people wandered around in an unruly way.

A century later Peter the Great tried to Westernize the country and in part succeeded (see introduction to Chapter 5). But he provoked a reaction on the part of the Slavophiles, who cleaved to an idealized image of the Slav union in the past, the very antithesis of the West.

In the eighteenth century Catherine the Great had foreign-policy successes, notably the conquest of most of Poland and the capture of Crimea from the Ottoman Turks. The latter achievement inspired Potemkin to conceive of the Greek Project, which was no less than the reconstitution of Byzantium as an independent Christian state after the conquest of the Ottoman Empire, based on a renewed Constantinople. Catherine's second grandson was named Constantine in expectation of his ruling there. He was entrusted to a Greek nurse; Catherine ordered medals to be struck with a reproduction of St Sophia.[8] Her last minister, Zuboff, added India to Turkey as another objective of this push south. Nothing came of it at the time, but it has perhaps inspired Zhirinovsky's conception of the 'Last Dash to the South'.

The nineteenth century saw more reasonable projects adopted and serious economic development begun by its end. But the good prospects ended with 1914. The Bolsheviks at first put in place the aim of igniting revolutions for Communism in the West. When these expecta-

7 Sir Halford Mackinder, *On the Scope and Methods of Geography*, Royal Geographical Society, London, 1951.

8 Nicholas Riyasanovsky, *A History of Russia* (4th edition), OUP, 1984, p. 266.

tions failed Stalin adopted the goal of making the Soviet Union the lodestar of the whole world, which Moscow was to lead to the promised land of Communism. A *Salvator Mundi* project with a vengeance, the military costs involved in maintaining the Cold War with the West from 1947 onwards eventually broke it apart in 1989–91.

But meanwhile Stalin had at least achieved one earlier unfulfilled project, that of Ivan the Terrible. For modern technology now allowed the construction of a totalitarian state, complete with GULAG, purges and witch trials. As Stalin told N. K. Cherkakov, the actor who played Ivan the Terrible in Eisenstein's film of the same name, the secret police, *Oprichnina*, was a 'progressive' idea. Ivan's mistake, in Stalin's view, was not to pursue his purges far enough.[9] This was not an error Stalin could be accused of making.

Indeed, it was revulsion against the Stalinist record that led Gorbachev to his idea of 'Communism with a human face', of *glasnost* and *perestroika*. This proved to be another impossible Russian project, as the Chinese have duly noted. One can have *glasnost* or *perestroika*, but not both together. The former leads to the collapse of Communism forthwith, the latter to its delayed collapse while saving one's face.

THE SOUL PITTED AGAINST LUXURY PLASTIC

Peter the Great tried to Westernize Russia, which by reaction induced Slavophilism and the conservation of the 'Great Russian Soul', the very antithesis of the West. Even St Petersburg, his dazzling new capital, the Venice of the North, was built not organically, like Venice, but with Asiatic brutality on a swamp, killing nearly a million forced labourers from among the serfs. Catherine the Great

9 Paul Dukes, *A History of Russia, Medieval, Modern and Contemporary*, Macmillan, 1974, p. 53.

understood that it was wiser to refrain from action in this regard and that it was better simply to talk and to pretend.

Contemporary Anti-Westernism

The nineteenth-century debate between pro-Western and anti-Western parties continued until the First World War, but with the victory of the Bolsheviks no further debate was possible. The staunch anti-Western stance of the Communists, however, gradually promoted pro-Western attitudes, as an ever-increasing number of people lost hope in any substantial change, and finally, from the late 1960s onwards, the leadership became more and more cynical and society more and more corrupt (see below, 'Mafia Capitalism').

With Gorbachev at the helm of the Party, pro-Western attitudes became respectable, but at the same time the old debate between Russophiles and Westerners started up again. The prestige of the West rose in many people's eyes; much hope was pinned on Western help. The West gave the impression of knowing how to help Russia to its feet after the collapse of Communism. Western experts went in droves, set norms for the reforms and tied aid to the achievement of certain targets. The IMF and the World Bank were confident about their advice. Professor Sachs of Harvard University was appointed economic adviser to the reformist government, which now follows fewer and fewer of his suggestions. The Russian government has lost its trust in Western experts – or perhaps its nerve in the face of the increasing dissatisfaction.

Robert Ericson, head of the Harriman Institute at Columbia University, New York, thinks that the entire conception of the IMF and the World Bank of how to rescue Russia from the consequences of Communism and create a free-market economy is misconceived. In *The Bear Contained*, BBC Radio 4, 24.3.94, he quoted an old Russian saying about Communism: 'Building Communism was like taking an aquarium and making fish soup of it,' adding that rebuilding capitalism from Communism might be 'like taking the fish soup and trying to reconstitute the aquarium'.

The old economy started to decline fast; the development of the new was not able to keep pace with it; problems of livelihood overshadowed everything in everybody's mind – and what do human rights and democracy mean to those who have hardly anything to eat and no fuel to keep them warm through the long, bitterly cold Russian winter? Most people were lost in that new world, where they had no idea how to go about things, what to do, how to join in a 'new' society and how to conform to new practices.

The Soviet regime was bad, but most people knew their place. Everybody knew what he or she could do and what not; everybody was monitored; and practically the only way up was through the Communist Party. Stepping out of line was quickly punished, and justice was arbitrary. The people were treated like minors, whose father was the Party: a bad father, no doubt, a nasty, shabby drunkard who beat his children, but still a father. Salaries were very low, but at that very low level there was financial security for everybody. With a bit on the side (see below, 'Low-level Corruption'), most people eked out an existence.

With the Communist regime suddenly gone, everybody was free to act, but most people are still completely lost in this new world, where they have to behave as adults and take decisions formerly taken by others for them but do not know how to go about it: having got rid of their drunkard father, they have become orphans. Disillusionment, bewilderment and fear of the future are growing, just as is fear of the present as the streets have become more and more violent, ruled by gangs.

With the Soviet Union, the latest avatar of the Russian messianic empire, gone, national identity has been shaken, for even in the Brezhnev days of corrupt stagnation there was some ambient pride left in being a top republic among the other fourteen and a superpower in the world.

Western help was not forthcoming at the rate, and in the way, people had expected. Many people began to suspect that the West, and especially the USA, just wanted to have Russia running after it, without really having any hope of catching up. They found the role of the little lap dog, faithfully trailing its master, humiliating. The West does, indeed, like its economic and social superiority seasoned by moral superiority: only if its advice is followed will the pupil be rewarded. That has already caused resentment in many countries; Islamic fundamentalism, for instance, in part feeds off that resentment. Many nations, especially ones with a long history and a rich culture, know that they have values that the West lacks, and they want to preserve them and pit them against the inferior spiritual values, as they see them, of the West. Iran is a case in point, as are many other Islamic countries. Russians are proud of their soul and their emotional depth. They may admire and even envy the West but feel that people in the West are not quite real people: there is nothing much behind that polished exterior; they seem to be made of plastic, their existence an ontological anomaly; they seem empty strutting through their boutiquified cities, within the corrals of their pedestrian precincts – haughty but lost souls.

'There is that in the Russian soul which corresponds to the immensity, the vagueness, the infinitude of the Russian land; spiritual geography corresponds with physical. In the Russian soul there is a sort of immensity, a vagueness, a predilection for the infinite,' says Berdyaev, 'such as is suggested by the great plain of Russia. For this reason the Russian people have found difficulty in achieving mastery over these vast expanses and in reducing them to orderly shape. There has been a vast elemental strength in the Russian people combined with a comparatively weak sense of form.'[10] Berdyaev speaks of a phenomenon germane to Dostoyevsky's *gestaltlose Weite*, formless distances unfettered, undefined by form, as being real Christianity.[11] And now the Russians have to face up to the rigours of modernity: all shape and form, no internal space or yawning depth of the soul. All that counts is the unblemished, hard enamel of the surface.

10 Berdyaev, *The Russian Idea*.

11 Carl Schmitt, *Römischer Katholizismus und politische Form*, Klett-Cotta, Stuttgart, 1984, p. 55.

Enter the Saviour

Then comes a strange little man. They call him a buffoon both in the West and in Russian reformist circles (although the latest Moscow stance is that he is mad, a clinical case, perhaps a wistful reflection of the good old Soviet days when dissidents could be locked up in psychiatric hospitals). He claims that he, like everybody else, suffered in childhood, and he makes extravagant promises to restore public order, reoccupy the republics, double the standard of living in a couple of months and lead the Russians to a monstrous Torremolinos stretching for thousands of miles along the northern shores of the Gulf of Oman and of the Arabian Sea, as Russian soldiers with handy, small but efficient automatic weapons watch over the peace of the exhausted northerners.

The poor lumpenized masses are his constituency, and he is proud of it. He banks on the further degradation of the population and makes no secret of it; and his stock has been appreciating considerably in the past eighteen months.

In October 1992 an interview with him was published in the *New Times International*, in which he flaunted his brazen 'lumpenophilia'. The interviewer told him: 'It is very easy to make such extravagant promises to people. There is an enormous lumpenized mass which will buy them.' Zhirinovsky: 'It will buy them all right.' Interviewer: 'But, after all, the nation is not composed of lumpens alone. Lots of people retain common sense.' Zhirinovsky: 'They do. They vote against me, but they will be in the minority.' Interviewer: 'So far they are in a substantial majority. Do you reckon on the degradation of the masses?' Zhirinovsky: 'I most certainly do!'[12]

He has pitted himself against everybody: the remnants of the old *nomenklatura*, the '*nomenklatura* kids' among the reformers, the sleek, new Russian businessmen, the merciless *mafiosniki* and the implacable extreme right wing, way beyond him.

12 *New Times International*, October 1992, p. 11.

ON THE WINGS OF THE RUSSIAN RIGHT

If Zhirinovsky knew Lewis Carroll's *Through the Looking Glass*, he might, when told that he was a right-wing extremist, adopt the logic of the Red Queen and retort: 'You may call me a right-wing extremist, but I could show you right-wingers in Russia in comparison with whom I am the most stolid of moderates.'

In Pamyat circles – Pamyat is an ultra-nationalist, far-right group – Zhirinovsky is quite beyond the pale, but not because of his extremism; on the contrary, he is seen as a dubious cheat, a traitor, the agent of a global conspiracy against the rebirth of Russia and against God the Almighty. And as a nationalist he is quite unsatisfactory because he took part in parliamentary elections, which shows that he thinks in Western terms. Election anyway is a manifestation of levelling decadence. Moreover, his father was a Jew; so no right-wing extremist of the Pamyat stamp worth his salt would ever want to be seen rubbing shoulders with him. Dimitri Vasilyev, the head of Pamyat, is a staunch monarchist and wants the tsar back but will have nothing to do with any descendant of the Romanovs in Western Europe because their stock is no longer pure. Many decades of intermarriage have rendered them unsuitable for the task: a new dynasty must be found. And he rejects Nazism on the ground that it was born on the rubbish heap of Bolshevism.[13]

Fascist groups even further to the right are, for instance, the street bands of Alexander Barkashov, which concentrate entirely on violence.

All present-day conservative nationalist movements hark back in some way or other to their common ancestor, the Black Hundred (Chernaya Sotnya: *Enc. Brit.*, 11th edn, 1911, vol. 23, p. 910), who, as Walter Laqueur explains, 'are a unique phenomenon in the history of twentieth-century politics, as it was a halfway house between the old-fashioned reactionary movements of the nineteenth century and the right-wing populist (fascist) parties of the twentieth.

13 *Der Spiegel*, No. 8, 1994.

With their strong ties to monarchy and Church they largely belonged to the past, but unlike the early conservative groups they were no longer élitist.'[14] They had come to assume their new role during the crisis of tsarism in 1904–5. He speaks about 'them' because the Black Hundred was not a single organization but a 'somewhat catch-all term for various extreme right-wing groups that existed between, roughly speaking, the turn of the century and 1917,' explains Walter Laqueur. With the coming to power of the Bolsheviks the right went underground but was not entirely eliminated. Its ideas maintained their clandestine existence in the Soviet Union and were pursued openly by Russian emigrants abroad.

After the 'fall' of Trotsky and the indefinite postponement of 'world revolution' Stalin decided to make do with 'socialism in one country'; consequently the Soviet Union became increasingly national socialist and eventually was as nationalist as Russia had been under the tsars; Russian nationalism was subsumed under Communism, and the subterranean circulation of most right-wing ideas continued in that new packaging. That is why there had come to be such a strong Communist element in the new Russian right as it gradually emerged in the Gorbachev years.

All through the Soviet period the façade of internationalism was carefully maintained, but Russian nationalism was an additive in practically all Soviet policies and measures. A new Potemkin village was added to the existing stock. The successive Communist Party leaders varied as to the emphasis they laid on the internationalist epidermis or on the underlying Russian nationalist bone structure. The promotion of regional ethnic development in the republics continued on the surface – the Soviet leadership was quite confident that it would never get out of hand and could not weaken Moscow's hold over the republics. The local ethnic groups, however, were not deceived by the surface internationalism: they were experiencing the very strong nationalist strain in Moscow's rule all the time. Their

14 Laqueur, *Black Hundred*.

hostility to it may well have contributed later to sometimes precipitate declarations of independence as well as to the self-assertion of one republic against another – in the Caucasus, for instance. Regional ethnic-nationalist ideas had also been 'firmed up' in their opposition to Russian chauvinism in the Soviet period. A very strong Russian nationalism was equally experienced in the Communist satellite countries of Eastern Europe. Without this Russian imperialist chauvinism, Communism as such might have gained marginally more support. Outside observers, say in the West, were often oblivious of what became a very important factor later, at the end of the Gorbachev era, and has remained so since the collapse of the Soviet Union.

Both Soviet ideology and the Black Hundred-type of thought were strongly anti-liberal and anti-Western, which facilitated a 'tacit agreement' between them. The Soviet leadership probably noticed the further alienation of the nationalities and the ethnic groups in the republics and in the autonomous republics of the Russian federation respectively but were confident that it could be contained (as Khrushchev clearly thought that the inclusion of the Crimea in the Ukraine would spell no danger to the Russians living there).

As Walter Laqueur explains: 'Three centuries of Russian history were undone in a few days in August 1991 as the result of the weakness of the centre. To save the remnant, a spiritual as well as a political renaissance is needed, a return to the national and religious values of the Russian people. It is pointless to embrace Western values and to copy Western institutions. Russia had always followed a road of its own; political systems that functioned elsewhere were unsuitable for Russia.'[15]

As the new Russian right emerged under Gorbachev's *glasnost* it was carrying with it a sizeable Communist load, which it had taken on during seven decades. Its anti-Semitism survived unscathed the long years spent under the mask of anti-Zionism. Conspiracy paranoia

15 Laqueur, *Black Hundred*, p. ix.

was a strong feature of Stalinism, and it was congruent with the same tendency later in the right-wing movements as they came out of hibernation. Therefore it is not surprising that parts of the 'patriotic intelligentsia' allied itself with some of the KGB and of the high military command as well as with the staunch remnants of the ex-Soviet leadership in August 1991. That community of minds makes it also quite easy for pro-Soviet militants to switch to militant national-ism as the need arises.

The so-called red-brown elements straddle the two ends of the scale, so to speak, and will perhaps help the serpent to bite its own tail. Such a man is Alexander Prokhanov, geopolitical writer and editor of the militant paper *Zavtra*, formerly *Dyen* (the latter was banned after the defeat of the armed parliamentary revolt in October 1993 because of its closeness to the Rutskoy cause). The resurgent *Eurasianism*, pleading for a Eurasian–Russian Great Empire, finds new supporters every day. Nikita Michalkov, the inter-nationally well-known film producer, for instance, has given up being Yeltsin's adviser on cultural policy and has turned against the Western reforms and the Western concept of liberty in favour of Eurasianism.

Conservative (that is, Communist) elements around Rutskoy find it easy to mingle with the born-again Russian extreme nationalists, and ex-Red Army militants will probably be able to mix easily with resurgent Cossacks to follow one or another aspiring right-wing leader. The distribution of the forces thus generated will probably determine, to some extent at least, whether a new future political crisis will flare up into a civil war, how bitter it will be and, from the point of view of this book, how Zhirinovsky will fare in this struggle for survival of the fittest.

THE REFORMERS

The latest impossible project for Russia is to try to turn it into a liberal-democrat and consumer-capitalist country in a few years or one generation at the most. This was precisely the aim of first the Yavlinsky '500-day' plan for capitalism, which Gorbachev toyed with but then dropped, and then the Gaidar reform team's 'shock therapy' plan.

Shock therapy is the traditional IMF medicine for a developing or developed country in a crisis with over-swollen state spending and inflation. Cutting back the state sector and curtailing monetary growth can then bring down inflation and allow resources to switch to the private sector.

The trouble with this in Russia is that it is neither a developing nor a developed country but a profoundly misdeveloped one. After seventy years of Communism, with the ruination of its agriculture by forced collectivization in the 1930s and a bloated military–industrial complex, shock therapy does not right the financial economy by much, but it does derange the real economy, which is collapsing as a consequence.

Basically, the very infrastructure in Russia was misdeveloped – the oil and gas pipelines are rusty and leak, the roads are pockmarked, the airplanes of Aeroflot are unsafe to fly – while the environment is the most polluted in the world and partially radioactive to boot (fifty mini-reactors of a Chernobyl type were put within Greater Moscow, causing the distribution of radioactive dust all over the city). Of the numerous conditions needing to be met for a successful take-off into capitalist growth, Russia has but a few – an educated workforce, good scientists and engineers and access to abundant resources and energy – but the legal, fiscal and, above all, cultural contexts of capitalism are quite lacking.

People are hostile to private property, says Russian film maker Andrei Konchalovsky. 'In Russia people despise wealth. Just look at the way private farmers who strike out on their own are the subject of hostility from everyone else.'[16] This attitude, indeed, explains why the expropriation of the *kulaks*, the better-off farmers of tsarist Russia and the 1920s New Economic Policy, was possible in the 1930s, the lesser peasants and the policemen involved scorning them for being well-off. Such attitudes lead to rich farmers facing arson of their lofts or farm buildings and theft of their equipment and livestock. 'People here almost consciously reject the idea that they can be rich if they work hard,' Konchalovsky says, adding that illogical tax laws nobody could afford to obey (demanding up to 85 per cent of turnover for the taxman) could only encourage lying, cheating and bribery. 'Russians seem to prefer to be poor.'[17]

Such attitudes date from the tsarist epoch and are hard to eradicate. The reform team of Yegor Gaidar and his men, Boris Fyodorov and Anatoly Chubais (still in power as head of the privatization process, the one reform still going on), allowed a brief reign of macroeconomic policy from December 1991 to December 1992, when Victor Chernomyrdin, an old-style industrialist and head of Gasprom, took over from Gaidar as premier.

Chernomyrdin calls himself a reformer too – as do all Russian politicans except the Communists and ultra-nationalists. In fact, Chernomyrdin was keen to appoint a fellow Soviet *apparatchik*, Victor Gerashchenko, to the key post of head of the Russian Central Bank in July 1992. The new boss did a U-turn and began to issue credits to the state firms that the Gaidar team had cut. As controller of the distribution of credit, Gerashchenko is in a position to assume, in an economy become 'privatized' and subject to market forces, the role of the old Gosplan Five-year-planners in charge of the distribution of resources: the credit confers purchasing power in the market for those very resources.

Gerashchenko justifies his liberal use of credit by a novel argument: claiming to be no less monetarist than the Gaidar team, he does not

16 *The Sunday Times*, 1 May 1994, p. 23.
17 *The Sunday Times*, 1 May 1994, p. 23.

deny the fact that there is a link between money changes and price changes, postulated by the Quantity Theory of Money. He thinks that it is only of a different character than usually thought. Money increases, far from stimulating price rises, stimulate production and so enable demand to be satisfied more easily, thereby countering inflation. This is veritably monetarism *à la Russe*.

The aim, of course, has been to keep Russian workers in work by ensuring a flow of finance to their employers and so preventing Zhirinovsky from coming to power. But one cannot use *Alice in Wonderland* economics to avert *Through the Looking Glass* (darkly) geopolitics. Printing money to chase goods, mostly in the wrong lines of production, means hyper-inflation in the prices of those goods people want.

Gaidar made a comeback in April 1993 as deputy premier for reform. He was able to force a measure of financial discipline on the Russian Central Bank by means of advocacy from younger, reform-minded bankers so that Russian inflation fell from over 20 per cent per month in early 1993 to under 10 per cent for a while in early 1994. But the sharp cuts in credit to state firms meant that his influence was greatly resented by them and he lost his job, as did his ally, Boris Fyodorov, Minister of Finance, after the December 1993 election.

A return to Gerashchenko-economics took place for a while in early 1994, leading to expectations of a resurgence in inflation by 1995 unless the bank's chairman's wings are clipped by Chernomyrdin.

Gaidar, Fyodorov and Chernomyrdin are not really feared by Zhirinovsky because they have all been tried and have visibly failed. The one reformer with an unblemished reputation is Gregory Yavlinsky, whose Centre for Economic and Social Research has prepared a report on economic reform for the Nizhny-Novgovorod region, whose governor, Boris Nemtsev, is a physicist-turned-reformer and is pioneering a grass-roots reform, privatizing farms with foreign help and pushing for new industries out of defence conversion. It indicates the appeal of the Liberal Democratic Party of Russia (LDPR) that, even so, it obtained 18 per cent of the vote there in the December 1993 election.

Yavlinsky is, then, the one serious centrist candidate for the presidency, explicitly opposed to the rapid brand of reform applied so far and with a fresh-faced appeal to many voters, who, however, never taps the groundswell of nationalism stirring in Russia as Zhirinovsky incomparably does.

MAFIA CAPITALISM

The Soviet Union under Stalin established law and order on the streets in its own way. Gangsters were put in the GULAG, where they often became guards. By a curious paradox every subsequent Soviet or Russian leader has unwittingly, except possibly in Brezhnev's case, encouraged the rise of gangsterism. Khrushchev released from the GULAG the 'thieves' elders', as they are called, who formed gangs engaged in the usual repertoire of drugs, gambling and prostitution.

In Brezhnev's time a new generation of gangsters emerged that exploited the shadow economy that was springing up in the interstices of the command administrative system. It became common for moonlighting firms to operate businesses with the bribed connivance of daytime bosses, using state materials to produce goods for the black market. This was doubly illegal because it was misappropriating state assets and because capitalism of any sort was banned. Such shadow businesses were hence good targets for mafia-type extortionists.

Perestroika and *glasnost* were a new boon to the gangsters, who were able to strengthen their international links. The Caucasus peoples, especially the Azeri, the Chechen and the Georgian and Tambov gangs, provided many of the leading *mafiosi* of Moscow and the main towns. Dealing in arms, caviare and 'out of legal hours' alcohol, one of their most profitable lines was drugs from Central Asia sold in the West. Uzbekistan has 3,000 poppy fields, and Kazakhstan is a world leader in cannabis production. In Tajikistan opium and cannabis have replaced dollars as the side currency. Italian and Russian mobsters plan to have 40 per cent of the world's drug traffic under their control by 1997.

A further extension of the mafia's activity into armaments was made possible by the break-up of much of the Red Army and yet again by Gorbachev's prohibition of alcohol from 1986 onwards. Prohibition ruined many fine vineyards but did not stop the production of vodka, which carried on in the black economy. 'As soon as the state ... let the reins drop and lost control of vodka, political troubles inevitably followed. Problems that had earlier been hidden emerged into the open.'[18]

Prophetic words – for by 1992 the USSR had ceased to exist and the Russian and Caucasian mafia gangs began to go legitimate in certain activities in the rapidly spreading private economy. Komsomol holiday camps became training grounds for contract killers recruited from the disintegrating army.[19] Extortion of other private firms under threat of contract murder became common. Some 90 per cent of the private sector is now under mafia control;[20] some 40 per cent of the existing Russian economy is also.[21] The banking sector has been targeted. Ten senior bankers were killed in 1993 for failing to extend further 'loans', while Moscow's senior godfather himself and a Duma member were gunned down in April 1994. The murder rate has reached Lebanese proportions, which, with inter-gang killings and contract murders, is twenty-five times the UK rate.[22]

The chaos associated with *perestroika* allowed tens of thousands of corrupt factories and trading firms to team up with the big mafia and sell billions of dollars' worth of Russia's precious materials, mostly from the Baltic states and ports, notably St Petersburg, but also from

18 Andrei Pokhlebkin, *A History of Vodka*, Verso, 1991, p. 175.
19 *Daily Mail*, 19 March 1993.
20 *Focus*, January 1994, p. 44.
21 *The Sunday Times*, 1 May 1994, p. 7.
22 *Focus*, January 1994, p. 42.

the Black Sea ports and the Far East. In 1988 scrap-metal exports became legal when Russian technology could not reprocess it. This loophole has been fully exploited. The mafia has also diversified into scrap-metal export and energy, a third of whose exports are estimated to be contraband. Through forgeries and bribes for police and customs officials they began to sell copper, zinc, aluminium and other strategic materials in vast amounts, keeping the proceeds in the West for fear of a clean-up campaign at home.[23]

There are now between 3,000 and 5,000 gangs operating right across Russia from St Petersburg to Vladivostock, two cities of intense mafia activity. Racketeering, like prostitution, was deemed not to exist in the Communist paradise, and neither is illegal. But even smugglers and those held on murder charges often get off, since 70 per cent of the police force is corrupt. One policeman in St Petersburg apparently refused a US$700,000 bribe to be turned.[24] Where one refused, how many would accept?

St Petersburg has only a twenty-four-man squad, with deficient facilities, to tackle the mafia; 5,000 is the minimum needed. Mayor Anatoly Sobchak has called for the Defence Ministry to take over the task, but it refuses, saying that Interior Ministry troops should do so.[25] Zhirinovsky wants a special task force, recruited from the army and carefully vetted, to take up the job, with results expected within three months or the top man loses his job. This approach is what is required, indeed, and is the most popular policy he advocates. If he could be seen to tackle at least the small-fry *mafiosi* hitting the kiosks, shops and restaurants, between 70 and 80 per cent of which pay 10–20 per cent of their earnings as extortion, according to a special report commissioned by Yeltsin, then a Zhirinovsky presidency would immediately enhance its appeal. The big-time mafia fleecing of the nation's resources would be harder to stop, but a dictatorship

23 *Newsweek*, 5 October 1992, p. 18.
24 *Newsweek*, 5 October 1992, p. 18.
25 *Independent*, 3 May 1994, p. 10.

such as Zhirinovsky advocates, with 100,000 being shot within three months, is probably the only way a dent could be made here. Mussolini cleaned up Italy in a brutal way.

The Russian attitude to private wealth has always been a troubled one, regarding it as sinful, although there are some 7,000 dollar millionaires in Russia. This attitude, to which film maker Andrei Konchalovsky ascribes much of his country's woes, he captures thus: 'In Russia, the more wealthy a man is, the further he is from God, so when you steal from him you are bringing him closer to God.'[26] Soulful gangsters dispense salvation along with extortion and mayhem.

The scale of the mafia fleecing of Russia is shown by figures collected by the Institute of International Finance (IIF), the world banking community's think-tank. The IIF estimates that US$90 billion has been earned by Russians selling materials and energy to the West since 1991, of which US$40 billion has not been repatriated.[27] A further source of profit is the printing by rogue elements in the KGB's successor agency of counterfeit currency, especially US dollars. Some US$10 billion–$15,000 billion is circulating in Russia illegally, according to the head of the regulations department of the Russian Central Bank, Viktor Melnikov, a sum greater than the total value of roubles in circulation.[28] Many of these dollars must come from counterfeit sources.

The outward-bound direction of the Russian mafia is making Western police uneasy, since the intention is to engage in similar activities in, say, Germany, the UK and the USA. Toughened by

26 *The Sunday Times*, 1 May 1994, p. 23.

27 *Financial Times*, 19 April 1994, p. 2.

28 Russian TV Channel, 20 April 1994. Mr Melnikov is reported by BBC Monitoring, Caversham, as saying US$10 million–$15 million, but this is contradicted by the next clause and must have been a mishearing. That Russian dollars are over US$10 billion is attested by IMF officials independently.

survival in a totalitarian state, it is convinced that it is far more ruthless than local mobs – indeed, is matchless. In a sinister echo of Khrushchev's 'We'll bury you' threat, one Russian gangster says: 'We'll overwhelm you. We'll overwhelm you and your neighbours in the common European home.'[29] The West cannot be said not to have been warned. If Zhirinovsky comes to power and wages a campaign against the mafia, this could accelerate its exodus to the West, much as tightening in Italy is leading to Italian mafia migration abroad.

LOW-LEVEL CORRUPTION

Corruption in Soviet society spread far beyond the *mafiosi* and the criminal rings. It involved a large section, probably the majority, of the population. Such activities, though illegal, were in the domain of socially acceptable illegality.

There were three basic kinds. You could expect payment or gifts for services, the provision of which was part of your job. A nurse in a hospital could expect payment for performing her ordinary duties, such as giving meals to patients (or at least giving reasonable meals to patients), a doctor for treating a patient in a health service that was supposed to be free. (But the doctor himself had to pay a laboratory assistant for a routine blood test done for a patient of his in the hospital, for instance.) Domestic repairs that were supposed to be provided free by a housing-estate management were not done, or at least not done properly, unless every time the workman was given some extra money, which meant an income over and above his salary.

What did those people do who were not in a service profession but worked in a factory? They had the opportunity of stealing materials, tools, etc., from the factory and either using them or selling them. Or they could use the factory equipment for producing articles that they

29 *Focus*, January 1994, p. 48.

could sell privately. In agriculture state farm workers could sell privately produce that was the property of the state.

As people were generally badly paid, even though the necessities were inexpensive – basic foodstuffs, transport, homes and average clothing – a very large number of people did not find it easy to make ends meet if they wanted anything above the absolutely basic. The slightest luxury was far beyond their means. And what they were able to afford made for a very drab life indeed. (Zhirinovsky complains in his writings and in his speeches, perhaps insincerely, about the poverty he suffered as a child: he had no toys, no books, had to eat the bad canteen food that his mother brought back from work. He hopes to give the impression that he has shared the general hardship of the ordinary Russian citizen and that this will bring him closer to his potential constituency.)

An illegal income was not considered criminal: it was generally accepted, but it still meant a frail public morality. From the higher echelons of an illicit income the jump to the lowest grade of actual criminality was not great. And nobody considered stealing state property a real crime when done on a small scale, nor the system of taking small bribes. The state itself was seen as a racket of some sort, run by a very small circle of privileged people. And the frail public morality proved fertile ground for 'development' when the walls of the Soviet structure began to crumble, for those who were ready.

All in all, ways of getting extra cash involved a very high percentage of the working population – probably well over half of them. Those in positions of power had, of course, the best opportunities.

RULER AS CLOWN

The reason why Zhirinovsky is considered unlikely to become president by many in Russia and the West is that he is a clown, a court jester. There is, however, a long tradition of the buffoon in Russian politics, upon which he is drawing.

During the Soviet period the tradition was banned, although Khrushchev quite consciously, and Brezhnev unconsciously, had their decidedly clownish sides. Khrushchev banged the table at the UN with his shoe to make a point – country-bumpkin behaviour that contributed to his downfall. But his successor developed his own absurdities, conferring on himself literary awards for unreadable tomes that accumulated unread on the book shelves, while overloading his chest with medals for supposed deeds in the Great Patriotic War, in which he and his cronies turned the tide. A whole culture of political jokes emerged to lampoon him and his corrupt court. But, whatever they did, they kept on the whole to the leaden Soviet style of public speaking.

Zhirinovsky breaks with all that dramatically. The more outlandish his utterances, the more he distances himself from the Soviet times and associates himself with the tsarist world. In Peter the Great's time there was the day of the fools, 1 April, when the jester with his cap and bells was king.

Zhirinovsky is flaunting his Russian soulfulness with his rages and antics, such as pelting Jewish demonstrators from the Russian legation in Strasbourg in March 1993. He is expressing his contempt for the West and all its decorum of hypocrisy. Undignified and boorish he may be, but he is for real, the epitome of everything that Communism tried to expunge from the Russian character. Far from hurting him electorally, his clowning is a help – a comic diversion for the Russians in their desperation and a reminder of the absurdity of their situation and of life.

An anecdote that can, perhaps, drive this home is told by Christabel Bielenberg, a British woman married to a German lawyer from Hamburg who was a liberal opposed to the Nazi regime. In late 1932 they attended a Nazi meeting out of curiosity to find out about the phenomenon. Halfway through Hitler's speech Bielenberg jacked his future wife out of the crowd and said loudly, within earshot of the organizers: 'You may think that Germans are political idiots, Chris, and you may be right. But of one thing I can assure you: they won't be so stupid as to fall for *that* clown.'[30] Three months later Hitler became Chancellor of Germany.

30 Christabel Bielenberg, *The Past is Myself*, Corgi Books, 1984, p. 22.

THE NEAR-ABROAD OR
FORMER SOVIET UNION OUTSIDE RUSSIA

A RÉSUMÉ OF RUSSIAN IMPERIALISM

Zhirinovsky evinces a great respect for history – before 1914. He seems to think that only if a country was independent before then has it a right to exist today. Hence the importance of establishing Russia's acquisitions before this crucial watershed. It is these territories that he has in his sights in an imagined recreation of the empire of the tsars, a fantasy he would like to turn into a reality. The Russian state has always been an expansionist one. Its original home around Kiev in the tenth century was under one three-hundredth of its present extent. In 1462 it covered 15,000 square miles. By 1914 it occupied 8,660,000 square miles, the ethnic Russians establishing dominion over more than a hundred very different nationalities.[1]

Expansion was several times punctuated by a 'Time of Troubles', in 1603–14, 1917–20 and, most spectacularly, 1989-91, with massive relinquishment of territory. But Russia has always begun to expand again, now into Abkhazia, prised from Georgia, and it is re-establishing control over Tajikistan and Belarus.

Russian imperialism has been not just a practical matter of self-defence and self-assertion, the peasant habit of coveting

---

1 *Russian Imperialism from Ivan the Terrible to the Revolution*, ed. Taras Hunczak, Rutgers University Press, 1974, Foreword, p. 1.

that extra strip of territory, but also a messianic affair. 'Messianic consciousness is more characteristic of the Russians than of any other people except the Jews. It runs all through Russian history down to the Communist period.'[2] After the fall of Constantinople in 1453, Russia assumed the leadership of Orthodoxy and became the Third Rome with the mission to lead the faithful. 'The Russian religious vocation is linked with the power and transcendent majesty of the Russian state, with a distinctive significance and importance attached to the Russian tsar. There enters into the messianic consciousness the alluring temptation of imperialism.'[3]

It is estimated that Russia was adding 50 square miles per day to its territory for four centuries before 1914. This encroachment came as a series of responses to outside invasion, such as that of the Tatars, Germans, Poles and Swedes. New territory was seized for security reasons. But then this territory required its own security zone. Adding security zone to security zone, Russia expanded to its natural limits, the Baltic, the Arctic, the Pacific Ocean, the Altai, the Pamirs, the Caucasus and the Carpathian mountains. Even then the expansionist habit led to the acquisition of Alaska, Finland and, southward beyond the northern Caucasus range, Georgia, Armenia and Azerbaijan.

The Expansion of the Tsarist Empire

After Ivan the Terrible had taken the last Tatar strongholds in the east (the Crimea was not incorporated until 1783, Kazan in 1552 and Astrakhan in 1556), the way was clear for expansion to Siberia. The Cossacks, under their heroic leader

2 N.A.Berdyaev, *The Russian Idea*, (reprint) Greenwood Press, 1979 p. 8.
3 Berdyaev, *The Russian Idea*, p. 9.

Yermak, went around the Urals in 1581. By 1649 the Russians had reached as far as the Pacific rim.

Russia experienced a grave 'Time of Troubles' in 1603–14, when its territorial integrity was severely shaken. But, as usual in Russian history, trouble prompted the Russians to expand, and a Cossack rebellion in Ukraine enabled this ancient heart of Rus to be rejoined with Russia in 1654. Peter the Great acquired Estonia, Livonia (part of modern Latvia), the mouth of the Neva, on which he built St Petersburg, and part of Karelia from the Swedes by 1721. Catherine the Great seized Crimea in 1783, subjugating the Crimean Tatars who had previously owed allegiance to the Ottoman Sultan, and gained the Black Sea coast by the Dnieper by 1792 in fighting back the Ottoman Turks.

To the west Russia obtained the lion's share of Poland under Catherine in three partitions of the country, carried out with Prussia and Habsburg Austria, in 1772, 1793 and 1795. The 1793 gains brought the bulk of White Russia (now Belarus) to rejoin its eastern areas already in Russia, after having been Polish for centuries, while the 1795 acquisition brought into the empire Lithuania, which had also been in Poland since the Union of Lublin in 1569.

In 1809 Finland was taken from Sweden, after a successful one-year campaign against the Swedes, and incorporated in the empire as an autonomous Grand Duchy, the tsar being its Grand Duke. The Finns cooperated with the Russians in quelling repeated Polish revolt, but they were to resent the Russian yoke as much as the Poles when a misguided policy of Russification began in the 1890s. Pushing southwards across the northern Caucasian mountains, Russia took Georgia by stages in 1801–10 and Daghestan and northern Azerbaijan in the same decade, occasioning a successful war with the Turks and

Persians, who recognized Russian sovereignty by 1813. As a result of the war Russia was in a position to straddle the entire Caucasus range, taking Armenia by 1828, although a famous Muslim rebellion in Azerbaijan under the legendary Imam Shamil did not die out until the early 1860s.

In the West, after repelling Napoleon in 1811–12 the Russians occupied Bessarabia in 1812, which, with part of Moldavia taken in 1829, forms the core of modern Moldova. After acquiring Alaska in 1799, the Russians erected Fort Ross in northern California.

In a long process of piecemeal absorption the Kirghiz steppe was incorporated in the empire from 1731 to 1734, bringing areas of modern Kazakhstan and Uzbekistan and Turkmenistan under Russian tutelage. They were not fully acquired until 1865–76, when conquest of the khanates of Kokand, Bokhara and Khiva brought the whole of Central Asia, including Kyrgyzstan and Tajikistan, under the tsar. This was done to pre-empt interference in the region by the British, pushing up from India into Afghanistan, and as a compensation for the sale of Alaska to the United States in 1867, for only US$ 7,200,000. Indeed, the Great Game between Russia and Britain in Central Asia set the pattern for subsequent geopolitical rivalries across the Eurasian continent, notably the Cold War (1947–89). Turkey and Persia were great players in the game then. The Russians justified seizure of Central Asia on the ground that they would save the people there from tribal disunity and dismemberment at the hands of Turkey and Persia, though it is not recorded if the Central Asians themselves appreciated Russia's public spirit in this regard.[4]

4 Nicholas Ch. Riyasanovsky, *A History of Russia*, 4th edition, OUP, 1984, p. 390.

In 1847 the energetic Count Nicholas Muravyev, known later as Muravyev-Amyursky (that is, of the Amur) became the Governor General of eastern Siberia. He promoted Russian advance in the Amur and secured gains from China, which was beset by war with Britain and France and by internal rebellion. In 1858 China ceded the left bank of the Amur and, in 1860, the Ussuri region. The Pacific coast began to be settled, the town of Nikolayevsk on the Amur being founded in 1853, Khabarovsk in 1858 and Vladivostok ('Ruler of the East') in 1860. In 1875 Russia yielded the Kuril Islands to Japan in exchange for the southern half of the island of Sakhalin,[5] which, however, it was to be forced to relinquish to Japan after losing the 1905 war to it. The Trans-Siberian railway, begun in 1891, was supposed to commence the integration of the vast empire as one common economic space. By the 1880s the tsarist empire reached its zenith, including one sixth of the land area of the globe, until then the largest territorially contiguous empire in history.

The Shattering of the Tsarist Empire and its Supersession by the Soviet Union

The First World War gave this vast structure a terrible battering, which proved fatal by 1917. The Soviet Union emerged in its wake. The Bolsheviks had to give up Poland (not without a fight), the Baltic states, Finland and Bessarabia, which rejoined an enlarged Romania in 1918–19. Ukraine, White Russia, the Transcaucasus Federation (to be dissolved into the separate states of Azerbaijan, Armenia and Georgia) and Central Asia broke away with independence movements. But after winning

5 Paul Dukes, *A History of Russia, Medieval, Modern and Contemporary*, 2nd edition, Macmillan, 1990, p. 140.

the Civil War of 1918–20 the Soviets reimposed Russian control over them by 1924, with the Georgian Stalin, the connoisseur Commissar for Nationalities, urging and executing a Great Russian chauvinist policy. This time it was not the supposed benefits of benign autocracy that were invoked to justify Russian rule but the blessings of the international fraternity of workers and peasants uniting in their own state. Proletarian solidarity was the ideological carapace of the Soviet state and could justify indefinite extension beyond Russia's geographical limits.

In 1939 Stalin made a pact with Hitler that enabled him in June 1940 to incorporate the Baltic states and Bessarabia, which with Trans-Dnestr constituted the Soviet Moldovan Republic or what is modern Moldova. In 1945 victory in the Second World War enabled the Soviet Empire to extend 'from Stettin in the Baltic to Trieste in the Adriatic', to use Churchill's graphic phrase in his 'Iron Curtain' speech at Fulton in 1946, marking the onset of the Cold War. Even after the loss of Tito's Yugoslavia in 1948, the Soviet Empire in Central Europe incorporated over 100 million people, living in Eastern Germany, Poland, Czechoslovakia, Hungary, Bulgaria and Romania (which asserted a certain independence by the 1960s under Ceauşescu). In the guise of socialist brotherhood, Moscow by then ruled an empire of 400 million over a vast expanse of territory, nearly one fifth of the world's land area, eclipsing even the tsarist empire as the largest territorially contiguous empire in history.

The New 'Time of Troubles'

The events of 1989–91 were traumatic for the Russians. First in 1989 Central Europe broke away, as country after country had a liberal and nationalist revolution. Then the USSR itself cracked open in 1990, as Lithuania declared its independence, and finally dissolved in August–December 1991, as one Soviet republic after another declared its independence. The 25 million Russians living in the Near-Abroad became justifiably apprehensive. From being colonial masters they became at best second-class citizens in the non-Russian republics, and often, as in the Baltic states, not citizens at all unless they could pass stringent language and residency tests. By 1993–4, after experiencing harassment and economic misery, the 7 million Russians in Kazakhstan, mostly in the north, and the 11 million in Ukraine, mostly in the east, began to cast longing looks at Russia, desiring their reincorporation – which in turn makes Kazakhs and Ukrainians apprehensive about Russian intentions. Some Russians have been returning, but enough remain to cause inter-ethnic tensions.

This astonishing collapse has left the Russians stunned and in disarray, particularly as their command state economy is sliding into chaos as well. A 'Time of Troubles' is upon them with a vengeance. The question remains whether Russia can keep itself together with *de facto* independence emerging in its outer regions, such as the Russian Far East, Daghestan and the other north Caucasus republics. Yet the urge to expand has already reasserted itself. Abkhazia, with Russian troop support, has gone independent from Georgia, and this formerly western province of Georgia has returned to the Russian fold in all but name. Tajikistan and Belarus have been brought under economic and military control; Azerbaijan, north Kazakhstan and east Ukraine are also coming within the ultra-nationalist sights. Zhirinovsky's rhetoric seems to offer a further extension of Russia's borders to the historic frontiers of 1914, with even Alaska added as a fine flourish. The ardent desire for extra land, the Russian geopolitical obsession *par excellence*, is renewing itself in Zhirinovsky, who echoes the saga of centuries of endless expansion.

THE GENERAL CONCEPTION OF THE NEAR-ABROAD

The concept of the Near-Abroad was made up by the Russians immediately after the collapse of the Soviet Union in order to distinguish the newly independent republics from other independent countries of long standing around them. Clearly, it affords less status and, because virtually everybody in Russia considers these republics integral parts of Russia, it may bode ill for the independence of these new states. Neither the British nor the Americans use the expression 'Near-Abroad' officially; they want to avoid getting into the invidious position – in the event of Russia reoccupying, say, the Baltic states – of having in any way condoned such an action.

On 13 December 1993, the very day news was coming through of a stunning electoral victory for the LDPR, the text of an interview with its leader on Serbian TV, Belgrade, was published. An interviewer, Jasmina Stamenić-Pavlović, asked Zhirinovsky: 'What are your party's main slogans?' He replied: **Over a year ago we took a moderate stance regarding all issues, of a rightist-centre patriotic orientation. We are against the restoration of the USSR; we are against the CIS; we favour the restoration of the Russian state as a homeland for all. That is the formula we believe in. National divisions imply constant war, constant friction, constant border issues, accusations, retaliation; of course, all of this is unacceptable. To create new states today, at the end of the twentieth century, that is too expensive and tragic. (Serbian TV, Belgrade, 13.12.93)**

We must force our republics to return. How? And we should not be goodnatured towards them. Kindness is a wonderful quality in a human being, but it's bad for the state. We buy from Uzbekistan third-rate cotton at world prices. We should trade in this way: in exchange for your crappy cotton, we will give you two Zhigulis [small cars] and goodbye. They'll starve – then let them starve. Tribal societies should starve. Why should they be sated at the expense of our civilized Russian nation? (*Kuranty*, 16.11.93)

An interviewer for *Izvestiya* accused Zhirinovsky of publicly proposing the restoration of the tsarist empire by war, abolishing the republics of the Near-Abroad and turning them into provinces ruled by Russian government generals. There will be no war. All these territories – the Baltics, Bessarabia, Caucasus – historically belong to Russia. I proceed from the beginning of history, and you from the end. We need not conquer them. Everything is very simple. We have only to stop supplying timber to Ukraine and all mines of the Donbass are bound to collapse. If we stop supplying everything which we currently supply to Ukraine, the Kravchuk government will crumble in three months. Stop aid, including military aid, to Tajikistan and you'll have Rakhmonov fleeing to Moscow and begging, 'Admit us as a Russian province.' (*Izvestiya*, 30.11.93)

As for ex-Soviet states, Russia supported and fed them under the Communists. Ukraine was the only one to manage it alone, and with great difficulty ... Stop helping them, and they won't last a month. Why should we inflict suffering upon ourselves? Let's make others suffer. (*Izvestiya*, 30.11.93)

We Russians have helped all the republics much too much; we have built everything for them. And since everything we put there is being destroyed, we do not want to help them any more. (*Die Zeit*, 4.2.94)

The flow of refugees [Russians returning from the republics that have become independent] is easy to stop; if we threaten the regions from where Russians are driven out with doing the same thing to their indigenous people in Russia, that will suffice.

Take, for instance, Azerbaijan. Of 500,000 Russians who lived there a mere 100,000 remain. Now, how many Azeris are hanging about Russia at present? One million. So for a start we must evict 400,000 Azeris from Russia to Baku and tell them that if they dare bully Russians again, we'll give back the whole million. The same applies to other regions. Don't forget that there is no democracy without violence. (*Izvestiya*, 30.11.93)

We must all become citizens of Russia. But by Russia I understand the whole of the territory of our state, from the Baltic to the Pacific, from Kushka to Murmansk and from Kishinev to Kamchatka. So I'd like us to return to the old name of our state. Then it would be clear what we were talking about ... As a lawyer, I regard the 1977 Constitution as valid in this country. Under that Constitution, we have existing external state borders, and the Baltic republics, *inter alia*, are part of our country. (Soviet Television, 31.5.91)

Ex-Soviet Union republics, Georgia, Azerbaijan, Armenia or the Central Asian republics – they want to be included in Russia. We don't want that because there's no profit to be together. (Oesterreich 1 Radio, Vienna, 22.12.93)

I am against even a single metre of Soviet territory coming under the jurisdiction of an alien, foreign flag. I should therefore like to see questions of sovereignty resolved in the economic sphere. Economic sovereignty, economic power only, should be given to all regions, oblasts and republics, so that they – to put it in down-to-earth language – choke on that power and ask the centre to take back a part of it. That is the model that is needed – not to reject claims by regions and territories for economic powers but, on the contrary, to give them as many as possible. (Soviet Television, 22.5.91)

I want to tell you bluntly whose side I'd take; in Georgia I will be defending the interests of the Abkhaz people and the Ossetians. In the quarrel between Azerbaijan and Armenia I will tell you bluntly that I'd take the Armenian side.

The Russian president must have a clear-cut position on all these problems. Then the peoples of Russia and the whole of the USSR will calm down. Today, when there is anarchy, when power is paralysed and when the economy and culture have disintegrated, civil war is effectively on our ethnic periphery, and our state continues to disintegrate. (Soviet Television, 22.5.91)

Russia's soldiers will once more stand guard over the 1975 border of the Soviet Union, and once we have put them there, they will not move back a single step. (*Financial Times*, 14.12.93)

The republics wanted independence; they'll beg us on their knees to let them belong to Russia. We will make them provinces. (*La Stampa*, 16.12.93).

The frontiers of the USSR as of 1975, recognized by the world community, will be restored and Russian flags will fly over the cities of Kazakhstan, Central Asia, the Transcaucasus, etc. (ITAR–TASS, World Service Radio, 2.4.94)

Imperialism and colonial policy are foreign notions. We have no such things here. It was normal for us to have colonies. It was good, it was right. (*New Times International*, February 1992)

I will introduce an economic blockade to force the Baltic region to return to Russia. I would use the military as a means to solve the problem of Kazakhstan. Against the Ukraine I would use some military means and some economic measures. (Interview with Zhirinovsky, *Aftenposten*, Oslo, 4.11.91)

I'll bury nuclear waste along the border. I'll move the Semipalatinsk test site to your area. You Lithuanians will die from diseases and radiation. (*Time*, 17.2.94)

Moldova and the Baltic republics will be reduced to the size of Liechtenstein, and the Ukraine must give us back the whole of its southern and eastern regions. (*Frankfurter Allgemeine*, 16.12.93, quoted from *The Last Dash to the South*)

As a possible future president of Russia I want to raise the Russian issue, not because I want the Russian nation to lord it again, but because we have raised all the ethnic issues as they relate to all regions but have forgotten about the Russian people – 155 million Russians whom nobody needs!

They find themselves in a particularly sorry plight in the national republics – 25 million Russians there have become second-class citizens. For this reason I should very much like to see the new president of Russia be not only president of Russia but also president for all Russians living on the territory of the USSR and all Russian speakers and to take under his protection all the small peoples. (Soviet Television, 22.5.91)

Here one cannot fail to speak about the ethnic question and

the state borders. When I spoke on Friday [19 November, 1993] some people said: 'The Baltics and Moldova are far away; I live in the Urals and as a pensioner I want a normal, calm life.' But you are not going to live a quiet and calm life in the Urals or in Magadan if we do not have normal borders.

For example, all of us together built Novotallinsky port [Estonia] under the Communists; it cost 4 billion roubles. It is no longer ours. Now we are building another port, in Leningrad Oblast – more billions of our money. So you pensioners are not going to live better if we are going to lose territories, ports, roads, communications, the southern regions where it is warmer and better. We are all linked together. (Russia TV Channel, Moscow, 23.11.93)

Just look who has suffered most today. Again, it is pensioners of Russian nationality. Why? Well, the Baltics are trying to avoid pensions. Or take the Transcaucasus or Central Asia. They have lost more than anyone. Or take servicemen. They have served their term and are now outside the borders of Russia. Not only can they not receive their service pension, but they are not allowed into any form of activity, since they served, allegedly, in an army of occupation.

To prevent this, to prevent millions of our fellow citizens suddenly, at the end of their lives, from becoming occupationists or colonists, we must have a correct state policy. If people such as Travkin [head of a neo-Fascist party, the Democratic Party of Russia] have a good knowledge of how to build pigsties, we have great need of this. But the State Duma will not be building pigsties. It will be building a new Russian state. And here, experience in building pigsties is not applicable; it is terrible. (Russia TV Channel, Moscow, 23.11.93)

With the change of leadership in Russia, many nonprofessional politicians got into political life. They are considered amateurs by those who oppose them. On the other hand, they are clean of mistakes made during the Soviet regime.

SLAVIC REPUBLICS AND MOLDOVA

President Mircea Snegur of Moldova recalled in mid-December 1993 that in pre-election speeches Zhirinovsky had made covetous remarks about his republic.

The Republic of Moldova is none other than a province of Russia with an already-appointed governor – the commander of the 14th Russian Army stationed in Tiraspol. (*Commersant Daily*, 15.12.93)

Tiraspol is the capital of Trans-Dnestr, a Russian military base on the left bank of the river Dnestr, the rest of the republic being on the river's right bank. The commander of the 14th Army is General Alexander Lebed, a strong supporter of Zhirinovsky's party.

Moldova [alongside the Baltic republics] **will be reduced to the size of Liechtenstein.** (*Frankfurter Allgemeine*, 16.12.93)

In answer to the question 'How can Russia get Ukraine back?' It is all quite simple. **We will stop deliveries of timber to Ukraine and all the mines of the Donbass will collapse. In fact, we will stop supplying anything: in three months the Ukrainians will be on their knees begging us to take them back.** (*Frankfurter Allgemeine*, 14.12.93)

Ukraine must give us back the whole of the eastern and southern parts. (*Frankfurter Allgemeine*, 16.12.93)

Russia will not feed Ukraine as western Germany feeds eastern Germany. (*Die Zeit*, 4.2.94)

Zhirinovsky said of Nikita Khrushchev, the former First Secretary of the Communist Party, that he **was to blame for the loss of Crimea, which had been developed at the expense of all the people** (Russia TV Channel, Moscow, 23.11.93). Khruschchev, who was the First Secretary of the Ukrainian Communist Party in the 1940s, handed over the Crimea to Ukraine in 1954. To him this must have seemed a wholly formal procedure without any possible consequences; little did he know. It is now, of course, a highly contentious issue with Russia, since the majority of the population there is, in fact, Russian, and they do not want to belong to Ukraine – it may even become the cause of a war between the two states.

According to Zhirinovsky, President Yeltsin paid 1 billion roubles in fuel for the Black Sea fleet. His comment on that: **I will take the money from them both for the fuel and for the fleet.** (*Die Zeit*, 4.2.94)

The map on which he redrew the frontiers in Central and Eastern Europe shows the annexation of the Baltic states and of Moldavia, Ukraine and Belarus. As for Russian expansion to the south, he affirms in his book that **reaching the Indian Ocean is vitally important for the Russian nation, on which depends its survival.**

THE BALTIC STATES

On Western ambassadors to the Baltic republics, which he intends to abolish: **They are going to leave the same way they came.** (*The American Spectator*, March 1992)

Lithuania will understand this [the strength of the union] **through economics. Give them an opportunity to separate, but**

only in the 1940 borders. But who in Europe will buy Lithuanian cheese? We need it, but there no one does ... The other way is back to the union. Who, for example, will reconcile the Chechen and the Ingush? Only a Russian governor. (Interview with Zhirinovsky, *Leningradskaya Pravda*, 25.6.91)

In the autumn of 1991 Zhirinovsky asked the Baltfax correspondent to inform the three Baltic state presidents of the time, Landsbergis, Gorbunovs and Ruutel, that he was very displeased with them. Tell them that when I become president of the confederation next spring, they will have to pack their bags. I shall establish a Baltic province. I will have a governor in Riga who will rule Estonia, Latvia and Lithuania. (Russia's Radio, 5.9.91)

Latvia should belong to Russia. Lithuania will become a small independent state, an enclave. (*Die Welt*, 29.1.94)

Instead of the three Baltic republics, there will be one province headed by Governor-General Alksnis (TASS, 8.7.91). Colonel Alksnis from Latvia is a prominent advocate of the restoration of the Soviet Union and supported the August *coup* plotters in 1991 one month after Zhirinovsky made this statement.

The Baltic republics will be reduced to the size of Liechtenstein. (*Frankfurter Allgemeine*, 16.12.93)

I love the Balts. We would gladly live together [with the Balts]. All problems can be settled. God save us from hatred.

[The Balts] are a nice, cultured nation. And you need us. We won't build any frontiers, and Russians would gladly learn Estonian and Lithuanian if only the most favourable solution can be reached ...

Lithuania would speak Russian, Polish and Lithuanian; Estonia would speak Estonian and Russian; and Kaliningrad could speak Russian and German. Just as in Finland, where people use both Finnish and Swedish. And [interethnic] relations are normal there.

I say I love the Balts. I have a slightly negative attitude towards the southerners [presumably the former Soviet southern republics] because there are too many criminals among them.

But our party cherishes the warmest feelings towards the Baltics. It was the journalists who portrayed us as enemies of the Baltic states. I met Landsbergis [former Lithuanian Supreme Council chairman] and I met representatives of the Latvian Supreme Council. I tried to call Arnold Ruutel [former Estonian Supreme Council chairman] in January 1991, but he was busy. I was everywhere, in Tallinn, in Parnu, in Riga – I was everywhere, and I know everything.

We have the best attitude towards the Baltics. I say, I love you all, Estonians, Latvians and Lithuanians, and all Russians who live there. The Baltics is a region of the highest culture and the broadest cooperation – no soldiers, no shooting, mere economy, culture and festivals. (BNS, Tallinn, 14.12.93)

Zhirinovsky was then asked if he was ready to speak to the Baltics in the language of sovereign countries instead of the language of provinces. It's a completely different issue. If Estonians, Latvians and Lithuanians are able to build their countries without discrimination and in compliance with international law, we are ready [to let them do it]. But if they jeer at Russians, depriving them of voting rights, and steal from Russia what belongs to Russia, then we will be forced to use defensive means.

As economists and lawyers, we understand that the Baltics have the cold Baltic Sea to their west and Russia to their east. You have only two options; to sail to Sweden or to live at peace with Russia, but the peace must be just. You should not steal from Russia. If you steal, we will try to prevent it. If you try to deprive Russians of their rights, we will respond with such steps that you will have no electors left to stage elections. For we will always support any Russian, Pole or German who has Russian citizenship. If you use force to deprive them of voting rights, evict them from apartments, dismiss them from jobs, we will use economic methods only to square all accounts with the Baltics, and your countries will collapse two weeks after I have become the president of Russia. There will not be a single Baltic country if you continue your thievish policies. (BNS, Tallinn, 14.12.93)

This irredentist position began to influence Russian foreign policy very soon after the LDPR's stunning victory in mid-December 1993. The Russians had agreed to withdraw the 10,000 troops they had in Latvia and the 3,500 troops in Estonia by August of 1994; this was confirmed at the US–Russian summit in early January 1994.

Then on 18 January 1994 Mr Andrei Kozyrev, the Russian Foreign Minister, indicated that Russian troops would stay in the Baltic in spite of these commitments. He told a conference on Russian policy towards the countries of the CIS and the Baltic states that complete withdrawal of troops 'from this region' would be against Russia's interests because it would create a security vacuum and would leave local ethnic Russians undefended. 'We should not withdraw from these regions, which have been in the sphere of Russian interests for centuries, and we should not fear these words,' TASS quoted him as saying. His confidence in expressing the words is obviously attributable to the wild words on the same and kindred subjects uttered by Zhirinovsky.

Estonia: **If they don't behave, we'll switch off their lights.** (*La Stampa*, 16.12.93)

When I speak about closing borders to whom do I mean this should apply? Only those who rob us. We and you Russians will have total freedom. You will be able to move in any direction. But some sections of the border – say, the Caucasus – could be made stronger or even closed.

In the Baltic there should be tight customs crossings. At present they are growing rich by stealing our non-ferrous metals, timber and so on. At the same time their living standards are getting worse and worse.

They have more and more suicides. In Estonia, where Russians are deprived of electoral rights, where they have no incomes and there are many unemployed, the number of suicides is greater among Estonians. That is proof of the viability of the Russian nation, of the fact that it is more resilient and that it is not a colonizer.

In the free Estonia of today the Estonians are doing away with themselves. They cannot stand it; they are ashamed that Estonia and other independent states are living on the proceeds of robbing and thieving from Russia . . . Only after two and a half years were flimsy customs posts finally put up. Money was spent on this. Our money – from your pockets, pensioners. They should have been made to do this – the Estonians, Latvians and Lithuanians. But borders with Russia are not to their advantage. They benefit from open borders. And why? To steal (Russia TV Channel, Moscow, 23.11.93). Zhirinovsky commented after this that a vote for the LDPR would combat this deplorable problem.

Estonia should be part of Russia, since there are many Russians living there. However, Tallinn should remain a city-state. (*Die Welt*, 29.1.94)

The new Tallinn port cost 4 billion roubles. And they gave it away as a show of good will. And now we are building our own in Luga, breaking our backs in the process. Meanwhile the Estonians keep stealing. A nation of 900,000 and every one of them is a thief! A nation of thieves!

Politics is the art of deception, and we shouldn't be hindered by this factor. However, while we're good-natured and preen ourselves before world opinion, our people will starve and live in misery. (*Kuranty*, 16.12.93)

The LDPR has a representative in Estonia, Petr Rozhok, who asserts that Estonia continues to be an ancient Russian territory. According to him, neither the peace treaty of Uusikaupunki of 1721, confirming Russian occupation of Estonia, nor the Helsinki Treaty of 1975, also doing so, has been repealed.

The 3,000 Russian troops and tens of thousands of retired Russian servicemen and reservists living in Estonia should know, he says, that they are living in an ancient Russian territory. He has appealed to these servicemen to form defence units. Nevertheless, he has been persuading Zhirinovsky not to use phrases such as 'Let us bring our tanks' but to threaten Estonia with economic sanctions only in order to secure its reunion with Russia.

The Estonian government has brought a criminal case against Mr Rozhok, who has been charged for instigating ethnic hostility. Zhirinovsky promptly, on 9 February 1994, voiced explicit threats against each and every one of the 900,000 ethnic Estonians (there are 600,000 Russian Estonians in Estonia) if the government proceeded with legal action against his representative in the country. He said: **I warn the Estonian government that if even a hair should fall from the representative of the LDPR, Petr Rozhok, the Estonian government will have to think about the fate of 900,000 Estonians. I'll swap one Rozhok for 900,000 Estonians. If Rozhok is put into an Estonian jail, an end will come to Estonia and Tallinn** [Estonia's capital]. **We will implement such measures that the Estonians will forget that they are Estonians** (BNS, 9.2.94). The premier, Mart Laar, stated on 10 February 1994 that the origins of anti-Jewish leaflets that were being distributed in Estonia must also be investigated. They might have some connection with the LDPR, he claimed.

Mr Laar said that it would benefit Zhirinovsky to use tranquillizers from time to time: 'Zhirinovsky's irritation has set us pleasantly in the company of all those East European nations with which he has already expressed his annoyance.' **The Baltics are Russian land. I will destroy you. I will start burying nuclear waste in the border zone of Smolensk Oblast; the Semipalatinsk will be transferred to your area. You Lithuanians will die of disease and radiation. I will remove the Russians and the Poles. I am God. I am a tyrant. There will be no Lithuanians, Latvians or Estonians in the Baltics. I will act like Hitler in 1932. The champagne you are quaffing today is your own wake** (*National Affairs*, 3.10.91).

It may well be that such wild statements do not make the same horrifying impression on his Russian audience – his sole concern – as they do on us, who are accustomed to euphemisms and extreme verbal circumspection – which does not mean that they do not send a chill down the spines of Lithuanians, of course.

THE CAUCASUS

When a hundred or two hundred years ago the Georgian tsar sent his delegation, Georgia was perishing, awash with blood spilt by alien invaders. This treaty says: with Russia for eternity. It was Georgia that was asking – but today they reject us and today the Transcaucasus military district troops there are occupants. If we were not there, there would have been no Georgia or Armenia on the political map of the world. I say this as an Eastern expert . . . The maps of the general staff of the Iranian and Turkish armies do not feature Georgia – all this is shaded there as provinces, or *vilayets*, of Turkey and Iran. The word 'Batumi' is not written there – it is Batum-Kale, Sukhum-Kale – and it is because the Soviet troops are there that Georgia and Armenia exist . . . So, let them stop and think about the future of their countries and not strive for independence . . . let Georgia and Armenia die for the edification of all the peoples of the Soviet Union. They will die within a year; these two republics will disappear. It is a matter of great regret for me, but it will happen because they are situated in a region in which they will not be able to stand on their own two feet. (Soviet Television, 22.5.91)

There were no states in the Caucasus; it was just a tract of wilderness (*New Times International*, October 1992). Here Zhirinovsky bends history to his own ideas. The Caucasus in the early nineteenth century, when Russia conquered it, was no tract of wilderness. Of course, he may simply be ignorant of this fact.

When Azerbaijan and Georgia crawl back on their knees, imploring to join Russia, they should be quarantined for as long as possible. (*Izvestiya*, 10.11.93)

The Caucasus must be cut off from Russia, separated by a Berlin Wall. We must confine ourselves to observation, while selling weapons to all factions. The Caucasus was conquered by Russia and not assimilated – we must never forget that. In the past there were no modern weapons of mass destruction, so the tsar needed the Caucasus as a buffer, as an outpost, but now we have no need for the Caucasus. Let them sort things out between themselves while our diplomats and secret agents keep tabs on them from a distance. (*Le Monde*, 23.12.93)

During the build-up to the December 1993 election Zhirinovsky condemned the Civic Union, a party headed by the chief of the Russian Union of Entrepreneurs and Businessmen. It appeals for peace, stability and calm, but its leader, Arkady Volsky, is responsible for the ruin of Russia's industry and bloodshed in Nagorno Karabach. (Russia TV Channel, Moscow, 23.11.93)

We don't need to fight ... We should simply not get involved. They will kill each other: Armenians–Azerbaijanis, Turks–Armenians, mountain peoples–Turks, Afghans–Tajiks, Tajiks–Uzbeks, etc. And then they, or more likely the survivors, will run to beg from Russia some status for district rights (*Kuranty*, 16.12.93). Zhirinovsky's designs southwards take in the Caucasus and Central Asia as one vast stretch of murky, mainly Turkic, disturbance.

Events in the Caucasus demonstrate that, without Russia, civil war breaks out: Armenia against Azerbaijan, Georgia against Abkhazia and Ossetia. The same thing will happen along the southern border of Russia: Uzbeks, Tajiks, Kazakhs – they will all fight one another. There will be no Russian troops in these regions. The only thing we can do is to sell arms. If these peoples want to buy weapons, they can only do it in Russia. We do not want a new Afghanistan. But what do we see there? No government, no president, towns fight against one another, cities get destroyed, the transport breaks down ... The entire region will perish. Iran, Turkey, Afghanistan will interfere: it'll be an inferno, just like Lebanon or Northern Ireland. Then, twenty or thirty years later, they'll come in tears and beg us ... Russia could save the situation – chiefly by psychological means ... Both these regions and the international community will ask us; only if they pay for it will we put an end to the catastrophe – and reliably. (*Die Welt*, 29.1.93)

CENTRAL ASIA

Zhirinovsky has spoken of Uzbekistan, whose capital is Tashkent, as 'our Tashkent province'. This assault on the republic's independence was attacked in the local press, one Uzbek newspaper saying that his election speech employing the phrase 'fell like snow from the sky' (Ostankino Channel 1 TV, Moscow, 26.11.93).

I was born in Central Asia myself, you see. We regard it as Russia, not Central Asia. Initially, it was populated by Russians only, and Russians brought civilization there. The Kazakhs lived in nomad tents. They had no electricity, nothing, and all they had was cattle, sheep breeding, like all the primitive communal tribes. There was no state there. (*New Times International*, February 1992)

Let Muslim regimes rule in Kabul and in Tashkent. But our government supports the old Communists there. Why? The Komintern again (*Le Monde*, 23.12.93). (For Komintern and

Kominternism, see Chapter 6.) At the same time he regards as inevitable Russian domination of Central Asia as well as of the Middle East.

They will all fight among themselves and we will come in when they invite us (*Guardian*, 31.1.94). That is another piece of wish-projection on the part of Zhirinovsky. His audience, his constituency, is well aware of the danger of civil war in Russia, consequently the dream image he wants to present here is the opposite: a peaceful, and strong Russia that is asked to create order in the turbulent southern regions.

Kazakhstan is an artificial creation that can thrive only under Russian domination. (*Frankfurter Allgemeine*, 16.12.93)

I would ask Mum, 'Why do we have such bad housing conditions? Why can't we get an individual apartment?' Mum replied: 'We aren't Kazakhs ... Kazakhs get priority'. (*The Last Dash to the South*)

Stop aid, including military aid, to Tajikistan and you'll have Rakhmonov fleeing to Moscow and begging, 'Admit us as a Russian province.' (*Izvestiya*, 30.11.93)

As a matter of fact, Andrei Kozyrev, the Russian Foreign Minister, sounded more bellicose two months earlier than Zhirinovsky was here. Kozyrev, dressed in battle gear in Dushanbe (the Tajik capital) said: 'We will not give up Tajikistan without a fight.'

2

THE SECURITY ZONE AROUND THE NEAR-ABROAD

Russia has long had grave security concerns, which have intimately shaped its foreign policy and history. Bordering every one of the world's major geopolitical zones, Europe, the Middle East, Central Asia, the Far East and North America, it is keen to pre-empt enemies before they strike, including those from within.

Russian autocracy aimed to establish absolute internal security and external impregnability. Hence Ivan the Terrible's creation, at the discretion of the tsar alone, of what effectively came to be a secret police, the *Oprichnina*, who wore black uniforms and rode on black steeds, foreshadowing the Black Hundred (see Introduction). The Soviet Union aimed at total control over the population by forcing everybody to remain at home by means of the internal passport system; it was a criminal offence, for example, to travel to Moscow without permission, much as serfs in tsarist Russia could not move outside their villages. External security was assured by electric fences, border guards in turrets and pillboxes along thousands of miles of frontier. Foreign visitors were subject to the strictest customs searches and KGB surveillance. An all-enveloping calm was to reign over the Soviet lands.

But the Russians, whether in tsarist or Soviet times, still remained acutely anxious of what lay immediately beyond their borders – hence the idea of security zones to forestall threats lurking therein.

The Russians have been obsessed by conquerors and conspirators against their security for good reasons: the very real attempts made upon them by the Tatars, the Teutonic knights, the Poles, the Swedes, the Ottomans, the French, the British and, in this century, the Japanese in 1905, the Germans in 1914, the British, Americans, French and Japanese in 1918–20, the Japanese again in a little-known war in the Far East in 1936–9, the Nazis in 1941–5 and then the relentless Cold War.

Stalin occupied Central Europe in 1945 to repel and defeat the Nazis. He hung on to it ostensibly to spread the socialist gospel but, more fundamentally, to prevent another Nazi-style invasion. During the Cold War the Soviet Union was surrounded by Western military bases and missiles from Norway to Turkey and Iran, from Korea and Japan to Alaska and the Arctic. When it tried to install missiles in Cuba in 1962, the USA reacted with an hysteria that the Soviet leadership itself felt all the more strongly. On the other hand, such a reaction was not surprising, since Moscow infringed the not entirely tacit agreement between the two superpowers: the mutual recognition of their respective spheres of influence. The USA accepted Moscow's reassertion of power in its 'security zone' in parts of Central Europe by acquiescing in the suppression of the Hungarian revolution by Soviet troops in 1956. The USSR would presumably have been equally hysterical had the Americans done otherwise.

The spectre of a profound threat to the Soviet Union appeared in 1979. A fundamentalist Islamic regime came to power in Iran, and since there have always been close ties between Iran and Afghanistan (part of the present area of Afghanistan was historically Iranian land), the possibility that Islamic fundamentalism would spread from Iran was a reasonable assumption to make. The frail pro-Soviet Communist government and ruler were deemed unsafe by Moscow. The

Soviets applied the Kremlin's right, under the Brezhnev doctrine, to extend help to such a regime in the form of military intervention.[1] The Communist regime was seen as a stooge of the Kremlin by the fierce Muslim mountain tribesmen of the country, whose way of life for centuries had involved perpetual warfare and tolerated no outside overlord.

After the Soviet intervention by force, it turned out that the USA did not accept it as a proper application of the 'Brezhnev doctrine' to Afghanistan and provided massive help to the Mujahedin. The Soviet Chief of Staff voiced his objection to the venture, citing two British failures to conquer Afghanistan in the last century; he was clearly aware of the difficult terrain and the nature of the opponent. The Afghans inflicted only the second military defeat of the Bolsheviks and by far the most serious (the first was simply the failure of the victorious Red Army at the end of the civil war in 1920 to take Warsaw and turn Poland Communist, a quixotic adventure). The Soviet defeat undermined confidence in the regime not only among the population but also among the very leadership. In modern Russia change has often come after military defeat, such as the emancipation of serfs in 1861 after the Crimean War of 1854–6, the 1905 Russian Revolution, the Stolypin reforms after the Russian defeat in the war with Japan in 1905 and, most significant, the 1917 revolution after the defeat by the Germans in the First World War. And we know what happened after the Afghan defeat.

Soviet power had reached its maximum territorial extent in

---

1 There is a curious parallel here between not letting a Communist regime become renegade to Moscow and the tsarist law which forbade reconversion to another faith (Catholic, Protestant or Muslim) for those who had already converted to the Russian Orthodox faith.

the early 1980s, holding areas in Afghanistan. The Russian instinct to expand when in trouble defeated its purpose in the most spectacular way in Russian history. Yet by no means all Russians have learned this lesson. Modern Russia has inherited the security obsession, and Zhirinovsky fully exemplifies it. The countries of the Near-Abroad that he wishes to occupy are to be put in quarantine by having buffer zones around them, although he would refer to these as part of Russia and does not speak of buffer zones.

He is exploiting the special fears and resentments of the Russians that have accumulated over centuries, reaching a pitch in Soviet times, when Moscow was the negative centre of the Western world, feared, loathed and derided. The Russians have a curious sense of isolation in their vast land, unknown to the Scandinavians or West Europeans, who jostle against each other all the time. The Russians know that their neighbours fear them, not without good reason. Yet what the Russians really want is gratitude on the part of the countries occupied by them or drawn into their sphere of influence and, more generally, to be loved to the extent of being invited in to rule – or so Zhirinovsky and his ilk imagine.

TATAR AND TURK

Of the major invasions that have scarred the Russians' common memory, the first that lives on is that of the Tatars, under the notorious Gengiz Khan, and the Golden Horde he left behind. Russia suffered the Tatar yoke for more than two centuries after 1240. This coloured Russia's relations with Turkey and Central Asia thereafter. When Zhirinovsky says, 'Nothing would really happen to the world if the whole Turkish nation perished,' he is expressing a Tatar-tutored Russian hostility to all things Turkic and Mongol. The Central Asians and the Azeris, as well as the Turks themselves, surround the Russians, Zhirinovsky complains, and are a menace to civilization. A new pan-Turkic alliance is feared and needs to be forestalled. The Great Game played out by Russia and Britain in the nineteenth century across Eurasia, is being re-enacted, with Turkey and Iran as the latter-day foils to Russia.

The Turks are not only remnants of the Tatars in ultra-nationalist Russian eyes; they are the successors to the destroyers of Byzantium, the Ottomans who seized Constantinople in 1453. The great destiny of being the Third Rome, centre of the Orthodox faith, the Russians owe, paradoxically, to the Ottomans. But they have always feared that the Turks would one day do to them what the Ottomans accomplished with Byzantium. Fear of the Turks led Muscovy to build up a formidable army, which by the 1670s was 'much the largest in Europe', claims Hellie,[2] probably an overestimate, considering French and Ottoman capacities at the time. But the Russian army was certainly a force to be reckoned with by then. 'In the next decade massive Turkish thrusts [into the south of Russia] from the Black Sea were painfully checked at the price of making a wilderness of much of the Ukraine.'[3] Fear of the Turks was kept alive in a series of wars that the Russians lost or only perilously won; even Peter the Great was defeated and nearly overwhelmed by them. The Tatars of Crimea, the last remnants of the Golden Horde on Russian soil, were vassals of the Ottoman sultans and a thorn in the Russian flesh, kept at bay by the vigilant Cossacks for centuries. It was not until the time

2 R. Hellie, *Enserfment and Military Change in Muscovy*, Chicago, 1917, p. 226.

3 Perry Anderson, *Lineages of the Absolutist State*, Verso, 1974, p. 338.

of Catherine the Great that Russia took to triumphing against the Turks, occupying Crimea in 1783 and encroaching along the Black Sea coast, between the rivers Bug and Dnieper, by 1792. Despite the decline of the Ottoman empire thenceforward, it remained a redoubtable power. A dispute arose over the Holy Land under Turkish rule, and over Russia's championship of oppressed Orthodox populations under the Ottomans, that led to the outbreak of the Crimean War in 1854, in which the Turks fought bravely and successfully.[4] After suffering the reverse of losing Serbia and Bulgaria to Russian arms in 1877–8, the Turks gave them a drubbing in the First World War that the Russians have not forgotten.

Logically, Iran might seem the most frightening opponent of Russia today, with its fundamentalist Islamic regime. The ideology, indeed, is feared, but more in Turkic Central Asia, whither it spreads mostly from Turkey, oddly enough. Iran has never won a major war against Russia. It is Turkey that is really alarming in Russian nationalist eyes. The pan-Turkic threat of an alliance of a Turkic-speaking people, from Istanbul to Baku to Samarkand, Tashkent and Almaty (Alma Ata) in Central Asia, is what Zhirinovsky hopes to thwart with his Last Dash to the South, while, in order to round out the borders and obtain access to the Indian Ocean, Iran and Afghanistan are to be occupied as well. Zhirinovsky is determined to get in his retaliation first.

4 Nicholas Riyasanovsky, *A History of Russia*, 4th edition, OUP, 1984, p. 337.

BESSARABIAN STAKES

Another near-by state with a special relationship with the Roman Empire and its own brand of rival Orthodox Christianity is Romania, the land of Dracula, of Vlad the Impaler, who left his enemies to die on stakes. Romanians have a Latin language and are convinced that they descend from the Roman legionaries left behind in Dacia, the Roman province there in the third century, a fact impossible to establish, since recurrent nomadic invasion has left a gaping hole in the historical record of the next millennium of Romanian history.[5] In the thirteenth century Wallachia and Moldavia, Romania's two main provinces, fell under Ottoman vassalage. Bessarabia, a strip of fertile, vine-growing territory stretching between the Pruth and the Dnestr down to the Black Sea, has long been a bone of contention between the Russians and the Romanians. In modern times Russia took it in 1812 in the aftermath of expelling Napoleon. It was reunited with Romania in 1918–19 to form a Great Romanian state with Transylvania, populated by Romanians, Hungarians and Saxons.

In 1939 Stalin made a pact with Hitler, under one term of which the USSR could retake Bessarabia, which it duly did in June 1940. Realizing its strategic significance for the whole Black Sea area, Stalin detached the southern coastline and put it into Ukraine, while the remainder of Bessarabia, together with Trans-Dnestr, on the left bank of the Dnestr, hosting a strong Soviet garrison, formed the Moldovan Soviet Republic. In 1989 this became independent Moldova. Its national identity has been troubled by three developments. One is that national-

5 H. H. Stahl, *Les Anciennes communautés villageoises roumaines, asservissement et pénétration capitalistes*, Bucarest, 1969, pp. 1–45.

ists crave reunion with Romania; the second is that the Russians and Ukrainians of Trans-Dnestr want to rejoin Russia or Ukraine; the third is that 180,000 Turkic-speaking people, the Christian Gagauz, want secession in the south. After a war from 1989 until July 1992 between the right-bank Moldovans and Trans-Dnestr was brought to a close by the arrival of the Russian 14th Army 'Peacekeepers' an uneasy truce remains.

The commander of the 14th Army, General Alexander Lebed, proud possessor of the Cossack Cross for the defence of Trans-Dnestr, is a warm supporter of Zhirinovsky. Zhirinovsky himself is right behind the Trans-Dnestr Russian cause. The Romanians, among whom he would include the Moldovans, are 'Italian gypsies'. Romania is an 'artificial country'; it is Russians, not upstart Romanians, who are the true heirs of Rome. The Romanians are to be put in their place, losing Transylvania to Hungary and roaming around a truncated Moldavia and Wallachia in Zhirinovsky's future Europe. Bessarabia and Trans-Dnestr are to return to Russia. Moldova will be wiped off the map.

This boost to Hungary, this free present of somebody else's land, is coupled with a curious detachment towards the Hungarians on the part of Zhirinovsky; as Magyars, not Slavs, they do not seem to interest him. True, on passing through Budapest in February, he nearly missed a plane and called them 'the whore nation', but this is just his customary temper. There is no reason to infer any special Magyar irritation.

BULGARIAN BRETHREN

The Bulgars are Slav brothers for Zhirinovsky, fit to belong to his greater Slav union. As an Orthodox country, Bulgaria is targeted as a key state for pan-Slavism. But the Bulgarians, despite being liberated from Ottoman rule in 1878 by the Russians, are now averse to Russian domination, having endured four decades of it in the 1949–89 period, a sufficient inoculation against pan-Slavic temptations.

THE ALOOF CZECHS AND SLOVAKS

The Czechs were the least anti-Russian Catholic Slav people before 1939. But forty years of forced Communist rule, and the crushing of the Prague Spring in August 1968 (bringing to an end Dubček's Communism with a human face), make it unlikely that the Czechs and Slovaks hanker after union with Russia, when they cannot abide union even with each other. Zhirinovsky's 'Fascism with a human face' is not likely to go down well in the Czech republic, whose predecessor state, Czechoslovakia, was the sole liberal democracy in Central Europe surrounded by Fascist power between the two world wars.

THE LURE AND MENACE OF GREATER GERMANY

The one foreign country that Zhirinovsky respects, and even admires, is Germany. In this he is like many of his countrymen, who remember both the great contribution Germany has made to their civilization and the devastating invasions that it has successively inflicted upon the Russians.

The Hanseatic League of trading cities, along the North Sea and the Baltic, to which Nizhny Novgorod owed its preeminence in the Middle Ages, brought a rich trade in timber, fur, wax, honey and wines to medieval Russia, as well as valuable cultural links with the West. But the Teutonic knights, renowned at the time for their depredations and cold, methodical brutality, pressed ever eastwards in the early Middle Ages.

Every Russian knows the story of how Alexander Nevski beat them on the thawing ice of Lake Peipus in April 1242, into which the knights and their mounts sank (memorably evoked by Eisenstein's film of the same name).

The Romanov tsars renewed their line by marrying German princesses, giving Russia her greatest empress, Catherine the Great (1762–96). German thought and culture pervaded the St Petersburg court and intellectual life (Hegel having a huge influence), even more than French, although French was the international language of aristocracy in the eighteenth century. German settlers played a valuable part in improving industry, commerce and banking at this time. Zhirinovsky is insistent that the Volga and other Germans are very welcome in Russia and could facilitate a German–Russian alliance, which he strongly favours at times.

The reason why the last qualification is necessary in the case of Zhirinovsky and many other Russians is that the twentieth century has brought the horrors of two world wars, which the Russians attribute to German mischief in 1914 and German malice in 1941, as they also do the Bolshevik Revolution of 1917. The Bolshevik takeover, the Russians believe, would have been impossible if the Germans had not allowed Lenin through in a sealed train from Switzerland to St Petersburg in April 1917. In many Russian eyes a German Jewish thinker, Karl Marx, and his reputedly half-German follower, Lenin, visited this calamity upon Russia. It was defeat at the hands of Germany, first at Tannenberg in 1914 (a kind of re-enactment of the great battle of 1410 but going the other way), then more comprehensively in 1917, that gave Lenin his chance.

The Nazis were in some sense the successors of the Teutonic knights in Barbarossa (the name of the campaign), who laid waste wherever they invaded and, turning prisoners of war into slave labour, worked them to death. It cost Russia at least 20 million lives to oust the Germans in the 'Great Patriotic War' of 1941–5. Fear of another German attack accounted mainly for Russia's occupation of Central Europe in 1945 and hence for the Cold War. No country has traumatized the Russians so profoundly as Germany, and this legacy will never be forgotten or quite forgiven. Yet the phenomenal economic success of Germany after the war won the Russians' at first reluctant but then increasingly admiring respect. Stalin himself, in his last years, expressed regret that Germany had not remained an ally of Russia, for he was prepared for a long-lasting German–Russian *rapprochement*. Many Russians today would like nothing better than just such a *rapprochement*, for which German reunification has prepared the way. Zhirinovsky expresses the ambivalence of this attitude towards Germany when he talks alternately of establishing again a 'common border' and of 'annihilating Germany in World War III'.

One way such a border could be re-established is if Russia gave back its enclave Königsberg (Kaliningrad) in East Prussia, between Lithuania and Poland. An old Hanseatic League town, and home of Emmanuel Kant, Königsberg was seized by Stalin in 1945 and repopulated by Russians. (Either the German inhabitants fled to Germany or, of those who remained, one part died of hunger and cold while the rest were deported to Siberia.) The common border would still come about only if Lithuania and Poland were truncated, both of which possibilities Zhirinovsky has contemplated. Kaliningrad is of little use to Russia, except as a garrison.[6] However, the Russian armed

---

6 It is not quite such a garrison town as Lermontov describes in *A Hero of Our Times*. Times have, indeed, moved on. Littered with scrap metal and the debris of an empire, Kaliningrad is a dump in the literal sense of the word.

forces regard it as very important in that role. It is estimated that there are 200,000 Russian troops there with very modern weapons, and troops withdrawn from the Baltic states, Poland and Germany are stationed in the area. A formidable military force is being built up, which causes concern not only to the Balts and the Poles but also to Germany and Sweden. Zhirinovsky's plans are, therefore, hardly likely to please the Russian military high command.

Zhirinovsky may well have territorial concession to Germany as his trump card with which to woo the Germans to his cause. There is no doubt that repossession of Königsberg (as it would be immediately renamed) would be an offer that the Germans would find difficult to resist, genuine and heart-felt as their abdication of irredentist aspirations now is.

LITHUANIAN AND POLISH REVERBERATIONS

The two states enclosing Kaliningrad, Lithuania and Poland, played an unusually significant role in early Russian history. Russia developed its original Byzantine identity in a contest with Lithuania, a large, backward state on the Baltic only belatedly converted to Christianity, which by the late fourteenth century had an empire stretching from the Baltic to the Black Sea, including White Russia and Ukraine. The distended Lithuanian state was largely Russified in language and customs. In 1386, however, it allied itself with Poland, and after failure in 1399 against the Mongols the Lithuanians joined the Poles to win the great battle of Tannenberg against the Teutonic knights in 1410. Lithuania redirected itself westwards towards Poland and came heavily under its influence long before its formal inclusion into Poland with the Union of Lublin in 1569.

Zhirinovsky considers Lithuania the one Baltic state with a

right to exist, albeit in a truncated form. Although Russia occupied it in 1914, this was only by reason of its earlier incorporation into Poland, whose Lithuanian east was incorporated into Russia in 1795 in the Third Partition of Poland. Since an independent Poland should cease to exist, having been Russian in 1914, so its incorporation of Lithuania in 1569 should be annulled by tolerating an autonomous Lithuania today, he reasons.

Poland has long had a complex relationship with Russia. A powerful state in the Middle Ages, Poland made a bid for the control of Russia at the 'Time of Troubles' in 1603–14.

The Poles backed a pretender to the failing line of the Ruriks, the false Dimitri, who ruled for a brief period. The Poles then backed a second false Dimitri without success. After his fall the Poles declared war upon Moscow, and Russia finally rallied against the threat of occupation by heretical Catholic Poles with the new Romanov dynasty, established in 1613.

Poland remained a source of disruption in Russian eyes until it was partitioned in three stages, in 1772, 1793 and 1795. Despite Russia's subjugation of Poland, the Russians remained afraid of a Polish conquest of their Russian lands, which actually occurred in a 'Time of Troubles' in 1917–20. The Red Army marched on Warsaw, but in a heroic resistance the Poles, helped by the French, repelled them. This gave them a reprieve for twenty-five years.

Poland is feared by the Russians, not just on its own account, as the intruder at times of troubles, but also as occupying the historic route taken by Western invaders, latterly Napoleon and Hitler. For more reasons than one, nervous Russian nationalists have always wanted to subjugate Poland; Zhirinovsky, at least verbally, is promising this to them.

FINLAND THE BRAVE

Finland was for centuries the easternmost province of Sweden. The army of Charles XII of Sweden was defeated by Peter the Great at Poltova in southern Ukraine in 1709. In 1808–9 Alexander I fought and defeated· Sweden. Russia took over Finland, Finland becoming a Grand Duchy, with the tsar as Grand Duke. The Finns were given considerable autonomy at first, and good fighters were used by the Russians to quell periodic Polish revolts. But from the 1890s St Petersburg followed a policy of Russification that swiftly alienated the Finns, who thenceforward gave sanctuary from the attention of the tsarist police to many Russian revolutionaries, notably Lenin and senior Bolsheviks. For several crucial months of counter-revolution in the summer of 1917 Lenin took refuge in Helsinki, from where he was able to direct preparations for the October Revolution. The revolution proved to be of benefit to the Finns, who took their chance to become independent.

Finland is now about to become a member of the European Union. Zhirinovsky's call for the Russian occupation of Finland is a rhetorical flourish and probably not much more than that. By talking of reincorporating Finland, Poland and Alaska (which was Russian between 1799 and 1867), he is reminding his listeners that his aim is to recreate the glories of tsarist Russia, not those of the Soviet Union. Even he must realize that the West would not tolerate occupation of any one of these territories, but for the moment his only concern is to maximize his appeal to Russian voters.

AREAS THAT FORMED PART OF THE
OLD TSARIST EMPIRE

Zhirinovsky, like Hitler before him, is fond of cartography. He was interviewed in December 1993 by Rolf Gauffin, the former Swedish ambassador to Moscow, who was visiting the capital for the Italian geopolitical review, *Limes*. On the wall behind the LDPR's leader was his party's emblem, a stylized map of the former Russian Empire, which included Finland and Alaska. It was surmounted by an eagle and the words 'Liberty and Law'. **'Liberty and Law ... and Russia,'** declared Zhirinovsky, placing his pointer on Alaska.

This interview yielded another even more interesting map, the continent of Europe as seen by Zhirinovsky. Its salient features, drawn sketchily by him with a pen, involve:

1. Poland to be divided between Germany and Russia;
2. Germany to take over Austria, the Czech republic and Slovenia;
3. Russia to take over the Baltic republics (apart from Tallinn and Kaunas);
4. Bulgaria to take over Macedonia and parts of Greece, Turkey and Romania;
5. Russia to take over Ukraine, Moldova and probably Slovakia;
6. The UN out of the former Yugoslavia;
7. The final flourish ... Zhirinovsky arrogantly signs his own name.

This map was published in *Le Monde*, the French daily, on 29 January 1994. It was republished in colour in *The European* of 3–8 February. He told Gauffin: **This Greater Germany and the new Russia will one day form an alliance that will neutralize Europe.**

Zhirinovsky said that the return to Germany of Königsberg would be **a present from Russia** (*The European*, 3–8.2.94)

The map shows Poland once again divided between Russia and Germany. This would be the fifth partition of Poland. All the Poles get as compensation is Lvov, capital of western Ukraine.

The Baltic states are swallowed up by Russia. But Tallinn, capital of Estonia, escapes this fate and becomes a city-state like Liechtenstein or Luxembourg. Kaunas, former capital of Lithuania, also becomes a city-state. Germany repeats its adventures of the 1930s and obtains Austria and the Czech Republic as well as its half of Poland; meanwhile Belarus, Ukraine and Moldova become parts of Russia, as does Slovakia.

As an alternative, Zhirinovsky says, Slovakia could be the nucleus of an eastern European economic community. The LDPR leader expresses his firm advocacy of Slav interests in a 'greater Bulgaria', which would absorb areas of Greece, Turkey, Romania and the former Yugoslav republic of Macedonia.

Hungary would take Transylvania from Romania, which, Zhirinovsky states, **is not a country, but only a space where Italian gypsies live.** Croatia and Serbia would divide Bosnia between them. For Zhirinovsky **the whole of the Transcaucasus is a nest of bandits and crooks of no interest to Russia.**

Here, as in Central Asia, there will be **all-out war.** All this is highly reminiscent of the 1930s and, in particular, of the Nazi–Soviet pact of August 1939, which made certain the outbreak of the Second World War. This pact, negotiated by Foreign Minister Ribbentrop of Germany and Stalin in the Kremlin, involved the Fourth Partition of Poland and the confirmation of, or agreement to, territorial changes very much in the spirit of Zhirinovsky's map. The LDPR leader likes to dissociate himself from Hitler, who was, of course, the guiding spirit behind the pact on the German side. It is not hard to see why the publication of Zhirinovsky's map should have set off alarm bells once again in all of Europe's chancelleries in early 1994, nor why he has a lot to live down if he wishes to make clear to the world that he's not a 'Russian Hitler' (*Le Monde*, 29.1.94, *The European*, 3–8.2.94).

On the famous map showing the borders of central and East European countries redrawn by Zhirinovsky, western Poland is annexed to Germany, but Poland gets back some of the territories annexed by the Soviet Union after the Second World War that now are part of Ukraine. A month or so later, during his visit to Poland, he repudiated any earlier suggestion that Poland would have to cede territory to Russia. How about Poland? **Well, Prussia used to be a German state which included Breslau (Wrocław) and Stettin (Szczecin); these areas should be annexed to Germany. Poland can have the area around Lvov, in compensation for the loss of territory along its western frontier** (*Die Welt*, 29.1.94).

I would not like anybody to think, even theoretically, that the Polish borders should be changed, ever; we are for a strong Poland, so that Russia and Poland can be good neighbours (UPI, 12.3.94). This statement is, however, somewhat weakened by another of his announcements made at the same time: **Poland can never be a corridor for foreign armies for aggression towards Russia** (MON, 12.3.94).

Zhirinovsky was a guest of Janusz Bryczkowski, leader of the Polish right-wing National Front. Bryczkowski announced in his opening speech of the first congress of his party that it was 'ideologically associated' with Zhirinovsky. He added, moreover, that the guarantor of borders in Europe was a strong Russia: 'Let no one think that NATO is the guarantor of our borders.'

Russia has no territorial claim and its army would never go west, stated Zhirinovsky, adding that there was a need for pan-Slavic solidarity, in which both Russia and Poland would have an immense role to play (MON, 12.3.94). Elaborating this suggestion: **If Poland and the other Slavic countries want it, Russia will be ready to establish a political alliance** (UPI, 12.3.94).

What does such a plan entail? **There would be our common army with equal rights – not a situation where Poles will be shining the shoes of German officers. They are drawing you into NATO to turn you into cannon fodder** (UPI, 12.3.94). Bryczkowsky was invited to attend the World Congress of Slavonic Nations in Moscow in April.

When in Warsaw in March 1994, Zhirinovsky hobnobbed with Janusz Bryczkowski, who not only regards Zhirinovsky as 'Poland's great friend' but also sees him as Russia's future president. Bryczkowski himself intends to run for the presidency of Poland. Zhirinovsky plans to set up a pan-Slavic union under Russian leadership, stretching from the Adriatic to the Baltic. **We have enough potential to become the most powerful community on this planet. We have the largest territory and our reserves are sufficient for Europe's development for the next three hundred years ... I want Poles to be rich and drive Mercedes and Lincolns instead of cleaning their windows ... Polish soldiers should be a part of the Slavonic army with equal rights** instead of allowing themselves to be dragged into a situation where they would be NATO's cannon fodder ... (On Polish–Russian relations) **May there always be only flowers and the smiles of Polish girls, the most beautiful** in the world, between us ... The best borders are sea borders. May the Baltic Sea be the common border of Russia, Poland and Germany. In all conflicts up to now these three countries have been the losers, while others have won. Now we want the opposite to happen. (The Warsaw Voice, 20.3.94)

We have no use for either Poland or Finland today, he said in answer to a question in an interview given to *Der Spiegel*, 51, 1993. When the interviewer asked him, 'What about tomorrow?' he did not give a direct answer but went on about the Russian people not wanting to be irritated day after day by television pictures of people on warm beaches asking for Coca-Cola when in Russia the temperature is 20 degrees centigrade below freezing.

Finland wants Karelia back. As for that, I say that if Finland wants Karelia, then Finland must come into Russia. We will not take one single step westwards – they'll all come back to Russia one day. Then he assured the Finns that he had nothing against Finland but at the same time warned them: Keep away from NATO and all the other military alliances that are directed against Russia otherwise Russian and German troops will fight on Finnish territory. (*Izvestiya*, 5.4.94)

The Finns: They are afraid of me. (*La Stampa*, 16.12.93)

FROM PRAGUE TO BUCHAREST

Zhirinovsky invokes the heritage of the Soviet liberation of Czechoslovakia and Central Europe as a whole from Nazism in 1944. Why did they enter Prague on 9 May? Why did millions shed their blood? Today they insult us there. They have erected a monument to Bandera; they have erected monu-

ments to SS men. What about our army and the older generation? They are spat upon today. Why did they shed their
blood? (Soviet television, 31.5.91)

The Czech Republic will one day belong to Germany ...
One day Slovakia will belong to Russia ... Hungary wants to
protect its population in Romania. (*Die Welt*, 29.1.94)

On 8 February 1994 Zhirinovsky gave an interview on
Czech television in which he confirmed that he had been
invited by the Czech Republican Party, led by Miroslav Sladek,
to visit the Czech Republic, a visit that was several times
postponed, given the Czech government's express hostility to
it. This is easy to understand in the light of his many aggressive
utterances about Central Europe, echoed in this very interview,
in which Zhirinovsky made a verbal attack on President Vaclav
Havel as well as painting a lurid picture of the Czechs' future:
If Vaclav Havel feels unhappy about my visit, then I am also
unhappy about the fact that playwrights can become presidents
of certain countries.

This is not right. I am not going to write theatre plays, I am
not going to write *The Cherry Orchard* if I am not Chekhov.
Why, then, is a playwright a president? Your country is dying.
I can assure you that in ten years' time there will be no
Moravia, no Sudeten. In ten years' time the entire Czech
nation will curse Havel, as the Russian people are cursing
Gorbachev. All, including me, used to applaud him – after
Chernenko we saw Gorbachev as a good option. Nowadays
we curse that villain.

The same situation will exist in your country. Vaclav
Havel will die, and in ten years' time young Czechs will
curse him. They will be forced to speak German; they will
be forced to forgo their mother tongue; they will be forced

to attend Holy Mass in German churches and to clean the boots of German officers. This will be the Czechs' fate in a few years' time.

We do not want this. We intend to call a congress of Slavonic nations on 2 and 3 April. We are 300 million. We will live in our East European community and will not serve Western Europe. (Czech TV1, Prague, 8.2.94)

Zhirinovsky makes frequent visits to the Balkans, especially to his beloved Serbia. To do this he has to fly via Budapest. In February he burst into Budapest airport two minutes before take-off for a flight back to Moscow. The check-in for the morning flight was already closed. 'I am a Member of Parliament. Hold the plane! I have to leave,' he shouted in Russian. Startled officials of MALEV Hungarian Airlines, after some hesitation, requested the plane to wait. As other passengers gaped in astonishment, Zhirinovsky ordered his aides to bring forward a motley collection of baggages, cardboard boxes and what appeared to be paintings in foam wrapping. Airport security guards gathered around him nervously as he searched for his ticket, berating his assistants for incompetence. He finally found it in his own pocket. As a small mountain of luggage began to accumulate, MALEV officials baulked at loading it on to the plane. 'I have a first-class ticket. I want to take that luggage on the plane,' Zhirinovsky shouted at a flustered check-in clerk. 'If something is lost or broken, I will have your head,' he warned the attendant. A MALEV official stepped forward and told Zhirinovsky that it would be impossible to load so many things on to the plane. 'You'll see what is impossible when I become president,' Zhirinovsky retorted. Approached by reporters, he whirled round to vent his wrath. 'You have a whore-house in your country. Imbeciles!' (*Guardian*, 17.2.94)

Romania, an artificial country – did not exist before the First World War. Consequently, Dobrudja belongs to Bulgaria. The rest of the land will belong to Romania. The population there comes from Italy. (*Die Welt*, 29.1.94)

Zhirinovsky was ordered out of Bulgaria in late December 1993 after publicly urging Bulgarians to replace President Zelyu Zhelev with the Russian politician's own aide. Mr Zhirinovsky proposed the candidature of Mr Svetoslav Stoilov, a Bulgarian living abroad and one of Zhirinovsky's advisers, for the presidential office. He went on to say that Mr Stoilov was his adviser on economic matters. **I'd like, and it would also be in Russia's interest, to see Mr Stoilov, who is an outstanding economist, as Bulgarian president** (BTA News Agency, Sofia, 26.12.93). According to the LDPR leader, it is just such a president that Bulgaria needs. And the relations in the Balkans will stabilize only after he steps into office. Zhirinovsky's nominee is quite unknown in Bulgaria.

My expulsion was an act of jealousy by Zhelev. People were coming to greet me, to embrace me, to say, 'Long live Zhirinovsky, Russia's future president.' They kissed my hand, something they have never done to Zhelev (*New York Times*, 30.12.93). Zhirinovsky's statements are unserious, according to President Zhelev. The fact that Zhirinovsky wants to make Bulgaria the sixteenth republic is self-evident. 'As for this, he is a bit late: he should have brought forward this proposal ten or fifteen years ago, when the Communists were in power and shared these views,' Dr Zhelev said.

Thrace should be returned to Bulgaria by the Greeks. And Dobrudja belongs to Bulgaria; but this is actually not our problem. (*Die Welt*, 29.1.94)

MUSLIM NEIGHBOURS

The majority of mankind is interested in dissecting the Muslim world. The Muslim peril has to be eliminated. The Russian Army's last march to the south would lead it to the shores of the Indian Ocean and to the Mediterranean and would mean liberation for 20 million Kurds, hundreds of thousands of Baluchis and Pushtuns. (*Los Angeles Times*, 4.3.94)

Nothing would happen to the world if the entire Turkish nation perishes, although I do not wish that upon it. (*The Last Dash to the South*)

In Ankara the plans for a Greater Turkish State have long since been prepared. Pan-Turkism threatens Russia, since it has a large Turkic-speaking Muslim population and also a Persian-speaking one; that is a good inducement for Afghanistan, Iran and Turkey to move north ... And Russia loses everything – the 'great and talented' Turkish nation is worthy of living right in the centre of the world, in the scented region, on the shores of six seas; the weak and powerless Russia, however, must perish. Is that foreseen in the history of humanity? No, that is not possible. (*Die Zeit*, 14.1.94)

In the past Russia saved the world from the Ottoman Empire, which collapsed as a result of thirty wars with Russia. Without Russia perhaps the whole of Europe would have been made Turkish ... Millions of people have been grateful to this day. Should then Russia not be able, and not be duty-bound, to perform her last gesture: the Dash to the South? So that Russian railways may reach there: Moscow–Delhi, Moscow–Kabul, Moscow–Indian Ocean, Moscow–Teheran, Moscow–

Baghdad, Moscow–Ankara, day and night, for the economy and for the development of culture? (*Die Zeit*, 14.1.94)

The Turkish 'democratic' way, which made it possible for the Turks to get everywhere in Europe, is much worse for us. It is 'Kominternism', whereas fundamentalism is nationalism (*Le Monde*, 23.12.93). Zhirinovsky does not like 'Kominternism' because he identifies it with internationalism, which is, as he puts it, like living in a 'communal' apartment with common bathrooms and a lot of intermingling, whereas nationalism is a self-contained apartment where you are safely behind doors and you let in only such visitors as you want to see. (See also Chapter 6.)

Zhirinovsky's attitude towards Turkey is implacable; he has not one good word for it. This may be due to his resentment for having been arrested in Turkey (see Introduction to Chapter 6) and then deported in his younger days or may be simply a political matter, echoing and reinforcing anti-Turkish attitudes in Russia. In his Moscow press conference after his visit to Strasbourg in early April 1994, he declared: **The Turks hate all Slavs** (ITAR–TASS, Moscow World Service Radio, 15.4.94).

They will all fight among themselves and we will come in when they invite us (*Guardian*, 31.1.94). That is another piece of wish-projection on the part of Zhirinovsky. His audience, his constituency, is well aware of the danger of civil war in Russia; consequently the dream image he wants to present here is the opposite: a peaceful, and strong Russia that is asked to create order in the turbulent southern regions.

That will be the moment when Russian soldiers will reach the shores of the Indian Ocean. (*Guardian*, 31.1.94)

All we want is three countries: Afghanistan, Iran and Turkey.

Russia can play an historic role in saving the world from the spread of Islam, from the spread of international terrorism. (*Time*, 27.12.93)

If in Afghanistan we had had the tsar's flags instead of the red flag, we would have won. (*La Stampa*, 16.12.93)

Russian troops were right to enter Afghanistan; what was wrong was that they did so under the red flag. (*Russia Express*, No. 73, 2.3.92)

Iran can take over Azerbaijan; Armenia and Georgia will belong to Turkey. These three states [Azerbaijan, Georgia and Armenia] have never been independent. (*Die Welt*, 29.1.94)

With Japan, Mongolia and China we have no territorial problems. (*Die Welt*, 29.1.94)

3

THE RUSSIAN–SERBIAN AXIS

RUSSIAN PAN-SLAVISM

If pan-Germanism was an obvious geopolitical dimension of Nazism leading to the *Anschluss* of Austria, the seizure of the Sudetenland from Czechoslovakia and Memel from Lithuania in March 1939, it might be thought that pan-Slavism is the dimension of Zhirinovsky's programme that would initially be the most dangerous force should he come to power. A new union of all Slav states, or at least of those espousing the Orthodox faith, lies behind his trips to the Balkans and would justify the annexation of eastern Ukraine and Belarus.

Pan-Slavism harks on about the ancient Slavic nation but, in fact, is of recent origin. Like pan-Germanism, it does not seriously predate the eighteenth century as a political force of any moment. The forced Westernization of Peter the Great profoundly humiliated the Russians and provoked a nationalist backlash that took proto-pan-Slav directions. Russia's outstanding liberal thinker in the nineteenth century, Alexander Herzen, stated, 'Slavophilism or Russianism, not as theory or teaching, but as the offended national feeling . . . [was] a reaction to the foreign influence that existed from the moment Peter I [the Great] caused the first beard to be shaved.'[1]

The Slavophiles of Herzen's time looked back nostalgically

---

1 Taras Hunczak (ed.), *Russian Imperialism from Ivan the Terrible to the Revolution*, Rutgers University Press, 1974, p. 84.

to the Moscow period of 1340–1703, which they saw through rose-tinted spectacles. As Berdyaev says, 'Interruption is a characteristic of Russian history. Contrary to the opinion of the Slavophiles, organic is the last thing it is. Russian history has been catastrophic. The Moscow period was the worst in Russian history, the most stifling, of a peculiarly Asiatic and Tatar type, and those lovers of freedom, the Slavophiles, have idealized it in terms of their own misunderstandings of it.'[2]

The Napoleonic invasion prompted a wide debate concerning whether Russia was right to become a European nation after the Western fashion or to foster and develop its Slav uniqueness, bringing together the Slav peoples in a new brotherhood, itself a notion borrowed from the French Revolution and German Romantic ideas of nationalism.

While the Westerners took their cue from Peter the Great and, deriding Russian backwardness, stressed the need to emulate the West, the Slavophiles extolled the virtues of the Slavs, especially the eastern Slavs under Russia's rule, including the Ukrainians and White Russians. Russia was, for them, superior to the decadent materialism of the West, personified by the bourgeois menace of England and Holland.

The Slavophiles delved into Russian history, searching for organic unity, which they found in a myriad of institutions and characteristics designed to enhance their self-esteem. The people, the *narod*, were organized by the *mir*, the village council, to which all land reverted on death for reallocation among the peasants. *Sobernost*, or wholeness, was its *Leitmotif*; the humility and communality of the Russian spirit, they

---

2 N.A.Berdyaev, *The Russian Idea* (reprint), Greenwood Press, Westport, 1979, p. 3.

deemed, set them apart from the West, where egoism and individualism prevailed. The focus of the Slav brotherhood, for them, was the Orthodox Church, with its universal message of truth, love and internal freedom – associated with external submission to the tsar.

Constantine Aksakov gives a good description of the ideal Slavophile commune: 'A commune is a union of the people who have renounced their egoism, their individuality, and wish to express their common accord; this is an act of love, a noble Christian act . . . a commune thus represents a moral choir . . . a brotherhood . . . a triumph of human spirit.'[3]

CONTRADICTIONS OF PAN-SLAVISM

Slavophilism had arisen independently in Bohemia, Poland and the Slav lands under the yoke of Turkey, Serbia, Croatia and Slovenia. But the Polish Slavophiles regarded themselves as the natural leaders of the Slav peoples as Catholics and as Western-ers, despite their suffering the indignity of foreign occupation at the hand of the Russians.

The Russian Slavophiles, of course, saw themselves as the obvious leaders, the Russian empire having the vocation to incorporate all Slavs, not just the Poles in 1772–95, under its hegemony; Herzen talks of 'Slavophilism or Russianism' indis-criminately. This is the nub of the contradiction of Slavo-philism, since non-Russian Slavs are none too keen on this Russian interpretation of the matter. Pan-Slavism is a complex idea, aspiring to an impossible project, the union of highly disparate peoples, the main divide being between the Catholic Slavs of Poland, Bohemia, Slovenia and Croatia and the

3 *Russian Imperialism from Ivan the Terrible to the Revolution*, p. 86.

Orthodox ones of Russia, White Russia, Ukraine, Bulgaria and Serbia.

THE SERBIAN EXCEPTION

When Serbia and Montenegro declared war on their occupiers, the Turks, in 1876, pan-Slavism ceased to be a vague sentiment confined to intellectuals and came alive among the general public. Pan-Slavic committees were formed and sent 5,000 volunteers, ranging from nobles to peasants, and including 800 former Russian officers, to fight in the Serbian army, which was headed by another Russian volunteer, General Mikhail Cherniayev. But the Turks defeated the Serbs, as they had the Bulgarians, also in 1876.

Pressure mounted on the Russian government to intervene. Russia declared war on Turkey in 1877, obtaining victory by 1878 and the independence of Serbia and Bulgaria. It is the memory of Russian volunteers and armies then that kindled the cheers for Russian peacekeeping forces when they came to Bosnia in spring 1994.

Pan-Slavism became entrenched among educated strata of society, especially the army, the Church and a section of the gentry, even though the tsars and the high nobility tended to disdain it, when they did not use it as a cloak for extending Russia's power, as in 1877–8. The mass of the peasantry was still largely unaffected by, if not indifferent to, other Slav peoples, whose languages and countries they knew little about.[4] Indeed, the greatest pan-Slav affair, as it was presented at the time, Russia's participation in the First World War on Serbia's side against Austria–Hungary and the German Empire up to

4 ibid.

1917, became highly unpopular with the peasant conscript soldiers, leading to mass desertions and the revolution of 1917.

MODERN PAN-SLAVISM

Under the Soviet Union pan-Slavism was officially frowned upon, although it remained an undercurrent, giving reality to 'proletarian internationalism' among its Slav republics and with Bulgaria. In one way the Soviet epoch gave pan-Slavism a covert boost. One achievement of the Soviet regime that can hardly be disputed is its education of the Soviet population, largely illiterate in 1917. Pan-Slavism could be comprehensible only to educated people, knowing some history of Russia, Ukraine and the former Yugoslavia and being acquainted with their religious and cultural heritage. This is by now true of many Russian citizens. Zhirinovsky has been able to benefit from this in rekindling pan-Slavism on a wider, more popular, basis. But he has implicitly redefined it as a union of Orthodox Slav peoples. Under the aegis of the LDPR Party Congress in April 1994 there was a World Congress of Slav Orthodox and Christian Nations.

Every time Zhirinovsky is acclaimed by an enthusiastic crowd in Belgrade, the TV shots back home are priceless in establishing him as the 'coming man', already representing Russia's interests abroad. The Russians crave to be loved by foreigners, not pitied by them. The Serbs, in a material plight worse even than that of the Russians, manifest love and gratitude towards them in a highly gratifying way. Every Serb cheer for Zhirinovsky warms the Russians' hearts and not least on behalf of Zhirinovsky himself.

There is another, and particularly poignant, link between Zhirinovsky and the Serbs. Dobrica Ćosić, a Serb nationalist intellectual, in his speech on the occasion of becoming a member of the Academy in 1977, said: 'Internationalism has ruined the Serb nation.' This fits in exactly with Zhirinovsky's views on the effect of internationalism on Russia, as he explained in his article published in *Izvestiya* on 28 August 1993 (see Chapter 6). Ćosić criticized the internationalism of Tito's Yugoslavia for much the same reasons as Zhirinovsky uses for condemning the Soviet 'Kominternism'. In addition, Ćosić, in the same speech, argued that the Serbs always win the war and lose the peace. The dire consequences of his views – no doubt shared by many other of his countrymen – are only too painfully obvious now in Bosnia.

THE ROLE OF ORTHODOXY

There are suggestions that the Greek Orthodox Church may be one determining factor in the shaping of Russian society and in the evolution (or lack of it) of its political order.

The role of the Orthodox Church at present is unclear. It certainly plays a part in efforts to reconstitute Russia as it was before the onset of the Soviet Communist regime. It is a tradition that people can go back to. However, it is difficult to say how strong religious faith is in Russian society after many decades of persecution by the Bolshevik authorities and as a result of the concomitant secularization of society.

There are those who argue that persecution saved the Orthodox faith from the kind of secularizing forces that have been eroding Western Churches during the same period by the shifting of emphasis to the political and moral aspects of religion at the expense of purely spiritual values, the core tenets of faith, the inner life, the pilgrimage of the soul through life towards God. In Protestant and, perhaps to a lesser extent, in Catholic countries of the West religion is being gradually absorbed by society and by social and political institutions. The slow erosion of dogma by detached rationalism and by science is emptying faith of its content. Christianity is reduced to its generally accepted moral values – or so goes the reasoning. Materialist pursuits undoubtedly weaken the role of faith in people's lives: the transcendental, spiritual hope of religion is replaced by short-term 'realistic', 'realizable' hopes of achieving material and social objectives. On the other hand, the persecution of religion may push the Church into the role of representing national objectives, that is, representing aspirations to national identity, and in the long term that may be to the detriment of the Church: when nationalist objectives have been achieved people may slowly turn away from religion. That danger threatens the Russian Church probably less than, say, the Polish Catholic Church or, more significantly, the Serbian Orthodox Church, which is at present closely identified with the Serbian cause of expansion.

The idea of Orthodox brotherhood plays an important part in bolstering Russian support for the Serbs. That is certainly exploited by Zhirinovsky, as the religious factor in the Balkan conflict is thought to become more important. There is another aspect of Orthodoxy that has influenced Russian history throughout the centuries. As a result of the fall of Constantinople to the Ottomans, the role of Byzantium as the champion of the Christian faith against the infidel fell vacant. Ivan III, by marrying the niece of the last Byzantine emperor, assumed that role and declared Moscow the successor of Byzantium: the Third Rome. The messianic spirit resulting from this new legitimacy of Moscow has been kept alive ever since in one form or another. It can be argued that Communism, shedding any Christian aspect, continued this mission by trying to construct a terrestrial paradise, justifying expansionism and moral superiority on the basis of it. Berdyaev maintains that 'Messianic consciousness is more characteristic of the Russians than of any other people except the Jews.'[5]

What are those aspects of the Orthodox faith that may also have influenced Russian society in its adherence to autocratic rule and have facilitated its acceptance by the population? It is remarkable that in Orthodox iconography the image of Christ the King (Pantocrator) has always been much more prevalent than in Western Christianity. A second point is that the Orthodox Church has never accepted the idea of Purgatory, which was devised by Western Christianity in the Middle Ages to play a mediating role between damnation and salvation. The propensity for extremes has always been held to be an important feature of the Russian character.

ZHIRINOVSKY MAKES HIS FIRST TRIP TO SERBIA

At a press conference in Belgrade's Jugoslavija Hotel on 30 January 1994 Zhirinovsky warned Western politicans that **bombing Serb positions in Bosnia would be a declaration of war against Russia** (Tanjug, Belgrade, 30.1.94).

Speaking in detail about the ways to solve the conflict in Bosnia-Hercegovina, he said that there were three ways to end it: the foreign troops should leave the territory of former Yugoslavia and let the Slav nations solve their problems on their own; **the status quo should be accepted**; or **Russian troops should be allowed in**. The latter course is exactly what happened in late February – yet another instance of Russian

5 Berdyaev, *The Russian Idea*, p. 8.

foreign policy, this time with Western approval, taking a leaf out of Zhirinovsky's book.

We are supporting the Serbs and our standpoint is that the Serb lands – the Serbian Republic [in Bosnia-Hercegovina] and the Republic of Serbian Krajina – should be within the Republic of Serbia, he said, adding that he would be happy if Russia and Serbia had a common border. (Tanjug, Belgrade, 30.1.94)

On 30 January 1994 Zhirinovsky arrived in Subotica from Slovenia, on his way to Belgrade. He had been invited to Serbia by the Serbian Democratic Party of the Serbian Lands (the leading party in the Serbian Republic in Bosnia-Hercegovina). After a brief traditional Orthodox ceremony Zhirinovsky addressed Subotica's citizens. **I am visiting your country for the first time, but I come here as a representative of the victorious party at the Russian elections, as a representative of Russia, which has chosen a new course. This course is the obligation of Russia to help the brotherly Serbian people. Our enemies are our common enemies, and you ought to know that they will be punished for all the evils committed against the Slav people** (Montenegrin TV, Podgorica, 30.1.94).

A new era is beginning, Zhirinovsky said. His words were accompanied by chanting: 'Russia! Serbia!' He stressed that the enemies of the Slav people were now trembling in Paris, Bonn, London, Washington and Tel Aviv.

Commenting on the war the Serbian people were waging on the territory of the former Yugoslavia, Zhirinovsky said that **all the barbarians who had settled on the sacred Serbian soil had to accept the fact that this land belonged to the Serbian people or leave it** (Hungarian Radio, Budapest, 30.1.94).

THE WEST IS BLAMED FOR WAR IN FORMER
YUGOSLAVIA

On 31 January 1994 in Vukovar, in the Republic of Serbian Krajina, Zhirinovsky said that **the West – because of applying double standards – was most to blame for the war in the former Yugoslavia.** On the one hand, the republics that seceded from the former Yugoslavia were recognized and, on the other hand, the Serbs were not granted the right to self-determination.

The West must be punished for this, and Russia will do its utmost to have war criminals punished, Zhirinovsky said at a press conference held in the partially rebuilt Dunav Hotel after the rally. Amidst an ovation from several thousand people in Vukovar, the guest of the Serbian Democratic Party of the Serbian Lands promised that **the great Russia will be the protector of all Serbs** and spoke about the **creation of a joint Slav state from Vladivostok to Knin** (Tanjug, Belgrade, 31.1.94).

SOLIDARITY WITH ZHIRINOVSKY'S
'SERBIAN BRETHREN'

On 1 February, in Podgorica, Zhirinovsky told a meeting of several tens of thousands of its residents that there were 300,000 Russian soldiers in Germany. **If the Germans have lost their appetite for war, if necessary we will transfer those 300,000 soldiers from Germany into the Balkans and help the Serbs** (Tanjug, Belgrade, 1.2.94), he said to a standing ovation and frequent shouts of 'Russia! Russia!' and 'Vladimir! Vladimir!' **The world should be told what Russian military might is. We have state-of-the-art weaponry, which others do** not have, the leader of the Russian liberals said, recalling the battles won by the Russians in past eras and during this century.

Zhirinovsky stressed that again Russia had a great historic mission, that of preventing the Slav peoples from being converted to Catholicism or Islam. Let the Catholics stay in Paris and Madrid, he said. Russians and Serbs have two enemies now – Catholicism and Muslims. Religion is used as the final weapon, Zhirinovsky stressed.

Addressing his audience mainly as brother Serbs, although he occasionally mentioned Montenegrins, Zhirinovsky also announced that he would convene an assembly of the political parties of Slav states in early April 1994 in Moscow to proclaim the idea of forming an East European community.

We are one nation; we have one religion. If they have formed a European Union in the West, we will form an East European community. Territorially, it will be ten times larger than the European Union. We are spiritually stronger than the West. We have the greatest economic potential.

He stressed clearly in Podgorica that any possible bombing of the Serbs in Bosnia would mean a declaration of war on Russia and that in the post-war period the Serbs in the Balkans would get everything they need from Russia. With the victory of his party, Zhirinovsky said, the Russian people have determined a new course in policy, particularly towards the events in the former Yugoslavia ... The world wants to divide the Balkans into many little statelets, so that the West can Catholicize half the peninsula and Islamize the other half. They are trying to destroy our Orthodox religion, and your only fault is that you are on the borders with the West, and therefore the attacks on you are all the fiercer ...

As for the sanctions, they can keep them in force. Russia has all you need and will buy everything you can offer. As for defence, if there is an attack, you should not give it so much as a thought. Russia has not only state-of-the-art weapons, but also a secret sonar weapon – as it is called – which it will use for its own defence and for the defence of its Orthodox brothers on the territory of the former Yugoslavia. (For more on his 'secret weapon' see Chapter 5.) **Russian might has to be displayed to the world so as to force it to leave the Slavs to live in peace. Russia will make it clear that Serbia should not be taken lightly.**

At the end of his speech, Zhirinovsky called on Russians and Serbs to **become closer in all aspects. Russians, who will pay for everything, should have holidays on Adriatic beaches** (Tanjug, Belgrade, 1.2.94; Serbian Radio, Belgrade, 1.2.94).

AIR STRIKE ON SERBS WILL BE THE 'BEGINNING OF THE THIRD WORLD WAR'

In an interview with Czech TV on 8 February 1994 Zhirinovsky replied to a question about his views on the possibility of an air strike against the Serbian troops shelling Sarajevo. He said, **We oppose violence. To bomb Serbian towns is the same as bombing Russian towns. If this terrible thing takes place, we will lodge our protest with the countries whose pilots are involved in the bombing. The same thing will consequently happen to their towns – bombs will fall on towns of the countries that attack Bosnia** (Czech TV, 8.2.94).

In an address to the State Duma on 9 February Zhirinovsky said that bombing of the Serb positions in Bosnia would be the **beginning of the Third World War.** Zhirinovsky's address was connected with his recent tour of former Yugoslavia. According to him, **millions of Serbs are appealing to Russia for protection.**

After a brief outline of the country's history Zhirinovsky said the people living there were **a single Orthodox people, some of whom were once forcibly converted into Islam and Catholicism.** Vladimir Zhirinovsky called on the Duma to take a unanimous position on the matter and threatened that **the countries whose pilots dare to bomb the Serb positions will be completely eliminated** (ITAR–TASS, Moscow, 9.2.94).

PLANS FOR GREATER SERBIA AND THE ALLIANCE OF SLAV PEOPLES

Srdjan Djurić, the editor of the *Eye of the World* programme of the Independent Television Studio B, Belgrade, had an 'exclusive' interview with Zhirinovsky, the text of which was published in the Belgrade-based journal *Večernje Novosti* on 28 January 1994. In it Zhirinovsky said: **All armies, including that of NATO, should be withdrawn from the territory of the former Yugoslavia. The existing situation needs to be strengthened, and the Yugoslav peoples themselves need to decide their future. Territories populated by Serbs or Croats must stay under the control of Serbs or Croats, while the Muslim issue is an artificial one. You do not have any Muslims.**

The blockade must be lifted and then everything will take a normal course. There will be Slovenia, Croatia and Greater Serbia, and that is it. Bosnia-Hercegovina, Montenegro – it is all Serbia. Nothing else will be necessary. Let there be three states: Slovenia as one entity and Croatia – if they are such great Catholics – and the rest will be Greater Serbia, whose borders will be shared with Bulgaria, Romania and Hungary. You have access to the Adriatic; it is all normal.

Djurić then said: 'Your idea of a confederacy of Orthodox countries has been given a lot of publicity in Serbia. How do you envisage this? Which countries would it comprise? What would be its purpose?' Zhirinovsky replied: We need to think about the fact that in this world, which has fallen apart, there are no longer two blocs; there is no bilateral balance, and no fanatical ideology lasts for ever. All this has gone down the drain. Essentially, this was violence. However, if we were to try uniting into some kind of alliance of states, as Orthodox Slavs, this would make us stronger, give us a common language with you. We are one tribe. You remained in the Balkans, the Poles proceeded to the north-west, the Russians to the north-east; our civilization started there. The Russians went on their way, the Poles on theirs and you stayed here. Then they hacked Yugoslavia to pieces, gave some to the Italians, Austrians, Germans and Turks. They are all barbarians. They came from here 500 years ago; they conquered the Byzantine Empire and kept you in blood and torture for 500 years until Alexander II liberated all of you.

That is why we could now form a Slav alliance of Slav states. The Balkans, [the] Czech [Republic], Slovakia, Poland, Russia – these would make a very good foundation because we share a common language and culture. The Serbs, the Ukrainians and the Russians are all Orthodox. It would be easier for all of us. It would be better. It would all be one expanse of territory because this is a single territory, one territory, a huge territory. If you were in New Zealand and someone else were in Argentina, how could you unite? Whereas in this case everyone is here. You. The Bulgarians. Only the Hungarians and the Romanians are in the way . . . There is a clear border with the Ukraine, Belarus and Russia.

We could save a lot on transport – for example, from your ports on the Adriatic across all of Russia from Vud to Japan. There you are. Poland and Germany as well. Hamburg,

Warsaw, Moscow, Vladivostok: a Eurasian transit trade route, and everything will be fine. The language – Russian. You will be pleased to speak Russian more often than English. You even use the same alphabet as we do. We favour doing something. We are trying to accomplish something. However, the Slavs have always been weak. The Germans constrained you from the west, the north-east and the north-west. If a new Russia emerges, we will not allow them to go on constraining you. If you desire closer relations with Russia, so be it. If you do not, you are welcome – everything depends on you, on your wishes. If the Russians rule over the territory of the former Soviet Union, the situation in Serbia and former Yugoslavia will be stable. If the Serbs are at war – with Croatia and Bosnia – it will be an endless war. The same applies in our case. If you remove the Russian front, we too will have an endless war, just like Afghanistan. (*Večernje Novosti*, Belgrade, 28.1.94)

ON SERBIAN AND 'YUGOSLAV' LEADERS

In his interview with the Belgrade-based Independent Television Studio B's editor, Srdjan Djurić, Zhirinovsky was asked his opinion of the presidents of Serbia and former Yugoslavia. Zhirinovsky said, I do not know them very well personally. From the point of view of principles, they're all former Communists. I am not a Communist, and that is why it is obvious that there is no agreement on ideology. I am ready to support them if they take up a patriotic position – that is, where there are Serbs, that is Serbia. Zhirinovsky then asked Djurić the name of the current president of Yugoslavia, since Milošević is the president of Serbia only. Djurić replied: 'His name is Lilić.' Zhirinovsky then continued: Who? Lilić? Who is he? We know of Milošević from Serbia, and the Muslims have Izetbegović. Who is this Izetbegović? What makes him a Muslim? And I know Tudjman, the Croat. There, we have heard of them – Tudjman, Milošević, Izetbegović – while the president of the united Serbia and Montenegro is not widely known ... We knew of Tito, Josip Broz Tito! That was all we knew – Tito – and nothing else. Nowadays you elect them and change them every year. For example, that American – where did he run off to? Djurić replied: 'You mean Panić [a Yugoslav American who stood unsuccessfully against Milošević in the last elections for the Serbian presidency]?' Zhirinovsky said: **Yes, Panić. That was his fate. He came for a while, he was here, and then he went back to where the greasy sandwiches are** (*Večernje Novosti*, Belgrade, 28.1.94).

The second stage of his visit to former Yugoslavia at the end of January was Serbia. He arrived from Slovenia, via Hungary, at the town of Subotica, just south of the Hungarian–Serbian border. Subotica was, until recently, a town with an ethnic Hungarian majority.

In his speech he explained that it was the duty of Russia to help the brotherly Serbian people. As he put it: **Our enemies are our common enemies and you ought to know that they will be punished for all the evils committed against the Slav people.** And he stressed that the enemies of the Slav people were now trembling in Paris, Bonn, London and Washington (according to Hungarian Radio, he also added Tel Aviv to the list of towns). Commenting on the war in which the Serbs were involved, he said that all the barbarians who had settled on sacred Serbian soil had to accept the fact that this land belonged to the Serbian people or leave it (Montenegrin TV, Podgorica, 30.1.94). Later that day, in Belgrade, he focused on more immediate issues.

Bombing Serb positions in Bosnia would be a declaration of war against Russia.

The Russian Army is still in Europe – it is not threatening anyone.

We are supporting the Serbs, and our standpoint is that the Serb lands, i.e. the Serbian Republic in Bosnia-Hercegovina and the Republic of Serbian Krajina, should be within the Republic of Serbia. He added that he would be happy if 'Russia and Serbia had a common border'. (Press conference, Belgrade, 30.1.94)

I promise you that I will very soon make radical changes in policy. I have already demanded that [Foreign] Minister Kozyrev should say clearly to the entire world that the Russian government and the Russian parliament are on the side of the Serb people (Zhirinovsky's speech in Bijeljina, as reported by Tanjug, Belgrade, 31.1.94). A few days later Kozyrev did indeed change his attitude more or less along the lines Zhirinovsky suggested in response to NATO's threat of air strikes.

Catholics from the West, Muslims from the East, enemies from the North – they all want to take a chunk of Greater Serbia for themselves and they think that we will agree to it. We will never agree to it, and Russia will help you. It will punish those who wish to divide the Serb land.

This policy has been going on for a hundred years now. Every fifty years they start a war in the Balkans or somewhere else, and each time the victims are the Serb and the Russian peoples. Our message to the whole world today is that a new historic era is in the making. Once and for all, we shall put an end to the policy of playing games with the destinies of the Serb and Russian peoples (Zhirinovsky's speech in Bijeljina, as reported by Tanjug, Belgrade, 31.1.94). This is a good example of Zhirinovsky's skills in demagoguery. He identifies with the Serb sense of being a beleaguered nation, constantly under attack from all sides, the self-pity of the aggressor.

His success in Serbia did not seem to be marred by the fact that his relations with the Serb leader, Milošević, are not particularly cordial. In Slovenia he announced, **He must go**, describing him as an incorrigible Communist. Both politicians are populists, but Zhirinovsky is the real thing. He is willing to incur the wrath of politicians with pronouncements like: **I have no wish to be of service to any politician.** He points out that he always has the little man in mind. That is one way in which Zhirinovsky distances himself from the entire former political élite, who spoke about the people *ad nauseam* but certainly did not want to hear what they had to say. (We remember the famous slogan of the demonstrators in the then East German city of Leipzig in autumn 1989 who shouted: 'We are the people' – the people the leadership had always been talking about and through whom it had tried to justify its actions, saying, 'The people want, or will not tolerate . . .') The memory of that is, of course, still very much alive in Russia, so that Zhirinovsky has to do more than simply talk about the people: he must publicly dissociate himself from other politicians, especially from the Communists, to have any kind of credibility. He takes this line also with the present 'democratic' Russian leadership, accusing them of having been Communists, which indeed is true of most of them.

No doubt Milošević was comforted by Zhirinovsky's dreams of a Slavic empire stretching **from the Adriatic to Vladivostok** and the promise that Serb territory will be extended – presumably by Zhirinovsky if he becomes president of Russia – to include all lands **wherever its citizens live.** (The word 'citizen' is clearly used loosely, since ethnic Serbs living in Bosnia and Croatia, etc., are not Serb but Yugoslav citizens.)

All foreign troops must leave [the former Yugoslavia]. **And the Serbs, Croats and Bosnians should keep their present borders. The UN troops must withdraw so that the fighting factions are able to settle the conflict between themselves.** (*Die Welt*, 29.1.94)

ZHIRINOVSKY'S SPEECH TO SERBS IN CROATIA

Obviously showing signs of a drinking session or two, Zhirinovsky addressed two thousand of his fellow **brothers by blood and faith** who had been waiting for him for hours in the Croatian city of Vukovar on 2 February 1994.

Who dares say it? Who dares claim falsely that Serbia is a small country? It's not small! It's not small! Three times it has waged war! Here is an old country that has an emperor in heaven! Serbia, our dear mother, gave birth to us all. Long live Serbia!

We Slavs cannot continue to be the victims of the struggle to save Western civilization from the barbarians. The time has come to repay us for all our sacrifices. There are 300 million of us altogether.

I assure the governments of some Western countries that using force will not help them. If a single bomb falls on the towns of Bosnia, I warn that this means a declaration of war on Russia, and we will punish them for it. My name, Vladimir, means 'ruler of the world'. Let us Slavs rule the world in the twentieth century. (*Daily Mail*, 2.2.94)

The bombing of Serb positions round Goražde inflamed

Zhirinovsky's wrath towards NATO and the West in general. NATO's action is against Russia. For the most part, it serves the interests of Germany in the Balkans. It is against Christians, against the Slav people, Zhirinovsky said, adding: If I were president, we would bomb those bases in Italy. They bomb one town; we bomb another town (MON 11.4.94).

The official Russian reaction was not as wild, but Sergei Sakhrai, Russian Deputy Prime Minister, told reporters in the lower house of the Duma: 'I think the bombing was targeted not so much at Serb positions ... as at the internal political position in Russia ... The national-patriots benefited from this ... It is a blow a blow to reforms in Russia.' Such statements, in their curiously illogical way, look as if the Russian official position and Zhirinovsky were drawing closer together.

4

THE FAR-ABROAD

ATTITUDES AND PLATITUDES

Under Western Eyes

One thing that is preventing the gravity of the situation that is developing in Russia from being realized fully in the West is a range of concepts, distilled here but quite inappropriate in a Russian context. The Russians have always been very different from other Europeans, and seventy years of Communism have made them even more so. The unprecedented crisis that they are now enduring is not, despite the new trappings of liberal democracy, making them like the West at all. It is, rather, bringing out their more louche qualities in darkened hues, at which use of *chiaroscuro* Zhirinovsky is an adept.

Westerners talk of moderates and extremists. In the West someone like Zhirinovsky inhabits the 'lunatic fringe'. Westerners are not aware quite how extreme the unfolding situation in Russia is, where what would be an extremist position to Westerners is a commonly held outlook. In the extremist situation, the extremist is king.

Westerners also attribute the success of extremist politics to the 'protest vote'. The notion of the protest vote is readily applicable to a crisis in the West. In the early 1930s, for example, Germany, having lost a world war, was engulfed in a chronic economic crisis. A humiliated nation, with 40 per cent of its people out of work and a fragile democracy, gave rise to a protest vote for Hitler, one third of the electorate casting their lot for Nazi totalitarianism in 1932. This situation was not in the same league as Russia's position today. The Russian crisis is very much graver. Germany in 1933 was a country with the most advanced economy in Europe, whose woes were easily remedied by state spending on *Autobahns* and armaments. By 1936 unemployment was down to 2 per cent, and the economy was booming. Russia's agony is that its present economic plight is the outcome of seven decades of intensive misdevelopment.

Nobody really knows how to rescue a broken-down, misdeveloped economy. Many pretend to, not least the IMF and the reformists. But IMF shock therapy has not succeeded in stabilizing the financial economy of Russia, while it has certainly succeeded in destabilizing its real economy. The leaders in Moscow are trying one desperate expedient after another to rectify the situation, without effect.

In this crisis everyone becomes a protest voter, the pro-reformers trying to turn Russia into a capitalist country in a hurry and protesting against the Communist heritage, the Communists protesting the loss of the Soviet empire and the Soviet Union itself, and the ultra-nationalists protesting against the degradation of the nation. When every voter is a protest voter, the likes of Zhirinovsky do well. For in Russia what is there not to protest about? An economy in ruins, a society breaking down for lack of public morality and falling into the clutches of the mafias, an environment polluted and partially radioactive, a health service in disarray, a rise in epidemics and a death rate that is decimating the population, the best scientists and engineers leaving the country and only the mafias functioning successfully in fleecing the country of its resources and salting away their ill-gotten gains abroad. The country is going to the dogs, and everybody knows it. This type of crisis, so much more profound and desperate than Germany's in the 1930s, breeds the politics of despair and the geopolitics of fury. Hence Zhirinovsky's outbursts, contrary to all that is politically correct in the West, are heard with glee by many sections of the population.

Under Eastern Eyes

When Zhirinovsky goes to Strasbourg, as he did in early April 1994, and chucks plants from the Russian Consulate at Jewish demonstrators, he is giving them what they deserve, according to many Russians, who blame the Jews for the Bolshevik Revolution and Communism, that thought-child of Karl Marx and Leon Trotsky. The more aggressive Zhirinovsky's utterances against the West, the more he rises in the esteem of ultra-nationalists.

Displaying contempt for the West serves the purpose of distinguishing and distancing Zhirinovsky from the present leaders of the Russians as well as from what we must now call the previous generation of reformers: Gorbachev and his *entourage*. What the Russians see as the failure of the West to help Russian reforms promotes an anti-Western attitude that has been there latently at least from the time of Peter the Great and his forced modernization (i.e. Westernization).

There is, however, another source of anti-Western attitudes, the influence of early Romanticism in German eighteenth-century thought. This exerted influence on intellectuals in the first place and then percolated down through society. Soviet anti-capitalism and anti-imperialism tried to make use of that latent propensity, with some success at first, but later it was much weakened by the ever more apparent failure of Communism to overtake capitalism. One of the most important points of the anti-Western movement in nineteenth-century Russia was the argument that Westerners were winning the competition in the economic and political sphere, but in the process were losing their soul. The concept of the 'Russian soul' is still important in present-day Russian consciousness; it is reinforced now that Russians can travel more easily to the West and see what they regard as inauthentic in the Western character: artificial, 'plastic' personalities, without the existential depth of Russians. That feature was noticed in the nineteenth century by, among others, Dostoyevsky and was linked with a German early Romantic perception of the French in particular by J. G. Hamann. As a matter of fact, it was the French themselves who noticed it even earlier. *A mesure que la société se perfectionne, l'homme se dégrade* (to the extent that society perfects itself, man degenerates).

In the later Brezhnev years many Russians, having lost faith in the capacity of Communism to overtake the Western countries, turned into 'occidentophiles'. The wheel had turned to sympathy towards the West, and that transformation engulfed the Soviet leadership as well – Gorbachev was clearly one who wanted to learn as much as he could from the West and to apply the medicine to Soviet society and economics. He did not realize, however, that you cannot take the best features of a capitalist society and those of Communism and work out a Third Way. The Third Way was much talked about in the Communist countries of Central and Eastern Europe around 1989 but has since been abandoned by most politicians as a hopeless quest. Zhirinovsky, however, still seems to hang on to that idea when he advocates not destroying the good features of the command economy and at the same time promoting a free-market economy (see Chapter 5).

In the 1980s many Russians were listening to Russian-language broadcasts from the West and learned something about Western society. In both Western publications and broadcasts there was criticism of the evil effects of the Soviet-style command economy and of the lack of freedom in economic life as well as in the development of society. The advantages of the free market and democracy were extolled; little mention was made, however, of the difficulty of the transition from Communism to capitalism. That gave the wrong impression to untutored listeners, who imagined that once the Soviet system was abolished everything would be fine and the West would help Russia. When, following the changes in 1991, the West dragged its feet and the expected help was not forthcoming, of course a new disillusionment with the West set in, and that is still growing. Zhirinovsky makes good use of it, and that is one of the reasons why he does not mind disparaging remarks about him in the Western media. In a television programme broadcast by BBC 1 (*Panorama*, 28.1.94) he said explicitly to the British journalist interviewing him: **Go on calling me Fascist and compare me with Hitler. The more you do it, the more votes I'm going to get in the next election.**

THE WEST AND FOREIGN COUNTRIES IN GENERAL

The twenty-first century will be **our century**, he predicts. **We are washing away these scabs, this dirt that has accumulated over the whole twentieth century. Sometimes this causes blood. This is bad.** But blood, he adds in a final gruesome flourish, may be necessary **in order finally to wash away this contagion that was introduced into the centre of Russia from the West to poison the country and undermine it from within – through Communism, nationalism, cosmopolitanism, through the** influence of alien religions, alien ideas, an alien way of life. We will put an end to this (*The New Republic*, 14.2.94).

If the European, Asian and American great powers refuse to acquiesce in Zhirinovsky's last dash to the south, Zhirinovsky has pledged to make life very unpleasant (*National Review*, 21.3.94). He has never specified what his measures might be, but nuclear blackmail and the abrogation of arms-control agreements are among those measures that he has mentioned.

I feel neither particular sympathy nor particular antipathy towards any foreign statesmen. (*Der Spiegel*, 51, 93)

We must divide the spheres of influence. It is like two girls and two blokes. The men have to decide which girl is theirs and then there are two couples, everything is friendly. Until they decide what belongs to whom, they will fight. (*The Times*, 21.12.93)

On relations with the West, Zhirinovsky said that any Western country could help Russia, but Russia did not need aid. Russia is a country with abundant resources, and it is prepared to develop equable economic relations with all states. I understand Western businessmen who have misgivings in view of the economic situation in Russia. (ITAR–TASS, 22.12.93)

At a press conference in Karinthia (Austria) Zhirinovsky warned the West against interfering in Russian affairs. If certain Western circles were to provoke a civil war in Russia, nuclear and chemical weapons might get out of control ... Russia has far more dangerous weapons than nuclear weapons ... these weapons are 'Elipton' weapons, with which the entire world could be destroyed. (Oesterreich 1 Radio, 22.12.93)

We must ask ourselves, with whom are we interested in good relations? What does the West do for us? Westerners come here to buy cheap resources, to conquer our markets, to pay us slave wages. The West takes everything from us: the material products of Russia and the brains of our people. That's enough of that. (*The Times*, 21.12.93)

He aims to reverse **Gorbachev's and Yeltsin's policies of giving everything to the West** (*Financial Times*, 9.12.93). Generally speaking, he rides on the rising tide of disillusionment about the West in Russia. That is partly due to the tacit suggestion on the part of the West that once Communism and a command economy is eliminated, prosperity will emerge and the Russians will be received into the community of the well-to-do élite of the world. It is a view that has never been expressed in so many words, but people in Russia and other Communist states could not possibly have comprehended the difficulty of the transition, and before the collapse of Communism Western broadcasts rarely mentioned the size of the task. Hope was stressed at the expense of sweat and tears. Also listeners in Communist countries were assured of Western help by implication rather than by detailed explication. Similar suggestions by implication were given, for instance, to the Bosnians and the Croats at the beginning of the disintegration of Yugoslavia. Many Western countries were very reluctant to recognize the independence of former Yugoslavia's successor states. It was that very reluctance (based on practical political considerations) that awakened hopes in Croatia and Bosnia, since it clearly seemed to say: 'We are unwilling to rush into it because if we do recognize their independence, then we will bear some responsibility for promoting or defending it,' a fatally naïve misinterpretation.

Why should we care about what Britain or France thinks

about us? Sort out your problems. Keep away from us. (*The Times*, 21.12.93)

Today our main weapons are made up of the fleet and the army. This is real power! The best borders are sea borders. England was a sea power with the best sea borders! Mongolia has no sea borders: it is a shabby state! Today we have no colonies. The colonies provided England with the lion's share of its profits. Today we receive nothing from colonies and yet feed beggarly appendages. We should be thinking about colonies ... I will struggle for Britain's disintegration. Let there be separate Irish, Scottish and Welsh peoples. They've suffered enough under imperial England. (*Independent* Magazine, 2.4.94)

At a press conference in Moscow after his visit as member of a Russian delegation to Strasbourg, Zhirinovsky lashed out against the West and said that if Russia joined the Council of Europe, **a struggle will be waged against us for your money.** He also took an anti-NATO stance, saying: **We are glad that the country's political leadership has taken a correct step in that direction** [non-cooperation with NATO]. **We support the president's decision not to sign the Partnership for Peace programme** (ITAR–TASS, Moscow, World Service, 15.4.94). President Yeltsin did not, in fact, refuse to sign it but simply put it off until a later date, which, of course, may result in Russia's not signing it. Zhirinovsky has always been adamant that Russia should not join any Western organization because he regards such a step as limiting Russia's freedom of movement and leading to further damage inflicted on Russia by the West.

Though it no longer has an opponent [the Warsaw Pact],

NATO is drawing close to Russia's borders. It wants to send its troops to the Baltic countries and Transcaucasia, the Black Sea, the Barents Sea and the Balkans. (*Warsaw Voice*, 20.3.94)

His visit to Strasbourg incensed him – against the West in general. His heaping insults on Jewish demonstrators and throwing flower pots at them made a bad impression, something that he would normally shrug off or even welcome, but this time he may have felt that he had gone too far. However, at the Moscow press conference he vented his anger against the West, culminating in a tirade against **the Zionists and Americans.** Britain also came in for criticism. The British, he declared, **plundered the world first of all, yet now have become conservative, protecting their plunder, and have foisted their language on the whole world.** (*Warsaw Voice*, 20.3.94)

You send us the clothes you do not want to wear and the food you do not want to eat (*The Times*, 21.12.93). The anti-Western stance expressed in these statements is due as much to the topic of the day as to trying to bolster the self-respect of a population that knows itself to be at the centre of an empire, however tottering, and is now completely disorientated by changes that baffle it, as they baffle its leaders. The 'food you do not want to eat' probably refers to the meat sent by Britain some months earlier as food aid and found by the authorities to be unfit to eat, probably also to bolster self-respect.

I am an internationalist twice over – both as far as my primary education is concerned and as far as my secondary education is concerned. I can speak to the president of France *tête-à-tête* in his mother tongue. When we are told that our leaders have *tête-à-tête* meetings, it is untrue – interpreters are by their side. But, as for me, I will speak to him *tête-à-tête* –

and with Kohl in German and with Bush in English. I have already had *tête-à-tête* conversations with them in Bonn. I removed the members of my delegation, asked the diplomats of the German Foreign Ministry to leave, and I had a *tête-à-tête* chat with Herr Schaefer, the deputy Foreign Minister of the Federal Republic of Germany, and Herr Genscher, the German Foreign Minister. So, I am not just theorizing now; I have already done it ... In foreign policy we must move from a West–East relationship to a North–South relationship. It is a safer and cheaper one, giving us friends who possess a high degree of culture and technology: North America, northern Europe and Japan. Our friends today are not, unfortunately, remarkable for their culture or their riches. It is as though we have opted on purpose for the poorest, the weakest, and, in the final analysis, we ourselves have become like them. As the Russian proverb puts it: you become like those with whom you keep company. (Soviet Television, 22.5.91)

We have no use for those American false images that are thrust upon my people on television day by day ... We do not want Pepsi-Cola at all, or chewing-gum. (*Der Spiegel*, 51, 93)

On arriving in Helsinki to take part in a parliamentary seminar on the prospects for Russian membership of the Council of Europe, Zhirinovsky said: We do not need your Council of Europe; we do not ask for it. On the contrary, it is you, who need us. (ITAR–TASS, Moscow, World Service English broadcast, 4.4.94)

If I accept the invitation of that politican [a conservative South African politican], it does not mean that I have anything against Negroes ... My heartfelt desire is that the last Russian soldiers should soon leave Germany; but the American soldiers should also leave. There should be no foreign military base in Germany. Germany must have freedom without any limitations. (*Der Spiegel*, 51, 1993)

I greet Paris as the town of Arabs. In ten, twenty years things will be all over for France ... The same goes for Germany: the Turks will be in charge there. Only Russia remains a white country, the country of natural democracy, where there are human rights for all, without discrimination (French TV Antenne 2, Paris, 10.4.94). This was said during Zhirinovsky's visit to the Council of Europe in Strasbourg as a member of the delegation of the Russian Parliament. He was not allowed to go anywhere else in France, which upset him.

The new Russian state, he says, will help France rid itself of American and Zionist influence. (*The New Republic*, 14.2.94)

Ethnic Germans should not leave Russia in future; on the contrary, German farmers could come and find fortune with us. (*Der Spiegel*, 51, 1993)

Austria and Slovenia should be one country. Germany, Austria and Slovenia should have access to the Adriatic. That is the wish of the German people. (*Die Welt*, 29.1.94)

Thrace should be returned to Bulgaria by the Greeks. And Dobrudja belongs to Bulgaria; but this is not actually our problem. (*Die Welt*, 29.1.94)

THE USA

I am against Zionists, Americans and American influence ... American Jews make America strong, but Russian Jews make Russia weak. They do that on purpose, so that they can emigrate to Israel. They should stay here ... Our greatest problem are the Americans and the Zionists ... When I come to power I'll put things in order and throw out the Americans and the mafia. (*Die Zeit*, 4.3.94)

We should maintain ordinary relations with America, remembering that it is our main competitor and is not interested in Russia's prosperity and might. (*Rossiyskaya Gazeta*, 3.12.93)

Zhirinovsky seems to be convinced that the United States will offer no resistance when Russia starts to reclaim Alaska. And the reason for that is because it will perish of its own accord, just as the USSR has. (*New Times International*, October 1992)

Like a chameleon, Zhirinovsky is likely to adopt such attitudes towards the USA as are suggested by the mood of his country, as he perceives it. At the moment he is hostile because the general mood is hostile to America. He can be quite candid about this. President Clinton refused to meet Zhirinovsky during his visit to Moscow, so he tried to turn the snub to his advantage, declaring: President Clinton showed himself to be a weakling. This is a gift, as anti-American feeling is growing in Russia because the people know that Clinton supports the disintegration of Russia (AP, 15.3.94). Zhirinovsky advised Clinton to go home to Arkansas and play the saxophone there. He added that the USA was clearly in a bad way and that under his leadership Russia would mount a massive aid effort to help it. He warned Clinton: Don't make the mistake Napoleon and Hitler made: withdraw from Europe (*La Stampa*, 16.12.93). And he offered further advice through Nixon: Don't support the losers in the last elections. There is no future in it. Another of his messages to Clinton was, he told reporters after his meeting with Nixon: **Don't be afraid of me. There is no reason to be afraid of my party.** The inscription in the copy of his own book that he asked Nixon to give to Clinton is: '**I don't want to be misunderstood by you.**' He criticized the United States for backing **radical democrats, who are all former Communists and are destroying the country.** (AP, 15.3.94)

Zhirinovsky has accused the Western powers of launching their third attack against Russia this century, the first two being the two world wars. **It was all the same to them who ruled Russia, tsars or Communists. Their goal was to destroy Russia. The country this time is being undermined by a peaceful invasion of pretty slogans about democracy and human rights** . . . **The Americans are clever. They know it is better to come here with chewing-gum, stockings and McDonalds.** (*The Vancouver Sun*, 9.4.94)

His prognosis for the USA is that some time in the next century its population will perish, swamped by blacks and Hispanics, and it will go the way of the USSR. He writes: **We will not gloat when California joins Mexico, when a Negro republic is created in Miami and when the Russians take back Alaska,** or when America dissolves into a **Commonwealth of New States** (*The New Republic*, 14.2.94). **The factories will close down. There will be no medicine, no food, and you Americans will emigrate to Europe, to Japan and to Russia.** (*La Stampa*, 16.12.93)

JAPAN AND ASIA

Zhirinovsky's plans about Japan are sometimes difficult to understand. Generally speaking, his stance is hostile without, however, directly threatening Japan. On the other hand, he wants to discourage aggression on the part of Japan. His general attitude may be summarized as follows: **Was Hiroshima and Nagasaki not enough for you? Do you want to have another nuclear holocaust? No? In that case forget about the Kurils.** (*New Times International*, October 92)

We won't give up a metre of land [on the Kuril Islands]. We are ready to accept new land at the request of the masses. We will run out of border posts. (Warsaw Voice, 20.3.94)

The Sea of Okhotsk between the Russian mainland and the Kurils should fall under Russian jurisdiction, and a 200-mile (320-kilometre) protective fishing zone should be created. Not a single foreign ship will enter that sea, so that all the sea food will get on to the tables of the Russian people. (AP, 13.12.93)

Zhirinovsky has proven willing to change his line on several key issues in his quest for power. The Kurils are a case in point. His firm stand against returning the islands was a major factor in his obtaining strong support in the December 1993 elections in the Russian Far East. However, in an interview with the *Wall Street Journal Europe* in 1990 he saw things differently. In those days he advocated a sweeping overhaul of Soviet foreign policy, including the realignment of various borders based on bargains and trade-offs. The Kurils were a problem for the Communists for ideological reasons but not for him and the LDPR.

Zhirinovsky was asked by an English reporter what he wanted to do about the Kuril Islands dispute in January 1993. **I would bomb the Japanese. I would sail our large navy around their small island, and if they so much as cheeped, I would nuke them ... and we Russians haven't forgotten English** treachery during the war. You're a small island, so you watch out, too. (*Financial Times*, 14.12.93)

On relations with China: **We want it to develop its activity towards the south.** (Warsaw Voice, 20.3.94)

With Japan, Mongolia and China we have no territorial problems. (*Die Welt*, 29.1.94)

President Clinton is a coward. AIDS is a plague from the United States. If Germany and Japan don't stop harassing Russia, bombs will fall on their cities. (AP, 6.2.94)

CENTRAL AND WESTERN EUROPE

Zhirinovsky addressed two thousand activists of the far-right German People's Union (DVU) at a rally in the Bavarian town of Passau on 2 October 1993. The DVU, headed by German extremist Gerhard Frey, campaigns against foreign immigrants and for the reclamation of old German lands from Poland.

Our borders must shift closer together. Germany and Russia should again have a common border ... When I am in the Kremlin and one of you Germans looks askance at us Russians, you will pay for everything that we Russians have rebuilt in Germany. And the same goes for the Japanese. We will create new Hiroshimas and new Nagasakis. I will not drag my feet over using nuclear weapons. You know what Chernobyl meant for our country. You will get your own Chernobyl in Germany. (Reuter, 13.12.93)

On a visit to Austria in late December to meet a friend, former Carinthian timber merchant Edwin Neuwirth, Zhirinovsky gave his views on the future of Europe. **We have** dissolved the Warsaw Treaty, but NATO continues to exist. NATO must also be dissolved. All foreign troops must be withdrawn. Europe must be shaped in the same way as Austria. Austria might become the capital of the whole of Europe as a single country. German, Russian, English, French – that is all. (ORF TV, 21.12.93)

During his visit to Poland in early 1994 Zhirinovsky changed his tune about the fate of the country. This time he was polite and made no threatening remarks. In fact, he repudiated his earlier comments that the eastern part of Poland should be ceded to Russia. **I would not like anybody to think, even theoretically, that the Polish borders should be changed, ever; we are for a strong Poland, so that Russia and Poland can be good neighbours.** Zhirinovsky emphasized that Russia had no territorial claims and its army would never go west. However, he also declared: **Russia would not allow Poland to be used as a corridor for foreign aggression against Russia.** (MON, 12.3.94)

The so-called Oder–Neisse Line is not the last word in history. (*Frankfurter Allgemeine*, 16.12.93)

I am not threatening anyone, but I am warning everyone that if there is any danger to Russia, I shall harden my policies, said Zhirinovsky during his visit to Poland. **We took Berlin in 1945 and then gave it back again. Now the Germans live well and we do not. Why did we conquer Berlin then? We ought to have forced millions of Germans to work for us.** (*Frankfurter Allgemeine*, 16.12.93)

The opinion he is expressing here is reminiscent of the current Serb nationalist tenet expressed by Dobrica Ćosić, whom many see as the ideological mentor of Milošević, in his inaugural lecture at the Academy in 1977: 'Serbs are victorious in wars and are defeated in peace.' Another idea expressed by Ćosić reminds us again of Zhirinovsky: 'Internationalism has destroyed the Serb nation.'

The German magazine *Der Spiegel* ran a special issue about Zhirinovsky, which obviously pleased him for its publicity value. However, he objected to a couple of points. **My picture on the cover is very nice. But if I see my photograph next to Hitler's again, and if I am again compared to Hitler, then I see a bleak future for *Der Spiegel*. I can see it being wound up. We will sue *Der Spiegel* for damages to the tune of 100 million marks.** (*Der Spiegel*, 24.1.94)

The question of north Prussia and Königsberg [Kaliningrad] will in any case be solved in accordance with the wishes of Germany ... The area of Königsberg must not be a bone of contention between Russia and Germany. (*Der Spiegel*, 51, 1993)

Gerhard Frey, a Munich businessman who makes no attempt to conceal his nostalgia for Hitler's Third Reich, runs a flourishing business selling Nazi memorabilia. He is a friend of Zhirinovsky, who visited him in December 1993. Herr Frey, publisher of a right-wing nationalist newspaper, *National-Zeitung*, constantly casts doubt on the existence of Nazi war crimes and promotes the rehabilitation of Hitler's *Wehrmacht* as the 'best soldiers in the world'. He wrote in the late December issue of his paper that if Zhirinovsky came to power, Russia would negotiate with Germany over the return of its lost province of East Prussia, which has been Polish and Russian territory since the end of the Second World War, which established the Oder and Neisse rivers, hundreds of miles west of the East Prussian city of Königsberg, as Germany's eastern border. 'The Russian

Liberal Democrats offer negotiations over East Prussia and envisage a revision of the crying injustice of the Oder–Neisse Line through negotiations as a just solution,' Frey wrote.

The area of Königsberg also belongs to Russia ... One day we can return Königsberg to Germany. We want to give back everything the West wants. (*Die Welt*, 29.1.94)

Germany does not really need foreign troops, and I cannot see any proper reason to have foreign troops stationed on the territory of the Federal Republic and, on the other side, to put German soldiers under foreign command. Germany is not a protectorate but an important power ... I like to have a healthy military capable of the defence of Russia, and I also represent the interests of the army. No one can be more for peace than I. But it cannot be in the interests of Russia and Germany, and, for that matter, of almost the whole world, if Russia is deprived of power. Then the world will have to dance to the tune of the world policeman. (*Spotlight*, 7.3.94)

Zhirinovsky has a habit of making contradictory statements about the same subject. When his visa application was refused by the German consulate in Sofia, he threatened Germany with stationing 300,000 Russian soldiers on German soil after coming to power. He also told the perplexed German consular official that the First World War started with the assassination in Sarajevo of the heir to the Habsburg throne. And you know how World War II came about? He added that preventing him from going to Germany might lead to World War III (DPA, January 1994).

In reply to a question about the relations between Russia and the Nordic countries he declared: There will be festivals, festivals and only festivals. (*The Times*, 21.12.93)

THE MIDDLE EAST

The majority of mankind is interested in dissecting the Muslim world. The Muslim peril has to be eliminated. The Russian army's last march to the south would lead it to the shores of the Indian Ocean and to the Mediterranean and would mean liberation for 20 million Kurds, hundreds of thousands of Baluchis and Pushtuns. (*Los Angeles Times*, 4.3.94)

I like [Saddam Hussein] as a person. Kuwait was to Iraq as Crimea is to Russia. Both should be back where they belong. (*The Times*, 21.12.93)

Zhirinovsky's outrageous remarks are not accidental; they are the object of the exercise or in any case were until he made a name for himself. He simply follows the principles of advertising.

We need close ties with the Arab states, including Iraq and Syria. (ITAR–TASS, 13.12.93)

Zhirinovsky made a speech to armed volunteers whom he sent to defend his hero, Saddam Hussein, in January 1993. I wish you a safe return, though some of you may die there. You will die for a noble cause (*Independent*, 25.1.93). Were these volunteers told, perhaps, that they would take part in a new Gulf War?

You are going to defend Iraq, a victim of reckless aggression by America and Israel ... We will blow up a few Kuwaiti ports and aircraft, plus a few American ships in the Gulf. (*Financial Times*, 14.12.93)

Iraq? I'm the best friend of the Iraqi people. (*La Stampa*, 16.12.93)

Saddam Hussein invited me on one occasion. Had the Israelis done so, I'd have gone there too. (*Der Spiegel*, 51, 1993)

I personally met Saddam Hussein . . . He listened to me, and asked questions (*Guardian*, 7.1.94). This quotation from Zhirinovsky's book gives a good idea of the general style of that work, which, apart from some outrageous remarks, is written mostly in a somewhat pedestrian prose.

I have never sent volunteers to fight in Iraq. It was a cultural exchange: the boys went to see the museums in Baghdad. (*La Stampa*, 16.12.93)

Russia ought to be willing to **blow up a few Kuwaiti ports and aircraft, plus a few American ships**, to defend an old ally, Iraq. (*New Yorker*, 27.12.93)

Zhirinovsky's planned 'dash to the south' would appear to involve a severe blow to the Middle East. **The break-up of the Muslim world will benefit most of humanity. It will also free Europe from the Israeli trap.** (*Guardian*, 7.1.94)

According to Zhirinovsky, Russia is losing its position in the Middle East, where **Iraq is its most reliable ally**. To the east and south Russia ought to be building relationships with Japan, China and India. **As for the allied relationship with India, it will depend largely on whether Russia helps it repel the Muslim threat.** In Zhirinovsky's view, access to the Indian Ocean should become a goal of Russia's foreign policy to the south. Afghanistan, Iran and Turkey would have to be 'neutralized', which, according to him, **will be applauded in Europe.** (Zhirinovsky's statement to the press, INTERFAX, 24.11.92)

Good relations continue between Zhirinovsky and Saddam Hussein. At the time of the LDPR's congress in April 1994 an official of the Iraqi Ba'ath party brought greetings from Hussein. Zhirinovsky sent his warm greetings to Baghdad in return and reiterated **his support for the just struggle being waged by the Iraqi people** (INA News Agency, Baghdad, 3.4.94). The wording of this message is very much in the Soviet style. Zhirinovsky does his best to distance himself from the Soviet period, and in his speeches he strikes a note that would have been quite alien to the official style of Communist politicians. But when it comes to formulas, he necessarily falls back upon the only vocabulary he knows, just as everybody else in the country does. Vocabulary is the ballast that the new Russian politicians find most difficult to shed.

THE THIRD WORLD

I suggest that a different foreign policy, a radically different foreign policy, will be a source of money. Yesterday you learned from the mass media that Mengistu Haile Mariam fled from Ethiopia. This is a regime in which we invested billions. He fled – but who will return our billions to us? What will bring them back from Africa, from Latin America and from Asia? It is, after all, an impossible foreign policy to pursue. We invested billions, we got our people killed – and the regimes have collapsed. Some foreign policy! (Soviet Television, 22.5.91)

With Khrushchev the ideas of the Komintern poured out in a cascade. The Communist movement regained vigour. We put ourselves out to aid 'the Egyptian brothers'; the Cuban saga commenced. Khrushchev tried to assume the functions of the pope of the Komintern, 'to learn to live' with a billion Chinese. (*Le Monde*, 23.12.94)

5

RUSSIA

MOMENTS OF RUSSIAN HISTORY USED OR ABUSED BY ZHIRINOVSKY

Which are the events of Russian history that are still very much alive in the minds of present-day Russians and therefore influence political behaviour? And which are the memories (real or imagined) that a demagogue can exploit because they have become more important since the demise of the Soviet Union, as the entire nation has been deprived of spiritual sustenance – something that Russians have always needed and have always been proud to need?

The Byzantine Moment

Russian nationhood, and the consciousness of it in particular, was founded on Prince Vladimir's conversion to the Greek Orthodox Christianity of Byzantium in the tenth century. As so often in Russian history, conversion was by force, with troops driving people into the rivers for mass baptism. By linking itself to Byzantium Russia joined Europe, inheriting Roman traditions but, in its case, those adopted by the eastern half of the Empire surviving 1453, when Constantinople fell to the Turks, Byzantium disappeared, and Russia assumed the role of the Third Rome. Russia formed its national character by borrowing Byzantine art (icons) and architectural features and the Cyrillic script modelled on the Greek alphabet.

The Nomadic Moment

As if in doubt about the best place from which to rule Russia and to defend it from attack, the Russians, like nomads, kept moving their capital around – it was first Kiev, then Vladimir, and, after an interval, Moscow by 1340, then it moved from Moscow to St Petersburg between 1703 and 1715 and then, of course, back to Moscow in 1917. What provoked the original Russian people to commence their restless expansionism were the invasions by waves of nomadic Mongols from the ninth century onwards. The Russian state has encountered, from its inception, a variety of nomadic incursions (hostile or otherwise) along its southern frontier, but in the thirteenth century the invasion of the Mongols was an incomparably more important experience, which is still, as it always has been, a source of trauma in the Russian psyche. The Tatar occupation and vassalage lasted for more than two centuries and developed in the Russians a sense of insecurity that has lurked in the collective mind ever since. The long struggle against the nomads and then against the Golden Horde, the state that the invading Tatars came to form, has bequeathed Russian folklore a series of mighty heroes and colourful events. For a while – perhaps for a very long while – the Tatar invasions cut Russia off from Europe and turned its face towards Asia. Scratch a Russian, goes the popular saying, and you find a Tatar.

Ivan the Terrible

That you become like your enemy is the oldest truism in psychology. The fact that Ivan the Terrible (1533–84) was the ruler to seize the last Tatar strongholds, Kazan in 1552 and Astrakhan in 1556, says it all. While suspicion, a craving for security, secrecy, sentimentality and savagery are the raw meat of the Russians' history, their soulfulness and saving-the-world messianism, inherited from Byzantium, are its all-embracing sauces.

The treatment meted out to the Russians by the Tatars was relayed and redoubled by the Russian nobles *vis-à-vis* the peasantry, who became serfs, yoked to one spot, virtual slaves working up to three days per week on the lords' fields and paying two thirds of the produce from their own land in tribute. The regime was far harsher than its equivalents in the West and harsher even than those of the slaves in the US South. It became generalized, as Ivan the Terrible favoured the middling landowners against the greater, or *boyars*, whom he decimated. Indeed, he even denied them the right to travel. By the end of his brutal reign everyone in Russia could be deemed to be not only Slavs but also slaves, the derivation of the name.

The 'Time of Troubles'

Ivan's death led after an interval to ten years of utter chaos, when no one seemed to know what path to take. Preceding this turmoil, and perhaps precipitating it, there was the famous figure of Boris Godunov, who is thought to have murdered the legitimate heir, Dimitri, to seize power. During the 'Time of Troubles' several False Dimitris arose, aspiring to supreme power. Many people in Russia refer to the present period also as the 'Time of Troubles'.

Peter the Great

The most remarkable of the Romanov dynasty (1613–1917) was Peter the Great (1689–1725), a giant in stature and quite tireless, who was determined to correct Russia's backwardness and drag it into the modern Western world by means of 'shock therapy'. Barbarism was to be rooted out – if necessary, by barbaric means. Western technological and cultural influence became paramount. The capital was shifted again, this time to a city that he founded, St Petersburg, at the price of a million forced labourers' lives.

Peter the Great's forceful modernization was repeated early in the twentieth century by the Bolsheviks. Another attempt is now in progress.

Catherine the Great and Late Tsarist Russia

Catherine the Great (1762–96), wife of Peter III, whom she promptly usurped, surrounded herself with French and German luminaries in order to establish an enlightened despotism. The period stretching from her reign to 1917 was marked by a number of partial and sometimes aborted reforms, such as the emancipation of serfs in 1861, and by a great flowering of literature, the arts, science and mathematics. The invasion by Napoleon in 1811–12, which did not achieve its purpose, reinforced the Russians' age-old sense of insecurity and spurred them on to further conquests in order to secure their realm by adding ever more buffer zones (see Chapter 2).

By the eve of the First World War Russia was in full economic up-swing, but this was not accompanied by a comparable development of civil society and political institutions (the Duma, or parliament, was convened, only to be dissolved by the tsar).

War and Revolution

The decision by the last tsar, Nicholas II, to participate in the First World War turned out to be an unmitigated disaster for the Russians. A new (reputedly half-German) leader appeared via Germany, Vladimir Ilyich Ulyanov – Lenin – in a new 'Time of Troubles'. A fanatical revolutionary, he borrowed a Western idea, Marx's Communism, in order to elevate Russia to a leading role not only in Europe but in the whole world. He set out to destroy the Russian heritage accumulated throughout the centuries. Instead of emulating the West, like Peter the Great, he hoped that this time the West would emulate Russia.

Stalin

But Russian history took revenge on Lenin's ideals. At his death in 1924 the obvious successor to him – victor of the Civil War, the highly cosmopolitan and resolutely internationlist Jew, Trotsky – lost out to a new despot whose career eclipsed that of the harshest of the tsars: Stalin.

His rule, spanning virtually thirty years (1924–53) brought quick industrialization, the transformation and destruction of a flourishing agriculture, an extensive network of forced labour camps (GULAG), a vast and well-equipped army and air force and a victory over a new invader: Hitler.

The period following the Second World War, which was meant to clinch the success of Russia as a leading power, did, indeed, bring victory and at least a show of military parity with the USA. It resulted in the Cold War.

While the West thrived on the Cold War years, the Soviet economy became little more than a military–industrial complex, with a highly trained work force, making unending sacrifices for a future to come, fed and served by a civilian economy that did not fulfil its early promise in the Khrushchev years. By Brezhnev's time the whole country had settled into a quite comfortable and increasingly corrupt stagnation. World supremacy was not to be.

Gorbachev – Suicide Trip

A new period of reform started with Gorbachev (1985–91), who thought that the Soviet Union's society and economy, however drab, could be made liberal-democratic and efficient (hence *glasnost* and *perestroika*). His attempt was marked by the final decline of the Soviet political élite: they had forgotten that the basis of their power was coercion and repression. Reforms have been the main issue in Russian society since the collapse of the Soviet Union, resulting in the loss of two buffer zones: the satellite states of Central Europe and the Soviet republics. Russian expansion, which continued under Stalin, was suddenly put into reverse; and the loss of vast areas, coupled with growing economic chaos and a population that is completely baffled by developments, has undermined the self-confidence of most individual citizens as well as the nation as a whole.

The Russians, trying to obliterate the memory of the Soviet era, are harking back to Russian nationalism, the Orthodox Christian world (savagely suppressed by the Communists) and dreams of a Russian empire that existed until the First World War. The Russian leadership seems no less bemused by the sudden changes that it is striving to bring about. However they ring the changes on reform, the economy continues to deteriorate – except for its one highly efficient sector, the mafias.

And now a self-assured demagogue, Zhirinovsky, has appeared on the scene to pander to the dreams and wish-projections of a population in despair.

RUSSIA: ITS PAST AND PRESENT GRANDEUR

When the Soviet Union still existed, it was axiomatic for Zhirinovsky to proclaim Soviet nationalist sentiments.

Imperialism and colonial policy are foreign notions. We have no such things here. It was normal for us to have colonies; it was good, it was right. (*New Times International*, February 1992)

Russia once saved the world from the Ottoman Empire by sending its troops to the south. Seven centuries ago we stopped the Mongols. We have saved Europe several times: from the south, from the east, from the north and from the centre of Europe itself. The world should be grateful to Russia for its role as saviour. (*The Last Dash to the South*)

On 13 December 1993, the very day on which news came through of the stunning electoral victory of the LDPR, its leader was being interviewed on Serbian TV, Belgrade, by Jasmina Stamenić-Pavlović, who asked him: 'How do you see the future of your country, and is there a danger of Russia falling apart?' Zhirinovsky replied: Of course we wish to view the future with optimism. We wish to realize those slogans of which I spoke earlier; we want Russia to be a strong, powerful state. Realistically speaking, I think that these unstable times will go on for some time, this blood, this violence; however, I believe that, ultimately, we will reach the point at which the Russian people will calm down, the economy will recover and we will discard all these ideological scarecrows for which people are dying today. However, the coming years will be difficult, very difficult in every respect.

Russia will do only what is foreordained and will fulfil its great historical mission: to liberate the world from wars, which always begin in the south ... Otherwise Russia will be unable to develop, and will perish, and we will be crammed with nuclear stations and nuclear weapons that will destroy the whole planet. (*The Last Dash to the South*)

Zhirinovsky has been opposed to the Commonwealth of Independent States (CIS) from the outset. The goals of the CIS will mean the death of Russia. Russia will simply perish. Not right away but gradually, over the next twenty to thirty years, as new groups decide to secede. The only remaining Russians will be street-cleaners, sanitation workers, truck drivers – everyone else will have broken away. (TASS, 18.12.91)

My two years in the army (1970–72) were very useful to me. First, I got to know the army itself ... I had quite a good knowledge of the nationalities' problems before, but the Trans-caucasus region was different from Central Asia ... All Russia's problems are in the south. So until we resolve our southern problem we will not extricate ourselves from this protracted crisis, which will periodically worsen. (*The Last Dash to the South*)

Zhirinovsky has said that the LDPR is not anti-Communist and that it condemns not ordinary members but corrupt leaders. All nine Russian leaders from Nicholas II [1894–1917] to the present day have damaged Russia, but the coming elections could reverse this. Russia is now being run by an alliance between corrupt officials and mafia elements (Russia TV Channel, 23.11.93)

There was something good about tsarist Russia. There were merchants, there were courtiers, workers, civil servants. (*The Last Dash to the South*)

Give me a billion dollars and I will become president of Russia ... 'Never shall anyone humiliate the Russians' [on Zhirinovsky's posters]. (*Financial Times*, 14.12.93)

There will be no lonely women in my Russia ... We can't send everybody into the streets to sell vodka, lighters and condoms. (*US and World Report*, 10.1.94)

The Bolsheviks came to power during the night by using violence ... and rape. The next stage, the Stalin period, was a period when members of a party were being eliminated by that same party. It was not a struggle between two or three parties; there was just the one party on which Stalin depended. And the best members of the party were being eliminated. Compared with sexual morality, this reminds one of the problem of homosexuality, where there are relationships between representatives of the same sex.

Let's take another period, the Khrushchev period. It was different from Stalin's period. He was always smiling. But mostly he was alone. As for the people, we did not feel any pleasure. One can compare this with the problem of masturbation, when a person satisfies himself alone.

As for the periods of Brezhnev, Chernenko and Gorbachev, these were times of political impotence. These leaders wanted to perform, but they could not. They proposed things but they could not achieve anything, just as in the case of physical impotence. (Russia TV Channel, 26.11.93)

PAST AND PRESENT INJUSTICES
AND SUFFERING – THE MISTAKES OF THE
PRESENT LEADERSHIP

Mum worked in an institute cafeteria, and the lecturers would often tell her about the examinations and about how sorry they felt for the Russian kids. A Russian would give an answer and get a '2', and a Kazakh would give just the same answer and get a '4' ... Under Stalin's regime we were a closed country. That was a good thing in some respects – for instance, we were almost completely free of venereal diseases. And the level of morality in general was high. (*The Last Dash to the South*)

The present reforms are being conducted at your expense. The leadership wants you to die as quickly as possible, and you are already doing this. Zhirinovsky went on to say that for Russians the death rate now exceeds the birth rate and that children are dying because vaccine factories in other republics are not providing vaccines ... Today I wish mainly to address the older generation and, in particular, pensioners and veterans because they are the ones who are suffering the most. Chiefly they have been dealt a great psychological blow – they have the impression that they have lived their lives in vain, that everything has been bad, the Revolution, the war and everything they have done. Our party takes a different position. We do not blame the older generation for anything. On the contrary, we bow down to you and say to all of you that you have done well. You are leaving us a normal country, a good economy in principle, great cities, fine transport, fine science and culture. You did everything you could and now you have the right to a dignified old age. (Russia TV Channel, 23.11.93)

For decades you have been deceived, made fools of and stuffed full of a variety of dogmas. I shall represent all those who have received, and still receive in these terrible years, only 200 roubles and live in two-room apartments. You are made to do nothing but work – work so that those at the top get rich. If I do not win the election, I will not be the loser. You, the inhabitants of Russia, will be the losers (Soviet TV, election speech, 22.5.91). Zhirinovsky never misses an opportunity to hammer home the fact that his unhappiness, poverty, etc., were the same as that of the Russian common man. Another point he emphasizes is that self-pity, both in his case and in that of the Russian people in general, is justified. Self-pity and self-flagellation have for a long time been the two national psychological sports in Russia, as witnessed by nineteenth-century Russian literature. The Soviets wanted to do away with self-pity and put pride and confidence in its place. They succeeded to a certain extent, but as soon as it became clear that their pride and self-confidence were without real foundation, a large part of the population quickly reverted to their former psychological habits.

The Oslo *Aftenposten* reporter interviewing Zhirinovsky on 4 November 1991 said that when Zhirinovsky's monologues start to deal with the injustice done to the Russian people, he scales the heights. He gesticulates with his hands, and his words come like bullets from a machine-gun.

Talking to *Izvestiya* on 30 November 1993, Zhirinovsky said: Do you think the Soviet Union could have collapsed all on its own? It was the price our society had to pay for letting the Communists stay in power in National Democrat disguise. There is certainly some conspiracy behind this process in the country. Don't tell me that the Soviet Union was degenerating and its economy was decaying. The situation was carefully planned as part of the strategy to destroy Russia.

Zhirinovsky was asked: 'Who harboured and implemented this strategy?' Russia's rivals, who dream of destroying Russia, with its powerful economy, huge armed forces and scientific achievements. (*Izvestiya*, 30.11.93)

In Ankara the plans for a greater Turkish state have long since been prepared. Pan-Turkism threatens Russia, since it has a large Turkic-speaking, Muslim population and also a Persian-speaking one; that is a good inducement for Afghanistan, Iran and Turkey to move north ... And Russia loses everything. The 'great and talented' Turkish nation is worthy of living right in the centre of the world, in the scented region, on the shores of six seas; the weak and powerless Russia, however, must perish. Is this foreordained in the history of humanity? No, that is not possible. (*Die Zeit*, 14.1.94)

There are specific geopolitical factors that have played a part in the development of the Russian soul. Russia is situated in bad climate zones, with bad neighbours. For 700 years there have always been wars ... The Tatar yoke for 300 years ... With Turkey alone, thirty wars. With others, dozens, hundreds of wars. That is why there is something animal-like about 'Russianness'. Our intention to tame that instinct is the central point of our programme. That's why we need a strong army, so that no one should be in Russia's way. (*Soziologische Forschungen*, No. 7, 1993)

In the spring Boris Yeltsin's regime will collapse. Tens of millions of hungry and unemployed Russians will sweep him aside. Russia is moving towards total economic collapse (Soviet TV, 31.5.91). This is a prophecy that he never stopped repeat-

ing but returned to with renewed vigour in spring 1994, issuing
dire warnings about a new revolt against Yeltsin, similar to
that of October 1993, but linking it also with strong rumours
about Yeltsin's worrying state of health.

**Why did the Soviet troops enter Prague on 9 May 1945?
Why did millions shed their blood? Today they insult us there.
They have erected a monument to Bandera; they have erected a
monument to SS men. What about our army and our older
generation of citizens? They are spat upon today. Why did
they shed their blood? The Russians are the most humiliated
and insulted nation.** (Moscow Radio, Home Service, 11.6.91)

**The Russians everywhere will become a national minority
being slowly annihilated. There will be a slow assassination of
the Russian nation because there is no purely Russian territory ... the Russian people will perish.** (*New Times International*, February, 1992)

**He has consistently criticized the inconsistent and passive
stand of Russia's ruling circles with regard to Iraq.** Zhirinovsky's group of deputies will **raise the issue of lifting sanctions against Iraq and press for a change in Russia's diplomatic
policy, among others, within the framework of the UN.**
(ITAR–TASS report, Moscow World Service, 2.4.94)

In reply to the question of why the August 1992 *coup* failed,
Zhirinovsky said: **That was no *coup d'état* in the proper sense
of the word. Two or three groups at the centre of power were
fighting with each other. That's why the *coup* could not be
planned and executed like a military operation. And that's why
it failed.** (*Die Welt*, 29.1.94)

RUSSIA'S PRESENT POLITICAL AND ECONOMIC PROBLEMS AND HOW ZHIRINOVSKY PROPOSES TO REMEDY THEM: WHAT TO DO FIRST?

No Communists and no 'Democratic Russia' – we must be just Russians, at last. (*Die Zeit*, 14.1.94)

Industry? We shall be obliged to manufacture and sell a lot of weapons. (*La Stampa*, 16.12.93)

I have a whole concept [for improving the living conditions of soldiers]: it consists in a plan for training, and in a plan for creating congenial everyday living conditions and in the use of armies abroad ... Soldiers under contract for hard currency could perform tasks assigned by the world community. You will ask, where will you get the resources to implement such grandiose plans? What about the sale of weapons abroad? Why destroy our tanks and weapons and, in the process, become poorer and poorer. (*Krasnaya Zvezda*, 30.5.91)

We cannot permit alien religions to destroy the minds of the young generation of Russians. (*The New Republic*, 14.2.94)

There are many ways of improving the economic life of the country. Take taxes. Many of our traders suffer from them. When I say, 'We must deal a blow against crime,' I mean that only Russian citizens in possession of a licence should trade on Russian territory. (Mayak Radio, Moscow, 8.12.93)

Intellectuals are not Zhirinovsky's favourite breed. In fact, he despises them as much as Hitler did. He knows that they will never support him, but he shrugs this off by saying: **How many votes do they have? Indeed, Moscow intellectuals are against me. There are 100,000, 1 million, 3 million, 10 million** of them. But I'll need a 55-million electorate. (*New Times International*, October 92)

Millions of southerners will go home, and you will breathe freely. Because it is not so much commercial kiosks that irritate you as those inside them. When healthy Russian lads, from your regions, are standing there with honest Russian faces they are too ashamed to deceive you. For, you know, it is mainly aliens and fly-by-night southern *mafiosi* who are the swindlers, burglars, rapists and killers. (Mayak Radio, Moscow, 8.12.93)

Russia's move to the south is primarily a defensive measure, a counter-measure, because today there is a threat from the south, from the direction of Teheran, which is constructing plans for the pan-Islamic seizure of vast territories, from the direction of Ankara, where plans for a greater Turkic state were prepared long ago ... Nothing would happen to the world even if the entire Turkish nation perished, although I do not wish that upon it ... The principle of division [within Zhirinovsky's Russia] will be purely territorial inside the country: *guberniyas*, oblasts, provinces ... The blending of peoples as a result of the economy, the dominance of the Russian language and the Russian rouble, the dominant position of the Russian army as the most combat-capable; these are historical facts. We must ensure stability throughout our region for Russia and for the world community as a whole. (*The Last Dash to the South*)

New armed forces can be reborn only as the result of a combat operation. The army cannot grow stronger in barracks (*Die Zeit*, 14.1.94). In his book Zhirinovsky then goes on to describe how maintaining the army and extending Russia's frontiers will have all kinds of other beneficial effects: they will stimulate the economy, transport and communications, and at the same time it will be possible to transport raw materials and foodstuffs to help industry. Russia will become rich. There will always be enough people to work in industry as the people from the south migrate north in search of work. This particular daydream about the future of Russia is, no doubt, modelled on the migration of people to Western European countries in the period after the Second World War, first from the poorer south European countries and later from Turkey, North Africa and Asia. This combat operation envisaged for the army stands in stark contrast to other descriptions of how the dash to the south could be achieved peacefully; far from being forced, people in the south will gladly submit to Russian rule. **What is wrong with a state-controlled economy? It has its drawbacks, but why destroy it? A huge number of plants and _kolkhozes_ are working and producing output that we all need.** (*The Last Dash to the South*)

We advocate the principle of a mixed economy: the public sector should not be artificially broken up, nor the development of the private sector speeded up. Let everything develop naturally. Equal opportunities should be created both in the public and in the private sectors. Let the collective forms of economic activity (collective and state farms, auxiliary enterprises and agrobusinesses) and private activity, in the form of farms, peasant households and farmsteads, exist in the countryside. (*Rossiyskaya Gazeta*, 3.12.93)

In Russia there will be order – but only our order. What's happening right now is the destruction of the nation ... There will be a military coup here ... the army's role will be to save

the fatherland ... The people are not satisfied ... I will come to power. (*Time*, 17.2.92)

I think the pensioner will support us; he will be at peace. He will have a roof over his head. He will always have something to eat, something to wear ... And it [i.e., Zhirinovsky's accession to power] will mean that some of the population will live very well because people will have the opportunity to work honestly and, after that, to enjoy a secure old age. Because there will be no more revolutions and *perestroikas* in our country, we will put an end to the uncertainty ... The path to victory is the implementation of ideas via the success of the party and its leader. These are all interconnected ... We need to hold elections, but free elections, so that everyone who wishes to can participate in them. The voters should decide how much each party is worth. Second, we need to adopt a very concrete programme that is tied to the state. We have to prevent national divisions in Russia. There should be no Tataristan or Yakutia. Only territorial units should exist, as in every other country in the world. Third, we need to take a step back in the economy. We must strengthen the state sector, while in the private sector those who manufacture products should be given the chance to develop. We have to stop providing aid in every direction, in every respect, and we have to stop the conversion of the military industry. (*The Last Dash to the South*)

We must establish strong Russian borders. If someone owes us something and does not have the money to pay, we must confiscate their property. (Serbian TV, Belgrade, 13.12.93)

The frontiers of the USSR, recognized by the world community as of 1975, will be restored, and Russian flags will fly over the cities of Kazakhstan, Central Asia, the Transcaucasus, etc. (ITAR–TASS, World Service Radio, 2.4.94)

Zhirinovsky emphasized during his 1993 election campaign that Liberal Democrat deputies in the Duma **will never allow Parliament to act in such a way that anyone could dissolve it or even raise the issue of disbanding it. Moreover, never again in the history of Russia will anyone dare to fire at parliament. We shall never allow such a monstrous act. Also, such a blasphemy as presenting awards and titles only two days after this vile victory** [the taking of the White House in October 1993] **as a reward for Russians killing Russians in the capital of Russia is, of course, terrible.** (This particular turn of phrase; 'is, of course, terrible', is a favourite with Zhirinovsky. In certain sections of his book it is a rhetorical *ostinato*. It may come off better in live speech – he is known to be an orator.) **We shall try to put right that mistake, to rescind these titles and awards. I think the recipients will themselves lay down these titles and awards.** (Moscow TV, Ostankino Channel, 17.12.93)

In the same TV address he promised that the Duma would **raise the question of releasing Aleksandr Rutskoy, Albert Makashov and Vyacheslav Achalov** (who took part in the defence of the White House in October 1993, although, perhaps significantly, he does not mention the name of the leader of the Parliament, Ruslan Khasbulatov, who is a Chechen) **from Lefortovo prison.** He quickly added, for effect, that **those who initiated *perestroika*, ruining our economy and destroying our state, will be brought to book.** That was a promise he kept and successfully fulfilled in February 1994; he was present at Rutskoy's release from prison, took credit for it and announced: **The choice for president at the next elections is between Rutskoy and me.**

Another promise of his, which President Yeltsin kept for him, was made in the same speech: **Boris Nikolayevich Yeltsin will often be on holiday ... You'll see very little of him. Parliament will work very well.**

Zhirinovsky has always opposed the Commonwealth of Independent States on the grounds that it is harmful to Russian interests. **The goals of the Commonwealth of Independent States will mean the death of Russia. Russia will simply perish. Not right now, but gradually over the next twenty or thirty years, as new groups decide to secede.** (Zhirinovsky's press conference, as reported by TASS, 18.12.91)

Who will be our next president? The people must elect him. The choice is between me and Rutskoy (*Die Zeit*, 4.3.94), he said, after Rutskoy, one of the leaders of the rebellion against Yeltsin and his government in October 1993, was released from prison with an amnesty. That was a great humiliation for Yeltsin: he ordered the attack against the White House, defended by rebel parliamentarians, in order to have a parliament that he could control. The elections in December produced a new parliament against which he was as powerless as he had been against the previous one. That was predicted by Zhirinovsky, who on the night of the election said: **The moral and political climate in the country has turned against the state. No state in the world would permit the creation on its territory of such a large number of organizations with the declared aim of destroying that state. Nobody should allow this. Whereas democracy presupposes the existence of parties, newspapers, democracy appears also to assume the opposite process – banning parties and newspapers, not applying certain laws and introducing new laws. As we understand it, things can follow only one path – either everything is banned for decades,**

and nothing is permitted, and we all become serfs again; or else everything is permitted, and we have bacchanalia, anarchy, and nobody knows anything. (Soviet Television, 22.5.91)

If I were president, with my first decree I would subordinate the armed forces to myself and put them on a state of military alert; secondly, I would give every officer military rank up to colonel, and I would also give them the right to obtain a car made in the fatherland. (TASS, World Service in English, 18.12.91)

There are no laws today. As the ancient Greek philosopher Plato said, long before Russia or Europe existed: 'Any state where the force of law does not operate, where some force does not operate, will perish.' And how we are perishing today. (Soviet Television, 22.5.91)

Decisive steps are needed. We must not cut the army and the Ministry of Security troops. We must get the officers' corps and the Ministry of Security to fight crime in the toughest way. We must allow, temporarily, field courts-martial to be organized. If a criminal group is caught red-handed, its leader must be shot and killed immediately, on the spot, and the members of the group must be sentenced to different jail terms within three days. Only such decisive measures, which, of course, will be temporary – for six months – will enable us to get on top of crime. Otherwise it will get on top of us. (Mayak Radio, 8.12.93)

In this country today the words 'soldier', 'officer', have almost become swear words. It is absolutely necessary to save the army from indiscriminate criticism, to create the best material conditions for servicemen. (*Krasnaya Zvezda*, 30.5.91)

The conversion of factories to civilian production must be stopped. The military–industrial sector must again produce submarines, which, when exported, will earn us $200 million apiece ... In Russia there will be order – but only our order. What's happening right now is the looting of the nation. (*Time*, 17.2.94)

I will immediately declare a dictatorship – the country cannot afford democracy for now. I will stabilize the situation in just two months. (*Time*, 27.12.93)

I shall put all the strikers behind bars, train the racketeers and send them abroad to defend our national interests there, bring in cheap manpower from abroad and compel [the labour force] to work like hell for a hundred roubles a month. (*New Times International*, February 1992) (Another instance of 'their order' and of playing to a gallery unaccustomed to the nuisance caused by strikes to the public – strikes were unheard of in Soviet times.)

If I come to office next April, of which I have no doubt, in May those who signed the agreement at the creation of the CIS in Alma Ata will be in prison charged with staging a *coup d'état* ... For some reason Russians are not supposed to have their own state, where they are born, where they live, where their forebears died and where they founded cities. (TASS, 8.1.92)

Zhirinovsky's party, the LDPR: The people elected the party for the sake of stability (speech in Belgrade, 30.1.94, as reported by Tanjug.) As for trade with Russia: **Whoever wants to export goods to Russia must first send us what they wish to sell. If they are good, we will pay. Whoever wants to buy our goods must pay first, and then we will despatch the articles** paid for . . . What about banks? **I have nothing whatever to do with banks.** (*La Stampa*, 16.12.93)

In one of the few remarks he has made about parliamentary alliances he stated that he **wants to have links with the Women of Russia party**, which is regarded as being part of the 'Communist bloc'. (*La Stampa*, 16.12.93)

I will raise up Russia – Russia that is now prostrate . . . I dream of the day when Russian soldiers can wash their boots in the warm waters of the Indian Ocean. (*Frankfurter Allgemeine*, 16.12.93)

His plans when he gets into power: **5,000 gangs will be eliminated in Russia.** (*Frankfurter Allgemeine*, 14.12.93)

In reply to a question about how he is going to fulfil his promise to feed the nation in seventy-two hours: **It is very simple, really: I shall order 1.5 million troops into the former GDR, brandish arms there, nuclear arms included, and there'll be enough food to go around.** (*New Times International*, October, 1992)

Words like 'republic', 'autonomy', must go . . . There should be forty or fifty regional units in Russia; the central government must concentrate on questions like foreign policy, finance, defence, transport, communications, energy supply, ecology. (*Der Spiegel*, 51, 93)

The political system of Russia will soon receive first aid in the form of the LDPR . . . The mighty vessel of the LDPR has set sail on the expanses of the oceans, and all unseaworthy tubs have been left behind. (ITAR–TASS report, Moscow Radio World Service, 2.4.94)

THE FUTURE: ZHIRINOVSKY'S RUSSIA

Just before the December 1993 parliamentary elections, in a television programme, Zhirinovsky outlined how he sees the future of Russia and what kind of state it is going to be under him. The state, he said, is essentially the treasury and the army. If the treasury is empty and there is no army, then there is no state. The treasury is empty because it has been robbed by those who are seated before you today and ask with horror, 'How can it be that our state has collapsed? How can it be that our economy has collapsed?' But it is they who have done this, all of them except our party ... Television will be different, he announced. We shall ban all commercial advertisements. They will be allowed only in the newspapers. There will be no sneakers, no chewing-gum, no beaches. We have eight months of winter. We need fur coats and not ... beaches and cooling drinks. You will be able to watch good Russian films. Ninety per cent of all news on our television channels will be about Russia, in the good Russian language. You will be spoken to by Russian presenters with good, kind, blue eyes and fair hair. This can all be done quickly. (Moscow TV, Ostankino Channel I, 7.12.93)

He clearly wants an economy – perhaps some form of market economy – but without the irritation of consumer desires. He does not want people to be goaded into buying things, which he finds intrusive, disturbing to the minds of ordinary citizens. His dream of a market economy is of one with a human face, without commercial pressure and the consequent social pressure. He promises the 'human face', if not in so many words, in every field. His plans are for Russian expansionism with a human face: **the sound of bells of Russian Orthodox** churches on the shores of the Indian Ocean and of the Mediterranean will bring peace to those peoples. (*La Stampa*, 16.12.93)

How do I see Russia? I do not see Russia weeping . . . I see a proud Russia, a Russia wherein the glorious traditions of its army will once again be realized, where talented Russian engineers and industrialists will provide examples of the latest technology . . . We have a huge number of inventors, rationalizers . . . Russian mercantile traditions must be restored . . . This is how I see Russia. It will have the world's strongest army, strategic forces, missiles with multiple launchers. Our space-combat platforms, our 'Buran' spaceship and 'Energiya' rockets: these are the country's rocket shield . . . We have no rivals . . . Russians, a proud people; the twenty-first century will belong to us despite everything. In the next seven years we will finally put an end to all revolutions, all the *perestroikas*. We will put an end to Yeltsinism and Burbulisism. And we will enter the twenty-first century changed and pure . . . We must pacify the south for ever, so that there are vacation centres, youth camps, sanatoria and preventative treatment centres there on the shores of the Indian Ocean and the Mediterranean Sea . . . A single economy and a single legal and political structure would create favourable conditions for the development of all trades and for the culture, education, life and family structure that everyone wants. (*The Last Dash to the South*)

The division into spheres of influence continues. The main danger to Russia is concentrated in the south today. All our troubles have always originated, and will continue to originate, from there. The south is a highly unstable region – fire-spitting, controversial, riotous. Its future promises us conflicts and wars that would make Dushanbe and Sukhumi [the Tadjik and

Georgian civil wars] **look like child's play. We must calm this region down; and the world community will ask us to do so** (*Izvestiya*, 30.11.93). This will be carried out by a revived Russian army, **the final division of the world by means of shock therapy – suddenly, quickly, effectively.** (*The New Republic*, 14.2.94)

The fact that I have never been a Communist is the reason for my success in the elections. (Moscow TV, Ostankino Channel 1, 13.12.93)

I promise to adopt measures to put an end to the anti-Communist bacchanalia in particular regions and particular areas – within the framework of the law, of course. This anti-Communism should not be permitted. We are leaping from one extreme to another. Communism – we are all, so to speak, for this, but now there is a section of the population who are anti-Communists. The words 'Russian' and 'Communist' have now almost become insults. 'Officer' likewise has become an insult. That cannot be permitted. (Soviet Television, 22.5.91)

As a flexible politician, he wants to please everybody, to be all things to all men – even the Communists. **To save Russia we will definitely abandon narrow party interests and are ready to form blocs with any force** (*Independent*, 15.12.93). He manifests too great a readiness for political alliances to inspire confidence. With his characteristic and almost disarmingly candid disregard of niceties he indicates clearly that it does not matter with whom he is to join forces, since they will not be around for long once he has got into power. Is his abrasiveness towards other political figures and forces based on the calculation that whoever is in influential position now will soon disappear from the political scene, and that his constituency is the only important factor in his type of direct 'democracy'? Or is his style the result more of taste than of calculation – that is, is he really spontaneous and authentic, and is that his advantage over his rivals?

The Russian people have three choices. We can choose what we have now by voting for Gaidar and Yavlinsky, which will not suit many people, or we can choose to go backwards by voting for the Communists, which also does not suit many people. My party represents the third choice ... Less democracy! More economy! That is our slogan. Look at China. I admit it was not very democratic to use tanks against the students, but the main thing is that the country itself still exists. And they do not have shortages of food and medicines, as we have ... 'You will be fine with me.' [Campaign slogan] I am waiting in the wings. My moment has nearly arrived. (*Financial Times*, 14.12.93)

The Turkish 'democratic' way, which made it possible for the Turks to spread everywhere in Europe, is much worse for us. It is 'Kominternism', whereas fundamentalism is nationalism (*Le Monde*, 23.12.93). He does not like 'Kominternism' because he identifies it with internationalism, which is, as he puts it, like living in a communal apartment with common bathrooms, whereas nationalism is like living in a self-contained apartment, where you are safely behind doors and you admit only such visitors as you choose. (See also Chapter 6.)

POLITICAL FIGURES AND RIVALS

Khrushchev ... had absolutely no education in the humanities ... Andropov too was an uneducated person ... so all Russia's rulers have lacked a classical education ... even Lenin ... I realized that these dull-witted, sometimes simply stupid, people reached the heights thanks merely to the system that allowed them to do so. (*The Last Dash to the South*)

With Khrushchev the ideas of the Komintern poured out in a cascade. The Communist movement regained vigour. (*Le Monde*, 23.12.93)

Zhirinovsky's party was, from its earlier days in March 1990, organized on a broad scale, a fact that fed suspicions that he had special finance from the existing organs of power, notably rogue elements in the KGB. **Local party branches have been formed on the entire territory of the Soviet Union, from the Kamchatka peninsula to Moldova. The party has announced its existence in all the countries where liberal parties are available, that is, in about forty countries. In fact, the party has entered into contracts with practically all liberal parties. We have formed our political image as a moderate party of the centrist trend, seeking no social upheavals.** (Moscow Radio, World Service, 18.4.91)

Zhirinovsky made the point in the June 1991 election campaign that, at forty-five, he would be Russia's youngest president. **The bad old days of gerontocracy. How do Russia's new leaders differ from the old ones? They enjoy the same old privileges ... Once again there is total deception, and they are making fools of you.** (Soviet Television, 6.6.91)

Zhirinovsky claimed that the West is supported by democratic Russia and that the government, **who are fulfilling Western orders and embezzling, do so less because of a tendency towards corruption than because they realize that they will not remain in power long.** (INTERFAX report on Zhirinovsky's speech, 7.5.92)

Russia's Foreign Minister [Shevardnadze] was not a Russian. He is now the leader of a different state [Georgia]. That's why he was in such a hurry to withdraw our troops from everywhere and to sign all those treaties, of no use to us; they were anti-state and anti-Russian in nature. He wanted an opportunity to pull his republic out of the USSR and become its leader, (Russia TV Channel, Moscow, 26.11.93)

Boris Yeltsin is occupying my place only temporarily. I have already won. (*Time*, 17.2.92)

Zhirinovsky is often accused of being a Fascist. But he actually hurls the charge of Fascism at a great number of his political rivals, by implication not even exempting Yeltsin himself. In 1991 Zhirinovsky alleged that, when abroad, Yeltsin failed to visit Soviet war memorials. This has been denied by a representative of Yeltsin, who asked Zhirinovsky to apologize. Zhirinovsky's apology was as follows: **Wherever Yeltsin is there is war. There is Fascism. There is counter-revolution** (Soviet Television, 6.6.91). Yeltsin's representative replied: 'I am horrified at what will happen to Russia if such a president is elected.' Zhirinovsky repeated that a Yeltsin victory would generate civil war in Russia and soon a military *coup*, the latter half of which prediction was borne out two months later, in August 1991. Zhirinovsky was asked what post he would like in a future government if he were defeated. **If the winner is not Boris Nikolayevich Yeltsin, I'll occupy the post**

... I am an international-affairs specialist by profession. I am prepared to occupy the post of Russian Foreign Minister and will ensure a totally new direction for Russia's foreign policy. (Soviet Television, 6.6.91)

Komsomolskaya Pravda's representative invited Zhirinovsky, during the June 1991 election campaign, to name just one person other than himself in whom the country could believe. **Let the Russian people show through free elections in whom they wish to believe,** Zhirinovsky replied. Yeltsin, he claimed, was avoiding face-to-face debate with him. **Let everyone's medical records be on public display. Let everyone see the parlous state of Yeltsin's health.** (Soviet Television, 6.6.91)

Yeltsin, he said, had the press in his pocket, along with an endless flow of finance for his campaign. **I'm starting to go sour. I need an enemy, somebody to fight with. The Communists and the democratic Russians are lying down – who can I fight with? I can't kick a man when he's down, understand? There is nobody to fight** (NTV, Moscow, 29.3.94). Hitler thought that the political leader of genius could identify a good enemy to give his followers: 'The art of leadership consists of consolidating the attention of the people against a single adversary and taking care that nothing will fragment this attention. The leader of genius must have the ability to make different opponents appear as if they belonged to one category (*Mein Kampf*). Mao Tse-Tung would not have agreed with Zhirinovsky's chivalrous sentiments concerning not kicking a man when he is down. As Mao said, there is absolutely no better time to do it. **The elections of 12 June are not free. They are elections for just one person. It is just another political comedy.** (Soviet Television, 6.6.91)

In the same election a correspondent of the newspaper *Kuranty* asked Zhirinovsky why he had said in an interview that, if he became president, he would allow a Fascist party to be formed, with the implication that he would be its Führer. **I'll answer in the way that I, a republican presidential candidate, want to ... Today there are very many parties that do not bear the name 'Nazi' – the popular fronts and so on – but whose actions are, precisely, Fascist and Nazi ... I am a fierce opponent of Fascism, but today Fascism and the ground for it are prepared by such papers as** *Kuranty*. (Soviet Television, 6.6.91)

After the December 1993 parliamentary elections, his attitude seemed to have softened toward Yeltsin. **Boris Nikolayevich [Yeltsin] has changed lately. He is drawing closer to patriotic forces; he is identifying with Russia more openly. In the past few years his own staff have led him, again and again, into error – advisers like Gaidar, Burbulis, Chubais, Kozyrev. He himself did not want all the things that we have experienced as very negative.** (*Der Spiegel*, 51, 1993)

He is good to me: he reads a page of my book every day. (*La Stampa*, 16.12.93)

Yeltsin has no conceptions. He is like a doctor who has put on a white apron and plans to operate but has no medicine and no ideas. You don't need a big brain to break up collective farms. They [the Democrats] are destroyers. Other forces are needed for creative purposes. We – our party – can provide such forces. We will sell weapons and will not shy away from this fact. Two whole years – in two whole years the Democrats managed to sell only two diesel-powered submarines. (*Kuranty*, 16.12.93)

After meeting us, he [Yeltsin] is now moving in our direction.

He has amended his foreign policy and removed some anti-Russian elements from the government: Burbulis and Gaidar. (Warsaw Voice, 20.3.94)

Everybody is dropping Yeltsin. Not me ... When things get bad I'll take a bag, put a few apples in it and buy a bottle. And when we've had a drink or two I'll ask him: 'Boris Nikolayevich, why didn't you join me for a TV discussion before the elections?' (*Die Zeit*, 14.1.94)

I am not a Fascist. On the contrary, I have always made efforts in the struggle for human rights. Throughout my life I have not allowed myself a single extremist sortie. Some people even accuse me of being too soft towards Communists, but I am confident that the solution of all political disputes should be entrusted to the voters, to their verdict. (ITAR–TASS, 13.12.93)

It would be nice for the LDPR to cooperate with the political movement 'Women of Russia' – gentle, neutral [and regarded by many as allied to the Communists]. (Russia TV Channel, Moscow, 12.12.93)

Gorbachev: He destroyed the country. (*La Stampa*, 16.12.93)

Gorbachev should go back to where he came from, to his village near Stavropol, where he was once sitting at the wheel of a tractor. (*Der Spiegel*, 51, 1993)

Gorbachev's political ideas resulted in the state's and the economy's collapse. He should have introduced reforms in a different way. He should have made use of the existing power structures of the Communist Party, especially the KGB, and through just those structures carried out the democratization of the economy in the first place and then, as a second stage, the democratization of politics. (*Die Welt*, 29.1.94)

Yakovlev can retire to Canada, where he was ambassador for many years ... And Shevardnadze? He will go on being the commander of the besieged city of Tiflis until one day he gets a bullet in his forehead, fired by a Georgian patriot. (*Der Spiegel*, 51, 1993)

THE ARMY

What an army needs is armed conflict, both inside and outside the country. Only wars will revive the Russian army. (*Economist*, 18.12.93)

If I don't rule, then no matter, let the military. In any case, they would be better than Yeltsin's democrats. (*Financial Times*, 14.12.93)

If I were president ... with my first decree I would subordinate the armed forces to myself and put them on a state of military alert. (TASS, World Service in English, 18.12.91)

A key theme in his pre-election campaign was the need to strengthen the Russian army (which may explain why so many soldiers, including, apparently, the Taman division, which played a key role in putting down the October rebellion in Moscow, appear to have voted for him). In 1991 Mr Zhirinovsky won the nickname 'the Nuclear Robin Hood', on account of a proposal to use the army to feed his hungry compatriots. How? **By sending nuclear armed troops into the former East Germany. They would come back with enough food to go round.** He also advocates that the army deport millions of 'southerners' – code for Caucasians and Central Asians – from Russia. He argued in a pre-election broadcast that field courts-martial should be organized to shoot criminal gang leaders on the spot. **This would allow local Russian lads,** with honest Russian faces, to take over from the southerners as kiosk owners and market tradesmen. (Radio Moscow, 14.12.93)

After I become president, I shall place the army on high combat alert. Bandits from national armed units who do not hand in their weapons within seventy-two hours will be shot. (TASS, 8.1.94)

I do not rule out the use of our armed forces under the United Nations flag, for large payments in foreign currency, in different parts of the world, as is being done today by the multinational forces in the Near East and as may happen in Africa. A foreign policy of that sort would be profitable. We put everything into Iraq, and Iraq was smashed, and we have now lost everything. We would not invest in anyone, but we would be ready to make available our valiant armed forces so that, in fulfilment of UN resolutions, they could be used somewhere as a sort of police force. (Soviet Television, 31.5.91)

Our party believes that all the combat operations that have been carried out by the tsarist army, the Soviet army and the present Russian army are justified. They have all been in accordance with the military doctrine of our Russian state, and all those who were decorated deserved their awards. So one may, with honour and dignity, wear decorations received under the tsar, under the Communists and under the present regime, since the army must stand aside from the political course of the grouping that is temporarily in power. It performs its sole duty, that of protecting the fatherland. (Russia TV Channel, Moscow, 24.11.93)

Wherever our soldiers have been – in the Soviet–Finnish

War, in Afghanistan or in any other region, in Africa, in Cuba – they have done everything correctly. All the officers who fought, all the things that they did, were lawful. It was all correct, and they should always receive the necessary recognition from citizens ...

I should very much like to see a return to the time when civilians stood aside if an officer was walking along the street, and I should like people to look respectfully at an officer of the new Russian Volunteer Army. He, and even more his family, should never want for anything ...

We do not want Russian officers and men to be used anywhere as cannon fodder. If there is a need for them to take part in armed conflict, then we may provide military and technical assistance, but only on a contract basis and at a high price, and we may sell our equipment very dearly. The requesting nation must pay for the Russian equipment to demonstrate the greatness ... and the power of Russian military thinking and the potential of Russian military factories ...

I have paid great attention to the military profession, and I will say candidly that, ever since I was a child, I have nurtured the tenderest feelings for our army as a state institution, regardless of the uniform. My grandfather – Pavel Ivanovich Makarov – was a soldier in the tsarist army and he wore a uniform. I don't know whom he supported, Reds or Whites, but the uniform was that of the old tsarist army. I was myself an officer in the Soviet army and served the two years in the Caucasus. But in what army will my son be an officer or an ordinary soldier? How are we to nurture patriotic feelings if a grandfather, father and son serve in different armies, in different uniforms, with different emblems? It's monstrous. In that sense it's hard for us to bring up the younger generation and even harder to do so in a patriotic spirit. (Russia TV Channel, Moscow, 24.11.93)

Zhirinovsky claims that Russia has developed a new secret weapon, the Elipton, which kills people by eradicating their brains. He claims to have tested this weapon in Bosnia on fifteen Bosnian Muslims who are all now dead. He also announced his intention to conduct further trials of the weapon in the Belorussian city of Brest, although no report has so far emerged of his having done so. He boasts of the weapon that it is **purely ecological. It destroys opponents without leaving any contamination.** (Warsaw Voice, 20.3.1994)

THE LIBERAL DEMOCRATIC PARTY
OF RUSSIA

Neither I nor our party has ever given any support to the present political regime. This is a 100-per-cent guarantee that we are different. (Mayak Radio, Moscow, 8.12.93)

We do not want to be supported by any particular group in society. In our party there are workers, company directors, students, members of the Academy, soldiers, generals ... We do not believe in being oriented towards any class. (*Die Zeit*, 14.1.94)

We are the main party in opposition to the existing regime, he declared triumphantly, having received practically dictatorial powers from his party at the party congress. (ITAR–TASS, Moscow Radio, World Service, 2.4.94)

We are in favour of a market economy, but one that would not strike a blow at the majority of our citizens, the state sector and the military–industrial complex ... Let military

plants ... turn out market products; let them continue to sell. These plants should be converted gradually to peaceful production when the foreign market is saturated and they stop buying weapons ... The foreign market demands weapons. (Zhirinovsky's campaign statement, TRUD, 11.6.91)

I represent the party that won Russia's first free elections. Our party came first. The Russian people elected this party knowing that it was the party of a new Russia, the party of a new foreign policy, the party of cooperation with the Serb people. (His speech in Bijeljina, reported by Tanjug, Belgrade, 31.1.94)

Our stance is firm: we are against the Soviet Union, against the CIS; we are for a mixed economy without the destruction of the state sector either in the cities or in the countryside; we are against the dissolution of *kolkhozes*. We are for defending all Russians and for secure borders. All the mafias that originate in the south must be eliminated: all Russian cities must be cleansed of them. A terrific blow must be dealt against crime. That is what we proclaimed in our manifesto, and that is still valid. (*Der Spiegel*, 51, 1993)

I say it quite plainly: when I come to power, there will be dictatorship (said during his 1991 presidential campaign – AP, 18.3.94). In the same speech he stated that he **might have to** shoot 100,000 people, but the other 300 million will live peacefully.

Some 22,000 billion roubles [$13 billion] are not being used in Russia today. Let the money be used by political forces interested in developing the country. It is unreasonable for you to invest in your needs or in the needs of one or two ailing or old men. That's not how you'll save the country (AFP, 15.3.94).

This was said during a meeting with banking officials. At the time he was, or wanted to give the impression of being, short of funds, and he appealed to them for subsidies. With this request he may simply have wanted to reinforce his earlier assertion that his party is supported by ordinary citizens.

Asked about party funds: **We have more than 1 billion roubles in our party treasury. It all comes from simple people: contributions of 5,000, 10,000, 50,000 roubles arrive daily. You can check it at the main Post Office. Not a single rouble comes from shady sources ... The world does not need to be afraid of us. There will never be any danger for others from Russian soil: no territorial claims, no military occupation, perfect observance of international treaties. Russia will be a civilized European country, open to the world, without any GULAG, without repression or Stalinism, or – God forbid – Fascism. Only democracy ... We are against the Communists, just as we are against the ruling block, Russia's Choice. But we have nothing against allying ourselves in coalition: they can have two or three smaller ministries – at most.** (*Der Spiegel*, 51, 1993)

In the large cities, where the more cultured, better educated, more prosperous classes live, we will not do so well. But in small cities, the rural areas of Russia, among the poor, among the young, among the military personnel, we will be supported (*Financial Times*, 9.12.93). He was proved right in that prediction. From the very beginning he has staked his political success on the vast rural expanses of Russia and on the support of the poorer sections of society or on those who have had little to expect from the reforms. In 1992, in reply to a statement of Alexander Yanov – 'It is easy to make such promises to people. There is an enormous lumpenized mass which will buy them' (referring to Zhirinovsky's promises of

quick economic upturn, the re-establishment of Russia's prestige and the elimination of corruption and gangsterism) – he
said, laconically: **It will buy them all right.** His clearsightedness
verges on the cynical, something of which he is not in the least
ashamed. When Yanov pointed out that the nation is, after all,
not composed of lumpens alone and that lots of people retain
common sense, he replied: **They do, they will vote against me,
but they will be in the minority.** So does he bank on the
degradation of the masses? **I most certainly do!** he declared.
(*New Times International*, October 1992)

**The same political force is still in power. Its name is the
Russian Social Democratic Workers' Party** [the pre-revolution-
ary party that split into Bolsheviks and the less extreme
Mensheviks]. **But its Bolsheviks won in October 1917 and the
Mensheviks have won now. If you want real changes, you
should vote a new political party into power. Out of nine parties,
the only new one, the only one with an untarnished record, the
only party with clean hands and a clear conscience – we are
unsullied and unmarked by a single drop of blood – is the Liberal
Democratic Party of Russia** (Russia TV Channel, 23.11.93).

Menshevik means minority, whereas *bolshevik* means majority. This did not stop Lenin from calling his party Bolshevik,
even though his faction was in the minority at the last congress
of the Russian Workers' Social Democratic Party in 1903.
Lenin would have thought that he was in the majority morally
because he was right and the other faction was wrong. This
way of calculating majorities was exhibited by a later Bolshevik
leader, Nikita Khrushchev. In 1959 he lost a crucial Presidium
vote. He simply took the matter to the Politburo, the highest
organ of the Soviet state, and overturned the decision. When
somebody complained that this was not constitutional because

the opposing side were in the majority in the main forum of the Presidium, where it was appropriate for the decision to be taken, Khrushchev replied: 'That was purely a numerical majority.'

There are nine political blocs – I am referring to political parties – and eight of them are headed by members of the former ruling CPSU [the Communist Party of the Soviet Union]. All eight. There is one exception – the Liberal Democratic Party of Russia. As its chairman, I am sitting here before you. It is the only one. (Russia TV Channel, Moscow, 23.11.93)

The LDPR treasurer and number two in the party, Viktor Kobelev announced on 16 February 1994 that he was quitting the parliamentary faction of LDPR, then said that he and Zhirinovsky had ironed out their differences, although he admitted that their relations remained troubled (UPI, 17.2.94). On Kashpirovsky: **He was never in our Party. He made a statement** [not to represent the party in Parliament] **under the influence of Zionists and Ukrainian nationalists** (Warsaw Voice, 20.3.94). Anatoli Kashpirovsky, a well known faith healer and hypnotist in Russia, was elected as an LDPR deputy to Parliament in December 1993. He has since left the party to be an independent, along with Kobelev and three other LDPR deputies. Much as Zhirinovsky wishes to distance himself from the Communist period, having been brought up in it, he is permeated by Soviet methods, such as the retrospective amendment of history. The second part of Zhirinovsky's statement also needs interpretation. He was making a vague slur: Kashpirovsky is a Ukrainian Jew. This was probably in response to a private reference by Kashpirovsky to the widely held view that Zhirinovsky himself is a Russian Jew.

6

ZHIRINOVSKY ON
ZHIRINOVSKY AND THE WORLD

Zhirinovsky's past life is a subject upon which he has pronounced at length in his book, *The Last Dash to the South*, and elsewhere. Before assessing his party and explaining how it was created, a brief account of his career up to that time will help to explain how such a relatively obscure figure in 1989 has been able to take advantage of the new Russian polity that has arisen out of the débris of the Soviet Union to further his keen ambition to preside over his country's future.

Born in Alma-Ata, capital of Kazakhstan, in 1946, he had a Russian mother and, in all probability, a Russian–Jewish father. Wolfovich, his patronymic, derives from Wolf, a common Jewish name. He admits that the name Wolfovich 'sounds strange to Russian ears'. He denies being half-Jewish, which, in a country where anti-Semitism is rife, is what he would be likely to do. The Kazakh authorities claim that his father's name on his birth certificate was Eidelshtein. But Zhirinovsky also denies this. It is known that he applied for an Israeli passport at one point in the mid 1980s and that his application was accepted. He did not take it up as a new opportunity came his way. There is also evidence of his having attended meetings of Shalom, a Jewish cultural organization founded in 1989; he became the head of several of Shalom's committees, the other members of which took it for granted that he was as Jewish as themselves.[1] He takes pains to point

1 *International Herald Tribune*, 7 March 1994, p. 1.

out that he is not Jewish and also makes remarks which have a decidedly anti-Semitic ring to them. True, he couches them as merely anti-Zionist, but for decades 'anti-Zionism' was simply the Soviet code word for anti-Semitism.

In *The Last Dash to the South* he describes at length his unhappy childhood, in a family of four, living in one room (where Zhirinovsky himself was born). His father was killed in a car accident. Then, at the age of four, his life was made worse when his 38-year-old mother took as a live-in lover a loutish 23-year-old technical student. Zhirinovsky claims that no one celebrated his birthday until he was 12. He also claims that when he was 2 or 3 he was forced to board at the home of a child-carer.

At the age of 17, in 1964, he managed to enter Moscow's prestigious Institute of Oriental Languages, where he graduated in Turkish, which is one of four foreign languages he knows, the others being French and, rather less well, German and English. He describes these years as lonely ones, having been a poor provincial among his probably more polished fellow students. He admits to several abortive sexual experiences, which may have increased his penchant for brooding and self-pity.

In subsequent years, especially when he set out to follow what he describes in his book as his destiny to become a big-time politician, he made a point of stressing his sense of isolation and his self-pity, both in Alma-Ata and in Moscow, well aware of the prevalence of these traits in the Russian population at large. Like every Russian male, after graduating from the Institute he completed the usual two years of military service, in his case in the Caucasus, a particularly sensitive posting for a Russian soldier. He may have conceived his suspicion and dislike for Caucasians in general during these years. He graduated as a Soviet army officer, of which he remains inordinately proud.

It was during this period that his fascination with all things military was stirred: **I love the army**, he says.

He also declares his love for the KGB. And at this time it is quite possible that his love took a practical shape. Most students at the Institute, and many officers in the old Soviet days, were approached by the KGB to act as informers. Given Zhirinovsky's predilection for behind-the-scenes activities, it may well have appealed to his patriotism to serve the KGB as informant; such a temptation may have been irresistible to him. His participation in a trade delegation to Turkey as long ago as 1969, when he was only 23, is often cited as an indication of long-standing intelligence connections, for such Soviet trade delegations were heavily infiltrated by KGB men and their stooges.

It is the view of Oleg Kalugin, who worked for twenty-five years in KGB intelligence, seven of them in counter-intelligence, that Zhirinovsky was recruited by the KGB. 'There is no evidence, but he was obviously infiltrated into the system early on. Look, for instance, at when he was a student and was allowed to travel outside the country freely, even though he was single, with no family. His was the first party to emerge after Communism. He was received by the former KGB chairman, and his party manifestos were printed in the *Pravda* printing house. It is very difficult to get access to it unless you have the support of the Party and its henchmen, the KGB. I believe he has immense support from the old structures.' Kalugin recalls seeing Zhirinovsky, as far back as 1990, 'roaming the halls of the Kremlin as though he was one of the Party élite. I remember having several conversations with him and thinking he was a borderline psychotic.'[2]

2 *The Sunday Times* Magazine, 1 May 1994, p. 27.

Much of his professional life – for example, his time as a trainee in the foreign-broadcast section of the state radio and in the State Committee for Foreign Economic Relations – was spent in jobs that would almost certainly have required extensive KGB vetting and monitoring.

After taking evening courses in law at Moscow State University, he finally obtained long-standing employment as a lawyer at the age of 29 in 1975. He worked for Inyurkollegiya, a state-run law firm. One of about fifty lawyers in the concern, he was assigned the task of tracking down Soviet citizens whose relatives in the West had left them alimony, pensions and legacies. He was regarded as well-organized, competent and energetic, becoming the head of the firm's trade union, an important post in a Soviet company.

But his interest in politics led him to make strident pronouncements to the other lawyers in the firm, which made them wary of him. 'He would come into my office repeatedly to talk about politics,' said Yevgeny Konlichev, his immediate superior at Inyurkollegiya.[3] 'He was especially indignant that Russia was surrounded by Turkic people in the south.'

At this time, in the early 1980s, the Soviet Union must have seemed politically solid, even if economically stagnant. Anyone ambitious to become a politician would have had to join the Soviet Communist Party. Mr Konlichev states that Zhirinovsky tried to become a member, even pressing his superiors at the firm to recommend him for Communist Party membership. This Zhirinovsky denies, as he would now do whatever the truth. Mr Konlichev's account of why the firm refused to do this is as follows: 'He was very emotional and gratuitously, not constructively, critical,' he says. 'His ideas were disorganized,

3 *International Herald Tribune*, 7 March 1994, p. 1.

and he insisted fiercely on them,' which is true to this day. 'His character, the remarks he made, the way he related to people – these did not fit the code of Communist behaviour.'

Indeed, from this time onwards he tended to vent anti-Communist sentiments; it is, of course, likely that he shared with the Communists no beliefs, except Soviet nationalism. But rancour at their rejection of him must have fuelled his anti-Communist passion.

In spring 1983 came a rupture with Inyurkollegiya, when he was caught accepting what the firm regarded as improper gifts from a client. Mr Konlichev says that the rift was brought about by an inheritance case from West Germany. Zhirinovsky's Soviet client had a relative who had died in West Germany and left him, as part of his inheritance, special vouchers permitting him to stay at an exclusive resort. As a sign of his gratitude, the client gave Zhirinovsky the vouchers. According to Konlichev, Zhirinovsky insisted that he had returned the vouchers unused, but Konlichev and other managers in the firm became convinced that he had returned them only after the matter was discovered. 'This was the last straw,' states Konlichev. It was decided that 'unless he wanted more trouble he'd better go'.

Zhirinovsky denies that he did anything improper, and, indeed, no charges were brought against him. Konlichev's account of the case may not be the whole truth, since, from Brezhnev's time onwards at least, small-time corruption was endemic; salaries were low; and people supplemented their pay with 'gifts' that they expected to get from clients as a matter of course. It is at this time, when he was out of work, that, Israeli officials state, he applied for and was sent an invitation to emigrate to Israel. However, the Mir publishing house, an enterprise with more than 600 employees, needed someone with a legal background and offered him a job, so he remained in Russia.

Just as at Inyurkollegiya, he did well at first. But within a year or two his strong political views, in particular his vehement anti-Communism, attracted the attention of the local Communist Party's headquarters. The ideological chief of the Party's branch office contacted the head of Mir, Vladimir Kartsev, urging him to dismiss his wayward employee. Mr Kartsev, despite being a Communist himself, refused on the grounds that the law did not allow dismissals for political reasons. Again, there is probably more to this than meets the eye. As Mr Kartsev would well know, dismissals (and rather worse) for political reasons were very common in the Soviet Union.

Zhirinovsky aspired to become the Mir workers' representative, as he had been at Inyurkollegiya. In 1987 he stood as candidate for the council of Moscow's Dzerzhinsky District, named after the first head of CHEKA, the Secret Police in 1917, a forerunner of the KGB. The local Communist Party officials did not welcome his candidacy and rewrote the rules to disqualify him.

These were now the days of *glasnost* and *perestroika*. The struggle against the local Communists was to stand Zhirinovsky in good stead, much as Yeltsin's contest with the Soviet Politburo and Gorbachev did at this very time, when he was mayor of Moscow. Zhirinovsky tried to become one of Mir's fourteen-member employees' council, an innovation of *perestroika*, but was thwarted by Kartsev, who ran a vigorous campaign against him. Zhirinovsky, nevertheless, called his own campaign a 'victory', which in a sense it was. For this experience at canvassing helped to develop his oratory and his own brand of demagoguery (which is what politics 'is 70 per cent about', in his view). He honed the themes that he still exploits today – for instance, better conditions for the workers (in Mir's case, by shifting its line of production from scientific titles to popular books, the higher profits of which would go straight to the firm's employees rather than being invested in the business). He was prefiguring his rhetoric on the electoral stump – where he would promise higher pensions, cheap vodka, a war against crime, the renewal of Russia's military might and his country's resumption of its proper place in the world.

Kartsev then left Mir, and Zhirinovsky made an unsuccessful attempt to replace him as its head. But now he had opening up to him a wider field than the relative backwater of Soviet publishing. The era of *glasnost* was seeing a proliferation of new groups and organizations. From late 1987 Zhirinovsky began to attend as many meetings as he could, so that he could practise his oratory. It was at that time that he joined Shalom, and he explains his participation in the Jewish organization's activities. 'What did I want to use Shalom for?' he told a newspaper correspondent in 1991. 'To have a chance to speak.' The same is true of his attendance at meetings of the far-right-wing anti-Semitic and ultra-nationalist group Pamyat, which is closer to his political standpoint.

FROM PRIVATE CITIZEN TO PARTY LEADER

Getting himself known about in this way paid off. The crucial stage of Zhirinovsky's ascent in Russian politics was in the offing. In early 1989 he joined forces with Vladimir Bogachev, a self-styled composer and poet whom he met at a congress of one such organization, the Democratic Union. Bogachev was impressed by his oratory, his legal skills and his linguistic abilities. Bogachev saw him as the figurehead of a new party he was setting up, the Liberal Democratic Party (LDP) of the Soviet Union. At the party's founding congress in March 1990 Zhirinovsky was elected chairman and Bogachev his deputy.

This success, however, proved short-lived. He aroused the mistrust of his colleagues because they suspected that he had links with the Communist regime and the KGB in particular. Seven months later, at the party's second congress in October, it voted for his expulsion.

Zhirinovsky's connections with the Communists in 1990–91 have never been proved and are, of course, strongly denied by him. But not only are ex-party colleagues convinced that they existed; certain Russian politicians, including Gorbachev and Anatoly Sobchak, mayor of St Petersburg, also think that he was funded and backed by members of the KGB in mid-1990. For he reacted to the reverse of being ejected from the LDP of the Soviet Union by establishing his own party, which he still heads, the Liberal Democratic Party of Russia (LDPR), in the autumn of 1990.

Sobchak claims to have documentary proof that Gorbachev and others decided at a Politburo meeting in early 1990 to instruct the KGB to set up Zhirinovsky as a stalking horse, a sham 'opposition figure', to outflank Yeltsin and give Soviet politics the appearance of multi-party pluralism without disturbing Communist supremacy. The projected upshot was that Zhirinovsky's party would split the democratic vote and scupper Yeltsin.[4]

Gorbachev denies this and suggests that rogue elements in

4 Sobchak is expected to publish a book on the contemporary Russian scene in summer 1994.

the KGB were responsible. He told a Russian newspaper in January 1992: 'Beyond doubt, someone recognized his talents and plans to use them in the future.' If Gorbachev puts the matter of his KGB sponsorship 'beyond doubt', then it is highly likely to be so, because he is the one man who is in a position to know. All that he is denying is that the person in question was himself.

Vladimir Nazarov, an independent journalist and early biographer of Zhirinovsky, explains who financed the Liberal Democratic Party of Russia in 1990: 'In the archives of the Communist Party, deputies found an agreement between the management department of the Central Committee of the Communist Party of the Soviet Union and the company owned by Andrei Zavidiya (who had run for the vice-presidency in the Zhirinovsky election campaign in June 1991). The Bolshevik leaders granted the company an interest-free credit of 3 million roubles . . . Now it is clear who foots the LDPR's bills.'[5]

Later on the LDPR may well have had to diversify its sources of finance. The big state firms in the military–industrial complex are likely to be one set of backers. Some speculate that Abkhaz drug smugglers are another, in gratitude for LDPR militants' support in the Abkhaz independence movement's war against the Georgians. Abkhazia used to be a province of Georgia and is now of uncertain sovereignty. A third possible source of finance was the East German Communist Party. It is rumoured that the East German Communists misappropriated, and then at least partly transferred to Russia, a sum of DM 4 million. By early 1991 Zhirinovsky had arrived at centre-stage on Russia's political scene, which was threatening to escape its Soviet management. In the electoral contest for Russia's presi-

5 *New Times International*, October 1992, p. 12.

dency in June 1991 he won more than 6 million votes, or 8 per cent of the total, running third behind Yeltsin and Nikolai Ryzhkev, ex-Soviet premier and Communist candidate. That election assured Yeltsin of his presidential mandate, but the force that could succeed him emerged in the very hour of his electoral triumph, which was to be dramatically confirmed two months later by the failure of the August *coup* plotters and by his own successful defence of the White House (the seat of the Russian Parliament).

A ONE-MAN THINK-TANK

Zhirinovsky's party was from the outset called the Liberal Democratic Party of Russia. Like Yeltsin, he had anticipated the collapse of the Soviet Union and had positioned himself well to shine in its emerging polity. The party has representatives not just in the regions, autonomous republics and military districts of Russia but also in the republics in the Near-Abroad, including in military bases there, where he prides himself on being highly popular. These very representatives stir up trouble with local authorities, which gives Zhirinovsky ideal opportunities to keep himself before the public eye. A firm believer in the dictum that any publicity is good publicity, he wants to remain the most talked-about politician in Russia, to which end his becoming the most notorious politician in the world is a useful adjunct. Hence his flow of wild talk.

He likes holding press conferences at which he expresses indignation at some slight incurred by Russians in the Near-Abroad, whereupon he can give vent to his anger in a torrent of abuse. For instance, when his representative in Estonia, Rozhok, was detained in January 1994 for stirring up inter-ethnic strife, Zhirinovsky said at a press conference, to the cheers of his own militia: **I warn the Estonian government that if even a hair should fall from Rozhok's head, the Estonian government will have to think of the fate of 900,000 Estonians. I will swap one Rozhok for 900,000 Estonians. If Rozhok is put in an Estonian jail, an end will come to Estonia and Tallinn. We will implement such measures that the Estonians will forget that they are Estonian.**

The LDPR has several Cossacks among its backers, especially in the Near-Abroad. General Alexander Lebed, commander of the 14th Army, holds the Cossack Cross for the Defence of Trans-Dnestr, where his army is stationed. He offers strong support to Zhirinovsky, encouraging the Cossacks to do so too. The Cossacks of the Don officially backed Travkin's Democratic Party of Russia, which is largely neo-Fascist, in the December 1993 elections. But with other military and naval commanders expressing support for Zhirinovsky, it may be possible for him to woo the Cossacks away from the electorally far less successful Democratic Party of Russia.

The LDPR has had its share of internal troubles; some deputies have complained about Zhirinovsky's outspoken extremism. Defectors have denounced him as a puppet, installed by reactionary elements in the KGB. 'If you want to know about Zhirinovsky,' says Leonid Alimov, 'just ask Kryuchkev,' naming the former KGB chief who was a *coup* plotter in 1991.[6]

In February 1994 a more serious challenge to Zhirinovsky's position was mounted when party treasurer Victor Kobelev defected with Alexander Pronin, another LDPR deputy and shadow minister. They threatened to reveal damaging secrets about Zhirinovsky and the formation of the party. After a brief reunion with Zhirinovsky, Kobelev defected again,

6 *Time*, 17 February 1992, p. 11.

threatening to depose Zhirinovsky at the party conference in the first week of April.

In fact, the conference turned out to be a triumph for Zhirinovsky, who was unanimously elected leader for ten years by the 343 delegates, with no new conference to be held until 1997, one year after the next presidential election. Kobelev and other defectors were simply not invited. But, said Kobelev afterwards: 'At the moment I am not using the material [against Zhirinovsky], which I am saving for a serious talk. But if he insults me personally, I will destroy him as a person and as a politician.'[7] Two other deputies left in early April, Vladimir Bortyuk and Vladimir Novikov, who respectively headed Oryol and Udmurtia regional branches of the LDPR.

A fifth defector, Anatoli Kashpirovsky, who left at the same time as Kobelev and Pronin, was a great asset to Zhirinovsky in the elections, as he is a well-known hypnotist and faith healer, widely believed to possess occult powers. Until a government ban was imposed, he exercised them on television to mass audiences. He campaigned vigorously for the LDPR in the media in December 1993 and was accused by rival parties of hypnotizing the electorate to vote for Zhirinovsky. Kashpirovsky's defection is certainly a blow but not a fatal one. A strong personality, he is now concentrating on his role as president of the Foundation for Researching the A. M. Kashpirovsky Phenomenon.[8] Zhirinovsky himself has given rise to the 'Zhirinovsky phenomenon'. A book of that title appeared in Moscow in 1992, a partisan work.[9] Obviously both Zhiri-

7 *The Times*, 7 April 1994, p. 12.

8 'Directory of Members of the Russian Parliament Elected in December 1993', BBC Monitoring, January 1994, p. 56.

9 *Fenomen Zhirinovskogo*, Kontrolling, Moscow, 1992.

novsky and Kashpirovsky have such massive egos that their coexistence in one party was never likely to last. In what is increasingly becoming a one-man band there is no room for those with independent minds. **The leader and the party are one and the same** (*New York Times*, 5.4.94) is Zhirinovsky's credo.

Kobelev's defection would be more of a nuisance if the material that he has were really damaging. But one reason why he may not have ventilated it already is that it is very likely to implicate him also as a long-time associate and LDPR treasurer. Even if it turns out that Zhirinovsky's KGB connections are proved true, and that dirty money has passed through the party's coffers, this would not necessarily hurt Zhirinovsky very much in Russia's volatile situation, since the people assume that all politicians are crooked. What they are looking for is a 'good' crook or godfather heading a 'white mafia' to combat the black mafia that is fleecing the Russian economy. Zhirinovsky has made this very project his number-one priority once he assumes power. He could answer any allegation against him of ill-dealing by claiming to be just such a figure, heading his white mafia to clean up Russia.

A lethal threat to his position, indeed, comes from the mafia, who recognize him as the one politician who might act forcefully against them by using a special police force set up against the mafia in place of an already corrupted police force. Contract killings are now commonplace. One St Petersburg mafia leader, 'Sasha', told a *Sunday Times* investigator: 'Look at Zhirinovsky. If he came to power and started interfering in our business, we would make one phone call to Moscow. That's all. And then no more Zhirinovsky.[10]

10 *The Sunday Times*, 17 April 1994, News Review, p. 8.

Zhirinovsky, however, is well aware of the danger and always goes around with a contingent of his own militia, Zhirinovsky's Falcons, with uniforms and machine-guns. At his weekly public meetings in Moscow and the provinces they flank him on the rostrum and prowl around the generally enthusiastic crowds, keeping an eye open for trouble. A contract taken out on Zhirinovsky would be more difficult to execute than one on other politicians or top bankers, ten of whom were killed in this way in 1993.

An official attempt to prevent Zhirinovsky's rise to power is under way with the help of the Russian Attorney-General's office. This office is considering a request to have Zhirinovsky indicted for violation of Article 71 of the Russian Federation Penal Code, 'Propaganda of War'. Such a violation is punishable by imprisonment for a term of between three and eight years. Zhirinovsky's alleged violation is his calls for a war against Turkey, Iran and Afghanistan in *The Last Dash to the South*.

One reason why Zhirinovsky campaigned successfully for a parliamentary amnesty for Rutskoy, Khasbulatov and the other leaders of the October 1993 *coup* attempt by the previous Russian Parliament is probably that he knew that this would improve his chances of not being indicted himself. If those who actually employ violence against the government and president are let out of jail, how can a politician who simply uses violent language be adjudged sufficiently criminal to be imprisoned? A large fine would not be a serious problem for Zhirinovsky, who always says that anyway the case would be dropped. Something far more decisive than an uncertain legal prosecution would be needed to stop his ascent to supreme power.

HIS THOUGHTS ABOUT HIMSELF, HIS PAST
AND HIS FUTURE

I am bad but good for Russia. (*Die Zeit*, 14.1.94)

My mother was Russian and my father a lawyer (*New Times International*, February 1992): a classic answer to a question about his ethnic origins. He was Russian, Wolf Andreyevich Zhirinovsky. My mother called him Volodya [short for Vladimir] (CSM, 24.12.93). It would have been easier if she had given me the name Vladimir Vladimirovich, but for bureaucratic reasons or because of the pedantry of the registry, I do not know which, I am called Vladimir Wolfovich. This name is not familiar to Russian ears (*The Last Dash to the South*). He is clearly uncomfortable with his name.

When a foreign journalist asked him to clarify his racial origins, he replied: Newspapermen made that up. I never said that my mother was a Russian and my father a lawyer. The simple fact is that I was answering questions at a rally. I read the question: 'What nationality was your mother?' I replied: 'Russian.' A little while later I was handed a piece of paper, and I read: 'What was your father's profession?' I replied: 'Lawyer.' What was I supposed to do? Just imagine what would have happened if I had got the question about what my father's profession was and I had answered: 'Russian.' They would have called me a lunatic. Zhirinovsky went on to outline his genealogy, all the way back to his great-grandfathers and great-grandmothers. All of them were pure Russians, no mixtures. Granted, my father's parents were from Poland, but Poland isn't a state really. It's a Russian province (*Current Digest of the Post-Soviet Press*, 12.1.94).

I've had thousands of blood tests. If you have specialists

who could find at least 5 per cent Jewish blood in me, I would be proud. But there is none. (CSM, 24.12.93)

Zhirinovsky is the common man personified. I myself am an ordinary citizen. I represent the middle stratum which earns two hundred roubles and lives in a two-room apartment. I am just like you, and I understand that these awful prices in commercial and cooperative stores are beyond our pockets ... Women of Russia ... I know things have been hard for you ... A few days before [my mother] died she said: 'Volodya, there is nothing to remember.' In all her seventy-three years she had not known a single day of joy ... I share all of your anxieties: the eternal lines, the shortages ... constant worry about how to feed the family properly ... You must be provided for. (Moscow Radio, 11.6.91)

I was born among Russians, so I consider myself to have been born in Russia itself. (*Financial Times*, 9.12.93)

It was a joyless childhood. All eighteen years ... Even my bed was not my own. I slept on a trunk ... Mum never had any time. She was working ... Sometimes I would not see her for days on end (*The Last Dash to the South*). I had no place to play. My clothes were bought at the market, the clothes of dead people (*La Stampa*, 16.12.93). I was always hungry. I was fed from the cafeteria in which my mother worked. The food was awful and, of course, it caused gastritis. In the flat there were no children's books, no toys, no papers, no telephone (*Die Zeit*, 14.1.94). Life forced me to suffer from the very day, the moment, the instant, of my birth. Society could give me nothing. (*Time*, 27.12.93)

In his description of suffering and joylessness he falls back upon another commonplace topic: suffering as preparation for great achievement. A painter or a composer may need the experience of misfortune to be able to create. It was the same with me. Being isolated by loneliness . . . has served the purpose of enabling me to understand better, and more profoundly, the political process. The constant feeling of not being satisfied has stimulated me. (*Die Zeit*, 14.1.94)

His descriptions of his deprivations in the emotional and social desert of his early life may be heartfelt, at least sometimes, but they may equally well be intended to conjure up in the minds of his audience and readers biblical images of prophets girding their loins in preparation for their mission, especially since he goes on describing the vague intimations of a barefooted youngster: I was not able to comprehend it then, but I felt instinctively that I was destined for a great role in politics. (*Die Zeit*, 14.1.94)

I remember in school that one girl had a ball-point pen and I didn't. Or I would visit a home where they had hot water, but we didn't. If I had lived in good conditions, warm and well-fed, maybe I wouldn't have become involved in politics. (*Wall Street Journal Europe*, 14.12.93, quoted from *The Last Dash to the South*)

Even in early childhood something dawned on me. It was a kind of ultimate idea that was like the intellect governing the world. Even when I was a small boy walking along the quiet street from home towards the Nikolskaya church and the Nikolsky market, there was something . . . thoughts of something great were hovering in my head . . . And this came to pass. This was no accident . . . An educated man with two university degrees who speaks European languages; where did he pop up from, this throwback to the prosperous Russia of the last century? (*The Last Dash to the South*)

Try to find another country that is being destroyed and plundered as systematically as Russia. I am not simplifying the matter. Each decision is a hard one. It's just that I'm an expert in what I am doing; I provide prompt answers to questions because I have them. I have been thinking about them for thirty years.

Why do you ignore the fact that Zhirinovsky graduated from Moscow University with honours, that he speaks four languages and has travelled extensively throughout Russia and the world? Hence my prompt solutions. (*Izvestiya*, 30.1.93)

Ideology won't get in my way! I am free of dogma. My political views have always been the same as they are now. I come from a long line of lawyers. My grandfather was a lawyer under the tsar. My father was a lawyer – before the war, under the Stalin regime. I am a lawyer, and my son is studying law. So that is one point. Throughout the world, 80 per cent of leaders are arts graduates. I have a double arts background. (Soviet Television, 22.5.91)

An American offered me $10 million to leave politics. I told him: 'Never.' I steer the boat here. I know the course. No one else knows. (*Die Zeit*, 4.2.94)

I was born in 1946, the year of the dog. Dogs are faithful, sincere and always at your service. My party will never betray our voters. (*Economist*, 18.12.93)

I have never been a Communist. Neither I nor our party has ever given any support to the present political regime. This is a 100-per-cent guarantee that we are different. (Mayak Radio, Moscow, 8.12.93)

I have never read *Mein Kampf*. (*Die Zeit*, 14.1.94)

I am not a Fascist. On the contrary, I have always made efforts in the struggle for human rights. (ITAR–TASS, 13.12.93)

He prides himself on being an expert in geography, which, as he put it, is his favourite occupation. He once gave the former French diplomat Rolf Gauffin a map with the new frontiers of Central and Eastern Europe drawn on it. He signed it – just as Stalin signed the map showing the partition of Poland in the German–Soviet pact of 1939.

Asked about his connection with the former KGB, he gave the categorical assurance: **I have no connections with the former or the present KGB. I would gladly have had connections with the KGB, as it was the most powerful political police in the world. Had I been connected with the KGB, I would be sitting in the Kremlin now and not in this small town on the shore of a lake** (quoted by Radio Slovenia, Ljubljana, 28.1.94). On another occasion, when asked the same question, he replied: **I never worked for the KGB. I might have gone further if I had.** (*The Times*, 21.12.93)

I represent the party that won Russia's first free elections. Our party came first. The Russian people elected this party knowing that it was the party of a new Russia, the party of a new foreign policy, the party of cooperation with the Serb people. (A speech in Bijeljina reported by Tanjug, Belgrade, 31.1.94)

Zhirinovsky is a real populist. He is willing to incur the wrath of politicians with pronouncements like: **I have no wish to be of service to any politician.** He points out that he always has the little man in mind.

Thousands of people have kissed my hands. (*La Stampa*, 16.12.93)

The leader and the party are one and the same. (*The New York Times*, 5.4.94)

I have never allowed myself a single extremist escapade in my life. (*Time*, 27.12.93)

There is no doubt that I'll be president of Russia because there are no other candidates. If elections are held this year, I'll get 55 per cent of the vote; if they are held in two years' time it will be even better because then I'll be 50, and the people will give me 70 per cent of the vote as a present ... There are no other candidates because all politicans who are in any way connected with those in power are responsible for poverty, inflation and organized crime ... Polls which say that I have only 6 per cent support for the presidency are silly nonsense; they also said that I would not get into Parliament. The press only publishes these figures because of the mafia, which wants to liquidate me and pays the papers to sully my reputation ... As soon as I get into the Kremlin I'll order the liquidation of organized crime – 10,000 *mafiosi* will be arrested and publicly executed ... When I go to the Russian provinces, people kiss my hands and throw themselves upon me to embrace me, for they know that I am the only one to stand up for the rights of the people – no one believes the slanders that you journalists publish, such as that I'm a Fascist, an anti-Semite and so on. (*Yediot Akhronot*, 16.3.94)

I am moderate in all things. (*Time*, 27.12.93)

Zhirinovsky concedes that he has a weakness: **My only vice is a weakness for frontier posts, for their being in place. If** some unclean force moved them inside Russia, Zhirinovsky's party would return them to their place, but within the framework of the law. (ITAR–TASS report, Moscow World Service Radio, 2.4.94)

REFLECTIONS ON RACE AND NATIONALISM

Nationalism? It's a disease just like Fascism. We'll get rid of it in the third millennium. (*La Stampa*, 16.12.93)

Apparently we must deal with minorities as America did with the Indians and Germany with the Jews. (*Time*, 27.12.93)

There is another important aspect of Zhirinovsky's ideology – his stance against any form of what he calls 'internationalism', political, economic or social. The internationalist approach of the former Soviet government is what he mainly objects to. The idea of internationalism has been spreading around the world for a century and a half. With the growth of capital, frontiers became weaker and weaker. Improvements in the means of transport and of communications have made the task of industrialists increasingly easier, the industrialists of all countries united. The 'spectre of Communism' appeared in response to that: the idea of a united proletariat haunted Europe; and this fraternity, like the fraternity of the Rothschilds and the Rockefellers, has remained alive and influential to this day through the force of its spirit and its ideology (*Le Monde*, 23.12.93).

He sees the history of Russia from 1917 onwards as a series of alternations between national and international policies, one or the other gaining the upper hand under successive leaders. [Lenin] put the internationalist interests of the working class above national interests ... But world revolution never took place. However, the reason for that was not, as some scholars would have us believe, because the idea was senseless. Had Trotsky been the leader, the idea would have been realized. The enormous potential of a gigantic country, its powerful army and the influence of the Komintern would have yielded results. But power in the USSR was seized by a 'Caucasian group', which had little connection with the Komintern ... Stalin tended to limit the activities of the Komintern, turning towards isolation from Europe, both from the Communist and from the capitalist part of it. (Le Monde, 23.12.93)

We should think about saving the white race because today the white race is a minority in the world. It is a minority that needs to be protected and saved. If we don't fight against this danger – the Islamic danger, the Asian danger – then in the future we will have a religious danger and, finally, religious wars where we will all be swamped by what is called the Yellow Peril. (Time, 27.12.1993)

The notion behind internationalism is that of mixture; nationalism comprises the notion of quality. Nationalism is like a self-contained flat and not a communal boarding house ... If we acknowledge that we are constructing a national state, with a national ideology and without any kind of 'Atlantism' or 'Eurasianism', then our first task is to establish national frontiers. They must be clearly defined and then locked tight (Le Monde, 23.12.93). The 'Eurasianism' to which Zhirinovsky refers here was originally a movement of Russian émigrés in the 1920s who thought that, for Russia, Asia would be more important than the West. It was one of the many anti-Western tendencies in Russia, and at the time of the collapse of the Soviet Union it was revived for that very reason. 'Atlantism' is the enemy of the 'Eurasianists'; it proposes an Atlantic empire of the USA and international Zionism, whose nefarious influence and aggressive hostility – so the theory goes – can be repelled only by the bastion of Eurasia, led, of course, by Russia with its old Soviet borders.

National Socialism unites the most important principles of socialism with national ideas. National Socialism has nothing in common with Hitlerism. Hitler has discredited National Socialism. In addition, in elaborating his doctrines he borrowed the idea of ... world revolution. Only a very tenuous line separates the idea of wanting a world revolution from striving for world domination. National Socialists do not need to dominate the world ...

The philosophy of a National Socialist is that of the common man, of the *petit bourgeois*, if you will, who wants a quiet life in his own apartment, a wife who loves him, healthy children, a secure job; on Sundays he wants to go out into his garden or to the country; and he wants a holiday once a year. He does not wish to bother anybody, but he does not wish to be bothered either. He is not a hero – not at all.

He does not long to plough the frozen earth with his tank in the name of who knows what ideal. A beggar causes him distaste, and he feels some resentment of the very rich. He wants to be sure that his daughter will not be raped in the street at night and that his son's head will not be bashed in with a bottle. He is absolutely not fanatical; unlike Hitler, he needs no cult or occultism. But he wants to be able to look up to his leaders and feel that, because of their intelligence, they deserve the position they have. (*Le Monde*, 23.12.93)

Division along ethnic lines brings about civil war, dredges up the complication and inexorability of the nationalities issue, which is the most intractable of issues and has not yet been resolved anywhere in the world – not in affluent Canada, in cultured France or in formerly fraternal Yugoslavia. Everywhere it takes on a bloody aspect. (Soviet Television, 22.5.91)

Our most vexed issue is the nationalities question. I graduated with distinction from the institute of the countries of Asia and Africa. My profession has a link with the inhabitants of the majority of Turkic-speaking regions – Kazakhstan, Central Asia, the Transcaucasus and the Near East. I could address the Turkic-speaking deputies in their own language at this very moment.

It would be nice for them if the president of Russia understood them and knew the culture and language of this multi-million-strong people of our country, of our Russia. So that they can understand me, I'll switch languages. [Continuing in Turkish] Today we may elect the president, but what sort of president he will be will depend upon you. [Resuming in Russian] I'll revert to Russian because I have great respect for it and I'd very much like the whole country to respect the Russian language, just as it is respected today in Europe and America, whereas in the Baltic and some other regions they have a very negative attitude towards it. (Soviet Television, 22.5.91)

There is no reason to fear Islamic fundamentalism. Islamic fundamentalism is the establishment of an order, of traditions that characterize peoples in the south: polygamy, respect for the old, submission, traditional crafts, the Koran. In what way is that bad for us Russians? (Le Monde, 23.12.93)

Fundamentalism is nationalism. (Le Monde, 23.12.93)

It is, in general, a question of saving the white race from a threat to its existence. The whites constitute 8 per cent of the total today. Do you think that 92 per cent will put up for very long with 8 per cent living in better regions, enjoying better diets and longer life expectancy? This 92 per cent will claim its rights yet. (*New Times International*, October 1992)

Blacks? America will ask us for help to put a stop to the propagation of coloured people. (*La Stampa*, 16.12.1993)

Russia is threatened by Islam and non-Russian ethnic groups. The Turks are taking over too much power in Germany and the Arabs in France, and blacks may soon take over 'white cities' in America. Whites would be very upset in that case, and that is what is happening in Russia. (AP, 15.3.94)

In reply to a question as to whether he was racist on top of everything else, Zhirinovsky said: Not at all. Why do you think so? I am talking about the threat to the white nation. If a robber intends to break into my house, do I violate his rights to rob my house if I try to stop him?

I am against . . . Zionists. Why am I anti-Zionist? Because of the October Revolution, of course. And because of the thirty Zionists in Parliament; one of them is actually called Sabbath. This Mr Sabbath is particularly bad. Why are Zionists so bad? Because they make Russia weak. They do that because they want to emigrate to Israel. But they should rather stay here. It is, in fact, easier for a state when there is only one nationality. Russia is, however, multinational and should stay so (*Die Zeit*, 4.3.94). Zhirinovsky uses the word 'Zionist' in the sense in which it was used in the USSR, where anti-Semitism was officially unacceptable, illegal. It is a widely held view that Communism in Russia was a Jewish plot.

Although we are not anti-Semitic, we won't tolerate an increase in the strength of the Jews. (*Financial Times*, 14.12.93)

People who call themselves Jews are provoking a wave of anti-Semitism ... To avoid anti-Semitism, we should increase the number of Russian faces on TV. (*Observer*, 19.12.93)

On Russian television there should be pretty girls with blond hair and blue eyes, women who speak good Russian ... Gaidar is half-Jewish, and the IMF forms part of an international Jewish conspiracy. (*Frankfurter Allgemeine*, 16.12.93)

About the Jews: You are the richest people on earth; I envy you. (*La Stampa*, 16.12.93)

I will never agree with a situation in which 2 million Russian Jews rule a country where another 150 million Russians simply have to obey them. (*Time*, 27.12.93)

GEOPOLITICS

With a consummate demagogue like Zhirinovsky it is not always easy to know which of his ideas are meant simply to find favour with his immediate audience and which should be seen as having a more general relevance to his policies. In any case, during his tour in the former Yugoslavia at the end of January 1994 he addressed two audiences: those present, or listening to broadcasts, and the audience back home, especially the Russian leadership.

Both Kozyrev, the Russian Foreign Minister, and his deputy, Vitaly Churkin, made statements that gave the impression that they were trying to catch up with Zhirinovsky. Andrei Kozyrev, however, took the trouble to deny this. In a statement made on 10 March 1994 he said that Russian foreign policy was not being formulated under pressure from Zhirinovsky. 'If we had not been accused of acting on Zhirinovsky's orders, we would have talked even tougher,' said Kozyrev.

Considering that the Russians have never managed to penetrate so far into the Balkans, we can only wonder what else Kozyrev hoped to achieve by tough talk. The Serbs must have been impressed by the promptness with which Zhirinovsky's promises were translated into action: Russian troops arrived in Bosnia, proving that the great Russian nation is, indeed, behind the Serbs. Marshal Tito, who resolutely opposed letting Russians into Yugoslavia for decades, must be turning in his grave.

In foreign policy we must move from an east–west relationship to a north–south relationship ... We will come to an accommodation with Germany. A strong Turkey and Iran are in the south, but Russian soldiers will no longer shed their blood in the Transcaucasus. We will reach accord with the Turks and with Iran. (Speech to the Russian Congress of People's Deputies, Russian TV, 22.5.91)

According to Zhirinovsky, Russia is losing its position in the Middle East, where **Iraq is its most reliable ally**. To the east and south Russia ought to bank on building allied relationships with Japan, China and India. **As for the allied relationship with India, it will depend largely on whether Russia helps it to repel the Muslim threat.** In Zhirinovsky's view, access to the Indian Ocean should become a goal of Russia's foreign policy to the south. In this case Afghanistan, Iran and Turkey will have to be 'neutralized', which, according to him, **will be applauded in Europe**. (Zhirinovsky's statement to the press, INTERFAX, 24.11.92)

All we want is three countries: Afghanistan, Iran and Turkey.

Russia can play an historic role in saving the world from the spread of Islam, from the spread of international terrorism. (*Time*, 27.12.93)

I had already begun to develop my own geopolitical concept ... The last 'dash to the south' and to Russian outlets on the shores of the Indian Ocean and the Mediterranean Sea is really a measure designed to save the Russian nation. For when other parties talk of cutting off Kazakhstan, Kirghizia and Central Asia, they do not realize that we are pushing Russia into the tundra, where mineral resources are all that can exist, where nothing can live and develop ... The development of civilization has always begun in the south. We may quite unnecessarily drive ourselves into barren regions and destroy the nation once and for all ... So the idea emerged of the last dash – last because it will probably be the last repartition of the world and must be carried out ... suddenly, swiftly and effectively. This will immediately solve all our problems, because we will gain tranquillity. We will also gain tranquil neighbours. Friendly India. Enmity will cease for ever. (*The Last Dash to the South*)

The future prospect which I envision is the gradual abandonment of the national-territorial division, which will help us to solve the nationality issue ... Order needs to be restored. (Zhirinovsky's campaign statement, TRUD, 11.6.91)

For North America there will be Latin America; for Western Europe there will be Africa; for China and Japan, there will be South-East Asia ... For Russia there will be only three states: Turkey, Iran, Afghanistan. It is a region of vitally important interests for Russia ... And further to the south the warm Indian Ocean ... If we unite the Russian north [with its heavy industry] with the south, where there are basic foodstuffs and raw materials for light industry, then, *yes*, we will have our market economy. (Zhirinovsky's article published in the LDPR newspaper, *Liberal*, No. 2, 1993)

One day Greater Germany, a new Russia and India will form a new *entente*. Then there will be no problems in the world. India and Russia will neutralize China; Russia and Germany can control Europe; and Russia and the Balkan states will solve all problems in the Balkans. (*Die Welt*, 29.1.94)

Zhirinovsky promises that if he comes to power, he will restore order in Europe by forming an alliance with Germany. Let the Germans move east to the Soviet–German border while we move south. He has also expressed his support for the liberation struggle of the Kurds with the help of **Cuban mercenaries and Russian weapons**. (Zhirinovsky's stump speech, INTERFAX, 7.5.92)

GENERAL VIEWS ABOUT THE WORLD

Fascism: A terrible disease that we have got rid of. (*La Stampa*, 16.12.93)

I am not a Fascist. On the contrary. I have always made efforts in the struggle for human rights. (ITAR–TASS, 13.12.93)

You are not a genuine Fascist [he said to Alexander Nevsorov]. You only want a civil war because, as a journalist, you want something to write about. You're not really brown like me. You're reddish-brown. (*Die Zeit*, 4.3.94)

During his visit to Slovenia he expressed his disapproval of the disintegration of the Slavic states into a host of 'statelets', adding that if this trend continues **the entire world will break up because the readjustment of borders in one case will encourage the same practice in another.** (Quoted on Radio Slovenia, Ljubljana, 28.1.94)

His reply to the question of which historical figures he most admires was: **For Russia, General Kutuzov; for France, De Gaulle; for Germany, Roosevelt.** When one of his aides pointed out that Roosevelt was American, he added with perfect unconcern: **Well, all right, Frederick the Great for Germany.** (*The Times*, 21.12.93)

That's all that politics is about – demagoguery . . . Politics is 70 per cent lies and terror. Without lies and terror, you can't do politics . . . But I personally always tell the truth. (*Time*, 27.12.93)

The commonest major blunder, and Russia's mishap, was that they gave us gifts for what should have been sold for money. Now we have modern arms, which cost more than 30 billion roubles, but we are not selling them. We have quit the market.

For instance, the Volga–Urals military district had 24,000 idle tanks. India wanted them, but we did not sell them to India, preferring to scrap them instead. That is what I am trying to draw attention to – the demolition of arms for which certain countries are prepared to pay hard currency. Saddam Hussein is now prepared to pay us $10 billion, Iraq's debt to Russia, but for the past two years no Russian leader has met him, no diplomat, no journalist. Except myself. What Hussein said to me was, 'Russian diplomacy is amazing. I told them, "Take this money, it's yours," but they wouldn't take it. . .

Why should we inflict suffering on ourselves? Let's make others suffer. (*Izvestiya*, 30.11.93)

THE WEST, ITS VALUES AND
ITS PRACTICES

In a TASS report (World Service in English, 18.12.91) Zhirinovsky claimed that the CIA is in the process of waging a weaponless 'third world war' against Russia. Instead of sending the technology Russia needs to overcome its current economic crisis, the USA is trying to poison the Russian people with **vodka, Pepsi and propaganda.**

INTERFAX, commenting on Zhirinovsky's speech (7.5.92), quoted him as saying that the West, after robbing Africa and Latin America, has now started robbing Russia. He also claimed that the West is supported by Democratic Russia and the government, who are **fulfilling Western orders and embezzling, not so much because of a tendency towards corruption, but because they realize that they will not remain in power long.**

The world should think twice before opposing us – after all, is it really desirable to have a third world war? (*Financial Times*, 14.12.93)

During his tour of the Balkans at the end of January 1994, Zhirinovsky found a good opportunity to air his anti-Western views. In a speech in Bijelijna he spoke of 'some foreign countries' – an expression reminiscent of old Soviet-style speeches – in a clear reference to the NATO decision to bomb Serbian artillery positions around Sarajevo if they were not withdrawn by the deadline stated in the ultimatum.

They have two standards of democracy. The destruction of

the Serbs and the Russians is, according to them, democracy, but when we are defending ourselves they call it Fascism. We are not going to fall for these double standards. I therefore wish the Serbs to become even stronger. I wish you courage, strength and optimism. Look ahead proudly, as a great nation. The great Russian nation is behind you. (Bosnian Serb Radio First Programme, reported by Tanjug, Belgrade, 30.1.94)

The Anti-Russian conspiracy of the West is an age-old theme in Russian political rhetoric. In Soviet days the talk was of the anti-socialist, reactionary machinations of the imperialists; now, following much the same line but without the ideological colouring, we hear of cunning Westerners going to Russia, exploiting it and creating havoc. Before the December 1993 elections, Zhirinovsky accused the (Russian) producers of a film about himself: **The film was intended to scare people, and I think it was paid for by Western services** (Independent, 10.12.93). In the film there was a picture of Zhirinovsky with the caption: 'I am the Almighty! I am a tyrant! I shall follow in Hitler's footsteps.'

Yours is a democracy that will not succeed. You won't intimidate me. You are all losers, he said in Strasbourg. He was furious because the French authorities did not let him go anywhere else in France . . . **We are ahead of you. Russia has more rights and liberties than you have in Europe . . . You** [the Council of Europe] **have members who use their armed forces to fight against democracy.** He was referring to Turkey and Britain. He also accused the West of **contaminating** Russia **with the Communist virus.** (Reuter, 12.4.94)

THOUGHTS ON WAR (NUCLEAR AND CONVENTIONAL) AND PEACE

Zhirinovsky has always favoured peace, as he affirmed on Radio Slovenia (28.1.94). We are for disarmament. Russia will destroy its nuclear weapons – after everybody else (*La Stampa*, 16.12.93).

The twenty-first century will be our century, he predicts. We are washing away these scabs, this dirt that has accumulated over the whole twentieth century. Sometimes this causes blood. This is bad. But blood, he adds in a final gruesome flourish, may be necessary in order finally to wash away this contagion that was introduced into the centre of Russia from the West to poison the country and undermine it from within – through Communism, nationalism, cosmopolitanism, through the influence of alien religions, alien ideas, an alien way of life. We will put an end to this. (*New Republic*, 14.2.94)

POSTSCRIPT:
WHO IS THIS MAN ANYWAY?

There is one thing everybody agrees on: Zhirinovsky is a great talker. He smothers his audience with torrents of words and cascades of banalities seasoned with dreams and threats. He is charismatic in so far as he can hold an audience and can handle his television programmes with exceptional skill; apart from that, what has he to offer, if that is the right word? What is he, people ask: a state-of-the-art Hitler or just a clown? Underneath all the nonsense, what is his actual stance: a back-to-basics 'petit-bourgeoisism', or does he aspire to be a nuclear Robin Hood? Is he an unscrupulous and cynical opportunist, who will accept a bribe, when all is said and done, or is he a stalwart, though misguided, Russian patriot? Since he wants to be all things to all men, he may be all of these or none. Kurt Tucholsky, a noted figure on the German literary scene, said about Hitler before 1933: 'The man is simply not there – he's just the clamour he provokes' (*Die Zeit*, 14.1.94). Should Zhirinovsky come to power, would his actions be as aggressive as his words are now, or will the words do the job of actions?

If you try to make sense of his stated plans, you do not find a coherent policy. His economic policy is to sell lots and lots of arms to more and more people, and there are subjects upon which, in the midst of a sea of words, he hardly touches. Could it be that he has a subtext, a hidden agenda, about which he talks only with his powerful backers (if any), a hidden game plan that, if laid over what he actually says, would reveal the 'figure in the carpet'? But, before we discuss that, let us see who is most apprehensive about Zhirinovsky's unexpected rise, and what have they done about foiling his scheme.

THE BLACK RAINBOW OF RUSSIAN HOPES

In the lands of the former Soviet Union there are two main groups that fear his ascent to power: his opponents in Russian political life, and most people in the former republics, now independent states, since his declared ambition is for Russia to repossess them.

Who would welcome his coming to power? First of all, his followers, who voted for his party in the December 1993 elections and, secondly, such backers as he may have – that is, backers who have at their disposal political or other means with which to promote him. This is one subject that Zhirinovsky does not talk about. He has distanced himself from the KGB and from any part of the Soviet power structure, but can we be sure that at least one section of the KGB does not support him? There have been suggestions that the KGB, recognizing his political talents, set his party up as a token opposition party when the Soviet Union was still in place, and then, seeing his erratic ways, threw him over. He has always strongly denied any links with the KGB, which he would do both if there were some or not. Perhaps he is still supported by these hidden backers with considerable influence and means at their disposal to help him establish countrywide organizations and even, as some people now suggest, rig the results of the December elections in his favour more successfully than other parties were able to do. Would they have provided him with the necessary funds for running a countrywide organization indispensable for rigging millions of votes?

As for other backers, this time abroad, who may have helped him financially? Saddam Hussein springs to mind; Zhirinovsky has always emphasized his friendship with the Iraqi leader, but he usually confines himself to generalities (helping him in his struggle against the West, sympathizing with his aim to reoccupy Kuwait, which, he says, has the same status for Iraq as Crimea has for the Russians).

The help of European extreme-right groups has also been suggested, but that could not be very substantial. Former German Communist Party funds are also mentioned. Or is it possible that he is backed by one or more mafia organizations inside Russia, despite his protestations against the mafia and gangsterism, the elimination of which is at the top of his agenda after coming to power? Or could there be a group of foreign *mafiosi* who hope to gain influence through the future president of Russia?

What has the West done so far to throw a spanner in his works apart from calling him a grotesque clown? Zhirinovsky's main propaganda complaint against the West is that, far from helping Russia, it wants to ruin it and make it serve Western interests.

True, the West has not done much in the economic sphere, and very little in the way of any other kind of real assistance. In days gone by Germany gave DM80 billion (about US$ 50 billion) to the Soviet Union, but that did not save either the Soviet economy or Gorbachev.

Then the new Russian government, after the collapse of the Soviet Union, embraced a plan for Western-type reforms that Gorbachev had shelved. That raised new hopes that things would improve. But so far reforms have not done anything to alleviate the crisis, and consequently the reformers' position has been considerably weakened. There has been some financial aid, a billion dollars here and there, some of which has probably ended up, through mafia pockets, in Western banks. Are those IMF and World Bank plans and schemes quite wrong? After all, no one has ever had the experience of making a capitalist giant out of a Communist superpower. It may be an impossible task, certainly if it is done simultaneously with changing a totalitarian political system into a democratic multi-party one.

The reformers have started backtracking, and Zhirinovsky can declare with satisfaction that they have heeded his advice. It does not look as if the West is going to do anything spectacular in the field of financial or economic aid to Russia. The standing of the West in the eyes of the Russian people has fallen considerably. They feel that it has deceived them by omission. The Western media have dilated about the advantages of the market economy and the excellence of democracy but have said little about the problems of transition. Anti-Western attitudes are gaining ground, and anti-Western organizations are mushrooming. So far so good, thinks Zhirinovsky.

LET'S GIVE HIM A LEG-UP!

Far from thwarting Zhirinovsky's schemes, the West has started putting one into practice. Zhirinovsky, in an interview given to *Krasnaya Zvezda* in May 1991, outlined a scheme according to which Russian soldiers under contract for hard currency could perform tasks assigned by the world community. He suggested such a peacekeeping role in other contexts, for the countries south of Russia; that is one of the plans outlined in his book, *The Last Dash to the South*. So Western reluctance to get involved on the ground in Bosnia gave an opportunity to the Russians to penetrate the Balkans as a peacekeeping force (with the enthusiastic support of the local Serbs, of course), and they hope that their 'Orthodox Slavic Brotherhood' with the Serbs will enable them to gain a firm foothold in the Balkans, which has been a Russian ambition for a long time (Tito's careful policies, to Stalin's fury, foiled that plan in the 1940s and 1950s). So, is Zhirinovsky's plan, including the hope of gaining access to the Mediterranean through Montenegro, for instance, in the process of realization?

What about the subjects on which Zhirinovsky is generally silent? We cannot tell whether his nuclear threats are just verbal flourishes, nor how he is going to make use of Russia's military and, especially, nuclear capacity.

FLYING KITES

What can his repeated recourse to the idea of unleashing a third world war mean? Sometimes he seems to be on the point of making it clear. On other occasions he appears to be flying kites.

In an interview that he gave to Alexander Yanov, which appeared in the *New Times International* in October 1992, we read that he said the following in reply to the question of how he was going to fulfil his promise to feed the Russian nation in seventy-two hours: 'It is very simple really; I shall order 1.5 million troops into the former GDR, brandish arms there, nuclear arms included, and there'll be enough food to go round.'

Yanov, to whom he appears to say things that he does not mention so frankly elsewhere, in his article in the *Los Angeles Times*, 4 March 1994, writes the following: 'Zhirinovsky does not believe that the current Russian crisis can be resolved in the domestic area. Like Hitler, he sees the "salvation of the nation" in war and conquest. But not in a nuclear war, and not in one with either the West or with China. His quarrel is with the Muslim world (the only exception being his current friend, ally and financier, Saddam Hussein). Its riches, and especially its oil, he promises, would save Russia. He recognizes that "some people" in Teheran, Ankara or Riyadh may object to their countries becoming Russian provinces, **but the whole world should think that if Russia needs it . . . it is for the best.** Besides, **the majority of mankind is interested in dissecting the Muslim world. The Muslim peril has to be eliminated.** This would supposedly be Russia's greatest service to modern civilization.'

But that is not all, although, as Yanov notes, this is Zhirinovsky's *Mein Kampf* in briefest outline. 'What does Zhirinovsky think the rest of the world would do while his armies marched to the oil fields of the Middle East in order to monopolize this vital strategic resource?' Zhirinovsky has a quite impressive answer to this. According to him, the rest of the world would do precisely what it did when Hitler's armies began to march around Europe – nothing. This is what Russia's 'nuclear shield' is all about: to ensure a new Munich on the part of the West. And, indeed, would any Western government risk annihilation for the sake of Turkey, let alone Iran?

Richard W. Judy, writing in the *National Review* (21.3.94), says: 'Zhirinovsky carries a big stick. If the European, Asian and American great powers refuse to acquiesce in Russia's "Last Thrust to the South" he will be prepared "to make life very unpleasant".' He has never stated precisely what unpleasant measures he might take, but his remarks imply clearly that he means 'nuclear blackmail, abrogation of arms-control agreements and other militarily hostile measures'.

There we have a plan hinted at strongly by Zhirinovsky.

First of all, like a 'nuclear Robin Hood' (Yanov's words) he can blackmail the West with nuclear weapons to provide food and, presumably, other kinds of help. The threat of a nuclear strike could also be used in the Middle East. Let us take one scenario. In agreement with Saddam Hussein, he would send Russian armies against Iran (having first made sure that Azerbaijan was under control – he is more than halfway there with the flexible former Communist Party chief, Aliyev, in the presidential seat). He would attack Iran from the north, while Saddam Hussein would attack from the west. They would probably succeed in subduing Iranian resistance and set up a Quisling government with the help of Iranian opposition to the *mullahs*, either in Iran, or abroad, or both. At that point he would go no further. The two aggressors would divide the oil loot; at the same time an independent (independent in the sense that Kazakhstan and the Baltic states were independent in Stalin's time) Kurdish state would be set up to spite the Turks. He would not attack Turkey; he would only supply arms, money, etc., to Kurdish rebels in Turkey. Would the West risk a nuclear war in defence of Iran? Probably not. Would it risk a nuclear war to defend the Turkish stand against the Kurds? That would not be a very attractive proposition either. Russia and Iraq could stop at that point and let the West get used to the *status quo*.

But what about his other plans, the incorporation of the Baltic states, Finland, Poland? In exchange for a 'free hand from Karachi to Constantinople', Zhirinovsky might be prepared to give up Russia's historically justified claims. In the east he would abandon its claim to the return of Alaska and cede ownership of the Kuril Islands to Japan. Then again, he could occupy the Baltic states or any other state outside NATO and threaten a nuclear attack if anyone showed any inclination to stop him. Would the West risk a nuclear war to save Romania, Slovakia or Hungary?

The West would probably rather let him get on with these plans so long as he did not go further. Could he not learn from Hitler's mistakes, stop after the first round and give the world a breathing space? But if the West does not acquiesce, what then? Here we have to go back to what Mao Tse-Tung said to the Finnish ambassador in 1955, quoted in the Preface (p.vii).

The next, possibly better, scenario: Zhirinovsky takes power. He does not go beyond a big push against the Russian mafia – at least those parts of it that are not his allies – but, through a dictatorship, settles down to establish his version of national socialism (see Chapter 6), his own version of 'back to basics', to satisfy the aspirations of the 'little man' or, rather, to give the impression of doing so. By the time people realize that what they expected is not happening they will be in no position to object: the dictatorship he keeps promising will be firmly in place, with some political 'liberties' perhaps – by comparison with the Stalin era, no racial persecutions except for a new, strict *propiska* system preventing Central Asians and Caucasians from coming to Russia proper (his 'Berlin Wall' along the north of the Caucasus), a Potemkin multi-party system, Potemkin elections of the Soviet era, etc. And then he will turn round and say: 'We have established Fascism with a human face,' and everybody will heave a sigh of relief.

What if Zhirinovsky were shot or otherwise eliminated from the race? Is it likely that in a ruined Russia, whose only strength is military, somebody else would take a leaf out of Zhirinovsky's book and implement some of his 'milder' policies? Vladimir Nazarov, Zhirinovsky's first independent biographer, said in 1992: 'Even if Zhirinovsky himself disappears from the CIS's turbulent political scene tomorrow, the

"Zhirinovsky phenomenon" will not. He may well be replaced by someone else, someone more intelligent, better-mannered, more restrained – and of Russian nationality.'

Russia is not likely to resolve ingrained national problems without a major disaster, and we should wonder who else will be dragged into it. On the other hand, it may be that Zhirinovsky, or someone more or less like him, is simply a tool, the 'hidden hand' of the Russian soul yearning for self-purification through the ultimate catastrophe, 'the figure in the carpet'.

So what is the point of asking whether Zhirinovsky is like Hitler?

Discover more about our forthcoming books through Penguin's FREE newspaper...

READ MORE IN PENGUIN

In every corner of the world, on every subject under the sun, Penguin represents quality and variety – the very best in publishing today.

For complete information about books available from Penguin – including Puffins, Penguin Classics and Arkana – and how to order them, write to us at the appropriate address below. Please note that for copyright reasons the selection of books varies from country to country.

In the United Kingdom: Please write to *Dept. JC, Penguin Books Ltd, FREEPOST, West Drayton, Middlesex UB7 OBR*

If you have any difficulty in obtaining a title, please send your order with the correct money, plus ten per cent for postage and packaging, to *PO Box No. 11, West Drayton, Middlesex UB7 OBR*

In the United States: Please write to *Penguin USA Inc., 375 Hudson Street, New York, NY 10014*

In Canada: Please write to *Penguin Books Canada Ltd, 10 Alcorn Avenue, Suite 300, Toronto, Ontario M4V 3B2*

In Australia: Please write to *Penguin Books Australia Ltd, 487 Maroondah Highway, Ringwood, Victoria 3134*

In New Zealand: Please write to *Penguin Books (NZ) Ltd, 182–190 Wairau Road, Private Bag, Takapuna, Auckland 9*

In India: Please write to *Penguin Books India Pvt Ltd, 706 Eros Apartments, 56 Nehru Place, New Delhi 110 019*

In the Netherlands: Please write to *Penguin Books Netherlands B.V., Keizersgracht 231 NL–1016 DV Amsterdam*

In Germany: Please write to *Penguin Books Deutschland GmbH, Friedrichstrasse 10–12, W–6000 Frankfurt/Main 1*

In Spain: Please write to *Penguin Books S. A., C. San Bernardo 117–6° E–28015 Madrid*

In Italy: Please write to *Penguin Italia s.r.l., Via Felice Casati 20, I–20124 Milano*

In France: Please write to *Penguin France S. A., 17 rue Lejeune, F–31000 Toulouse*

In Japan: Please write to *Penguin Books Japan, Ishikiribashi Building, 2–5–4, Suido, Bunkyo-ku, Tokyo 112*

In Greece: Please write to *Penguin Hellas Ltd, Dimocritou 3, GR–106 71 Athens*

In South Africa: Please write to *Longman Penguin Southern Africa (Pty) Ltd, Private Bag X08, Bertsham 2013*

READ MORE IN PENGUIN

HISTORY

Citizens Simon Schama

The award-winning chronicle of the French Revolution. 'The most marvellous book I have read about the French Revolution in the last fifty years' – Richard Cobb in *The Times*

To the Finland Station Edmund Wilson

In this authoritative work Edmund Wilson, considered by many to be America's greatest twentieth-century critic, turns his attention to Europe's revolutionary traditions, tracing the roots of nationalism, socialism and Marxism as these movements spread across the Continent creating unrest, revolt and widespread social change.

Jasmin's Witch Emmanuel Le Roy Ladurie

An investigation into witchcraft and magic in south-west France during the seventeenth century – a masterpiece of historical detective work by the bestselling author of Montaillou.

Stalin Isaac Deutscher

'The Greatest Genius in History' and the 'Life-Giving Force of socialism'? Or a despot more ruthless than Ivan the Terrrible and a revolutionary whose policies facilitated the rise of Nazism? An outstanding biographical study of a revolutionary despot by a great historian.

Aspects of Antiquity M. I. Finley

Profesor M. I. Finley was one of the century's greatest ancient historians; he was also a master of the brief, provocative essay on classical themes. 'He writes with the unmistakable enthusiasm of a man who genuinely wants to communicate his own excitement' – Philip Toynbee in the *Observer*

British Society 1914–1945 John Stevenson

'A major contribution to the *Penguin Social History of Britain*, which will undoubtedly be the standard work for students of modern Britain for many years to come' – *The Times Educational Supplement*

MCQs in Anatomy
A Self-testing Supplement to 'Essential Anatomy'

J. S. P. Lumley MS FRCS FMAA(Hon) FGA
Professor of Vascular Surgery, University of London;
Honorary Consultant Surgeon, St Bartholomew's Hospital,
London; Past Examiner in Anatomy for the Royal College of
Surgeons of England

J. L. Craven BSc MD FRCS
Consultant Surgeon, District General Hospital, York;
Examiner in Pathology for the Royal College of Surgeons
of England

Both formerly Assistant Lecturers at University College

THIRD EDITION

CHURCHILL
LIVINGSTONE

NEW YORK EDINBURGH LONDON MADRID MELBOURNE SAN FRANCISCO TOKYO 1996

CHURCHILL LIVINGSTONE
Medical Division of Pearson Professional Limited

Distributed in the United States of America by
Churchill Livingstone Inc., 650 Avenue of the Americas,
New York, N.Y. 10011, and by associated companies,
branches and representatives throughout the world.

First edition 1979
Second edition 1988
Third edition 1996

ISBN 0 443 04977 7

British Library Cataloguing in Publication Data
A catalogue record for this book is available from the British Library

Library of Congress Cataloging in Publication Data
A Catalog record for this book is available from the
Library of Congress

The
publisher's
policy is to use
**paper manufactured
from sustainable forests**

Produced by Longman Singapore Publishers Pte Ltd
Printed in Singapore

i

Contents

Preface to the Third Edition

The production of the third edition of *MCQs in Anatomy* is timed to follow the publication of the fifth edition of *Essential Anatomy*, its companion volume.

The new edition contains additional clinical material and the text has been revised throughout. The embryology chapter has been removed but the embryology of individual organs expanded where appropriate.

The format of the questions has been changed from four to five options. This is in keeping with the style of the majority of current MCQ examinations. It has also provided the opportunity to increase the assessment and the information included in each area covered.

J. S. P. L.
J. L. C.

Introduction

Objective testing
The perfect examination would be one in which the student was accurately assessed in his knowledge, comprehension, application, analysis and evaluation of material pertinent to the subject being examined. The use of the essay type question paper as the sole means of assessment has been criticised because of its reliance on subjective qualities.

For several years educationalists of many different disciplines have sought methods of objective testing which examined all the above mentioned qualities. In all objective tests the student has to choose the correct response out of one or more alternatives, his answers being either right or wrong. The subjective judgement of the examiner thus plays no part in this form of examination. Objective testing has been used extensively in the U.S.A. since the end of the Second World War, but introduction in the U.K. has been slow, and it has reached the universities generally via schools and technical colleges. However, multiple choice question papers are now in use in most medical schools and it has been necessary for both the medical student and his teacher to become fully acquainted with the uses and abuses of this testing technique. It is appropriate here to consider the merits of the various examination techniques and, perhaps most important, to compare objective testing with the traditional essay question.

The essay
Students and examiners have questioned the effectiveness of an essay paper in measuring the attainment of a number of years of study. The area covered by such an examination is very limited, the more so when a wide choice of questions is allowed. It thus encourages the students to 'spot questions' and to concentrate on only part of the syllabus. The marking of essays is time consuming and unreliable, there being variations in an individual examiner's reassessment of papers as well as between examiners. This variation makes comparison on a national level difficult and is further accentuated by what has been described as the deep psychological reluctance of examiners to allocate more than seventy per cent of the total marks allowed for any given essay question. However, the essay does determine the candidate's ability to write clear and legible English, it tests his ability to collect and quantitate material, and it assesses his powers of logic, original thought and creativity. In terms of cost the essay question is cheap to produce but it is expensive to mark.

The composition of objective questions

The objective form of examination is best composed by a panel of examiners, each having a complete understanding of the syllabus and a thorough knowledge of the field of study. The panel must first decide the parts of the syllabus to be covered by the examination, and the level of knowledge required by the candidate. The type of objective test and the number of options per question is decided and each member of the panel prepares a set of questions for the group to consider. A multiple choice question consists of a stem (the initial question) and four or more options; one of these options in the multiple choice question is correct and this is known as the key, the incorrect responses being known as the distractors. In the case of multiple response questions, there may be more than one correct response. (This form of question has also been termed multiple completion, multiple answer, multiple true or false and the indeterminate response by various authorities, but in most centres, and in this text, it will subsequently be referred to as a multiple choice question.)

Stem and options should be brief, using the minimum number of words, and the instructions should be clear and simple, the language used being appropriate to the verbal ability and requirement of the candidate. The question must be of some educational value. The words 'always' and 'never' should be avoided and the stem should preferably not be in the negative. There should be no recurrent phrase in the options which can be included in the stem. The key (the correct option or options) must be wholly correct and unambiguous. It is important for the correct response to be in different positions in each of a group of questions and some form of random allocation may be necessary. The distractors (the wrong options) are the most exacting and challenging part of objective question composition and the standard of an objective test is probably best assessed in terms of the quality of its distractors. They must always be plausible, yet completely wrong. They should be in a parallel style to the key and they should not contain clues. Common misconceptions form good distractors. 'None of them' or 'all of them' are not satisfactory distractors. Four options are thought by many authorities to be sufficient.

After the draft questions have been collected, it is advisable for a panel of examiners to assess their value and limitations. Inaccurate and irrelevant material is then excluded. Even the most experienced of examiners will find that a panel will offer constructive criticism on the majority of his questions. Ideally, once the panel has accepted a series of questions these should be pre-tested on a group of students and the results analysed. It is desirable for a question to have been pre-tested on 300 to 400 students before it comes into regular use in a qualifying examination. The difficulty of a question can be determined by calculating the percentage of students giving the right answer, and its discriminatory value (the ratio of correct/incorrect responses) calculated in a manner which takes into account whether or not the better students obtained the correct response. The facility value (difficulty index) records the percentage of correct responses and compares it with the total number of candidates. Additional information on the mean and range of distribution of the answers can also be obtained with a discriminatory index and a bi-serial correlation coefficient (relating the total candidate response to an option, with the results of the top 27 per cent and the bottom 27 per cent of the candidates to the same option). Figures for both the discriminatory index and the bi-serial correlation coefficient range from plus 1 to minus 1. Questions with factors of less than 0.20 should be rejected (unless a few difficult or easy questions are to be included). Values of 0.21 to 0.29 are of marginal discriminatory value. The values 0.30 to 0.39 show a reasonable discriminatory power of the option, whereas results greater than 0.44 indicate good discrimination by a question of the candidates under test. The effectiveness of the question is also measured in terms of the number of students attempting it — the value of a question certainly cannot be assessed if a large number of students leave it out. Computer printouts on a series of questions will also provide the ranking of students, the scatter of the results and a raw score (i.e. the number of correct, less the number of incorrect results).

The pre-testing, though very time consuming, greatly adds to the validity and reliability of the objective test. Using the results of these tests the panel can rephrase unsatisfactory questions and compile the definitive examination paper. The time allowed in the pre-test is not limited but the students are asked to note the time taken to complete the test; the time required for the final version is thus arrived at. This time should allow at least 90 per cent of the candidates to complete the paper. It is usual to start an examination paper with a few easier questions (i.e. with a low difficulty index) and similarly a few difficult questions can be included at the end. It has been found that a good (wide) range of results is obtained by setting a large number of questions with average discrimination rather than including a large number with high or low discriminatory indices. Testing of the questions should not stop after the pre-testing phase, the information gained from each subsequent examination should be used to review continuously all the question material.

Obviously a series of questions which have been pre-tested and shown to be satisfactory is of great value to the examiner. Such questions can be used repeatedly provided they have not been freely available to the students. Security is an important factor, particularly when the number of questions is small and does not cover the whole syllabus. For this reason it is advisable to have a large number of questions available. It is reasonable to assume that if a student is capable of memorising the correct responses to a large number of questions (even if these are known to him) he will also have a passable knowledge of the syllabus.

A satisfactory bank of questions takes three to five years to build. After this time the questions can be grouped into sections and, whenever an examination paper is required, questions can be chosen at random from each section. Continuous updating and revision of this material should be undertaken and new material added regularly. The history of each question in the bank should be recorded. Repetitive use of the questions over a number of years allows annual standards to be compared.

The student's approach to objective testing
Any student required to undertake an objective test for a qualifying examination or a postgraduate examination should ensure he has some

preliminary experience in this form of testing. It is essential for him to know and have sampled the style of questions used by his particular examining board.

In any objective test all the instructions provided must be carefully read and understood and the student's designated number marked in the appropriate section, otherwise a computer marking system will reject the paper — this will not impress the examining authority.

The type of objective test used in medical education does vary and some of these types have already been discussed. Whatever form the question takes in the objective test, it is essential that the student starts on his first quick 'run' through the questions by filling in all the answers he knows to be correct. On this first 'run' he should also mark (on the paper) the questions where he is fully acquainted with the material but is unsure of the correct response. On the second 'run' all his attention can now be given to this group of questions, in which he should be able to make an informed guess. Experience has shown that his chances of being correct in this situation are above average. He should, as one examiner expresses it, 'play his hunches'. The questions which he does not understand are probably best left unanswered as at best he can only hope for a 50 per cent chance of a correct response on a random basis in the true/false situation, and only a 25 per cent chance of a correct response in a four item multiple choice question. In multiple choice questions the marking is usually positive, a mark being given for a correct answer and none for an incorrect one. In multiple response questions (as in this text) a mark is given for each correct response, whether this be true or false, and usually a mark is subtracted for each incorrect response. Most examination systems have now abolished the use of a correction factor for guessing as this was found to have little effect on the ranking of the candidates, and it has also been realised that informed guessing is in itself a useful discrimination.

Lack of time is not usually a problem in medical objective testing. Since these tests are of the 'power' rather than the 'speed' variety, i.e. knowledge rather than ability against the clock is being tested. Excessive time may be a disadvantage to the candidate as repeated reassessment of the answers may distract from the correct response rather than produce improvement. In the multiple choice situation it has been found that one minute is usually necessary per question although more time is required to answer a question containing a number of distractors.

Transcribing 300 items from a question paper to an answer sheet (i.e. 60 questions each with 5 options) takes a minimum of 10 minutes and the habit of leaving such transcriptions to the end of an examination is best avoided since, if rushed, it may introduce unnecessary inaccuracies.

Etymological hazards

The rarity of absolutes in anatomy means that a large variety of adjectives and adverbs are commonly used in its description. These increase the difficulty of both setting and answering multiple choice questions. Although one can question the desirability of assessing knowledge which is dependent on the 'strength of an adjective', these adjectives do form the language of present day medical practice. This factor is borne out by their use in some questions and answers of the present text. Nevertheless, the examiner must avoid ambiguity and in addition his questions must not contain clues to the correct answer. Such terms as 'invariable', 'always', 'must', 'all', 'only', and 'never' should be avoided since they imply absolutes and are therefore likely to be wrong.

The terms 'may' and 'can' also give rise to ambiguity. In anatomy almost anything 'may occur' and statements using this phrase are unlikely to be completely wrong. If these terms are used and the student is able to answer that the question 'certainly may' or 'certainly may not', he has little chance of being wrong. The term 'sometimes' comes into the same category.

The adjectives and adverbs 'common', 'usual', 'frequent' (commonly, usually, frequently), 'likely' and 'often' are an integral part of everyday medical language but their use in the multiple choice question may also lead to ambiguity. Their meanings are very similar yet their values depend largely on the context of the question. Expressed as incidences they may well range from 30 to 70 per cent. They may be considerably modified by the addition of 'quite', 'most', 'very' and 'extremely'. The examiner must be particularly careful of his choice of these terms. The 'majority' implies more than 50 per cent, whereas the 'vast majority' implies nearly 100 per cent.

The term 'typical' is a useful one for multiple choice questions. Its meaning implies 'that which is found most commonly'. 'Characteristic' implies a time honoured anatomical feature, and 'recognised' an accepted textbook description. Further vague terminology used in medical practice yet best avoided in the multiple choice question includes 'associated with', 'accompanied by', 'related to', 'linked with' and 'lend support to'.

On the negative side, 'uncommon', 'unusual', 'infrequent' (uncommonly, unusually, infrequently), 'unlikely' and 'rare' are all terms commonly used yet their use in the multiple choice question must not give rise to ambiguity. As with their positive equivalents they are markedly influenced by the addition of such terms as 'most' and 'very'. The term 'significant' is best kept for its statistical use and the terms 'increased' and 'more' should be restricted to direct comparative situations.

In conclusion, words used in multiple choice questions, although giving rise to apparent ambiguity, remain those in common use in medical practice; both the examiner and the student must be fully conversant with their meanings and disadvantages in order to avoid any confusion. It is hoped that the questions which follow will also help in this regard.

How to use this book

The text, consisting of questions and answers
('true or false'), is arranged throughout in such
a way that all questions appear on left-hand
pages and all answers on right-hand pages.

In use the student may conveniently cover the
right-hand page with a blank sheet on which to
note down the answers for comparison.

I   The Structure of the Body

true or false

1   The cell membrane:
a   is approximately 7 nm thickness.   (   )
b   is capable of selective permeability.   (   )
c   allows passage of specific ions through
    carbohydrate-gated channels.   (   )
d   is activated by a secondary messenger system.   (   )

e   may discharge particles by a process of vacuolation. (   )

2   Covered cytoplasmic inclusions:
a   contain cytosol.   (   )

b   together comprise the cell cytoskeleton.   (   )

c   are concerned with the carbohydrate metabolism.   (   )

d   are concerned with the collection and transport of
    cellular elements and chemicals.   (   )
e   are involved in phagocytosis.   (   )

3   The cell nucleus:
a   is usually 4 to 10 μm across.   (   )

b   is the site of RNA synthesis.   (   )
c   is surrounded by a single layered membrane.   (   )

d   contains nucleoli responsible for the production
    of the mitotic spindles during cell division.   (   )
e   contains ribosomes.   (   )

4   Cells are united by:
a   desmosomes.   (   )
b   intermediate junction.   (   )
c   tight junctions.   (   )
d   gated junctions.   (   )
e   terminal junctions.   (   )

a **T**— The membrane is protein-lined double lipid layer.
b **T**— It actively regulates the internal cellular environment.
c **F**— The channels are protein-gated.

d **F**— Stimulation of the surface of the cell membrane activates the secondary messenger system, these mediators acting within the cell.
e **T**— The process of endocytosis.

a **F**— This is the cytoplasm outside the membrane covered inclusions.
b **F**— This is a heterogenous collection of filamentous structures within the cytosol.
c **T**— The endoplasmic reticulum carrying out this function also subserves lipid metabolism and detoxification.
d **T**— The Golgi apparatus subserves these functions.

e **T**— The mitochondria subserve this function.

a **T**— The cells vary from 5 to 50 μm, the limited size facilitates the rapid diffusion of metabolites through their structure.
b **T**— The nuclear DNA serves as a template for this process.
c **F**— The nuclear membrane has two layers, the outer being part of the endoplasmic reticulum.
d **F**— Nucleoli contain specific chromosome fragments responsible for replication of RNA.
e **T**— These can cross the nuclear membrane to sites of protein synthesis.

a **T**— Desmosomes are small button-like areas on the cell
b **T** membrane, they provide the strongest form of anchorage.
c **T** In intermediate junctions, the gap is retained but a cobweb
d **F** of filaments extends into the cytoplasm of the adjacent
e **F** cells. In tight junctions, the intercellular gap is lost; these are areas of great cellular permeability.

5   **Epithelial tissue:**
- **a**   gives rise to the sebaceous glands of the scalp.   ( )
- **b**   undergoes constant renewal in most regions of the alimentary tract.   ( )
- **c**   lining the urinary tract contains numerous goblet cells.   ( )
- **d**   lining the respiratory tract is keratinised.   ( )
- **e**   can be resistant to harmful metabolites.   ( )

6   **Exocrine glands:**
- **a**   typically discharge their contents directly into the blood stream.   ( )
- **b**   usually secretes in a holocrine manner.   ( )
- **c**   are of mesenchymal origin.   ( )
- **d**   are absent in stratified squamous epithelium.   ( )
- **e**   may be unicellular.   ( )

7   **Elastic fibres are:**
- **a**   prominent in hyaline cartilage.   ( )
- **b**   formed from fibroblasts.   ( )
- **c**   prominent in superficial fascia.   ( )
- **d**   prominent in aponeuroses.   ( )
- **e**   prominent in retinacula.   ( )

8   **Hyaline cartilage:**
- **a**   contains a few fine collagen-like fibres.   ( )
- **b**   is the bony precursor in cartilaginous ossification.   ( )
- **c**   unites the sphenoid and occipital bones in the child.   ( )
- **d**   forms the knee menisci.   ( )
- **e**   is particularly vascular in relation to joints.   ( )

a **T**— And to most other glands.
b **T**— The alimentary tract is lined by simple epithelium between the oesophagus and the anal canal.
c **F**— The transitional epithelium of the urinary contains few glands.
d **F**— The lining is mostly ciliated columnar epithelium with numerous goblet cells.
e **T**— It can serve as a selective barrier and can also be resistant to chemicals.

a **F**— This is the definition of an endocrine gland. Exocrine glands have ducts opening on to a surface.
b **F**— Most exocrine glands secrete without damage to the cell, i.e. merocrine or epicrine secretion, as do most endocrine glands.
c **F**— They are of epithelial origin.
d **F**— Sebaceous and sweat glands are common in this form of tissue.
e **T**— Goblet cells are unicellular.

a **F**— Hyaline cartilage contains many cells and a few fine collagen-like fibres in the matrix.
b **T**— And found mainly in some ligaments attached to vertebrae.
c **F**— This tissue is a mixture of fat and collagen fibres.
d **F**— These are formed mainly of collagen fibres.
e **F**— These are thickenings of the deep fascia related to joints and are formed mainly of collagen fibres.

a **T**— And is found in synovial joints and in costal cartilages.
b **T**— Ossification in mesenchyme takes place on a fibrous tissue model.
c **T**— Growth in length of the skull occurs mainly at this joint; bony fusion occurring after the appearance of the last molar tooth, about the 25th year.
d **F**— These are formed of fibrocartilage.
e **F**— It is an avascular firm tissue of chondrocytes in an abundant matrix.

9   **Long bones:**
a usually ossify in mesenchyme. ( )
b consist entirely of compact bone. ( )

c normally contain yellow marrow. ( )
d are organised in Haversian systems. ( )

e are covered with the acellular periosteum. ( )

10   **Cartilaginous ossification:**
a occurs in all long bones except the clavicle. ( )

b occurs in cartilage which has replaced a
   membranous model. ( )
c has its primary centres appearing at about the
   18th week of intra-uterine life. ( )
d secondary centres typically fuse at puberty. ( )

e is typical in the bones of the skull vault. ( )

11   **In the development of a long bone:**
a osteoblasts come to line the primary alveoli. ( )
b osteoblasts become the osteocytes. ( )
c ossification extends along the body of the bone
   as endochondral ossification. ( )
d the epiphyseal plate separates the metaphysis
   from the diaphysis. ( )
e circumferential growth is from the diaphyseal
   centre. ( )

12   **The epiphyses:**
a are all present at birth. ( )
b are formed in hyaline cartilage. ( )

c are present in all long bones. ( )
d contribute to growth in length and girth of long
   bones. ( )
e may occur at sites of muscle attachment. ( )

a **F** — Long bones usually ossify in hyaline cartilage.

b **F** — Compact bone is found in the body of the bone but cancellous bone occupies most of the ends of the bones.

c **T** — In the healthy adult the marrow is of the yellow variety.

d **T** — Bone is laid down in concentric layers centripetally. Small blood vessels are usually found in the middle.

e **F** — The thick fibrous periosteum contains many granular, bone forming, osteoblasts.

a **T** — The clavicle has a mixed mesenchymal and cartilaginous ossification.

b **T** — The cartilage is of the hyaline type.

c **F** — These usually appear in the 8th week of intrauterine life.

d **F** — Secondary centres usually appear between birth and puberty, and fuse about the 18th–20th year.

e **F** — These undergo mesenchymal ossification, usually starting at the 5th and 6th weeks of intrauterine life.

a **F** — Osteoblasts line the larger secondary alveoli formed by the

b **T** osteoclasts absorbing the calcified matrix of the cartilage.

c **T** — The cartilage model is gradually replaced by bone.

d **F** — The epiphyseal plate lies between the epiphysis and the metaphysis.

e **F** — This is by subperiosteal ossification.

a **F** — These are secondary centres of ossification and formed by

b **T** osteoblasts: only those of the knee are present at birth. Most of the remainder appear by puberty.

c **T**

d **F** — The increase in girth of a long bone occurs by the laying down of bone by the periosteum.

e **T** — Pressure and atavistic epiphyses also exist.

13   Primary cartilaginous joints:
   a   unite the lower end of the tibia and fibula.   (   )
   b   occur between the teeth and jaw.   (   )

   c   comprise the sutures of the vault of the skull.   (   )
   d   unite the two pubic bones.   (   )

   e   include the costochondral junctions.   (   )

14   In synovial joints the:
   a   articular surfaces are all lined by hyaline cartilage.   (   )

   b   fibrocartilaginous discs usually partially divide the
       joint cavity.   (   )
   c   hinged variety is exemplified by the
       metacarpophalangeal joints.   (   )

   d   stability of the joint is generally inversely related to
       its mobility.   (   )
   e   hip joint is of the saddle variety.   (   )

15   Striated (voluntary) muscle:
   a   contains alternating A and Z bands.   (   )

   b   fibres are multinucleate.   (   )
   c   is present in the upper part of the oesophagus.   (   )

   d   fibres are bound together by the sarcolemma.   (   )

   e   is predominantly supplied from lateral horn
       efferent fibres.   (   )

a **F** — Primary cartilaginous joints are found between the body
b **F**   of a long bone and its epiphyses. The unions in a, b, and c
         are all examples of fibrous joints.
c **F**
d **F** — The pubic bones are united by a secondary cartilaginous
         joint (symphysis).
e **T**

a **F** — The temporomandibular and sternoclavicular joints are
         exceptions and are both lined by fibrocartilage. Their discs
         completely divide the joint into two cavities.
b **F** — But see (a).

c **F** — These are ellipsoid joints capable of abduction, adduction
         and circumduction as well as flexion and extension. The
         interphalangeal joints are true hinge joints.
d **T** — The shoulder joint is the most mobile but most easily
         dislocated.
e **F** — This is ball and socket joint; the carpometacarpal joint of
         the thumb is a saddle joint.

a **F** — The muscle is formed of alternating A and I bands, the Z
         disc dividing the latter.
b **T** — The nuclei are peripherally arranged.
c **T** — Also in the anal canal. The remainder of the alimentary
         tract has smooth muscle in its wall.
d **F** — Fibres are surrounded by the sarcolemma and attached to
         their neighbours by the fibrous endomysium. Bundles are
         enclosed in the perimysium.
e **F** — The motor nerve supplying it is from the anterior horn
         cells of the spinal cord and brain stem.

16   **In muscular activity:**

a   a synergistic muscle is one that relaxes against
the pull of gravity.   (   )

b   a parallel arrangement of fibres provides a more
powerful movement than an oblique arrangement.   (   )

c   antagonistic muscles oppose the prime movers.   (   )

d   innervation is by the muscle spindles.   (   )

e   Impulses from sensory endings pass into the
posterior horn of the spinal cord.   (   )

17   **A nerve fibre:**

a   in the central nervous system has astrocytes
forming the axon sheath.   (   )

b   consists of an axon, usually covered with a
myelin sheath.   (   )

c   ends as 'boutons'.   (   )

d   in a peripheral nerve may be injured and then
recover.   (   )

e   in the central nervous system is devoid of
cellular inclusions.   (   )

18   **Neuroglia:**

a   exist only in the brain.   (   )

b   are cellular neural connective tissue.   (   )

c   have a phagocytic function.   (   )

d   produce myelin.   (   )

e   are concerned with the nutrition of neurons.   (   )

19   **The spinal nerves:**

a   are formed from dorsal and ventral roots, each
root with both sensory and motor fibres.   (   )

b   are distributed to the limbs partly through their
dorsal rami.   (   )

c   leave the vertebral canal via the intervertebral
foramina.   (   )

d   have ganglia on the ventral roots.   (   )

e   comprise 31 pairs.   (   )

a F— During muscular activity prime movers produce movement at joints while synergists steady other joints. Relaxation against gravity is known as paradoxical movement.

b F— In muscles of equal volume a parallel arrangement gives greater range of movement but less power than an oblique arrangement.

c T— And control the rate and range of movement.

d F— Primary innervation of a muscle fibre is by the motor end plate; muscle spindles are sensory stretch receptors.

e T

a F— Oligodendroglia cells have this function which Schwann cells perform in the peripheral nervous system.

b T— There are also many unmyelinated fibres.

c T— These are related to the processes and cell bodies of adjacent nerves, the union being called a synapse.

d T— Schwann cells play an important role in this regeneration. Little or no regeneration occurs in the central nervous system.

e F— Neurons possess large nuclei and prominent cellular inclusions.

a T— Neuroglia do not exist outside the brain and comprise

b T three different types of cells: astrocytes, oligodendroglia and microglia.

c T— The microglia are small mobile phagocytes and

d T oligodendroglia produce the myelin of the central nervous system.

e T

a F— The dorsal roots contain sensory and the ventral, motor fibres.

b F— The limbs receive their nerve supply from the brachial and lumbosacral plexuses, these being formed from ventral rami.

c T— The foramina are formed by adjacent vertebrae. The first cervical nerve passes laterally above the first vertebra.

d F— The ganglia are the neurons of sensory fibres and are found on the dorsal roots.

e T— 8 cervical, 12 thoracic, 5 lumbar, 5 sacral and 1 coccygeal.

20   The autonomic nervous system:
a   supplies the glands, smooth muscle and cardiac muscle.   (   )
b   rises from the special visceral column of the spinal cord.   (   )
c   has peripheral ganglia near the walls of the organ it supplies.   (   )
d   prepares the body for fight and flight.   (   )
e   has no distribution to the lower limbs.   (   )

21   The sympathetic nervous system:
a   has myelinated postganglionic fibres passing from the sympathetic trunk to the spinal nerves.   (   )
b   has trunks extending from the base of the skull to the coccyx.   (   )
c   has usually only five ganglia in the sympathetic trunk.   (   )
d   fibres passing to the head and neck leave the spinal cord in the 5th–8th cervical spinal nerves.   (   )
e   sends preganglionic fibres to the cortex of the suprarenal gland.   (   )

22   The parasympathetic nervous system:
a   receives its fibres from nuclei associated with the 3rd, 5th, 7th and 10th cranial nerves.   (   )
b   receives its pelvic outflow from the 2nd, 3rd and 4th lumbar segments.   (   )
c   has its peripheral ganglia usually in the walls of the organ being supplied.   (   )
d   sends an innervation to the suprarenal medulla.   (   )
e   carries no afferent fibres.   (   )

a T— It is not under voluntary control.

b F— It arises from the general visceral column. The special
visceral column of the brain stem supplies striated
(voluntary) muscle derived from the pharyngeal arches. *lung*

c T— Parasympathetic ganglia are situated in this position,
sympathetic ganglia lie in the sympathetic trunk, usually
away from the organ.

d T— This is a general description of sympathetic activity.
Parasympathetic governs more vegetative functions. It is
responsible for evacuation of gut and urinary bladder and
slows the heart rate.

e F— Peripheral smooth muscle (e.g. in the arterial walls and
glands such as sweat glands) receives autonomic
innervation.

Group B - 3μm dia   *G.p C - 2μm dia*

a F— The preganglionic fibres are myelinated, the postganglionic
are unmyelinated, these respectively representing the
white and grey rami communicantes.

b T

c F— The trunk usually has 3 cervical, 10 thoracic, 4 lumbar, and
4 sacral ganglia.

d F— Fibres passing to the head and neck come mainly from the
lung → first thoracic segment, synapse in the cervical ganglia and
are distributed mostly with the branches of the carotid
arteries, and the spinal and cardiac nerves.

e T— The medulla of the gland does receive a dense innervation
of these fibres.

a F— Although the 5th nerve distributes parasympathetic fibres
derived from the 7th and 9th cranial nerves it is alone in
having none at its origin. The others have.

b F— Pelvic outflow comes from 2nd, 3rd and 4th sacral
segments of the spinal cord.

c T— The exceptions are the cranial parasympathetic ganglia
which are separated from their organs.

d F— The suprarenal medulla receives preganglionic sympathetic
fibres.

e F— Afferent (e.g. pain fibres from the viscera) pathways are
present in both sympathetic and parasympathetic systems.
lung

23   The white blood cells:
a   have coarse granules when of the basophil variety.   (   )
b   have pale basophilic cytoplasm in the
     lymphocyte variety.   (   )
c   have lobulated nuclei in the neutrophils.   (   )
d   are most commonly of the neutrophil variety.   (   )
e   pass out of the blood stream and take part in
     the inflammatory response.   (   )

24   Red bone marrow:
a   is present in most bones at birth.   (   )
b   exists in the adult only in the long bones.   (   )

c   contains precursors of both erythrocytes and
     white blood cells.   (   )
d   contains precursors of blood platelets.   (   )
e   is composed of a coarse fibrous network.   (   )

25   Reduction of the blood supply to an area:
a   is known as ischaemia.   (   )
b   is a feature of the inflammatory response.   (   )
c   may lead to infarction.   (   )

d   is commonly the result of thrombosis.   (   )
e   may be the result of an embolus.   (   )

26   The lymph nodes:
a   receive afferent lymph vessels at the hilus.   (   )
b   have a fine reticular network of collagen fibres.   (   )
c   have a peripheral subcapsular space.   (   )
d   have an inner densely packed medulla.   (   )

e   are surrounded by an elastic capsule.   (   )

a **T**— White cells are nucleated and either granular (e.g.
b **T**   neutrophils) or agranular (e.g. lymphocytes).

c **T**
d **T**
e **T**— Being involved in the classical features of swelling, pain, redness and heat.

a **T**— Red bone marrow is present in most bones at birth, but
b **T**   fatty yellow marrow gradually replaces it in the shafts of
      long bones so that, in the adult, red marrow remains
      mainly in the vertebrae, ribs, sternum and flat bones.
c **T**— It contains precursors of all the cellular and noncellular
      elements of the blood.
d **T**
e **F**— It is composed of a reticular network of fine collagen
      fibres.

a **T**
b **F**— In this response blood flow is increased.
c **T**— This term indicates death of an area of tissue which may
      then become infected and putrified, a condition known as
      gangrene.
d **T**— Blood clotting on the wall of a vessel and occluding the
e **T**— lumen is called a thrombus. When the clot moves, it is
      called an embolus.

a **F**— Afferent vessels enter the convexity of the node and
b **T**   efferent vessels leave the hilus on the concave side.
c **T**— Into which the afferent vessels open.
d **F**— The outer cortex is densely packed with cells and follicles,
      the central medulla is loosely packed with cells.
e **F**— The capsule is fibrous and from it, fibrous trabeculae pass
      inwards.

II The Vertebral Column

27   In the vertebral column:
a   the individual vertebrae are all separately
    identifiable in the adult.   (   )
b   cervical vertebrae all have bifid spines.   (   )

c   thoracic vertebrae all have articular surfaces
    for ribs.   (   )

d   the articular processes arise near the junction
    of the vertebral body and its pedicles.   (   )
e   primary fetal curvatures are retained in the
    thoracic and sacral regions.   (   )

28   In the cervical region:
a   the atlas vertebra has no body.   (   )

b   the superior articular facets of the axis face
    anterolaterally.   (   )
c   the 6th cervical spine is the most prominent.   (   )
d   dislocation of the dens is prevented by the alar
    and apical ligaments.   (   )

e   the upper vertebrae lie behind the oropharynx.   (   )

29   The intervertebral discs:
a   are largely composed of hyaline cartilage.   (   )
b   the anulus fibrosus is formed of elastic tissue.   (   )

c   contribute about one quarter of the length of
    the vertebral column.   (   )

d   are found in all regions of the vertebral column.   (   )

e   may compress the spinal cord when injured.   (   )

a **F**— Five vertebrae fuse together and form the sacrum, and others form the coccyx.
b **F**— All have a foramen in the transverse process. C1 has no spine and C7 is not usually bifid.
c **T**— Lumbar vertebrae are identified by having neither a foramen in the transverse process nor articular facets for ribs.
d **F**— They arise near the junction of the pedicles and the laminae.
e **T**— Secondary curvatures develop after birth in the cervical and lumbar regions. These are the most mobile regions and the most liable to injury.

a **T**— This part becomes attached in early fetal life to the axis as the dens.
b **F**— The facets face upwards.

c **F**— C7 is called the vertebrae prominens.
d **F**— The main factor stabilising the joint is the cruciate ligament. If dislocation occurs, the spinal cord may be crushed.
e **T**— Radiographs of the atlanto-occipital and atlanto-axial joints are taken through the open mouth.

a **F**— The discs are fibrocartilage; the centre part is semi-solid,
b **F** the nucleus pulposus, and the outer part, the anulus fibrosus, the latter is formed of fibrous tissue.
c **T**— During the day the discs are compressed. During sleep, water is re-absorbed and the discs restored to their original size.
d **F**— There are no discs in the sacrai or coccygeal regions, nor is there one between C1 and C2.
e **T**— Large posterior central herniations may produce this complication. If the herniation occurs at the posterolateral angle, a spinal nerve may be compressed as it lies in the intervertebral foramen.

30 **The vertebral bodies are united by:**
  a anterior and posterior longitudinal ligaments.   (   )
  b intervertebral discs. (   )

  c ligamenta flava. (   )
  d intertransverse ligaments. (   )
  e interspinous ligaments. (   )

31 **In the vertebral canal the:**
  a dural covering of the spinal cord fuses with the
     periosteum of adjacent vertebrae. (   )
  b spinal cord of an adult ends about the level of
     the 2nd lumbar vertebra. (   )
  c internal vertebral veins have large branches
     draining the bodies of the vertebrae. (   )
  d spinal nerve roots can be followed into their
     intervertebral foramina where the roots fuse. (   )

  e spinal cord cannot be damaged if a needle is
     inserted between the 1st and 2nd lumbar spines. (   )

III Thorax

32 **The thoracic wall:**
  a has a cartilaginous skeleton. (   )
  b is cylindrical in shape. (   )
  c is bounded below by the 7th–10th costal
     cartilages and the 11th and 12th ribs. (   )
  d receives its cutaneous nerves via the brachial plexus. (   )

  e gives attachment to abdominal wall muscles. (   )

a T— The anterior ligament is a flat band attached to each
b T   vertebral body and disc. The posterior runs from the axis
        to the sacrum and is also attached to each intervertebral
        disc which itself unites the cartilaginous articular surfaces
        of adjacent bodies.
c F— The ligamenta flava, intertransverse and interspinous
d F   ligaments are accessory ligaments and unite the adjacent
e F   laminae, transverse processes and spines respectively.
        They have no attachment to the vertebral bodies.

a F— Between the bony-ligamentous wall of the canal and the
        dura is the fat-filled extradural space with the emerging
        spinal nerves and the internal vertebral venous plexus.
b T— In a child it ends at a lower level.

c T— The marrow of the vertebral bodies is one of the chief
        blood-forming sites throughout life.
d T— In the lower part of the canal, the nerves run with
        increasing obliquity before emerging through the
        intervertebral or sacral foramina. The dorsal root ganglion
        is situated near the point of fusion.
e F— The spinal cord is still present at this level; for a lumbar
        puncture the needle is inserted above or below the spine
        of the 4th lumbar vertebra.

a F— It has a bony-cartilaginous skeleton.
b F— It is 'conical' in shape, narrower superiorly.
c T— These form the costal margin.

d F— It is segmentally innervated via the ventral and dorsal rami
        of the 1st–11th thoracic nerves.
e T— Rectus abdominis, the external and internal oblique, and
        transversus abdominis muscles each gain attachment to
        the anterior or anterolateral part of the costal margin.
        These muscles play an important role in forced respiration.

33 **A typical rib:**
a articulates with the vertebral bodies in two places. (   )
b is attached to an intervertebral disc. (   )

c bears three facets for articulation with the
vertebral column. (   )

d has a costal cartilage which articulates with the
sternum by a synovial joint. (   )

e is grooved superiorly by the costal groove. (   )

34 **Intercostal arteries:**
a supply only the posterior part of the intercostal
space. (   )

b arise from branches of the subclavian artery and
the descending aorta. (   )
c arise from branches of the ascending aorta. (   )
d supply the spinal cord. (   )
e lie inferior to the accompanying nerve in the
intercostal space. (   )

35 **A typical intercostal nerve:**
a is a ventral ramus of a thoracic spinal nerve. (   )
b lies in the majority of its course deep to the
internal intercostal muscle. (   )
c lies in the majority of its course in the subcostal
groove. (   )
d supplies cutaneous branches to the skin of the back. (   )

e may supply abdominal wall skin. (   )

a **T**— Each typical rib bears two facets on its head for articulation
b **T**   with its own vertebra and the one above. The intervening
crest is attached by an intra-articular ligament to the
intervertebral disc.

c **T**— Two facets for the vertebral bodies described above and
one for articulation with the transverse process at the
costotransverse joint.

d **T**— That between the first rib (not a typical rib) and the
sternum is a primary cartilaginous joint, but the joints
between the 2nd and 7th costal cartilages and the sternum
have a synovial cavity.

e **F**— The costal groove, in which lie the intercostal vessels and
nerve, lies inferiorly on the internal surface of the ribs.

a **F**— Each space is supplied by a posterior artery and paired
anterior arteries. The lower two spaces have only posterior
arteries.

b **T**— The first two posterior arteries and all the anterior arteries
arise from branches of the subclavian; the remainder arise

c **T**   from the aorta.

d **T**— Spinal branches arise from the posterior arteries.

e **F**— The nerve lies inferior to its accompanying artery.

a **T**— It has cutaneous and muscular branches.

b **T**— Where the innermost intercostal is deficient, it lies against
the pleura.

c **T**— The artery and the vein separate it from the bone.

d **F**— The skin of the back is supplied by branches of the dorsal
rami.

e **T**— The skin of the anterior abdominal wall is supplied by the
7th to the 12th intercostal nerves.

36 **The diaphragm:**

a is attached to the sternum, costal cartilages, the psoas fascia the transversalis fascia, and the vertebral bodies. ( )

b is supplied by both the phrenic and intercostal nerves. ( )

c increases the horizontal diameter of the chest on contraction. ( )

d has an opening in the central tendon for the inferior vena cava. ( )

e contracts during micturition. ( )

37 **The diaphragm is pierced by the:**

a splanchnic nerves. ( )

b sympathetic trunks. ( )

c left phrenic nerve. ( )

d gastric nerves. ( )

e the lowest intercostal nerves. ( )

38 **During deep respiration:**

a inspiration is aided by the upper ribs being elevated by the scalene muscles. ( )

b inspiration is aided by approximation of the upper ribs. ( )

c expiration is due to the elastic recoil of lung tissue and the costal cartilages. ( )

d expiration is aided by relaxation of the abdominal wall muscles. ( )

e there is often fixing of the shoulder girdles. ( )

a **T**— Via the back of the xiphoid, the lowest six costal cartilages, the lateral and medial arcuate ligaments over quadratus abdominis and psoas respectively, and the right and left crura to the upper three (right) and two (left) lumbar vertebrae respectively.

b **T**— Only the phrenic is motor, the intercostal nerves supply sensory branches to the periphery.

c **F**— Contraction results in flattening of the diaphragm and an increase in the vertical diameter of the chest.

d **T**— This opening is to the right of the midline and also transmits the right phrenic nerve.

e **T**— Expulsive acts, such as micturition and defaecation, follow a rise in intra-abdominal pressure produced by simultaneous diaphragmatic and abdominal wall contraction.

a **T**— The splanchnic nerves pierce the crura.

b **F**— The sympathetic trunks pass behind the medial arcuate ligaments.

c **T**— The left phrenic nerve pierces the left dome of the diaphragm.

d **T**— The anterior and posterior gastric nerves are transmitted with the oesophagus through an opening in the muscular part to the left of the midline. Muscle fibres from the right crus of the diaphragm surround the opening.

e **F**— These lie superficial to the diaphragmatic attachments. The subcostal nerve passes behind the lateral cruciate ligament.

a **F**— In deep inspiration, the uppermost ribs are fixed by the scalene muscles. The scalene muscles only elevate the upper ribs in forced inspiration against an obstruction.

b **T**— Fixation of the upper ribs by the scalene muscles allows the intercostal muscles to raise the remaining ribs by movement at their costotransverse joints.

c **T**— The elastic recoil is a major factor in expiration, and this is helped especially in forced respiration by simultaneous contraction of the abdominal wall muscles which also fix the lower ribs.

d **F**— The abdominal muscles contract and push the liver and the diaphragm upwards.

e **T**— This allows serratus anterior and the pectoralis muscles to raise the ribs.

39   **The adult female mammary gland:**
a lies deep to the deep fascia of the chest wall.   ( )
b extends from the side of the sternum to near
the midaxillary line.   ( )
c has a subcutaneous and submammary plexus
of lymph vessels.   ( )

d develops from modified skin glands.   ( )

e has a lymphatic drainage which extends to the
anterior mediastinum.   ( )

40   **The adult heart:**
a is related posteriorly to the oesophagus, left
main bronchus and aorta.   ( )
b lies on the left dome of the diaphragm.   ( )

c in health weighs approximately 900 g.   ( )
d admits the great veins on its posterior surface.   ( )

e is totally enclosed by the serous pericardium.   ( )

41   **The right atrium:**
a is related to the central tendon of the diaphragm
at the level of the 8th thoracic vertebra.   ( )

b has a thin anterior endocardial fold "guarding"
the superior vena cava.   ( )
c has an auricle situated superolaterally.   ( )

d has the coronary sinus opening situated between
the fossa ovalis and the opening of the inferior
vena cava.   ( )
e has a fossa ovalis on the atrioventricular wall.   ( )

a **F**— it is a subcutaneous structure lying in the superficial fascia.
b **T**— And vertically from the 2nd to the 6th rib.

c **T**— These drain laterally to the pectoral nodes; superiorly to the infraclavicular and lower deep cervical nodes; medially to the parasternal nodes (some lymph vessels cross the midline to the nodes and the plexuses of the opposite side); and inferiorly to the anterior abdominal wall plexuses and the diaphragmatic nodes.

d **T**— It originates as an ectodermal downgrowth on the 'milkline' between the axilla and the groin.
e **T**— Lymph drains to the axilla, the deep cervical nodes and medially to the parasternal nodes and the opposite breast.

a **T**— The square base is separated from these structures by the pericardial sac.
b **F**— Inferiorly it is related to the central tendon of the diaphragm, to which the fibrous pericardium is firmly attached.
c **F**— 300 g is the average weight of the adult heart.
d **T**— The four pulmonary veins enter the left atrium posteriorly; the superior and inferior venae cavae enter the posterior part of the right atrium.
e **T**— The serous pericardium is a closed serous sac invaginated by the heart. It encloses a thin pericardial cavity.

a **T**— The inferior vena cava enters the atrium at this point. The wall of the atrium between the inferior and the superior venae cavae forms the right border of the heart.
b **F**— The superior vena cava has no valve. There is an anterior fold 'guarding' the entry of the inferior vena cava.
c **F**— The auricle lies superomedially against the beginning of the aorta. On the inner surface, a ridge (crista terminalis) separates the rough-walled auricle from the smooth-walled atrium.
d **F**— The sinus opening lies between the fossa ovalis and the opening into the right ventricle. The sinus opening is 'guarded' by an endocardial fold.
e **F**— The fossa lies on the interatrial wall, a remnant of the fetal foramen ovale.

42   **The right ventricle:**
   a forms most of the inferior surface of the heart.   (   )

   b is normally oval in cross section.   (   )

   c has a tricuspid valve in its inflow tract.   (   )
   d usually contains three conical papillary muscles.   (   )

   e possesses a pulmonary orifice guarded by a
      tricuspid valve.   (   ).

43   **The mitral valve:**
   a possesses two cusps.   (   )

   b 'guards' the right atrioventricular orifice.   (   )
   c is closely related to the aortic valve.   (   )

   d has no papillary muscle attachments.   (   )

   e lies on the posterior wall of the left ventricle.   (   )

44   **The coronary arteries:**
   a arise from the inferior aspect of the aortic arch.   (   )

   b each gives atrial and ventricular branches.   (   )
   c anastomose extensively with each other.   (   )
   d supply the conducting system of the heart.   (   )

   e supply the papillary muscles of the mitral and
      tricuspid valves.   (   )

a **T**— It forms part of the anterior and most of the inferior surface of the heart.
b **F**— The interventricular septum bulges into its cavity making it crescentic in cross section.
c **T**— The tricuspid valve has fine tendinous cords anchoring its
d **F** cusps inferiorly. These arise from two papillary muscles and from the interventricular septum directly.
e **T**— The pulmonary semilunar valve possesses three semilunar valve cusps.

a **T**— Each cusp consists of a double fold of endocardium and a small amount of fibrous tissue. Normally it is avascular.
b **F**— The left atrioventricular orifice is 'guarded'.
c **T**— The anterior cusp is larger and lies between the aortic and mitral orifices.
d **F**— Both cusps are anchored by tendinous cords to papillary muscles arising from the walls of the left ventricle.
e **T**

a **F**— The right coronary artery arises from the anterior aortic sinus and the left from the left posterior sinus immediately adjacent to the aortic valve.
b **T**— The right artery supplies most of the right side of the heart
c **T** and the left supplies the left side, but, although they
d **T** anastomose in the septum and apex, sudden occlusion of a large branch may result in death of heart muscle. The conducting system is supplied by the coronary vessels and damage to it may have rapid catastrophic consequences.
e **T**— Occlusion of the coronary vessels may cause death of a papillary muscle and its rupture.

45   **The atrioventricular bundle:**
a   forms part of the conducting system of the heart.   ( )

b   is formed of nervous tissue.   ( )
c   lies in the interventricular septum.   ( )

d   divides into two branches and then ramifies as
the subendocardial plexus.   ( )
e   bridges between the atrial and ventricular muscles.   ( )

46   **During the development of the heart:**
a   the venae cavae come to enter the caudal end
of the heart tube.   ( )
b   the oblique sinus of the pericardium arises
from the serous pericardium enveloping the major
arteries.   ( )
c   division into right and left sides is completed
prior to birth.   ( )

d   the pulmonary veins and venae cavae are
incorporated into the walls of the left and right atria
respectively.   ( )
e   there is very little blood flow to the developing lungs. ( )

47   **The ascending aorta:**
a   ascends as far as the right sternoclavicular joint.   ( )
b   lies intrapericardially.   ( )

c   has no branches.   ( )

d   is related posteriorly to the right main bronchus.   ( )

e   is related anteriorly to the sternum.   ( )

a **T**— The system comprises all of the tissues which convey electrical impulses to the cardiac muscle, viz. — the sino-atrial node, the atrioventricular node, the AV bundle, its branches and the subendocardial plexus.
b **F**— It arises from the specialised cardiac muscle cells.
c **T**— It lies in the membranous interventricular septum and divides into right and left ventricular branches.
d **T**— On the ventricular wall the subendocardial plexus consists of the Purkinje fibres.
e **T**— The AV bundle is the only continuity between the atria and ventricles, whose muscles are separated by a pair of fibrous rings encircling both atrioventricular valves.

a **T**— Bending of the heart tube occurs and the precursors of these vessels then enter posteriorly.
b **F**— This cul-de-sac is formed by the pericardial reflection around the pulmonary veins and inferior vena cava.

c **F**— During intra-uterine life the foramen ovale remains patent allowing oxygenated placental blood to flow from the right to the left atrium and bypass the 'functionless' lungs. The foramen usually closes at birth or soon after.
d **T**— Forming the smooth posterior part of their walls.

e **T**— The patent foramen ovale and the ductus venosus, between the pulmonary artery and aorta, ensure most blood bypasses the fetal lung.

a **F**— It is 5 cm long, ending at the level of the sternal angle.
b **T**— Within the fibrous pericardium enclosed in a sheath of serous pericardium common to it and the pulmonary artery.
c **F**— The right and left coronary arteries arise near its origin from the anterior and left posterior aortic sinuses respectively.
d **T**— And, inferior to this, to the right pulmonary artery and the left atrium.
e **T**— The sternum lies directly adjacent.

48   The arch of the aorta:

a   arches posteriorly over the root of the right lung.   (   )

b   is related, on its left side, to mediastinal pleura.   (   )

c   is connected to the right pulmonary artery.   (   )

d   is related to the left brachiocephalic vein superiorly.   (   )

e   is related anteriorly to the manubrium sternum.   (   )

49   The descending thoracic aorta:

a   ends on the front of the 12th thoracic vertebra.   (   )

b   is directly related to both the left and right pleura.   (   )

c   gives branches to the bronchi.   (   )

d   is related anteriorly to the pulmonary trunk.   (   )

e   has the thoracic duct on its left side.   (   )

50   The pulmonary trunk:

a   lies at its origin anterior to the root of the aorta.   (   )

b   is contained within a common sleeve of
     serous pericardium with the ascending aorta.   (   )

c   bifurcates anterior to the aortic arch.   (   )

d   is related to the left pleura and lung.   (   )

e   is closely related to both right and left
     coronary arteries.   (   )

a **F**— It arches posteriorly over the root of the left lung and reaches the left side of the 4th thoracic vertebra.

b **T**— Which separates it from the left lung. The left phrenic and vagus nerves lie on its left side.

c **F**— There is a fibrous connection to the left pulmonary artery — the ligamentum arteriosum, a fibrous remnant of the ductus arteriosus.

d **T**— As the vein crosses obliquely above the aortic arch. The brachiocephalic, left common carotid and left subclavian branches of the aorta lie behind the vein.

e **T**— The arch commences at the sternomanubrial junction and lies directly behind the manubrium.

a **T**— It descends from the left side of the 4th thoracic vertebra and inclines medially, passes through the diaphragm at the level of the 12th thoracic vertebra and becomes the abdominal aorta.

b **T**— Throughout its course it is in contact with the left pleura and inferiorly the oesophagus leaves its right side so that it is then directly related to the right pleura and lung.

c **T**— Two or three such vessels arise, together with posterior intercostal, subcostal, oesophageal and diaphragmatic branches.

d **F**— Its anterior relations from above downwards are the root of the left lung, the oesophagus and the diaphragm.

e **F**— The duct lies alongside the azygos vein to the right of the aorta.

a **T**— Then it ascends posteriorly and to the left.

b **T**— All contained within the fibrous pericardium.

c **F**— It bifurcates posterior to and to the left of the aorta within the concavity of the aortic arch.

d **T**— Both its anterior and left surfaces are related to the left pleura and lung.

e **T**— These vessels surround its base.

51 The brachiocephalic vein:

a   of both right and left sides is formed by the
union of the internal jugular and subclavian veins.   (   )

b   enters the right atrium directly.   (   )

c   on the right side is related to the right pleura.   (   )

d   on the right is related to the thoracic duct.   (   )

e   on the left, gains tributaries from the thyroid gland.   (   )

52 The azygos vein:

a   originates in the abdomen.   (   )

b   leaves the abdomen by the oesophageal opening.   (   )

c   drains into the right atrium directly.   (   )

d   receives both right bronchial and right posterior
intercostal tributaries.   (   )

e   receives small pulmonary tributaries.   (   )

53 The left phrenic nerve:

a   arises from the dorsal rami of the 3rd, 4th and 5th
cervical nerves.   (   )

b   descends through the thorax in the left pleural cavity.   (   )

c   receives sensory branches from the mediastinal
and diaphragmatic pleura and from the
diaphragmatic peritoneum.   (   )

d   passes through the caval opening of the diaphragm.   (   )

e   descends in the thorax posterior to the lung root.   (   )

a **T**— This occurs behind the respective sternoclavicular joint.

b **F**— The two veins unite behind the right border of the manubrium and form the superior vena cava.

c **T**— Separated from it only by the right phrenic nerve.

d **F**— The thoracic duct enters the origin of the left vein, a smaller right lymph duct often enters the origin of the right vein.

e **T**— Inferior thyroid veins unite to enter the left brachiocephalic vein.

a **T**— Usually by the union of the right subcostal and right ascending lumbar veins. On the left side the accessory hemiazygos is formed.

b **F**— It leaves through the aortic opening.

c **F**— It arches over the root of the right lung at the level of the 4th thoracic vertebra and enters the superior vena cava.

d **T**— The left intercostal and bronchial veins drain via the hemiazygos and accessory hemiazygos veins into the azygos vein.

e **F**— Venous blood from the lung parenchyma drains into the pulmonary veins.

a **F**— It arises from the ventral rami of these nerves, descends on the anterior surface of scalenus anterior and passes through the thoracic inlet.

b **F**— It has a long mediastinal course and is covered by the left mediastinal pleura.

c **T**— And gives motor branches to the diaphragm.

d **F**— The left phrenic nerve pierces the dome of the diaphragm, sending branches to its undersurface. The right phrenic nerve passes through the caval opening of the diaphragm.

e **F**— Both phrenic nerves lie anterior to the lung root.

54   The right vagus nerve during its course in the thorax:
  a lies posterolateral to the right brachiocephalic artery. ( )
  b is separated from the mediastinal pleura by the
     trachea.   ( )
  c contributes to the pulmonary plexus.   ( )
  d contributes to the oesophageal plexus.   ( )

  e gives off the right recurrent laryngeal nerve.   ( )

55   The gastric nerves:
  a both arise from the oesophageal plexus.   ( )

  b contain only fibres from the right and left vagi.   ( )
  c supply branches to the liver.   ( )
  d supply branches to the coeliac plexus.   ( )
  e supply branches to the pancreas.   ( )

56   The thymus:
  a is a glandular structure which normally atrophies
     shortly after birth.   ( )
  b lies posterior to the trachea.   ( )

  c contains large numbers of lymphocytes.   ( )

  d is derived from the fourth pair of pharnygeal
     pouches.   ( )
  e is derived from thyroid tissue.   ( )

a   T— As it descends in the thorax posterolateral to the
b   F   brachiocephalic artery it lies between the trachea and
              mediastinal pleura.
c   T— It gives branches to the pulmonary plexus before
d   T   terminating with branches of the left vagus in the
              oesophageal plexus.
e   F— This branch arises in the neck and loops upward around
              the right subclavian artery.

a   T— Both anterior and posterior gastric nerves arise from the
              oesophageal plexus and contain both vagal and
b   F   sympathetic fibres.
c   T— After descending through the diaphragm the anterior nerve
d   T   supplies the stomach, duodenum, pancreas and liver. The
e   T   posterior nerve supplies the stomach and branches to the
              coeliac plexus.

a   F— It is large at birth, but normally atrophies before puberty.

b   F— It lies in front of the trachea at the root of the neck. It is
              variable in size and may extend down, in front of the aortic
              arch and its branches, into the mediastinum.
c   T— It is a lobulated structure with a cortex in which
              lymphocytes are predominant and a medulla which
              contains thymocytes and concentrically arranged cells —
              Hassall's corpuscles.
d   F— It is derived from the third pair of pharyngeal pouches.

e   F

57   The thoracic oesophagus:

a   lies posterior to the trachea.   (   )

b   is directly related to the vertebral column
     throughout its course.   (   )

c   is related to the left atrium.   (   )
d   pierces the central tendon of the diaphragm at
     the level of the 8th thoracic vertebra.   (   )

e   is crossed by the left bronchus.   (   )

58   The thoracic trachea:

a   bifurcates at the level of the sternal angle.   (   )

b   is closely related to the azygos vein.   (   )

c   has complete fibrocartilaginous rings within its
     walls.   (   )

d   is related anteriorly to the thyroid gland.   (   )

e   ends at the level of the sternal angle.   (   )

59   The right extrapulmonary bronchus:

a   is longer than the left.   (   )
b   lies more vertically than the left.   (   )

c   lies posterior to the pulmonary artery.   (   )

d   lies posterior to the pulmonary veins.   (   )

e   lies below the arch of the azygos vein.   (   )

a **T**— With the left recurrent laryngeal nerve and the right vagus lying in the grooves between it and the trachea.

b **F**— Superiorly this is so, but inferiorly it is separated from the vertebral column by the thoracic duct, the azygos and accessory hemiazygos veins, the right posterior intercostal arteries and the thoracic aorta.

c **T**— Separated only by the pericardium of the oblique sinus.

d **F**— The oesophageal opening is surrounded by muscular fibres from the right crus of the diaphragm, and is found to the left of the midline at the level of the 10th thoracic vertebra.

e **T**— The left bronchus crosses the middle third of the oesophagus anteriorly.

a **T**— The bifurcation is at this level and that of the 4th thoracic vertebra, and lies to the right of and behind the pulmonary trunk bifurcation.

b **T**— In its lower part it is separated from the mediastinal pleura by the azygos vein.

c **F**— Its walls are formed of a fibrous skeleton strengthened by 15–20 incomplete hyaline cartilage rings (plates) and smooth muscle.

d **F**— The thymus is found in front of the trachea in a child and thymic remnants in the adult. The thyroid gland is in the neck.

e **T**— Its bifurcation, the carina is at this level and that of the 4th thoracic vertebra.

a **F**— The right bronchus is shorter but wider than the left.

b **T**— Inhaled foreign material more easily enters the right bronchus.

c **T**— The bifurcation of the pulmonary trunk occurs at the same level as the bifurcation of the trachea and results in both right and left pulmonary arteries lying anterior to the main bronchi.

d **T**— The pulmonary veins lie inferior to both the bronchus and the artery on both sides.

e **T**— The azygos vein ascends behind the right bronchus to enter the superior vena cava.

60 **The surface markings of the pleural sacs:**
a do not extend above the clavicle. ( )
b are similar on the right and left sides. ( )
c meet in the midline anteriorly. ( )
d extend to the 8th rib in the midaxillary line. ( )

e extend to the 12th rib in the paravertebral line. ( )

61 **The right lung:**
a is larger than the left. ( )

b is divided by fissures into the upper and lower lobes and the lingula. ( )

c possesses 10 bronchopulmonary segments. ( )

d is related to the oesophagus only in the lower part of its medial surface. ( )

e is related inferiorly to the liver. ( )

a **F**— On both sides the upper limit of the pleura sacs lies 3 cm
b **F** above the middle of the medial third of the clavicle. The
c **T** pleura meet in the midline at the level of the 2nd costal
d **F** cartilage. At the 4th costal cartilage the left pleura
deviates laterally and descends along the lateral border of
the sternum to the 6th cartilage. Whereas the right pleura
decends vertically close to the midline to this level. They
then both deviate laterally and reach the 8th rib in the
midclavicular line and the 10th rib in the midaxillary line.
e **T**— The pleural reflection on to the diaphragm often lies just
inferior to the 12th rib and lateral to the paravertebral line.

a **T**— The right weighs about 620 g and the left about 560 g.
(The heart has to be accommodated on the left side.)
b **F**— The oblique and horizontal fissures divide it into upper,
middle and lower lobes. The lingula is the thin antero-
inferior portion of the left upper lobe representing the
middle lobe of the left lung.
c **T**— The bronchopulmonary segments are functionally
independent units of lung tissue. In the right lung there are
three in the upper lobe, two in the middle and five in the
lower lobe. The left lung is divided into five upper and five
lower segments.
d **F**— The medial surface of the right lung is related to the
oesophagus throughout its thoracic course except where
the azygos vein crosses over the hilus of the lung.
e **T**— And is separated from it by the right dome of the
diaphragm.

62   The lung tissue:
a   receives its oxygenated arterial supply via
branches of the thoracic aorta.   (   )
b   has venous drainage into the azygos system of veins. (   )
c   has no lymph drainage.   (   )

d   has ciliated columnar epithelial lining throughout.   (   )

e   receives a nerve supply from the vagus.   (   )

63   The thoracic sympathetic trunk:
a   possesses 11 ganglia.   (   )

b   lies in front of the necks of the ribs.   (   )

c   has no direct communication with the lumbar
sympathetic trunk.   (   )

d   provides the greater and lesser splanchnic and
least splanchnic (renal) nerves.   (   )

e   is independent of the thoracic spinal nerves.   (   )

64   Thoracic lymph vessels:
a   lying in the chest wall drain to axillary lymph nodes. (   )

b   in the lungs drain to tracheobronchial nodes.   (   )
c   drain from the oesophagus to posterior
mediastinal nodes.   (   )
d   do not communicate with those draining the
abdominal contents.   (   )

e   all drain into the thoracic and right lymph duct. (   )

a **T**— The bronchial arteries arise from the descending thoracic aorta.

b **T**— Bronchial veins drain to the azygos and hemiazygos veins.

c **F**— There is a rich subpleural lymph plexus, and a deep lymph plexus accompanying the bronchi. They drain via hilar and tracheobronchial nodes to mediastinal lymph trunks.

d **F**— Ciliated columnar epithelium lines the extra- and the intra-pulmonary bronchi. The terminal respiratory bronchioles are however lined by nonciliated columnar (cubical) epithelium and the alveoli by squamous epithelium.

e **T**— As vagal branches pass through the pulmonary plexus they produce bronchoconstriction.

a **F**— It usually possesses 12 ganglia, one corresponding to each thoracic nerve.

b **T**— It lies alongside the vertebral column on the necks of the ribs.

c **F**— It is continuous above with the cervical (through the thoracic inlet), and below with the lumbar sympathetic trunk (below the medial arcuate ligament).

d **T**— The greater arises from the 5th–9th ganglia, the lesser from the 9th–10th and the least (renal) from the 11th. They descend the posterior thoracic wall, pierce the crura of the diaphragm and give branches to the coeliac and pre-aortic plexuses.

e **F**— Two rami communicantes pass to each spinal nerve.

a **T**— Lymphatics drain from the superficial layers of the chest wall to the axillary nodes and from the deeper layers to parasternal and intercostal nodes.

b **T**— The thoracic viscera drain to three sets of nodes; anterior

c **T** mediastinal, tracheobronchial and posterior mediastinal.

d **F**— Those vessels draining from the diaphragmatic nodes pass through the diaphragm to communicate with vessels draining the upper surface of the liver.

e **T**— The thoracic duct drains the left half of the chest viscera and the right lymph duct, when present, drains the right sided viscera.

65 **The thoracic duct:**
  a   arises in the thorax.   (   )

  b   ascends anterior to the vertebral column.   (   )
  c   drains into the left brachiocephalic vein.   (   )

  d   drains mainly thoracic structures.   (   )

  e   is joined by the right lymph duct.   (   )

IV Abdomen

66 **The lateral muscles of the anterior abdominal wall are:**
  a   supplied by the lower six thoracic nerves and
      the first lumbar nerve.   (   )

  b   contained within the rectus sheath.   (   )

  c   attached to the lateral margin of rectus abdominis.   (   )

  d   attached in part to the costal cartilages.   (   )

  e   each gain attachment to the pubic bone.   (   )

a **F**— It arises in the abdomen from the cisterna chyli and enters the thorax through the aortic opening of the diaphragm.

b **T**— Behind the oesophagus, to the left of the azygos vein.

c **T**— It arches forwards from behind the carotid sheath, anterior to the subclavian artery and enters the vein.

d **F**— It drains all the body below the diaphragm, and the left half of the body above the diaphragm through left mediastinal, jugular and subclavian lymph trunks.

e **F**— The right lymph duct is often absent but, when present, it enters the right brachiocephalic vein, draining lymph from the right side of the head, neck and thorax.

a **T**— The nerves mainly lie between the internal oblique and the transversus abdominis. Terminal branches pierce the rectus sheath and supply the rectus abdominis. Skin and peritoneum are also supplied.

b **F**— The rectus sheath of each side is formed by the aponeuroses of the three lateral muscles. The sheaths join in the midline to form a strong midline raphe.

c **F**— The aponeurosis of the internal oblique splits to enclose rectus abdominis in the umbilical region. The sheath is reinforced anteriorly by external oblique, and posteriorly by transversus abdominis.

d **T**— Both external oblique and transversus abdominis originate by fleshy muscle fibres from the outer and inner aspects respectively of the lower six ribs and costal cartilages. Internal oblique is attached laterally to the costal margin.

e **T**— Internal oblique and transversus by the conjoint tendon and external oblique by the inguinal ligament.

67 The inguinal canal:

a extends between a defect in the transversalis fascia and a defect in the external oblique aponeurosis.   (   )

b has an anterior wall comprising the external oblique aponeurosis and the internal oblique muscle.   (   )

c has its floor formed by the deep fascia of the thigh.   (   )

d has its posterior wall formed medially by peritoneum.   (   )

e is longer in the newborn than the adult.   (   )

68 The spermatic cord:

a has three fascial coverings.   (   )

b contains three arteries.   (   )

c contains three nerves.   (   )

d contains one muscle.   (   )

e is less well developed in the female.   (   )

a **T**— The deep inguinal ring is a defect in transversalis fascia laterally and the superficial inguinal ring a defect in the external oblique aponeurosis medially.

b **T**— The internal oblique reinforces the lateral part of the anterior wall. The internal oblique fibres arch over the cord, join with the transversus abdominis fibres and form the conjoint tendon.

c **F**— The floor is the upper surface of the inguinal ligament which is continuous with the deep fascia of the thigh and the aponeurosis of the external oblique.

d **F**— The posterior wall is formed by peritoneum and fascia transversalis. They are reinforced medially by the conjoint tendon, i.e. behind the superficial inguinal ring.

e **F**— In the newborn, the external ring lies almost directly over the internal ring; it is therefore shorter and less oblique than in the adult.

a **T**— The internal spermatic fascia is continuous with the transversalis fascia, the cremasteric fascia and muscle are continuous with the internal oblique, and the external spermatic fascia is continuous with the external oblique.

b **T**— The testicular, cremasteric and the artery to the ductus deferens.

c **T**— The genital branch of the genitofemoral nerve, the ilioinguinal nerve and sympathetic nerves.

d **T**— The cremasteric muscle which mediates the cremasteric reflex. The testis is drawn up when the skin of the medial side of the thigh is stimulated.

e **T**— The spermatic cord is formed as the testis descends through the inguinal canal into the scrotum. It is absent in the female.

69 **The testis:**
  a has the epididymus applied to its medial side.   ( )

  b is supplied by sympathetic nerves originating
     in the 10th thoracic segment.   ( )

  c is drained by lymph vessels passing to the external
     iliac lymph nodes.   ( )
  d descends into the scrotum just before birth.   ( )

  e is covered in the scrotum by one layer of fascia.   ( )

70 **The testis, in its embryological development:**
  a originates from coelomic mesothelium adjacent
     to the mesonephros.   ( )
  b gains contributions from the developing
     mesonephros.   ( )
  c is aided in its descent by the processus vaginalis.   ( )

  d does not normally complete its descent into the
     scrotum until three months after birth.   ( )
  e causes inguinal hernias to be more common
     in the male.   ( )

71 **The lesser omentum:**
  a is attached superiorly to the porta hepatis and
     the fissure for the ligamentum venosum.   ( )

  b extends inferiorly as far as the transverse colon.   ( )

  c separates the lesser sac (omental bursa) and
     greater sac of peritoneum.   ( )

  d forms part of the boundaries of the epiploic
     foramen.   ( )
  e embraces the portal vein.   ( )

a **F**— The epididymis is applied to its posterolateral aspect and is connected to the testis by about 20 deferent ducts.

b **T**— This is the consequence of its development from the coelomic mesothelium of the upper posterior abdominal wall. The corresponding dermatome includes the umbilicus.

c **F**— Drainage is to the para-aortic nodes in the region of the renal vessels.

d **T**— It descends the posterior abdominal wall and then the inguinal canal, preceded by the gubernaculum, prior to birth. It takes a covering of peritoneum, the processus vaginalis, with it. This becomes the tunica vaginalis.

e **F**— It is covered by four layers. From within outwards, the internal spermatic fascia, cremasteric fascia, external spermatic fascia and superficial fascia containing the dartos muscle.

a **T**— It develops from the coelomic mesothelium of the posterior abdominal wall. Tubules of the mesonephros

b **T** become the efferent ducts and the head of the epididymis. The mesonephric duct becomes the ductus deferens.

c **F**— Testicular descent is aided by the gubernaculum, a mesodermal mass attached to its lower pole. Descent into

d **F** the scrotum is usually complete at birth.

e **T**— The processus vaginalis may result in inguinal hernias appearing any time from birth onwards.

a **T**— Its 2 layers are formed from the left and right sacs of peritoneum covering the liver which meet along this line. The falciform ligament, formed in a similar way, passes from the liver to the anterior abdominal wall above the umbilicus. The ligament and lesser omentum are both remnants of the fetal ventral mesentery.

b **F**— It passes inferiorly, meets and encloses from above downwards the oesophagus, stomach and initial part of the duodenum.

c **T**— The lesser sac lies behind the lesser omentum and stomach, and communicates with the greater sac only by the epiploic foramen.

d **T**— This foramen is bounded anteriorly by the free edge of the lesser omentum, superiorly by the liver, posteriorly by the

e **T** inferior vena cava and inferiorly by the duodenum. The free edge contains the bile duct, hepatic artery and the portal vein.

72   **The mesentery:**

a   of the small intestine is attached obliquely along a line extending from the descending part of the duodenum to the left sacro-iliac joint. (   )

b   of the small intestine contains branches of the inferior mesenteric artery. (   )

c   of the transverse colon is attached horizontally to the anterior border of the pancreas. (   )

d   of the sigmoid colon lies over the promontory of the sacrum. (   )

e   of the sigmoid colon contains the inferior mesenteric vein. (   )

73   **The pelvic peritoneum:**

a   covers both the uterus and uterine tubes. (   )

b   condenses and forms the round ligaments of the uterus. (   )

c   covers the anterior surface of the rectum only in its upper third. (   )

d   covers the superior surface of the bladder in both sexes. (   )

e   can be palpated by means of a digital examination of the rectum. (   )

74   **The abdominal oesophagus:**

a   enters the abdomen between the right and left crus of the diaphragm. (   )

b   is enveloped by peritoneum. (   )

c   is closely related to both the anterior and posterior gastric nerves. (   )

d   is closely related to the left lobe of the liver. (   )

e   is surrounded by an external oesophageal sphincter. (   )

a F— Its oblique attachment extends from the duodenojejunal flexure (on the left side of L2 vertebra) to the ileocolic junction (overlying the right sacro-iliac joint).

b F— The arteries it contains are branches of the superior mesenteric artery which supplies derivatives of the midgut.

c T— Its horizontal attachment extends to the left across the descending part of the duodenum, the anterior border of the pancreas and the tail of the pancreas as it crosses the anterior surface of the left kidney.

d F— The sigmoid mesocolon is attached on the posterior pelvic wall along a ∧-shaped line whose apex lies over the left sacro-iliac joint.

e T— Conveying the vein to the posterior abdominal wall where it ascends to join the splenic vein.

a T— It covers anterior and posterior surfaces of the uterus and the tubes, and extends to the pelvic walls forming the broad ligaments of the uterus.

b F— The round ligaments of the uterus are remnants of the gubernaculum of the ovary.

c F— Anteriorly the rectum is covered by peritoneum in its upper two-thirds.

d T— And extends over the upper part of its posterior surface. In the male, the upper part of the seminal vesicles are also covered.

e T— The rectovaginal, or in the male the rectovesical, pouch of peritoneum can be palpated in this manner through the rectal wall. Pelvic peritonitis may thus be diagnosed.

a F— The oesophageal opening of the diaphragm lies within the fibres of the right crus to the left of the midline.

b F— Peritoneum covers only its anterior surface.

c T— The anterior gastric nerve is often within its wall and the posterior gastric nerve is adjacent to its posterior surface.

d T— It lies between the diaphragm posteriorly and the left lobe of the liver anteriorly.

e F— The lower oesophageal sphincter lies within the oesophageal wall. Competence of the sphincter is aided by the oblique angle of entry of the oesophagus into the stomach.

75 In the stomach, the:

a fundus lies above the level of the oesophageal opening. ( )

b body extends inferiorly to the angular notch. ( )

c right border is known as its greater curvature. ( )

d cardiac orifice is closely related to the aorta. ( )

e blood supply arises from midgut arteries. ( )

76 The stomach:

a is supplied in part by arteries arising from the splenic artery. ( )

b is supplied by arteries which each arise from branches of the coeliac trunk. ( )

c has a venous drainage passing equally to the portal and systemic venous systems. ( )

d is lined by columnar and squamous epithelium. ( )

e is totally covered by serosa (peritoneum). ( )

77 The duodenum:

a is almost completely covered by peritoneum. ( )

b lies behind the portal vein. ( )

c lies anterior to the hilus of the right kidney. ( )

d is crossed anteriorly by the superior mesenteric vessels. ( )

e is about 25 cm long. ( )

a **T**— The fundus is that part lying above the oesophageal opening.

b **T**— The body extends from the fundus to the angular notch, the lowest point of the lesser curvature.

c **F**— The greater curvature is the left border extending from the left of the oesophagus around the fundus and body to the pylorus.

d **F**— The cardiac orifice and the oesophagus lie between the diaphragm and the liver and are separated from the aorta by fibres from the right crus of the diaphragm.

e **F**— The blood supply is by the short gastric arteries, the right and left gastric arteries, and the right and left gastro-epiploic arteries; all of these are branches of the coeliac, a foregut artery.

a **T**— The short gastric vessels, supplying the fundus and the left gastro-epiploic, supplying most of the greater curvature, arise from the splenic.

b **T**— The left and right gastric, the left and right gastro-epiploic and the short gastric arteries each arise from branches of the coeliac trunk or the trunk itself.

c **F**— All blood from the stomach normally passes to the portal vein. There are, however, anastomoses with oesophageal veins.

d **F**— It is lined completely by columnar epithelium and contains three different types of glands. The cardiac glands secrete mucus only; the acid and enzyme secreting gastric glands are found largely in the body; and the pyloric glands in the antrum produce mucous and the hormone gastrin.

e **T**— Peritoneum invests the whole stomach, being reflected from it along the lines of the greater and lesser omentum, on its greater and lesser curvatures.

a **F**— Only its first and last centimetres are invested by peritoneum. The remainder lies retroperitoneally, only its anterior surface being covered.

b **F**— The ascending part of the duodenum is anterior to the portal vein, bile duct and gastroduodenal artery.

c **T**— Its descending part lies anterior to the right suprarenal, the hilus of the right kidney and the right psoas muscle.

d **T**— The root of the mesentery and the superior mesenteric vessels cross anterior to the horizontal part.

e **T**— It comprises the 1st part (5 cm), 2nd (8 cm), descending on the right of the vertebral column, 3rd (10 cm), running horizontally and the 4th part (3 cm), which ascends on the left side of the 2nd lumbar vertebra.

78   **In the small intestine the:**
  a   duodenojejunal flexure lies on the left of the first
       lumbar vertebra. ( )
  b   jejunum has a thicker wall than the ileum. ( )

  c   arterial arcades are less numerous in the jejunum
       than in the ileum. ( )
  d   root of the mesentery crosses the left psoas muscle. ( )

  e   jejunum lies above and to the left of the ileum. ( )

79   **The caecum:**
  a   is completely invested in peritoneum. ( )
  b   possesses a longitudinal muscle coat but no
       taeniae coli. ( )
  c   lies on the right psoas muscle. ( )

  d   has an ileocaecal orifice opening inferiorly. ( )
  e   lies adjacent to the right femoral nerve. ( )

80   **The appendix:**
  a   arises from the inferior aspect of the caecum. ( )

  b   has a mesentery. ( )

  c   is commonly absent. ( )
  d   usually lies retrocaecally. ( )

  e   is clothed in peritoneum. ( )

a   **F**— The root of the mesentery passes from the left side of the 2nd lumbar vertebra to the right sacro-iliac joint.

b   **T**— The jejunum is also wider. Its mucous membrane is thrown into circular folds with many villi but there are fewer aggregations of lymphoid tissue in the wall and less fat in the mesentery than in the ileum.

c   **T**— The jejunal vessels are larger, and the jejunal wall is more vascular than the ileal.

d   **T**— It then crosses in turn the aorta, inferior vena cava, right gonadal vessels, right ureter and right psoas muscle.

e   **T**

a   **T**— It does not generally possess a mesentery.

b   **F**— The longitudinal muscle is arranged in three bands, the taeniae coli, which converge on to the appendix.

c   **T**— It lies anterior to the iliacus and psoas muscles in the right iliac fossa.

d   **F**— The ileocaecal orifice opens to its medial wall.

e   **T**— The femoral nerve and the external iliac vessels lie on its medial side.

a   **F**— It arises from the posteromedial wall of the caecum 3 cm below the ileocaecal orifice.

b   **T**— Its peritoneal coat extends and forms its mesentery which connects it to the terminal ileum.

c   **F**— Absence of the appendix is extremely rare.

d   **T**— Though its mobility leads to great variation in its position, it most commonly lies retrocaecally.

e   **T**— This peritoneum is reflected from the appendix to form the mesoappendix.

81   The sigmoid colon:
  a extends from the pelvic brim to the third sacral
      segment.   (   )

  b is closely tethered by its peritoneal covering. (   )
  c lies in close proximity to both ureters. (   )

  d lies adjacent to the bladder in both sexes. (   )
  e is supplied by branches of the inferior mesenteric
      artery. (   )

82   The coeliac trunk:
  a arises at the level of the inferior border of the pancreas. (   )
  b has three main branches. (   )

  c is surrounded by a plexus of nerves. (   )
  d supplies the foregut and structures derived from it. (   )

  e supplies the lower oesophagus. (   )

83   The splenic artery:
  a reaches the hilus of the spleen by a retroperitoneal
      course. (   )
  b lies along the upper border of the pancreas. (   )
  c supplies branches to the stomach. (   )

  d supplies branches to the left adrenal gland. (   )
  e lies anterior to the left kidney. (   )

84   The superior mesenteric artery:
  a arises behind the body of the pancreas. (   )
  b supplies no bowel proximal to the duodenojejunal
      flexure. (   )
  c supplies the bowel as far as the left side of the
      transverse colon. (   )
  d ends by dividing into ileocolic and right colic vessels. (   )

  e lies posterior to the uncinate process. (   )

a **T**— At the third sacral segment it becomes continuous with the rectum. Its position is variable for it is attached by a mesentery to the pelvic wall.

b **F**

c **F**— Posteriorly it lies on the left ureter and is related inferiorly in both sexes to the bladder.

d **T**

e **T**— Sigmoid arterial branches enter the sigmoid mesocolon to supply the structure.

a **F**— It arises from the aorta just above the pancreas.

b **T**— After passing forward for 2 cm it divides into the left gastric, common hepatic and splenic arteries.

c **T**— These nerves and ganglia form the coeliac (solar) plexus.

d **T**— The coeliac trunk supplies the foregut, the superior mesenteric the midgut, and the inferior mesenteric the hindgut structures.

e **T**— Oeosphageal branches of the left gastric artery supply the lower third of the oesophagus.

a **F**— Its initial tortuous course along the upper border of the pancreas is retroperitoneal, but it reaches the hilus of the

b **T** spleen by passing in the lienorenal ligament.

c **T**— Its short gastric branches pass to the fundus of the stomach in the gastrosplenic ligament and its left gastro-epiploic branch passes to the greater curvature of the stomach.

d **F**— Its only other branches are several pancreatic branches.

e **T**— In addition, it is anterior to the left crus of the diaphragm and left psoas muscle.

a **T**— Its origin from the aorta is behind the body of the pancreas.

b **F**— The inferior pancreaticoduodenal artery supplies the lower duodenum as far as the duodenal papilla and also the pancreas.

c **T**— At this point its branch, the middle colic artery, anastomoses with the left colic, a branch of the inferior mesenteric artery.

d **T**— After giving 15–20 jejunal and ileal branches it ends in the right iliac fossa by dividing into these branches.

e **F**— It descends behind the body of the pancreas to emerge anterior to the uncinate process after which it gains the small bowel mesentery.

85 **The inferior mesenteric artery:**

a supplies the large bowel from the left part of the transverse colon to the upper anal canal. (   )

b continues as the inferior rectal artery in the pelvis. (   )

c anastomoses with branches of the internal iliac artery. (   )

'd is crossed over by the left ureter. (   )

e contributes to the marginal artery of the bowel. (   )

86 **The portal vein:**

a drains venous blood from the whole of the intra-abdominal alimentary tract. (   )

b receives the splenic vein as a tributary. (   )

c receives branches from the liver. (   )

d is closely related to the bile duct and common hepatic artery. (   )

e gains tributaries from the anterior abdominal wall. (   )

87 **The splenic vein:**

a lies posterior to the pancreas. (   )

b unites with the superior mesenteric vein. (   )

c has tributaries draining into it from the stomach. (   )

d drains into the systemic venous system. (   )

e has the inferior mesenteric vein as a tributary. (   )

a **T**— It supplies this distal part of the large bowel and upper anal canal by the left colic and sigmoid arteries, and by its continuation in the pelvis, the superior rectal artery.

b **F**— The inferior rectal artery is a branch of the internal pudendal artery.

c **T**— Its terminal branch, the superior rectal artery, anastomoses with the inferior rectal branch of the internal pudendal artery in the wall of the anal canal.

d **F**— The artery descends on the posterior abdominal wall with the left ureter on its left side, separated from it by the inferior mesenteric vein. The branches cross over the ureter.

e **T**— Ileal and colic branches of the superior and inferior mesenteric arteries form a continuous anastomotic arcade along the mesenteric border of the bowel.

a **T**— The venous drainage from all the alimentary tract, from the lower oesophagus to the upper anal canal and including

b **T** the spleen, pancreas and gall bladder is into the portal vein which is formed by the junction of the splenic and superior mesenteric veins. Blood then drains along the portal vein into the liver.

c **F**— Hepatic veins drain into the inferior vena cava.

d **T**— The portal vein ascends in the free edge of the lesser omentum behind the common hepatic artery on the left and the bile duct on the right. The vein is separated from the inferior vena cava by the epiploic foramen.

e **T**— These, the para-umbilical veins, anastomose with other veins of the abdominal wall to form a portosystemic anastomosis. When portal pressure is high the distended veins of the anastomosis are readily visible around the umbilicus — the caput medusa.

a **T**— It is formed in the hilus of the spleen by the union of

b **T** tributaries from that organ, the left gastro-epiploic and

c **T** short gastric veins. It passes to the right lying behind the pancreas.

d **F**— It unites with the superior mesenteric vein behind the neck (head) of the pancreas and forms the portal vein which drains to the liver.

e **T**— It enters the splenic vein behind the body of the pancreas.

88   A portal-systemic anastomosis occurs between the:
a   azygos and left gastric veins.   (   )
b   epigastric veins and the veins in the falciform
     ligament.   (   )

c   portal vein and the inferior vena cava.   (   )
d   portal vein and renal vein.   (   )
e   portal vein and the extra hepatic tributaries of the
     hepatic vein.   (   )

**89   The mucous membrane of the small and large bowel
        possesses:**
a   numerous lymph nodules.   (   )
b   a layer of smooth muscle.   (   )

c   columnar epithelium throughout its length.   (   )
d   a nerve plexus throughout its length.   (   )
e   secretory cells throughout its length.   (   )

90   The liver:
a   is attached to the diaphragm and anterior
     abdominal wall by the ligamentum venosum.   (   )

b   is totally covered by peritoneum.   (   )

c   is divided on the visceral surface into two lobes
     by the interlobar fissure.   (   )
d   has a fibrous capsule.   (   )

e   has an embryological remnant connecting it to the
     umbilicus.   (   )

a **T**— The portal venous system anastomoses with the systemic
b **T**   venous system at both of these sites and others which are
        the 'junctional' regions such as the recto-anal junction, and
        the bare areas of the gut, liver and pancreas.
c **F**— Neither the inferior vena cava nor renal vein have any
d **F**   connection with the portal venous system.
e **F**— There is no connection between the portal vein and these
        tributaries.

a **T**— Collections of lymph tissue occur throughout its length.
b **T**— The mucous membrane is divided by the muscularis
        mucosae, a layer of smooth muscle.
c **T**— The epithelial lining contains many goblet cells.
d **T**— The submucous (Meissner's) nerve plexus.
e **T**— Mucosal cells produce mucus throughout; in addition, the
        small bowel mucosa secretes hormones such as gastrin
        and secretin.

a **F**— This liver attachment is by a fold of peritoneum, the
        falciform ligament, extending from the anterior and
        superior surfaces of the liver to the diaphragm and anterior
        abdominal wall, and by the peritoneum bounding the bare
        area of the liver, and probably most important, by the
        inferior vena cava.
b **F**— Although largely covered by peritoneum the two layers of
        the coronary ligaments diverge to enclose a part of the
        diaphragmatic surface posteriorly which is bare of
        peritoneum.
c **T**— Containing the ligamentum venosum and the ligamentum
        teres.
d **T**— This is invaginated at the porta hepatis by the triad of
        portal vein, common hepatic artery and hepatic duct and
        forms a sheath around these structures in their intrahepatic
        course.
e **T**— The ligamentum teres is the obliterated left umbilical vein
        draining from the umbilicus to the left branch of the portal
        vein.

91   The liver:

a   drains by hepatic veins into the inferior vena cava.   (   )

b   has a lymph drainage to both the mediastinal and porta hepatis nodes.   (   )

c   is supplied by the phrenic nerves.   (   )

d   is directly related to the right suprarenal gland.   (   )

e   gains an arterial supply from the coeliac axis.   (   )

· 92   The bile duct:

a   enters the duodenum 10 cm beyond the pylorus.   (   )

b   lies between the portal vein and duodenum.   (   )

c   lies anterior to the inferior vena cava in part of its course.   (   )

d   usually has an opening into the duodenum separate from the main pancreatic duct.   (   )

e   receives the right and left hepatic ducts.   (   )

＼ 93   The gall bladder:

a   lies adjacent to the tip of the 10th right costal cartilage.   (   )

b   is closely related to the duodenum.   (   )

c   is supplied by a branch of the right hepatic artery.   (   )

d   is lined by squamous epithelium.   (   )

e   is usually completely covered with peritoneum.   (   )

a T— There are usually large right and left hepatic veins and several smaller branches draining blood from the liver directly into the inferior vena cava.

b T— The superficial (subperitoneal) lymph plexus drains through the diaphragm to anterior mediastinal nodes, and on its under surface to nodes in the porta hepatis. The deep plexus drains to the posterior mediastinal and porta hepatis nodes.

c F— Parasympathetic fibres from both vagi supply the liver via the anterior gastric nerve; sympathetic fibres supply it from the coeliac plexus along the hepatic arteries.

d T— The bare area of the posterior surface is closely related to the diaphragm, inferior vena cava and right suprarenal gland.

e T— Via the hepatic artery, this ascends in the lesser omentum to divide at the porta hepatis into right and left branches.

a T— At the duodenal papilla on the medial wall of the descending part of the duodenum.

b T— Behind the superior part of the duodenum it lies anterior to the portal vein.

c T— Behind the head of the pancreas it lies anterior to the inferior vena cava.

d F— Both these ducts open into the ampulla, whose entry into the duodenum is guarded by a sphincter of smooth muscle which may also guard the duodenal opening.

e F— These join in the porta to form the common hepatic duct and this is joined by the cystic duct to form the bile duct.

a F— Its fundus is in contact with the anterior abdominal wall deep to the tip of the ninth right costal cartilage.

b T— Its fundus and body lie immediately anterior to the descending and superior parts of the duodenum.

c T— The cystic artery.

d F— Columnar epithelium lines the whole biliary tract. In the gall bladder are numerous mucus-secreting goblet cells.

e F— It lies on the inferior surface of the liver with only its fundus and the inferior surface of the body covered with peritoneum.

94   The spleen:

a   lies deep to the left 9th, 10th and 11th ribs.   (   )

b   is separated by the diaphragm from the chest wall.   (   )

c   is closely related to the stomach.   (   )

d   is separated by the stomach from the tail of the
     pancreas.   (   )

e   is closely related to the left kidney.   (   )

95   The pancreas:

a   is completely invested in peritoneum.   (   )

b   usually has two major ducts.   (   )

c   is related to both the greater sac of peritoneum
     and the omental bursa.   (   )

d   lies anterior to the right and left renal veins.   (   )

e   is closely related to the bile duct.   (   )

96   The kidneys:

a   lie with their hila at the level of the 4th lumbar
     vertebra.   (   )

b   lie in a fascial sheath with their related suprarenal
     gland.   (   )

c   are related posteriorly to the lower ribs.   (   )

d   possess a hilus on their medial border in which
     the pelvis of the ureter lies anterior to the renal
     artery and posterior to the renal vein.   (   )

e   drain lymph to para-aortic lymph glands.   (   )

a **T**— It lies behind the left midaxillary line deep to these ribs
b **T**   being separated by the diaphragm from them and the left pleural sac.
c **T**— Its anterior surface is directly related to the greater curvature of the stomach.
d **F**— The tail of the pancreas extends in the lienorenal ligament to the hilus of the spleen.
e **T**— The posterior surface is closely related to the left kidney and suprarenal gland.

a **F**— It is covered by peritoneum anteriorly and inferiorly (the attachment of the transverse mesocolon) across the posterior abdominal wall from the duodenum to the spleen.
b **T**— The main pancreatic duct joins the bile duct in the ampulla and opens about the middle of the medial wall of the descending duodenum. The accessory duct draining the uncinate process may open separately into the duodenum proximal to the duodenal papilla, but frequently joins the main pancreatic duct.
c **T**— The transverse mesocolon which is attached to the border between the anterior and inferior surfaces of the gland separates these two peritoneal sacs.
d **T**— Both renal veins join the inferior vena cava behind the head of the pancreas.
e **T**— The bile duct extends posteriorly and passes into the gland as it approaches the ampulla; here it usually joins the pancreatic duct.

a **F**— Their hila lie close to the transpyloric plane, at the level of the 2nd lumbar vertebra.
b **F**— They are surrounded by perirenal fat and enclosed by part of the fascia tansversalis which separates each of them from a suprarenal gland.
c **T**— The diaphragm separates them from the 11th and 12th ribs.
d **F**— At the hilus of each kidney the renal vein, artery and pelvis of the ureter lie in that order from before backward.

e **T**— These lie around the origin of the renal arteries.

97   The left kidney:

a   is separated from the psoas major muscle by
the quadratus lumborum muscle.   (   )

b   is crossed posteriorly by the body of the pancreas.   (   )

c   has cubial epithelium with a brush border lining
the proximal convoluted tubule.   (   )

d   develops from the pronephros.   (   )

e   is closely related to the splenic vessels.   (   )

98   The ureters:

a   have an abdominal course which is different in
each sex.   (   )

b   lie anterior to branches of the lumbar plexus and
posterior to the anterior branches of the aorta.   (   )

c   have a pelvic course which is different in each sex.   (   )

d   turn medially over levator ani at the level of the
ischial spine.   (   )

e   gain a sensory nerve supply from the autonomic
nervous system.   (   )

99   The suprarenal gland:

a   on the right side lies on the right crus of the
diaphragm.   (   )

b   on the left side lies on the left crus of the diaphragm.   (   )

c   on each side is related to the inferior vena cava.   (   )

d   receives its nerve supply from branches of the
thoracic sympathetic trunk.   (   )

e   lies alongside the coeliac axis.   (   )

a **F**— The kidney lies anterior to both muscles and to the transversus abdominis muscle.

b **F**— The body of the pancreas passes in front of the hilus and middle third of the kidney. The tail of the pancreas lies in the lienorenal ligament.

c **T**— This part of the nephron (functional unit of the kidney) is responsible for water reabsorption.

d **F**— The secreting part of the kidney develops from the metanephros. The collecting system (beyond the distal convoluted tubule) develops from the ureteric bud of the mesonephric duct.

e **T**— These pass anteriorly to the hilus and middle part of the kidney.

a **F**— The abdominal course of each ureter is similar in male and female; their courses in the pelvis are different in the two sexes.

b **T**— Both ureters descend on psoas, crossing over the genitofemoral nerve and being crossed over by the gonadal vessels. On the right side, the ureter is also crossed over by the duodenum and the right colic and ileocolic vessels: on the left side by the left colic vessels and the sigmoid colon.

c **T**— In both sexes the ureter crosses the bifurcation of the
d **T** common iliac vessels in front of the sacro-iliac joint and descends to the ischial spine before turning medially. In the male the ductus deferens crosses over it at this point, whereas in the female it runs medially under the root of the broad ligament being crossed over by the uterine artery and lying close to the lateral vaginal fornix, before entering the bladder.

e **T**— These nerve fibres originate in the upper lumbar and sacral segments of the cord.

a **T**— The right gland is pyramidal, the left crescentic, and both have a rich blood supply from neighbouring arteries.

b **T**

c **F**— The inferior vena cava lies anterior to the right suprarenal. The two glands are separated by the coeliac plexus with which they are intimately connected, and by the aorta.

d **T**— Via the splanchnic nerves. Preganglionic fibres end in the medulla of the gland.

e **T**— The two glands are separated by the coeliac plexus lying in front of the aorta.

100 **The psoas major muscle:**
  a is attached to the middle of the sides of the
        lumbar vertebral bodies.   (   )

  b is attached to the lesser trochanter of the femur. (   )

  c receives its nerve supply from all the lumbar nerves. (   )
  d both flexes the hip joint and the trunk.   (   )

  e gains attachment to the femur by passing below
        the pubic rami.   (   )

101 **The thoracolumbar fascia:**
  a lies posterior to the muscles of the posterior
        abdominal wall.   (   )
  b gives attachment to both the internal oblique
        and transversus abdominis muscles.   (   )

  c is attached medially to the spinous processes
        of the lumbar and sacral vertebrae.   (   )
  d is attached medially to the lumbar transverse
        processes.   (   )

  e connects the iliac crest to the 12th rib.   (   )

102 **The lumbar part of the lumbosacral plexus:**
  a lies in the substance of psoas major.   (   )
  b is formed by the dorsal rami of all the lumbar nerves. (   )

  c has no cutaneous branches.   (   )

  d contributes to the sacral part of the lumbosacral
        plexus.   (   )
  e contributes nerve fibres to the sciatic nerve.   (   )

a **F**— It is attached to fibrous arches which cross the concave sides of the lumbar vertebrae, to the edges of the bodies of the lumbar vertebrae and the discs between, and to the lumbar transverse processes.

b **T**— As it approaches the femur, it is joined by the iliacus muscle on its lateral side.

c **F**— It is supplied by branches of the 1st and 2nd lumbar nerves.

d **T**— Contraction will produce flexion and medial rotation at the hip joint, or flexion of the lumbar region of the trunk on the femur.

e **F**— It gains the thigh by passing under the inguinal ligament, above the superior pubic ramus.

a **F**— It consists of three fascial layers which enclose the posterior abdominal wall muscles. The layers fuse at the

b **T** lateral limit of the muscles and become continuous with the aponeuroses of the internal oblique and transversus abdominis muscles.

c **T**— The strong posterior layer covers erector spinae and is attached to the lumbar and sacral spinous processes; the

d **T** middle layer is attached medially to the ends of the lumbar transverse processes; the thin anterior layer covers quadratus lumborum and is attached to the front of the base of the lumbar transverse processes.

e **T**— Superiorly it is thickened to form the lateral cruciate ligament.

a **T**

b **F**— It is usually formed by the ventral rami of the first four lumbar nerves.

c **F**— The iliohypogastric and ilioinguinal nerves arise from it and supply the skin of the anterior abdominal wall and the external genitalia; the genitofemoral nerve supplies skin over the genitalia and the femoral triangle; the lateral femoral cutaneous nerve supplies skin over the lateral aspect of the thigh. Peritoneum is also supplied.

d **T**— By the lumbosacral trunk which is formed by the 4th and 5th lumbar nerves.

e **T**— Via the lumbosacral trunk (L4, L5) which descends over the sacrum to join the lumbosacral plexus.

103   The abdominal aorta:

a   ends anterior to the body of the 4th lumbar
    vertebra.   (   )
b   has the cisterna chyli lying on its left side.   (   )

c   has the inferior vena cava lying on its right side.   (   )

d   is related anteriorly to the right renal vein.   (   )
e   lies in close relationship with the lumbar vertebrae.   (   )

104   The renal arteries:

a   arise from the aorta at the level of the 2nd
    lumbar vertebra.   (   )
b   are both related posteriorly to the crus of the
    diaphragm of the same side.   (   )

c   supply branches to the corresponding suprarenal
    gland and ureter.   (   )
d   give testicular (or ovarian) branches.   (   )

e   are of unequal length; the left artery is longer than
    the right.   (   )

105   The inferior vena cava:

a   is formed on the front of the 3rd lumbar vertebra
    by the union of the two common iliac veins.   (   )
b   leaves the abdomen via the caval opening of the
    diaphragm at the level of the 8th thoracic vertebra.   (   )
c   receives tributaries from both gonadal veins.   (   )

d   receives several hepatic veins.   (   )

e   lies to the left of the aorta.   (   )

a **T**— Here it bifurcates into the two common iliac arteries.

b **F**— The cisterna chyli lies between the right side of the aorta and the right crus of the diaphragm.

c **T**— The cisterna chyli and the right crus lie between the aorta and the inferior vena cava which also lies further to the right.

d **F**— The left renal vein crosses it anteriorly.

e **T**— It lies directly anterior to the bodies of the upper four lumbar vertebrae.

a **T**— Arising at this level, the right renal artery crosses the right crus of the diaphragm lying behind the head of the

b **T** pancreas and the inferior vena cava. The shorter left renal artery crosses the left crus lying behind the body of the pancreas.

c **T**— Each renal artery gives branches to the suprarenal gland and the upper part of the ureter.

d **F**— The gonadal vessels arise directly from the aorta at the level of the 3rd lumbar vertebra and course down the posterior abdominal wall crossing over the ureter, the genitofemoral nerve and the psoas muscle.

e **F**— The aorta lies to the left of the midline, hence the left renal artery is the shorter.

a **F**— It is formed in front of the 5th lumbar vertebra.

b **T**— The caval opening lies in the central tendon of the diaphragm to the right of the midline.

c **F**— The left gonadal vein drains into the left renal vein, the right is a tributary of the inferior vena cava.

d **T**— The hepatic veins usually comprise two or three large vessels and a variable number of smaller vessels. They enter the part of the vena cava which is usually embedded in the liver.

e **F**— The left ureter lies along its left side.

V   Pelvis and Perineum

106   **The ilium of the hip bone:**
  a forms two-fifths of the acetabulum.   (   )

  b has a subcutaneous upper border.   (   )

  c gives attachment to the rectus femoris muscle.   (   )

  d gives attachment to the adductor magnus muscle.   (   )

  e gives attachment to the inguinal ligament.   (   )

107   **The sacrum:**
  a is formed of four fused sacral vertebrae.   (   )

  b has foramina communicating with the central sacral canal.   (   )

  c gives attachment to piriformis on the lateral part of its dorsal surface.   (   )

  d gives attachment to the erector spinae muscles on the medial part of its dorsal surface.   (   )

  e is closely related to the rectum.   (   )

108   **The sacro-iliac joint:**
  a is a fibrous joint in a young person.   (   )

  b owes its stability to the neighbouring muscles.   (   )

  c allows only slight rotation and gliding movements to occur.   (   )

  d lies behind the bifurcation of the common iliac vessels and the ureter.   (   )

  e lies anterior to the sciatic nerve.   (   )

a **T**— It contributes the upper two-fifths of this articular surface. The ischium contributes the posterior two-fifths and the pubis the remainder.

b **T**— The iliac crest extends from the anterior to the posterior superior iliac spine and is subcutaneous throughout most of its length. Its uppermost part lies at the level of the body and spine of the 3rd lumbar vertebra. The line joining the highest points marks the supracristal plane and is a surface marking for a lumbar puncture.

c **T**— This strong flexor of the thigh at the hip joint is attached to the anterior inferior iliac spine and the adjacent ilium.

d **F**— This muscle is attached along the ischiopubic ramus.

e **T**— The lateral end of the inguinal ligament is attached to the anterior border of the ilium at the anterior superior iliac spine.

a **F**— Five vertebrae usually fuse and form it.

b **T**— Paired pelvic and dorsal foramina communicate by corresponding intervertebral foramina with the central sacral canal and convey ventral and dorsal rami of the sacral nerves.

c **F**— Piriformis is attached to the pelvic surface of the lateral mass of the sacrum.

d **T**— The erector spinae arises in part from this surface which also gives attachment to the thoracolumbar fascia.

e **T**— The lower part of its anterior (pelvic) surface lies in contact with the rectum.

a **F**— It is a synovial joint of the plane variety between the sacrum and ilium. In adults the joint cavity may be partly obliterated by fibrous adhesions.

b **F**— Stability is maintained almost entirely by very strong ligaments — i.e. the interosseous, dorsal and ventral sacro-iliac, the sacrotuberous and the sacrospinous ligaments.

c **T**— The weight of the trunk tends to rotate the promontory of the sacrum forwards, this being prevented by the sacrotuberous and sacrospinous ligaments. Such gliding movement as occurs is restricted by the sacro-iliac ligaments.

d **T**— The lumbosacral trunk, obturator nerve and psoas muscle are also anterior to the joint, separating the joint from the iliac vessels.

e **F**— Posteriorly it is covered only by the erector spinae and gluteus maximus muscles.

109 **The symphysis pubis:**
  a is a secondary cartilaginous joint. ( )

  b has its surfaces covered with fibrocartilage. ( )
  c allows little or no movement. ( )
  d gains most of its stability from accessory ligaments. ( )
  e is united by a fibrocartilaginous disc. ( )

110 **The lesser pelvis:**
  a in the female, has a relatively longer anteroposterior
     diameter at the pelvic inlet. ( )

  b has an outlet bounded by the ischiopubic rami
     and the sacrotuberous ligaments. ( )
  c has a cavity whose anterior wall is much shorter
     than the posterior. ( )
  d has a smaller subpubic angle in the female than
     in the male. ( )
  e in the female is generally circular in cross section. ( )

111 **The levator ani muscle:**
  a gains attachment from the fascia covering obturator
     internus. ( )
  b gains attachment to both the perineal body and the
     anococcygeal body. ( )
  c reinforces both the rectal and urethral sphincters. ( )

  d is supplied largely by sympathetic and
     parasympathetic nerves. ( )
  e forms all of the pelvic floor. ( )

a **T**— As are many other midline joints, such as the manubriosternal and all the intervertebral discs.
b **F**— Hyaline cartilage covers the joint surfaces.
c **T**— Except in the later stages of pregnancy.
d **F**— The joint is strengthened on all surfaces by interpubic
e **T** ligaments and by its attachments to the intra-articular disc. It possesses no accessory ligaments.

a **F**— During parturition the fetal head enters the lesser pelvis in the transverse diameter and emerges through the outlet in the anteroposterior diameter. The head of a postmature fetus may be too large and a Caesarian section may be necessary.
b **T**— The outlet is diamond-shaped and, in the female, the anteroposterior diameter is greater than the transverse.
c **T**— In both sexes the cavity is a short curved cavity whose posterior wall is about three times longer than the anterior.
d **F**— The angle is more than 90° in the female, and less in the male.
e **F**— The maximum diameter of the inlet is transverse and of the outlet anteroposterior. Hence, in normal labour the head undergoes partial rotation during descent.

a **T**— Laterally it is attached to the back of the body of the pubis, the fascia covering obturator internus and the ischial spine.
b **T**— Its fibres descend to the midline to meet the opposite muscle in a midline raphe. The anterior fibres pass around
c **T** the urethra and prostate (or the urethra and vagina) to the fibrous perineal body; the middle fibres pass medially around the rectum to the anococcygeal body; and the posterior fibres pass to the midline raphe and the coccyx. It provides muscular support for the pelvic viscera and reinforces the rectal and urethral sphincters.
d **F**— It is supplied by branches of the 3rd and 4th sacral nerves and the pudendal nerve and is under voluntary control.
e **F**— The two coccygei muscles contribute to the posterior part of the pelvic floor.

112 **The pelvic floor:**
  a   is formed by levator ani and coccygeus.   (   )

  b   separates the perineum from the ischiorectal fossae. (   )

  c   is covered superiorly by fascia.   (   )
  d   has the pelvic vessels and nerves on its
       undersurface.   (   )

  e   is gutter shaped.   (   )

113 **The rectum:**
  a   begins in front of the 1st sacral vertebra.   (   )
  b   has no mesentery.   (   )

  c   forms the posterior wall of a peritoneal pouch.   (   )
  d   in the male is related anteriorly to the seminal
       vesicles and prostate.   (   )

  e   is related anteriorly to the cervix.   (   )

114 **The rectum:**
  a   is related posteriorly to the 3rd, 4th and 5th
       sacral nerves.   (   )
  b   has a lining of stratified squamous epithelium.   (   )

  c   has a venous drainage into the superior
       mesenteric vein.   (   )

  d   sends lymph vessels to the superficial inguinal
       nodes.   (   )

  e   is a straight structure.   (   )

a **T**— It is formed by the two levator ani muscles anteriorly and the two coccygei posteriorly.

b **F**— It is a fibromuscular diaphragm separating the pelvic cavity above from the perineum and ischiorectal fossae below.

c **T**— The tough pelvic fascia covers it superiorly.

d **F**— Both the vessels and nerves lie on the superior surface of the pelvic floor. The pudendal vessels and nerves lie below.

e **T**— This gutter-like arrangement rotates the fetal head as it descends through the pelvis.

a **F**— It begins in front of the 3rd sacral vertebra.

b **T**— Its upper third is covered by peritoneum on its front and sides, its middle third on its front only, and its lower third lies embedded in the pelvic fascia.

c **T**— Its upper two-thirds form the rectovesical pouch in the
d **T**   male, and the rectouterine pouch in the female. In its lower part its anterior relations may be palpated by digital examination of the rectum. These are the vagina and cervix in the female, and the prostate, seminal vesicles and ducti deferentia in the male.

e **T**— On digital examination of the female, the cervix is palpable through the rectal wall.

a **T**— Also to the sympathetic plexus, the sacrum and the piriformis muscle.

b **F**— The lining is of columnar epithelium, containing numerous mucous glands and aggregations of lymphoid tissue.

c **F**— The superior rectal vein is a tributary of the inferior mesenteric vein. There are also important anastomoses with the inferior rectal branch of the internal pudendal vein.

d **F**— These nodes drain the lower anal canal. The rectal drainage passes along the superior rectal vessels to the pre-aortic nodes and laterally to the internal iliac nodes.

e **F**— It curves anteriorly as it descends and usually loops toward the left side of the pelvis.

115   The anal canal:

a   possesses an internal sphincter of voluntary muscle. (   )

b   possesses an external sphincter supplied by
parasympathetic nerves.   (   )

c   is adjacent to the ischiorectal fossa.   (   )

d   has a lymph drainage to both the nodes around
the common iliac vein and to the superficial
inguinal nodes.   (   )

e   is lined by both columnar and squamous epithelium. (   )

116   The urinary bladder:

a   has no peritoneal covering.   (   )

b   is lined with cubical epithelium.   (   )

c   is attached to the umbilicus.   (   )

d   is closely related to the pubic bones.   (   )

e   has a lymphatic drainage to the inguinal nodes.   (   )

117   The urinary bladder:

a   has a motor nerve supply from both the
sympathetic and parasympathetic systems.   (   )

b   has a sensory supply from both sympathetic and
parasympathetic systems.   (   )

c   has a venous drainage to the inferior mesenteric
vein.   (   )

d   is largely supported by the pelvic fascia.   (   )

e   lies in close contact with the vagina.   (   )

a F— The internal sphincter is an involuntary muscle and a
b F   continuation of the rectum's circular muscle coat. The
        external sphincter encircles the lower two-thirds of the anal
        canal and is arranged into deep, superficial and
        subcutaneous parts. It is voluntary muscle supplied by the
        inferior rectal nerves and is reinforced by the levator ani
        muscle.
c T— It is separated from it by the levator ani and the external
        sphincter muscles.
d T— The upper two-thirds of the anal canal drain to the nodes
        around the common iliac vein and the pre-aortic nodes.
        The lower anal canal drains to the superficial inguinal
        nodes.
e T— The lower one-third is lined with squamous epithelium. It
        joins that part lined with columnar epithelium at the
        dentate line.

a F— Its superior surface in both sexes is covered by peritoneum
        and the upper part of the posterior surface in the male.
b F— The mucosa is lined with transitional epithelium.
c T— The median umbilical ligament, a remnant of the urachus,
        ascends to the umbilicus.
d T— The anterolateral surfaces, though separated slightly from
        the pubic bones by a fat-filled retropubic space, lie close
        enough for bladder injuries to complicate pubic fractures.
e F— It drains to external and internal iliac nodes.

a T— Both sympathetic and parasympathetic fibres supply the
        bladder; the sympathetic is motor to the vesical sphincter,
b T   the parasympathetic to the bladder wall. Sensory fibres are
        found in both supplies.
c F— It drains via the vesical venous plexus to the internal iliac
        veins.
d T— Pelvic fascia surrounds the bladder and the fascial
        thickenings around its neck attach it to the pubis
        (pubovesical and puboprostatic ligaments) and to the
        pelvic wall (lateral ligaments of the bladder).
e T— It lies anterior to the vagina.

118 The uterus:

a is an anterior relation of the anal canal.   (   )
b is supported by the parametrium.   (   )

c is crossed laterally above its middle by the ureter.   (   )
d sends its lymph vessels to the common iliac nodes.   (   )

e lies in the line of the vagina.   (   )

119 The broad ligament of the uterus:

a extends from the uterus to the lateral surface of the
   bladder.   (   )
b contains the uterine tube.   (   )

c contains the suspensory ligament of the ovary.   (   )

d contains the round ligament of the uterus.   (   )

e contains parametrium.   (   )

120 The uterine tubes:

a lie in the base of the uterine broad ligament.   (   )
b in the adult are about 4 cm long.   (   )
c are lined by ciliated epithelium.   (   )
d extend to the medial surface of the ovary.   (   )

e are, when healthy, always patent.   (   )

a **F**— The anal canal lies posterior to the vagina.
b **T**— The parametrium consists of strong bands of pelvic fascia radiating from the cervix to the pelvic walls. The lateral (cardinal) ligaments are the largest.
c **F**— The ureter is a lateral relation of the lateral vaginal fornix.
d **T**— Some vessels also pass along the round ligament to the superficial inguinal nodes and some others may pass with the ovarian vessels to the para-aortic nodes.
e **F**— The uterus lies normally at right angles to the vagina.

a **F**— It is a double fold of peritoneum extending from the lateral pelvic wall to the lateral margin of the uterus.
b **T**— In the medial two-thirds of its free upper border lies the uterine tube.
c **T**— The suspensory ligament of the ovary lies in the lateral one-third of this border and contains the ovarian vessels.
d **T**— The round ligament of the uterus extends from the upper lateral angle of the uterus through the broad ligament to the deep inguinal ring, then through the inguinal canal and ends in the labium majus. It is continuous with the ovarian ligament and is a remnant of the gubernaculum of the ovary.
e **T**— This is thickened fibrous tissue which surrounds the supravaginal cervix in the base of the broad ligament.

a **F**— The tubes lie in the upper borders of the broad ligament.
b **F** In the adult they are usually about 10 cm long.
c **T**— The ciliated epithelium contains many mucous cells.
d **F**— Each tube ends laterally in the fimbria which curl around and overlap the lateral surface of the ovary.
e **T**— Recurrent infection may, however, cause narrowing or closure to occur.

121 The ovary:
   a lies on the anterior surface of the broad ligament.   ( )

   b is related on its lateral surface to the uterine tube.   ( )

   c lies on the lateral pelvic wall.   ( )
   d receives a blood supply from branches of the
      uterine artery.   ( )
   e has lymph vessels passing to internal iliac nodes.   ( )

122 The vagina:
   a usually lies at an axis of 45° with the uterus.   ( )
   b is related laterally to the ureter.   ( )

   c has a lymph drainage both to iliac and superficial
      inguinal nodes.   ( )
   d is lined with epithelium rich in mucous glands.   ( )

   e is covered in its upper posterior part with
      peritoneum.   ( )

123 The prostate:
   a is traversed by two ejaculatory ducts.   ( )
   b possesses lateral and median lobes.   ( )

   c is surrounded by a prostatic sheath and venous
      plexus.   ( )
   d drains via its venous plexus to the internal vertebral
      venous plexus.   ( )
   e is separated from the rectum by rectovesical fascia. ( )

a **F**— It lies on the back of the broad ligament attached by a double fold of peritoneum, the mesovarium.
b **T**— Laterally the ovary is related to the fimbriated end of the uterine tube, and is attached to one of the fimbriae.
c **T**— Related to the internal iliac artery and the ureter.
d **T**— These supplement ovarian arteries arising from the aorta just below the renal arteries.
e **F**— The lymph drainage is to para-aortic nodes at the level of the renal vessels. The lymph vessels pass with the ovarian vessels.

a **F**— It usually lies at an angle of 90° with the uterus.
b **T**— Laterally it is related to the base of the broad ligament containing the ureter and uterine vessels.
c **T**— Its upper two-thirds drain to internal and external iliac nodes, its lower third to superficial inguinal nodes.
d **F**— Its squamous epithelial lining containing no glands. The greater vestibular glands lie laterally.
e **T**— This is the uterorectal pouch (Pouch of Douglas) separating the vagina from the rectum.

a **T**— These two ducts and the urethra traverse the gland and
b **T** with fibrous septa divide it into a median lobe lying between the urethra and ejaculatory ducts, and two lateral lobes below and lateral to the median lobe.
c **T**— The prostatic sheath is formed of pelvic fascia. The surrounding venous plexus drains to the internal iliac veins
d **T** and the internal vertebral plexus through the pelvic sacral foramina.
e **T**— This strong sheet of fascia covers the seminal vesicles and the front of the rectum.

124   The ductus (vas) deferens:
  a   is a continuation of the canal of the epididymis.   (   )
  b   joins inferiorly with the head of the epididymis.   (   )
  c   ends by opening into the prostatic urethra.   (   )

  d   lies medial to the seminal vesicle.   (   )

  e   possesses a sacculated diverticulum.   (   )

125   The perineum:
  a   lies below the pelvic diaphragm.   (   )

  b   is bounded anteriorly by the inguinal ligaments.   (   )
  c   is bounded posterolaterally by the sacrotuberous
      ligaments.   (   )
  d   is bounded laterally by the ischial spines.   (   )
  e   contains anal and perineal triangles.   (   )

126   The ischiorectal fossa:
  a   is bounded superiorly by the levator ani muscle.   (   )
  b   is bounded laterally by the inferior pubic ramus.   (   )
  c   does not communicate with its fellow of the
      opposite side.   (   )

  d   is related medially to the anal canal.   (   )
  e   contains the seminal vesicles.   (   )

a T— It is a narrow muscular tube extending from the tail of the
b F   epididymis and, joining with the duct of the seminal
c F   vesicle, forms the 2 cm long ejaculatory duct which opens
        into the prostatic urethra.
d T— In its terminal part it descends posterior to the bladder and
        medial to the seminal vesicle.
e T— This is the seminal vesicle and it lies behind the base of
        the bladder.

a T— It is the diamond-shaped space between the pubic
        symphysis and the coccyx.
b F— It is bounded anteriorly by the ischiopubic rami,
c T   posterolaterally by the sacrotuberous ligaments and
        laterally by the ischial tuberosities.
d F
e F— A line joining the ischial tuberosities divides the perineum
        into an anterior urogenital and a posterior anal triangle.

a T— It is a wedge-shaped space, bounded superomedially by
b F   levator ani, laterally by the fascia on obturator internus
c F   and inferiorly by perineal skin. The two fossae
        communicate with each other around the anal canal and
        are separated by the anococcygeal body, the anal canal
        and the perineal body.
d T
e F— The vesicles lie above the levator ani and so are within the
        pelvis. The fat-filled fossa extends forwards towards the
        pubis and backwards towards the sacrum. The pudendal
        canal is on the lateral wall.

127 The urogenital diaphragm:
a is attached to the ischiopubic rami. ( )
b is attached to the anococcygeal body. ( )

c in the female, is pierced by the vagina as well
as the urethra. ( )

d has, between its two layers, the vesical sphincter. ( )

e gives attachment to perineal muscles. ( )

128 The superficial perineal pouch:
a is limited inferiorly by the urogenital diaphragm. ( )

b is continuous with the spaces in the scrotum
occupied by the testes. ( )

c has a membranous covering which provides a
fascial sheath around the penis. ( )
d contains the penis, testes and spermatic cords. ( )
e is traversed by the urethra in the male and the
urethra and vagina in the female. ( )

129 The penis:
a comprises two cylinders of erectile tissue. ( )
b contains a ventral corpus spongiosum which
expands anteriorly to form the glans penis. ( )
c contains corpora cavernosa which expand
posteriorly to form the bulb of the penis. ( )

d has a lymph drainage to the internal iliac nodes. ( )
e has veins draining to the prostatic plexus. ( )

a **T**— This double layer of fascia stretches across the pubic arch
b **F**   between the ischiopubic rami. Its posterior border is
        attached to the perineal body.
c **T**— In the female it is a less well-defined structure but attached
        to its inferior surface are the bulb of the vestibule, the
        greater vestibular glands and the small crura of the clitoris.
        In the male the bulb surrounding the urethra and the large
        crura of the penis are attached to its inferior surface and
        the adjacent ischiopubic rami.
d **F**— The urethral sphincter occupies this position. It is
        composed of voluntary muscle, supplied by the perineal
        branch of the pudendal nerve.
e **T**— In the male it also gives attachment to the bulb and crura
        of the penis.

a **F**— It lies between the urogenital diaphragm superiorly, and
        inferiorly the membranous layer of the superficial fascia
        which is continuous with that of the anterior abdominal
        wall.
b **T**— The membranous layer of superficial fascia passes over the
        scrotum to be attached to the posterior border of the
        urogenital diaphragm.
c **T**— The pouch contains the bulb and crura of the penis (and
        corresponding structures in the female) and the superficial
d **T**   perineal muscles.
e **T**— In the female, the greater vestibular glands are also found
        in the pouch.

a **F**— There are three longitudinal cylinders of erectile tissue.
b **T**— The unpaired ventral corpus spongiosum expands
        anteriorly and forms the glans penis, and posteriorly it
c **F**   forms the bulb of the penis. The two united, dorsally-
        placed corpora cavernosa diverge posteriorly and form the
        crura of the penis.
d **F**— It drains to the superficial inguinal group of nodes.
e **T**— Together with branches to the internal pudendal veins.

130 The male urethra:
a receives a midline ejaculatory duct. ( )
b receives two prostatic ducts. ( )

c traverses the whole length of the corpus spongiosum. ( )
d has the sphincter urethrae muscle surrounding its prostatic part. ( )

e is narrowest in its membranous part. ( )

131 The pudendal nerve:
a arises from the lumbar plexus. ( )
b traverses the greater sciatic foramen. ( )
c traverses the lesser sciatic foramen. ( )

d supplies levator ani and perianal skin. ( )

e supplies sensory fibres to the penis. ( )

132 The common iliac arteries:
a arise in front of the promontory of the sacrum. ( )
b have no branches other than the terminal internal and external iliac arteries. ( )
c lie in front and to the right of the internal iliac veins. ( )
d are closely related to the inferior vena cava. ( )
e are crossed at their origin by the ureters. ( )

133 The external iliac artery:
a ends behind the inguinal ligament at the midinguinal point. ( )
b lies on the psoas major muscle. ( )
c is crossed anteriorly by the ureter. ( )

d is crossed anteriorly by the gonadal vessels. ( )
e supplies blood to the anterior abdominal wall. ( )

a F— The posterior wall of the prostatic urethra is marked by an
b F   elevation, the prostatic utricle on each side of which enters
        an ejaculatory duct. Into the groove on each lateral side
        open the 20–30 prostatic ducts.
c T— The spongy urethra is some 16 cm long and it traverses
        the whole length of the corpus spongiosum.
d F— The sphincter urethrae surrounds the narrow membranous
        urethra and is formed of striated (voluntary) muscle. The
        sphincter lies between the prostate and bulb, and is
        supplied by the perineal branch of the pudendal nerve.
e T— Where it descends through the deep perineal pouch.

a F— It arises from the sacral plexus.
b T— It leaves the pelvis through the greater sciatic foramen,
c T   crosses the ischial spine and enters the perineum through
        the lesser sciatic foramen to pass forwards in the pudendal
        canal.
d T— Together with the external anal and urethral sphincters,
        perineal muscles and scrotal (labial) skin.
e T— Via branches of the dorsal nerve of the penis.

a F— They arise in front of the body of the fourth lumbar vertebra.
b T— They end by dividing, anterior to the sacro-iliac joints, into
        these terminal branches.
c F— They lie anterior and to the left of the internal iliac veins. The
d T   origin of the inferior vena cava lies behind the right artery.
e F— The ureters cross anteriorly the terminal bifurcation of the
        common iliac arteries.

a T— At this point it continues into the thigh as the femoral artery.
        It is palpable at this point.
b T— Throughout its course it lies anterior to the psoas muscle.
c F— It is crossed anteriorly by the testicular or ovarian vessels
        and the ductus deferens. The ureter crosses the bifurcation
d T   of the common iliac artery.
e T— The inferior epigastric artery arises just above the inguinal
        ligament, ascends the inner aspect of the abdominal wall
        medial to the deep inguinal ring, and enters the sheath of
        rectus abdominis. It anastomoses with the superior epigastric
        artery.

134   The cisterna chyli:
  a   drains directly into the left jugular vein.   (   )
  b   lies between the right crus of the diaphragm and
        the aorta.   (   )
  c   receives the right and left lumbar lymph trunks.   (   )
  d   receives lymph (chyle) from the abdominal
        alimentary tract.   (   )

  e   receives all the lymph from the anterior abdominal
        wall.   (   )

135   The sacral part of the lumbosacral plexus:
  a   is formed by the ventral rami of the 4th and 5th
        lumbar nerves and the upper four sacral nerves.   (   )
  b   lies on iliacus muscle.   (   )

  c   gives branches to the gluteal muscles.   (   )
  d   gives branches to supply the skin of the buttock
        and the perineum.   (   )

  e   supplies the coccygeal plexus.   (   )

136   The coeliac plexus:
  a   is formed of two interconnecting coeliac ganglia.   (   )
  b   receives branches from both vagal trunks.   (   )

  c   gives branches which end in the suprarenal medulla. (   )

  d   supplies branches to the alimentary tract and
        urogenital tract.   (   )

  e   conveys visceral pain fibres.   (   )

a F— It leads directly into the thoracic duct as it passes through
b T   the diaphragm between its right crus and the aorta.

c T— The lumbar lymph trunks are formed by the efferents of
d T   the para-aortic nodes; the intestinal lymph trunk is formed
        by the efferents of the pre-aortic lymph nodes. All drain
        into the cisterna chyli.
e F— Though the lower half drains into inguinal nodes, that from
        the upper part drains to axillary nodes and thence to the
        thoracic duct.

a T

b F— It lies in front of the sacrum on the surface of piriformis
        deep to the pelvic fascia.
c T— The superior and inferior gluteal nerves.
d T— The perforating cutaneous nerve supplies the skin of the
        medial part of the buttock and the perineal branch of the
        4th sacral nerve supplies the perianal skin. The sciatic and
        obturator nerves also arise from the sacral plexus.
e F— This is formed of the 4th and 5th sacral nerves. It lies on
        coccygeus and supplies the skin over the coccyx.

a T— Which lie on each side of the origin of the coeliac artery.
b T— It is a plexus of both parasympathetic and sympathetic
        nerves receiving branches from the thoracic sympathetic
        trunk via the greater, lesser and least splanchnic nerves
        and parasympathetic branches from the anterior and
        posterior vagal trunks.
c T— Presynaptic fibres from the sympathetic trunks pass
        through the plexus and supply the suprarenal medulla
        directly.
d T— Postsynaptic fibres pass with the aorta and its branches
        and supply the upper part of the alimentary tract, the
        kidneys and gonads.
e T— Afferent pain fibres from the viscera are conveyed by
        parasympathetic fibres through this plexus.

VI The Upper Limb

137 **The clavicle:**
   a has no medullary cavity.   ( )

   b is convex anteriorly in the medial two-thirds. ( )
   c laterally gives attachment to trapezius. ( )

   d stabilises the shoulder joint. ( )

   e articulates laterally with the coracoid process of the scapula. ( )

138 **The scapula has a:**
   a palpable inferior angle which overlies the seventh rib. ( )

   b lateral border giving rise to the serratus anterior muscle. ( )
   c costal surface divided by a projecting spine into supraspinous and infraspinous fossae. ( )
   d coracoid process giving attachment to the biceps muscle. ( )

   e glenoid cavity, below which the long head of the triceps muscle is attached. ( )

139 **In the humerus the:**
   a subscapularis muscle is attached to the greater tuberosity. ( )
   b greater tuberosity is separated from the lesser tuberosity by the intertubercular groove. ( )
   c upper end has a V-shaped tuberosity for the attachment of the deltoid muscle. ( )
   d olecranon fossa gives attachment to the medial head of the triceps muscle. ( )

   e axillary nerve lies medial to the anatomical neck. ( )

a T— Though a long bone, it is also atypical in its largely membranous development.

b T— The lateral third is concave anteriorly.

c T— Trapezius gains attachment to the posterior aspect of its lateral third.

d F— Its important functions are those of support to the upper limb and as an 'outrigger' which thrusts the scapula away from the chest wall, thus increasing the range of movement at the shoulder joint.

e F— The flattened lateral end articulates with the medial side of the acromion. Strong ligaments joining the clavicle to the coracoid process act as a fulcrum for movement.

a T— The scapula covers the posterolateral aspect of the chest wall over the 2nd to the 7th ribs and its subcutaneous inferior angle is an important surface landmark.

b F— The muscle arises from the dorsal surface of the medial border.

c F— The costal surface is concave and has no spine. The dorsal surface is divided in this way by a subcutaneous spine.

d T— Biceps is attached to the scapula by two heads; the short head to the coracoid process and the long head to a tubercle above the glenoid cavity.

e T— The other two heads are attached to the humerus, bordering the radial groove.

a F— The muscle is attached to the lesser tuberosity.

b T— The groove houses the long tendon of the biceps.

c F— The deltoid is attached halfway down the lateral surface of the body of the humerus.

d F— The fossa is for the olecranon process of the ulnar, the muscle gains attachment to the posterior aspect of the humerus below the radial groove.

e F— The nerve lies medial to the surgical neck and is susceptible to injury in fractures of the surgical neck or dislocation of the shoulder joint.

140 **The sternoclavicular joint:**
a   is a synovial joint.   (   )
b   is of the ellipsoid variety.   (   )

c   has joint surfaces lined by fibrocartilage.   (   )
d   owes most of its stability to its capsular ligaments.   (   )

e   lies anterior to the aortic arch.   (   )

141 **The acromioclavicular joint:**
a   is not a synovial joint.   (   )
b   typically contains a disc of hyaline cartilage.   (   )
c   gains its stability from its capsular ligament.   (   )
d   possesses no accessory ligaments.   (   )

e   lies in close proximity to the brachial plexus.   (   )

142 **The shoulder joint:**
a   has a scapular articular surface less than one-third
    that of the humeral head.   (   )

b   is surrounded by a tight capsular ligament.   (   )

c   usually communicates superiorly with the
    subacromial bursa.   (   )
d   depends for most of its stability on the capsular
    and accessory ligaments.   (   )

e   is closely related inferiorly to the axillary nerve.   (   )

a   **T**— It has a small range of movement.
b   **F**— It is a ball and socket joint capable of elevation,
        depression, forward and backward movement in a
        horizontal plane, circumduction and axial rotation.
c   **T**— Its joint surfaces are lined by fibrocartilage and a
d   **F**   fibrocartilaginous disc completely divides the joint into
        medial and lateral compartments. Stability of the joint is
        maintained largely by the intra-articular disc and accessory
        joint ligaments, particularly the costoclavicular.
e   **F**— Its immediate posterior relation is the origin of the
        brachiocephalic vein.

a   **F**— It is a synovial joint of the plane variety.
b   **F**— A disc is sometimes found but is rarely complete.
c   **F**— The capsule is relatively weak and the joint owes its
d   **F**   stability to its two accessory ligaments, particularly the
        strong coracoclavicular ligament.
e   **F**— The joint lies subcutaneously and overlies the
        supraspinatus muscle.

a   **T**— Even though the scapular articular surface is extended by
        the ring of fibrocartilage, the glenoidal labrum, around its
        margin.
b   **F**— The capsule is lax, particularly inferiorly, and allows for the
        wide range of movement at this joint.
c   **F**— The subscapular bursa communicates with the joint.

d   **F**— The lax capsule is of little support and the shallow glenoid
        cavity affords almost none. The short articular (cuff)
        muscles, subscapularis, supraspinatus, infraspinatus and
        teres minor by their close proximity are the major
        stabilising factors.
e   **T**— Which is thus easily damaged in downward dislocation at
        the joint.

143   The pectoralis major muscle:

a   has a clavicular attachment to the middle third
of the anterior surface of the clavicle.   (   )

b   has a costal attachment to the 3rd, 4th, and
5th ribs, near the costochondral junctions.   (   )

c   has an attachment to the upper part of the external
oblique aponeurosis.   (   )

d   is attached to the lateral lip of the lower part
of the intertubercular groove.   (   )

e   receives its nerve supply from the lateral and
posterior cords of the brachial plexus.   (   )

144   The serratus anterior muscle:

a   gains attachment to all of the ribs.   (   )

b   gains attachment to the medial border of the
scapula.   (   )

c   is attached by a group of accessory fibres to the
medial bicipital groove.   (   )

d   is an accessory muscle of respiration.   (   )

e   is supplied by the thoracodorsal branch of the
posterior cord of the brachial plexus.   (   )

145   Trapezius is attached to the:

a   occipital bone.   (   )
b   clavicle.   (   )
c   thoracic vertebra.   (   )
d   iliac crest.   (   )
e   acromion.   (   )

a **F**— The clavicular attachment is to the medial third of the anterior surface.
b **F**— This is the costal attachment of pectoralis minor.

c **T**— The sternocostal head is also attached to the anterior surface of the sternum and the upper six costal cartilages.
d **T**— The clavicular head lies anterior to the sternocostal head at this attachment.
e **F**— The lateral and medial pectoral nerves are branches of the lateral and medial cords of the plexus.

a **F**— It arises from near the angles of the upper eight ribs and, passing forwards over the medial wall of the axilla, is attached to the medial border and inferior angle of the
b **T** scapula.

c **T**

d **T**— When the scapula is fixed, contraction will lift the upper ribs upwards and downwards.
e **F**— It is supplied by the long thoracic nerve which arises from the ventral rami of the 5th, 6th and 7th cervical nerves. The thoracodorsal nerve supplies the latissimus dorsi muscle.

a **T**— Medially it is attached to the occipital bone, the
b **T** ligamentum nuchae and the thoracic spines, and laterally
c **T** to the clavicle, acromion and spine of the scapula.
d **F**
e **T**

146   The latissimus dorsi muscle:

a   is attached to the lower six thoracic vertebrae.   (   )
b   is attached to the lumbar and sacral vertebral spines. (   )
c   has no attachment to the chest wall.   (   )

d   is attached to the inferior angle of the scapula.   (   )
e   is a powerful flexor of the humerus at the shoulder
     joint.   (   )

147   The deltoid muscle:

a   is a unipennate muscle.   (   )

b   overlies the subacromial bursa.   (   )
c   is proximally attached to the clavicle, acromion
     and scapular spine.   (   )

d   is distally attached to anterior upper third of the
     humerus.   (   )
e   is supplied by the radial nerve.   (   )

148   The short articular (cuff) muscles of the shoulder joint:

a   comprise subscapularis, supraspinatus,
     infraspinatus and teres major.   (   )

b   provide the greatest stabilising forces at the
     shoulder joint.   (   )
c   provide maximal support to the inferior aspect
     of the shoulder joint.   (   )
d   are all attached to the greater tuberosity of
     the humerus.   (   )
e   are all supplied by branches of the posterior cord
     of the brachial plexus.   (   )

a **T**— It is attached to the spines and supraspinous ligaments of
b **T**   these vertebrae and also by the thoracolumbar fascia to
c **F**   the lumbar and sacral spines. It is also attached to the
          lowest four ribs where it interdigitates with external
          oblique.
d **T**— On the dorsal aspect.
e **F**— It is a powerful extensor of the humerus. With the arm
          raised above the head and fixed it will pull the trunk
          upwards.

a **F**— It is multipennate. Strong fibrous septa intersect the
          muscle and give attachment to its fibres.
b **T**— Which separates it from the short articular (cuff) muscles.
c **T**— From this wide proximal attachment the muscle narrows
          distally to be attached to the V-shaped deltoid tuberosity
          on the lateral aspect of the humerus.
d **F**

e **F**— It is supplied by the axillary nerve. It can act as an
          abductor, flexor or extensor at the shoulder joint.

a **F**— The three first named muscles and teres minor lie closely
          related to the capsule of the shoulder joint (cuff muscles).
          Teres major is separated from it by a space transmitting
          the axillary nerve.
b **T**— Their tendons blend intimately with the capsule of the
          joint and strengthen it considerably.
c **F**— This is the area of least support; shoulder dislocation is
          commonest in this direction.
d **F**— Subscapularis is attached to the lesser tuberosity, the other
          three cuff muscles to the greater.
e **F**— Both supraspinatus and infraspinatus are supplied by the
          suprascapular nerve, a branch of the upper trunk of the
          brachial plexus. The other muscles are innervated from the
          posterior cord of the plexus.

149   The axilla has:

a   an apex which communicates with the posterior
triangle of neck.   (   )

b   an apex bounded in part by the medial third of the
clavicle.   (   )

c   a narrow lateral wall.   (   )

d   a posterior wall formed by serratus anterior.   (   )

e   an anterior wall containing the clavipectoral fascia.   (   )

150   The axillary artery:

a   extends to the lower border of teres major.   (   )

b   lies posterior to pectoralis minor.   (   )

c   lies lateral to the medial cord of the brachial plexus.   (   )

d   lies medial to the axillary vein.   (   )

e   lies lateral to the short head of biceps.   (   )

151   The scapular anastomosis:

a   provides collateral circulation between the
subclavian and brachial arteries.   (   )

b   lies closely related to the neck of the humerus.   (   )

c   receives contributions from branches of the
thyrocervical trunk.   (   )

d   receives contributions from the subscapular artery.   (   )

e   receives contributions from the lateral thoracic
artery.   (   )

a **T**— The apex is bounded by the superior border of the scapula, the outer border of the 1st rib and the middle
b **F** 3rd of the clavicle.

c **T**— Its lateral wall is formed by the narrow intertubercular groove of the humerus to which latissimus dorsi and teres major of the posterior axillary wall and pectoralis major of the anterior wall are attached.
d **F**— Serratus anterior, lying in the thoracic wall, forms the medial axillary boundary. The posterior wall is formed by subscapularis, latissimus dorsi and teres major.
e **T**— The fascia splits around pectoralis minor and subclavius; pectoralis major is situated anterior to these structures.

a **T**— And becomes the brachial artery.
b **T**— The artery in the axilla is surrounded by the cords and branches of the brachial plexus behind pectoralis minor.
c **T**— The cords are named because of their relationship to the artery.
d **F**— The axillary vein lies medial to the artery.
e **F**— The short head of biceps and coracobrachialis lie lateral to the artery.

a **T**— This opens up when the upper part of the axillary artery is blocked.
b **F**— It lies, as its name implies, around the scapula.
c **T**— It is formed by connections between the suprascapular artery and deep branch of the transverse cervical
d **T** proximally and by the subscapular artery and its circumflex branch distally.
e **F**— This artery is too far anterior.

152 The brachial plexus:
  a is usually formed by the ventral rami of the lower
     four cervical and first thoracic nerves.   (   )
  b has its roots situated posterior to the scalenus
     anterior muscle.   (   )
  c contains three trunks which lie in the neck.   (   )
  d contains three cords which lie in the neck.   (   )
  e has a posterior cord which receives contributions
     from all five roots of the plexus.   (   )

153 The brachial plexus:
  a originates from roots which emerge in front of
     scalenus anterior.   (   )
  b forms cords which are closely related to the axillary
     artery.   (   )
  c gives branches from its lateral cord to the
     extensor muscles of the upper limb.   (   )
  d supplies the latissimus dorsi muscle from its
     medial cord.   (   )
  e supplies the pectoralis major muscle.   (   )

154 The biceps muscle:
  a is attached to the scapula.   (   )
  b has an intra-articular tendon.   (   )
  c is attached to the humerus.   (   )
  d has an aponeurosis passing to the dorsal surface
     of the radius.   (   )
  e is a powerful pronator of the forearm.   (   )

a **T**— These ventral rami form the five roots of the plexus and unite to form three trunks in the posterior triangle of the

b **T** neck. The upper two roots form the upper trunk, the middle root continues as the middle trunk and the lower

c **T** two form the lower trunk.

d **F**— The cords are formed in the apex of the axilla behind the

e **T** middle third of the clavicle by each trunk dividing into anterior and posterior divisions which then reunite. The posterior cord is formed from the posterior divisions of all three trunks.

a **F**— The ventral rami which form its roots emerge behind the scalenus anterior muscle, between it and scalenus medius muscle.

b **T**— The cords are named according to their arrangement around the middle part of this artery.

c **F**— All the extensor muscles of the upper limb are supplied by the posterior cord.

d **F**— Latissimus dorsi is supplied by the thoracodorsal nerve which arises from the posterior cord.

e **T**— Through the medial and lateral pectoral nerves.

a **T**— By two heads, the short to the coracoid process and the long to the supraglenoid tubercle.

b **T**— The tendon of the long head lies in the shoulder joint surrounded by a synovial sheath in the intertubercular groove.

c **F**— Its distal attachment is to the radial tuberosity and by the

d **F** bicipital aponeurosis to the deep fascia of the medial side of the forearm.

e **F**— It is a powerful spinator of the forearm and flexor at the elbow and shoulder joints.

155 **The triceps muscle:**
  a is attached to the infraglenoid tubercle of the
      scapula.   (   )
  b is attached to the borders of the radial groove of
      the humerus.   (   )
  c is attached to the ulnar olecranon.   (   )
  d acts mainly at the shoulder joint.   (   )
  e is supplied by the median nerve.   (   )

156 **The brachial artery:**
  a lies medial to biceps.   (   )
  b can be palpated over most of its course.   (   )
  c ends at the lower border of teres major by
      dividing into radial and ulnar arteries.   (   )
  d is crossed by the median cubital vein.   (   )
  e is crossed by the median nerve.   (   )

157 **The musculocutaneous nerve:**
  a is a terminal branch of the posterior cord of the
      brachial plexus.   (   )
  b descends in the arm between biceps and brachialis. (   )
  c supplies coracobrachialis.   (   )
  d supplies cutaneous branches to the radial side of
      the forearm.   (   )
  e ends up as the medial cutaneous nerve of the
      forearm.   (   )

158 **The radial nerve:**
  a is a terminal branch of the posterior cord of the
      brachial plexus.   (   )
  b lies posterior to the humerus between the medial
      and lateral heads of triceps.   (   )
  c passes anterior to the elbow joint.   (   )
  d supplies the skin of the medial and anterior aspect
      of the forearm.   (   )
  e supplies the supinator muscle.   (   )

a **T**— Proximally it is attached by three heads to **(a)** and **(b)**, and the lower part of the posterior aspect of the humerus
b **T** below the radial groove.

c **T**— Distally all its fibres are attached by a strong tendon to the olecranon.
d **F**— It is mainly an extensor at the elbow joint.
e **F**— It is supplied by the radial nerve.

a **T**— Throughout its course it lies medial to biceps covered only
b **T** by skin and fascia.
c **F**— It usually ends in the cubital fossa by dividing into radial and ulnar arteries.
d **T**— At its termination, but separated by the bicipital aponeurosis from the vein.
e **T**— The nerve accompanies the artery crossing anteriorly from lateral to medial in the mid upper arm.

a **F**— It is a terminal branch of the lateral cord of the brachial plexus.
b **T**— It then emerges lateral to these muscles and pierces the deep fascia in front of the elbow.
c **T**— It gives muscular branches to this muscle, biceps and brachialis.
d **T**— It ends as the lateral cutaneous nerve of the forearm and supplies both surfaces of the radial side of the forearm.
e **F**

a **T**— Arising as a branch of the posterior cord it descends obliquely through the posterior compartment between
b **T** these two heads of triceps. It then pierces the lateral intermuscular septum and lies anterior to the lateral epicondyle.
c **T**— Lying between brachialis medially and brachioradialis laterally.
d **F**— It supplies branches to triceps, brachioradialis and extensor carpi radialis longus, and to the skin of the lateral and posterior aspects of the arm and forearm by the lower lateral cutaneous nerve of arm and the posterior cutaneous nerve of forearm.
e **F**— This is supplied by the posterior interosseous nerve.

159 **The median nerve:**
  a   arises in the neck from the brachial plexus.   (   )

  b   lies lateral to the axillary artery.   (   )
  c   crosses the brachial artery.   (   )

  d   has no muscular branches in the arm.   (   )
  e   lies anterior to the biceps.   (   )

160 **The ulnar nerve:**
  a   is a terminal branch of the medial cord of the
       brachial plexus.   (   )
  b   descends to the elbow in the anterior compartment
       of the arm.   (   )
  c   descends with the long hand of the triceps.   (   )

  d   lies behind the medial epicondyle.   (   )
  e   supplies branches to coracobrachialis.   (   )

161 **The radius:**
  a   possesses a head which articulates with the
       scaphoid and lunate.   (   )
  b   gives attachment to the biceps.   (   )
  c   gives attachment to the triceps tendon.   (   )

  d   possesses a palpable styloid process.   (   )

  e   is attached to the ulna throughout the length of
       its interosseous border.   (   )

162 **The ulna:**
  a   gives attachment to the brachialis muscle.   (   )

  b   possesses a styloid process on the anteromedial
       surface of its lower end.   (   )
  c   articulates at its lower end with an articular disc.   (   )

  d   is palpable over the whole length of its posterior
       border.   (   )
  e   is related inferiorly to the extensor carpi radialis
       muscle.   (   )

a **F**— It is formed in the axilla from the medial and lateral cords of the brachial plexus.
b **T**
c **T**— Lying at first on its lateral side and then crosses the artery halfway down the arm to gain its medial side.
d **T**
e **F**— It lies medial to biceps and anterior to brachialis and triceps.

a **T**— It runs initially in the anterior compartment on the medial side of the upper arm then pierces the medial
b **F** intermuscular septum and continues in the posterior compartment.
c **F**— After piercing the medial intermuscular septum it descends between the septum and the medial head of triceps.
d **T**— At this point it is subcutaneous.
e **F**— It has no branches in the upper arm. Coracobrachialis is supplied by the musculocutaneous nerve.

a **F**— The head articulates with the capitulum of the humerus and the radial notch of the ulna.
b **T**— At the radial tuberosity.
c **F**— Triceps is attached to the olecranon of the ulna. Biceps is attached to the radial tuberosity of the radius.
d **T**— The styloid process, the lower end of the radius, and the radial head are all palpable.
e **T**— The fibrous interosseous membrane connects the adjacent interosseous borders of the radius and ulna.

a **T**— Brachialis is attached to the coronoid process of the upper end of the ulna.
b **F**— The small conical styloid process lies on the posteromedial side of the head of the ulna.
c **T**— The lower end, or head, articulates both with the lower end of the radius and with the articular disc which takes origin from the base of the ulnar styloid process.
d **T**— Together with the posterior part of the olecranon, the head and the styloid process.
e **F**— The extensor carpi ulnaris lies in the groove between the head and the styloid process.

163 The cubital fossa:
a is a quadrilateral space situated in front of the elbow joint. (   )

b is floored by the bicipital aponeurosis. (   )

c contains the median nerve. (   )
d contains the radial nerve. (   )

e is crossed by the medial cutaneous nerve of the forearm. (   )

164 The elbow joint:
a is lined by synovial membrane which is continuous with that of the superior radio-ulnar joint. (   )
b is strengthened by radial and ulnar collateral ligaments. (   )

c is strengthened by an ulnar collateral ligament. (   )

d owes most of its stability to the close proximity of brachialis and triceps. (   )
e is supplied by the posterior interosseous nerve. (   )

165 The proximal radio-ulnar joint:
a is of the condyloid variety. (   )
b occurs between the head of the radius and the radial notch of the ulna. (   )
c is stabilised mainly by the surrounding capsular ligament of the elbow joint. (   )

d owes its stability mainly to the annular ligament. (   )

e is separated from the elbow joint by a fibrocartilaginous disc. (   )

a **F**— It is a triangular fossa bounded proximally by a line joining the two epicondyles of the humerus and distally by the pronator teres medially and the brachioradialis laterally.

b **F**— The bicipital aponeurosis is an extension from biceps tendon, and lies in the roof of the fossa. It gains attachment to the deep fascia over the medial side of the forearm and to the posterior border of the ulna.

c **T**— The median nerve is the most medial of the structures

d **T** passing through the fossa. The brachial artery, the prominent biceps tendon, and the radial and posterior interosseous nerves lie laterally in this order.

e **T**— It is also crossed by lateral cutaneous branches and cubital veins.

a **T**— The elbow joint is of the hinge variety.

b **T**— The radial collateral is a strong triangular ligament attached to the lateral epicondyle proximally and the annular ligament distally.

c **T**— The ulnar collateral radiates from the medial epicondyle proximally to the coronoid process and the olecranon.

d **F**— The most important factors in stabilising the joint are the shape of the bones and strong capsule.

e **T**— It is also supplied by branches of the radial, median, ulnar and musculocutaneous nerves.

a **F**— It is a synovial joint of the pivot variety.

b **T**— The radial notch and the annular ligament from an osseofascial ring which encircles the head of the radius.

c **F**— This capsular ligament is attached to the upper border of the annular ligament and does little to increase the stability of the radio-ulnar joint.

d **T**— This is narrower below than above and thus holds firmly the head of the adult radius. (Dislocation is more common in the child as the head of the radius has a less conical shape.)

e **F**— The proximal end of the radius articulates directly with the trochlea of the humerus.

166   The distal radio-ulnar joint:

a   is a synovial joint of the pivot variety.   (   )

b   owes its stability mainly to the capsular ligament.   (   )

c   with the superior radio-ulnar joint allows both
    supination and pronation to occur.   (   )

d   pronation is a powerful movement because of the
    action of biceps.   (   )

e   is separated from the wrist joint by a
    fibrocartilaginous disc.   (   )

167   The interosseous membrane in the forearm:

a   connects the radius and ulna.   (   )

b   gives attachment to both flexor and extensor
    muscles.   (   )

c   has fibres directed downwards and laterally.   (   )

d   has little intrinsic strength.   (   )

e   is closely related to the termination of the brachial
    artery.   (   )

168   The anterior superficial group of forearm muscles:

a   all arise from the anterior surface of the lateral
    epicondyle of the humerus.   (   )

b   includes pronator teres.   (   )

c   are all supplied by branches of the median nerve.   (   )

d   may effect flexion at the elbow.   (   )

e   has attachment to the anterior surface of both the
    radius and the ulna.   (   )

a **T**— The head of the ulna articulates with the ulnar notch on the radius.

b **F**— This is usually weak. Stability is dependent on the articular disc which is attached to the styloid process of the ulna and the medial edge of the distal articular surface of the radius.

c **T**— These movements occur about an axis joining the centre of the radial head and the ulnar styloid process.

d **F**— Biceps is a supinator muscle, and in most people this is the stronger movement.

e **T**— The disc separates the two joint cavities.

a **T**— It is attached to the adjacent interosseous borders of these two bones.

b **T**— Both the deep flexor and deep extensor muscles gain attachment to it.

c **F**— Its fibres are directed downwards and medially.

d **F**— It is a strong membrane and thus a force transmitted upwards through the hand, as in punching, is transmitted to the elbow joint via the ulna as well as the head of the radius.

e **F**— But the anterior and posterior interosseous arteries are closely related.

a **F**— They have a common origin from the anterior surface of the medial epicondyle of the humerus.

b **T**— From radial to ulnar side, the muscles are pronator teres, flexor carpi radialis, palmaris longus, flexor digitorum superficialis and flexor carpi ulnaris.

c **F**— Flexor carpi ulnaris is supplied by the ulnar nerve whilst all others are supplied by the median nerve.

d **T**— Since all these muscles cross the elbow joint they produce weak elbow flexion in addition to their other actions in the forearm and hand.

e **T**— The pronator teres and the flexor digitorum superficialis are attached to both bones. The flexor carpi ulnaris is attached to the posterior subcutaneous border of the ulna.

169   The flexor digitorum superficialis muscle:
a   arises from both radius and ulna.   (   )

b   lies deep to the median nerve.   (   )

c   has four tendons in the hand which encircle
    the corresponding tendons of flexor digitorum
    profundus in the fingers.   (   )
d   is attached distally to the base of the distal phalanx
    of the fingers.   (   )
e   has its middle and ring finger tendons placed
    anterior to those of the index and little, when deep
    to the flexor retinaculum.   (   )

170   The ulnar bursa:
a   invests all but one of the tendons of the superficial
    and deep flexors in the forearm.   (   )
b   begins deep to the flexor retinaculum.   (   )
c   extends into the digital synovial sheaths around
    the tendons of all fingers.   (   )
d   extends into the digital synovial sheath around
    the tendon of the little finger.   (   )

e   does not usually communicate with the radial bursa. (   )

171   The brachioradialis muscle is:
a   attached proximally to the lower third of the
    lateral supracondylar ridge of the humerus.   (   )

b   attached distally to the dorsal aspect of the base
    of the 3rd metacarpal bone.   (   )

c   a flexor of the elbow.   (   )
d   a pronator of the forearm.   (   )

e   supplied by the posterior interosseous nerve.   (   )

a **T**— It arises from the common flexor origin, the medial aspect of the coronoid process of the ulna, the anterior oblique line of the radius and a tendinous arch which lies between them.

b **F**— The median nerve passes deep to the tendinous arch and passes distally deep to the muscle.

c **T**— The four tendons diverge in the palm, one passing to each finger. Over the proximal phalanx the tendon splits, and passing dorsally, encircles the corresponding tendon of

d **F** flexor digitorum profundus. It then gains attachment to the sides of the middle phalanx.

e **T**— And the former are more likely to be damaged in lacerations of the front of the wrist.

a **T**— The common synovial sheath, the ulnar bursa, lies deep to the flexor retinaculum. It commences 2–3 cm above the

b **F** wrist and ends in the middle of the palm, except for a

c **F** medial prolongation which extends around the tendons of the little finger as far as the distal phalanx. The tendons in

d **T** the remaining fingers have separate digital synovial sheaths deep to the fibrous flexor sheaths. A part of these tendons in the palm has no synovial sheath.

e **T**— The radial bursa invests the tendon of flexor pollicis longus from above the wrist to the terminal phalanx.

a **F**— This is the attachment of the extensor carpi radialis longus. The brachioradialis is attached to the upper two-thirds of the ridge.

b **F**— This is the attachment of the extensor carpi radialis brevis. The brachioradialis is attached to the lateral aspect of the lower end of the radius.

c **T**— Most strongly in the mid-prone position.

d **T**— It may also supinate the forearm, depending on the position of the hand.

e **F**— This nerve supplies the forearm muscles attached to the common extensor origin. The brachioradialis and extensor radialis longus are supplied by the radial nerve.

172 **The extensor digitorum muscle:**

  a is attached proximally to the anterior aspect of the lateral epicondyle of the humerus. ( )

  b covers the proximal phalanges by dorsal expansions of its four tendons. ( )

  c is attached to the bases of the proximal phalanges of the four fingers. ( )

  d has small tendinous slips to the dorsal expansion from the lumbrical and interosseous muscles. ( )

  e is supplied by the radial nerve. ( )

173 **The supinator muscle:**

  a forms part of the floor of the cubital fossa. ( )

  b is attached to the medial epicondyle of the humerus. ( )

  c is attached to the proximal end of the ulna. ( )

  d is attached to the proximal end of the radius. ( )

  e is supplied by the ulnar nerve. ( )

174 **The abductor pollicis longus muscle:**

  a is attached to the interosseous membrane. ( )

  b tendon passes deep to both extensor carpi radialis longus and brevis. ( )

  c is attached to the base of the proximal phalanx of the thumb. ( )

  d produces extension at the thumb's carpometacarpal joint. ( )

  e possesses a separate synovial sheath around its tendon. ( )

a **T**— This is the common extensor origin.

b **T**— It divides just above the wrist into four tendons. As each tendon passes a metacarpophalangeal joint it forms a

c **F** triangular dorsal expansion covering the proximal phalanx. At the apex of the expansion (distally) the tendon reforms and then divides into three slips; the middle is attached to the base of the middle phalanx, the outer two slips pass distally and gain attachment to the base of the terminal phalanx.

d **T**— These small tendons influence movements at the metacarpophalangeal and interphalangeal joints.

e **F**— The muscle is supplied by the posterior interosseous nerve.

a **T**— It obliquely crosses the apex of the cubital fossa after emerging from deep to brachioradialis.

b **F**— It is attached below the common extensor origin on the lateral epicondyle.

c **T**— It is attached to the supinator crest of the ulna and the area in front of the crest.

d **T**— Ulnar and humeral heads are attached to the anterior surface of the proximal third of the radius.

e **F**— It is supplied by the posterior interosseous branch of the radial nerve.

a **T**— It is attached to the posterior surface of the ulna and radius and the intervening interosseous membrane.

b **F**— The tendon is superficial to both carpal extensors.

c **F**— Its tendon is attached to the radial side of the base of the first metacarpal.

d **T**— It produces abduction and extension at this joint.

e **T**— As it lies in the most lateral compartment of the extensor retinaculum.

175 The extensor pollicis longus muscle:
a is attached to the interosseous membrane. ( )

b passes deep to the extensor retinaculum. ( )
c has a synovial sheath common with that of
extensor indicis. ( )
d is attached to the base of the distal phalanx of
the thumb. ( )
e is supplied by the radial nerve. ( )

176 The anatomical snuff box:
a is bounded anteriorly by the tendons of extensor
pollicis longus and brevis. ( )
b is bounded posteriorly by the tendon of abductor
pollicis longus. ( )
c overlies the scaphoid and trapezium. ( )

d contains the tendons of extensors carpi radialis
longus and brevis on its floor. ( )
e contains the basilic vein in its roof. ( )

177 The radial artery:
a passes superficial to brachioradialis. ( )

b lies lateral to the radial nerve in the forearm. ( )
c lies on the anterior surface of the lower end of
the radius. ( )
d passes between the two heads of the first
dorsal interosseous muscle. ( )

e terminates in the superficial palmar arch. ( )

a **T**— It is attached to the posterior surface of the ulna and adjacent interosseous membrane distal to abductor pollicis longus.

b **T**— Its tendon descends deep to the extensor retinaculum,

c **F** grooving the medial side of the dorsal tubercle of the radius. It has its own synovial sheath.

d **T**— It extends the terminal phalanx.

e **F**— It is supplied by the posterior interosseous nerve.

a **F**— Its boundaries are — anteriorly, the tendons of abductor pollicis longus and extensor pollicis brevis, and posteriorly,

b **F** the tendon of extensor pollicis longus.

c **T**— Together with the radial styloid process, the wrist joint and the base of the first metacarpal bone.

d **T**— Together with the radial artery.

e **F**— The cephalic vein overlies the snuff box.

a **F**— It lies deep to brachioradialis in the early part of its course, and medial to the radial nerve.

b **F**— The radial nerve is on its lateral side.

c **T**— It is subcutaneous here and the pulse can usually be felt.

d **T**— It leaves the dorsum of the hand by passing between the two heads of this muscle and then the two heads of the adductor pollicis muscle.

e **F**— It ends in the deep palmar arch.

178 The ulnar artery:
a gives rise to the anterior interosseous artery. ( )
b lies deep to the muscles attached to the common flexor origin. ( )
c lies medial to the ulnar nerve. ( )
d crosses superficial to the flexor retinaculum. ( )
e supplies the deep extensor muscles of the forearm. ( )

179 The radial nerve, in the forearm and hand:
a lies deep to brachioradialis. ( )
b reaches the dorsum of the hand by passing across the lower end of the radius. ( )
c passes deep to the extensor retinaculum. ( )
d supplies the skin on the lateral aspect of the dorsum of the hand and the dorsum of the lateral four digits. ( )
e has no muscular branches. ( )

180 The posterior interosseous nerve:
a arises at the level of the elbow joint. ( )
b lies in close relationship with the upper end of the ulna. ( )
c passes through the supinator muscle. ( )
d supplies all the extensor muscles. ( )
e supplies the elbow and wrist joints. ( )

a **F**— This is a branch of the common interosseous artery.
b **T**— Lying deep to these muscles it descends on flexor digitorum profundus with the ulnar nerve on its medial side.
c **F**— It is lateral to the nerve.
d **T**— Ending along the lateral side of the pisiform.
e **T**— It gives nutrient arteries to the radius and ulna, and by its posterior interosseous branch it supplies the deep extensor muscles in the forearm.

a **T**— It passes down the arm with the radial artery on its medial side throughout most of its length.
b **T**

c **F**— It passes superficial to the structure.
d **F**— It supplies the dorsum of the hand but usually only the lateral two and a half digits as far as the distal interphalangeal joints.
e **F**— Its posterior interosseous branch supplies most of the extensor muscles of the forearm.

a **T**— It arises from the radial nerve under cover of
b **F**   brachioradialis at the level of the elbow joint and pierces supinator. It then curves laterally around the neck of the radius.
c **T**— It passes between the humeral and ulnar heads of the muscle.
d **F**— It supplies all but extensor carpi radialis longus which is supplied by the radial nerve directly. Injury to the nerve produces wrist drop.
e **T**— Also the intercarpal joints.

181 **The median nerve in the forearm:**
  a passes between the heads of the pronator teres. ( )

  b lies deep to flexor digitorum superficialis. ( )

  c passes deep to the flexor retinaculum. ( )
  d is a posterior relation of palmaris longus. ( )

  e supplies all the forearm flexor muscles. ( )

182 **The median nerve in the hand:**
  a supplies all the short muscles of the thumb. ( )
  b supplies all the lumbrical muscles. ( )

  c lies superficial to the flexor retinaculum. ( )
  d terminates just distal to the flexor retinaculum. ( )

  e supplies the palmar surface of the lateral three
  and a half digits. ( )

183 **The ulnar nerve:**
  a is an anterior relation of the medial epicondyle
  of the humerus. ( )
  b enters the forearm between the heads of the
  pronator teres. ( )
  c lies on flexor digitorum profundus in the forearm. ( )
  d supplies the ulnar half of the flexor digitorum
  sublimus. ( )
  e supplies adductor pollicis. ( )

184 **The ulnar nerve in the hand:**
  a passes into the hand deep to the flexor retinaculum. ( )
  b supplies the dorsal surface of the medial two and
  a half fingers. ( )
  c supplies all the interossei. ( )
  d supplies abductor pollicis brevis. ( )

  e supplies adductor pollicis. ( )

a   T— As it passes between the two heads of pronator teres it lies
       superficial to the ulnar artery, being separated from it by
       the deep head of the muscle.
b   T— The nerve adheres to its deep surface but emerges lateral
       to its tendons above the wrist.
c   T— Where it lies between the tendons of flexor carpi radialis
d   T   laterally and flexor superficialis medially. It lies deep to the
       palmaris longus tendon when this muscle is present.
e   F— Flexor carpi ulnaris and the medial part of the flexor digitorum
       profundus are supplied by the ulnar nerve. The median nerve
       supplies the others.

a   F— Adductor pollicis is supplied by the ulnar nerve.
b   F— Only the lateral two lumbrical muscles are supplied by the
       median nerve.
c   F— It passes deep to the flexor retinaculum in company with
d   T   the superficial and deep flexor tendons where it may
       become compressed.
e   T— By palmar digital nerves which lie anterior to the digital
       arteries. These branches also innervate the nail beds and
       give articular branches to the joints of the fingers. The
       palmar branches supply the lateral two lumbrical muscles.

a   F— It lies posterior to the epicondyle.
b   F— This is the course of the medial nerve. The ulnar nerve lies
       between the heads of flexor carpi ulnaris.
c   T— Deep to the flexor carpi ulnaris.
d   F— In the forearm it supplies flexor carpi ulnaris and the ulnar
       half of flexor digitorum profundus.
e   T— Also the hypothenar, interossei, and 3rd and 4th lumbrical
       muscles.

a   F— It enters the hand superficially, anterior to the flexor retinaculum.
b   T— By a dorsal cutaneous branch which divides into digital branches
       supplying these fingers as far as the distal interphalangeal joints.
c   T— And the 3rd and 4th lumbricals.
d   F— This muscle is supplied by the recurrent branch of the median
       nerve.
e   T— The ulnar nerve supplies the adductor pollicis.

185 **The carpal bones:**
  a are arranged into proximal, middle and distal rows. ( )

  b which form the distal articular surface of the
    wrist joint are the scaphoid, lunate and pisiform. ( )
  c give attachment to the flexor retinaculum. ( )

  d give attachment to the extensor retinaculum. ( )

  e give attachment to the lumbrical muscles. ( )

186 **The metacarpal bone of:**
  a the thumb gives attachment to the lateral
    interossei muscles. ( )
  b the thumb articulates with the trapezium. ( )
  c the thumb gives attachment to flexor pollicis brevis. ( )

  d the index finger articulates with those of the
    thumb and middle fingers. ( )

  e the little finger articulates with the lunate. ( )

187 **The wrist joint:**
  a comprises the lower articular surfaces of the
    radius and ulna and the proximal row of carpal
    bones. ( )
  b usually communicates with the distal radio-ulnar
    joint. ( )
  c owes its stability to the neighbouring tendons. ( )

  d is an ellipsoid joint. ( )

  e contributes the major degree of flexion at the wrist. ( )

a **F**— They are arranged as a proximal row of three bones, the scaphoid, lunate and triquetral; a distal row of four, the trapezium, trapezoid, capitate and hamate; and an anteromedially situated pisiform.

b **F**— This surface comprises from lateral to medial, the scaphoid, lunate and triquetral.

c **T**— The flexor retinaculum extends from the pisiform and hamate bones medially to the scaphoid and trapezium laterally.

d **T**— The extensor retinaculum extends from the distal end of the radius to the medial side of the carpus, i.e. the pisiform, triquetral and hamate.

e **F**— These unite the long digital flexor and extensor tendons.

a **T**— Together with the opponens pollicis and abductor pollicis longus muscles.

b **T**— Its articular surface is saddle-shaped.

c **F**— Flexor pollicis brevis is attached to the flexor retinaculum and the base of the proximal phalanx of the thumb.

d **F**— The 1st metacarpal, unlike the 3rd metacarpal, has no articulation with the index finger; **(b)** and **(d)** increase the mobility of the thumb.

e **F**— The 5th metacarpal articulates with the hamate.

a **F**— The lower end of the radius and the fibrocartilaginous disc overlying the head of the ulna articulate with the proximal row of carpal bones. Only on rare occasions when this disc

b **F** is perforated does the wrist joint communicate with the distal radio-ulnar joint.

c **T**— Together with the capsular and the medial and lateral collateral ligaments which strengthen it. The shapes of the bones contribute minimally.

d **T**— This permits flexion, extension, adduction (ulnar deviation), abduction (radial deviation) and circumduction. No rotation occurs.

e **F**— Wrist movements take place at the radiocarpal (wrist joint), midcarpal and carpometacarpal joints. The midcarpal has particular effect in flexion and abduction.

188   The metacarpophalangeal joints:
a   are synovial joints of the hinge variety.   (   )

b   of the medial four digits are bound together.   (   )

c   may be abducted by the dorsal interossei muscle.   (   )

d   may be adducted by the palmar interossei muscles.   (   )

e   may be flexed by the lumbricals.   (   )

189   The palmar aponeurosis:
a   is strengthened deep fascia.   (   )

b   is firmly attached to the palmar skin.   (   )
c   is continuous proximally with the flexor retinaculum.   (   )
d   distally is continuous with the long flexor tendons.   (   )
e   is attached distally to the deep transverse
ligament of the palm.   (   )

190   The flexor retinaculum:
a   is attached to the lower end of the radius.   (   )
b   is attached to the lower end of the ulna.   (   )
c   is attached to the pisiform bone.   (   )
d   gives origin to the thenar and hypothenar muscles.   (   )
e   overlies all tendons, arteries and nerves
proceeding to the palm.   (   )

191   The palmar muscle spaces:
a   are two in number.   (   )
b   are each deep to the palmar aponeurosis.   (   )
c   are separated by intermuscular septa.   (   )
d   contain the thenar muscles laterally.   (   )
e   contain the lumbrical muscles centrally.   (   )

a   **F**— They are ellipsoid joints, allowing movement in two planes at right angles to each other, and circumduction.

b   **T**— By an extension of the strong palmar thickenings of these joints forming the deep transverse ligaments of the palm.

c   **T**— And by abductor pollicis longus and brevis and abductor digiti minimi in the case of the thumb and little finger respectively.

d   **T**— And by adductor pollicis in the case of the thumb. Thumb movements of abduction and adduction occur at the carpometacarpal joint.

e   **T**— The attachment of these muscles to both long flexor and extensor tendons flex the metacarpophalangeal but extend the interphalangeal joints.

a   **T**— It comprises the strong central, triangular part of the deep fascia.

b   **T**— And its apex is continuous with the flexor retinaculum. Its

c   **T**   base divides distally into four slips which bifurcate around

d   **F**   the long flexor tendons, gaining attachment to the fibrous

e   **T**   flexor digital sheaths and to the deep transverse ligaments of the palm.

a   **F**— It is a thickening of deep fascia gaining attachment to the carpal

b   **F**   bones, medially to the pisiform and hamate, laterally to the

c   **T**   scaphoid and trapezium.

d   **T**

e   **F**— The ulnar artery and nerve and the palmar branches of the median and ulnar nerves all cross it superficially. The median nerve lies deep to it.

a   **F**— There are three palmar muscle spaces separated by two

b   **F**   septa which pass deeply from the lateral and medial margins

c   **T**   of the palmar aponeurosis to the shafts of the 1st and 5th

d   **T**   metacarpal bones. The lateral space containing the thenar

e   **T**   muscles, and the medial, containing the hypothenar muscles, are covered superficially by the deep fascia of the palm. The central space, containing the long flexor tendons and lumbrical muscles, deep and superficial palmar arches and the median and ulnar nerves, is covered by the palmar aponeurosis.

192   The fibrous flexor digital sheaths:
a   are modifications of the deep fascia of the fingers.   (   )
b   are attached to the phalanges.   (   )
c   proximally, are continuous with the palmar
aponeurosis.   (   )

d   overlie the first phalanges only.   (   )

e   enclose the tendons of flexor digitorum profundus
only.   (   )

193   The muscles of the thenar eminence:
a   are all attached to the radial side of the flexor
retinaculum.   (   )
b   are all supplied by the radial nerve.   (   )

c   have abductor pollicis brevis lying most
superficially.   (   )
d   are all attached distally to the first metacarpal bone.   (   )
e   have an attachment to the base of the distal
phalanx of the thumb.   (   )

194   The interossei muscles:
a   are eight in total.   (   )
b   all arise by two heads from adjacent metacarpal
bones.   (   )

c   are all attached distally to the base of the
corresponding proximal phalanx and the dorsal
extensor expansion.   (   )
d   may flex the metacarpophalangeal joints.   (   )
e   may extend the middle and distal phalanges.   (   )

a **T**— Here the deep fascia is modified, forming these fibrous
b **T**   sheaths which make osseofascial tunnels by arching over
c **T**   the tendons and gaining attachment to the sides of the
phalanges. Proximally they are continuous with the palmar
aponeurosis.
d **F**— Each extends to the base of the distal phalanx and is lined
with synovial membrane.
e **F**— Both the long flexor tendons, superficialis and profundus,
are enclosed within these sheaths.

a **T**— And to its bony attachments.

b **F**— The recurrent branch of the median nerve supplies all of
them.
c **T**— Opponens pollicis and flexor pollicis brevis lie deep to the
short abductor of the thumb.
d **F**— Both abductor pollicis brevis and flexor pollicis brevis are
e **F**   attached to the base of the proximal phalanx of the thumb.
The opponens is attached to the body of the 1st
metacarpal bone. (N.B. The adductor pollicis, supplied by
the ulnar nerve, is not a muscle of the thenar eminence,
though it is a short muscle of the thumb.)

a **T**— There are four dorsal and four palmar muscles.
b **F**— These muscles are attached to the bodies of the metacarpal
bones, the palmar by a single head and the dorsal by two
heads, from adjacent sides of the metacarpal bones.
c **T**— Their main action is at the metacarpophalangeal joints
producing adduction (palmar) and abduction (dorsal). They
may also assist flexion at these joints.
d **T**
e **T**— By their attachment to the extensor expansion they help
the lumbricals to extend the middle and distal phalanges.

195   The lumbrical muscles:
  a   are each attached to a tendon of flexor digitorum
      superficialis.   (   )
  b   have each a tendon winding round the ulnar side
      of the corresponding metacarpophalangeal joint.   (   )

  c   are all supplied by the median nerve.   (   )

  d   produce flexion at the metacarpophalangeal joints
      of the finger.   (   )
  e   produce flexion at the interphalangeal joints.   (   )

196   In the veins of the upper limb the:
  a   cephalic vein has no valves.   (   )
  b   the cephalic vein crosses the anatomical snuff box.   (   )
  c   basilic vein commences at the medial aspect of
      the palmar venous arch.   (   )

  d   basilic vein pierces the clavipectoral fascia.   (   )

  e   median cubital vein lies deep to the bicipital
      aponeurosis.   (   )

197   Lymph drainage of the upper limb:
  a   comprises a superficial and a deep group of
      vessels and nodes.   (   )

  b   has no lymph nodes distal to the axilla.   (   )
  c   is entirely to the axillary groups of lymph nodes.   (   )

  d   deeper tissues drain to the pectoral group of nodes.   (   )

  e   is eventually into the internal jugular vein.   (   )

a **F**— Each is attached to a tendon of flexor digitorum profundus.

b **F**— The tendons pass round the radial side of the joints and are attached distally to the base of the proximal phalanx and into the fibrous extensor expansion.

c **F**— The radial two muscles are supplied by the median nerve and the ulnar two by the ulnar nerve.

d **T**— They extend the interphalangeal joints. When paralysed, there is a resulting claw-hand, partial or complete.

e **F**

a **F**— Numerous valves are found in the majority of upper limb veins.

b **T**

c **F**— The superficial venous arch lies dorsally, the basilic vein arising medially. The cephalic vein, arising laterally, approximates in position to the pre-axial border of the fetal limb.

d **F**— The basilic vein pierces the deep fascia just proximal to the elbow joint. The cephalic vein pierces the clavipectoral fascia.

e **F**— The vein is superficial to the aponeurosis which separates the vein from the brachial artery. The median cubital vein is often used for intravenous injections so the arterial relations are of clinical importance.

a **T**— The superficial vessels drain the skin and related structures and follow the large superficial veins. The deep vessels drain the muscles, bones and joints, and follow the deep vessels.

b **F**— A cubital node is sited posterior to the medial epicondyle.

c **T**— These are arranged in five regions of the axilla: pectoral, lateral, subscapular, central and apical nodes.

d **F**— Deeper tissues drain first to the lateral group of nodes and then to central and apical nodes. The pectoral nodes drain the tissues of the anterior chest wall, including the mammary gland.

e **T**— The apical nodes drain the other nodes and are continuous with the infraclavicular group of nodes. From the latter, lymph trunks emerge and drain into the internal jugular vein.

198   In the nerve supply of the upper limb:
a   the skin over the thumb is supplied by the
     C6 dermatome.   (   )
b   an injury to the lower trunk of the brachial
     plexus produces a characteristic clawed hand.   (   )
c   damage to the radial nerve in the radial groove
     produces wrist drop.   (   )
d   injury to the median nerve at the wrist produces
     loss of sensation of the front of the thumb, index
     and middle fingers.   (   )
e   injury to the axillary nerve produces impaired
     abduction of the humerus.   (   )

VII The Lower Limb

199   In the development of the lower limb:
a   the axial artery arises from the superior vesical
     artery.   (   )

b   lateral rotation of the limb occurs between the hip
     and knee regions.   (   )
c   the muscles supplied by the posterior divisions of
     the ventral rami have been carried on to the
     anterolateral aspect of the limb.   (   )

d   synovial joints are present between some of the
     bones of the pelvic girdle.   (   )

e   the posterior division of the anterior primary rami
     of L2, 3 and 4 give rise to the obturator nerve. (   )

200   The ilium:
a   gives attachment to the gluteus maximus muscles
     between the middle and posterior gluteal lines. (   )
b   is bordered posteriorly by the lesser sciatic notch. (   )
c   gives attachment to the rectus femoris muscle
     anteroinferiorly.   (   )
d   has a secondary centre of ossification appearing
     along its upper border at puberty.   (   )
e   gives attachment to sartorius.   (   )

a **T**— The little finger is supplied by C8.

b **T**— This is due to paralysis of the small muscles of the hand and of the long digital flexors.

c **T**— Due to paralysis of the long digital and carpal extensors.

d **T**— Also paralysis of the thenar muscles and the 1st and 2nd lumbricals.

e **T**— Due to paralysis of the deltoid, there is also loss of sensation over the attachment of this muscle.

a **F**— The axial artery is represented by part of the internal iliac artery and its inferior gluteal branch. The artery roughly follows the course of the adult sciatic nerve. The superior vesical artery is a derivative of the fetal umbilical artery.

b **F**— Medial rotation occurs, so that the plantar surface of the foot is directed backwards, and later downwards.

c **T**— They are innervated by the femoral and common peroneal nerves. The large muscles of the lower limb are used mainly in locomotion. When standing upright, the weight is carried by bones and ligaments.

d **T**— The sacro-iliac joint is synovial but becomes increasingly fibrosed in later life. The two pubic bones are united by a symphysis. In these joints movement is minimal. The ilium, ischium and pubis have cartilaginous joints and no movement occurs.

e **F**— This is the derivation of the femoral nerve, the obturator is derived from the anterior divisions of the same roots.

a **F**— This is the area of attachment of the gluteus medius muscle.

b **F**— The greater sciatic notch forms the posterior border.

c **T**— The reflected head is attached to this area above the acetabulum.

d **T**— The iliac crest epiphysis fuses about the 20th year.

e **T**— At the anterior superior iliac spine.

201   The obturator foramen:
   a   is bounded posteriorly by the iliac part of the
          acetabulum.   (   )
   b   transmits the inferior gluteal nerve.   (   )

   c   is separated from the pudendal nerve by the
          obturator internus muscle.   (   )
   d   transmits the obturator artery and nerve.   (   )

   e   transmits the superior gluteal artery.   (   )

202   The greater trochanter of the femur:
   a   is united anteriorly to the lesser trochanter by the
          intertrochanteric line.   (   )
   b   gives attachment to the piriformis muscle along
          its upper border.   (   )
   c   gives attachment to the quadratus femoris muscle.   (   )

   d   gives attachment to the gluteus minimus muscle
          along its anterior border.   (   )
   e   gives attachment to the gluteus maximus along its
          posterior border.   (   )

203   The lesser trochanter of the femur:
   a   gives attachment to the pectineus muscle.   (   )

   b   gives attachment to iliacus.   (   )

   c   gives attachment to the flexors at the hip joint.   (   )
   d   gives attachment to vastus intermedius.   (   )

   e   has a secondary centre of ossification which
          appears in the 10th year and fuses in the 18th year. (   )

204   The body of the femur:
   a   forms an angle of about 125° with the neck.   (   )

   b   gives attachment to the gluteus maximus muscle
          along the linea aspera.   (   )
   c   has no muscles attached to its anterior surface.   (   )

   d   gives attachment to the short head of biceps.   (   )
   e   gives attachment to adductor brevis.   (   )

a **F**— The ilium forms no part of the foramen, which is bounded by the ischium and pubis.
b **F**— The inferior gluteal nerve passes through the greater sciatic foramen.
c **T**— The pudendal canal is related to the medial surface of this muscle.
d **T**— The obturator vessels and nerve pass in the obturator groove and, through the foramen, into the thigh. The nerve supplies the adductor group of muscles.
e **F**— The superior gluteal vessels and nerve pass through the greater sciatic foramen.

a **T**— The intertrochanteric crest joins the structures posteriorly.
b **T**— Obturator internus and externus are attached to its medial surface.
c **F**— This muscle is attached to the quadrate tubercle on the intertrochanteric crest.
d **T**— And the gluteus medius is attached diagonally to the lateral surface.
e **F**— The femoral attachment of this muscle is to the gluteal tuberosity.

a **F**— This muscle is attached to the body of the bone below the lesser trochanter.
b **T**— Iliacus joins with psoas and is attached to the lesser trochanter and to the bone just below.
c **T**— Psoas is also a medial rotator.
d **F**— This muscle is attached to the anterior surface of the body of the femur.
e **T**— Centres for the head (1yr) and greater trochanter (5yrs) also unite with the body at this time.

a **T**— This is less in the female. The body is inclined medially at an angle of about 20° with the vertical.
b **F**— This muscle is attached to the gluteal tuberosity between the linea aspera and the quadrate tubercle.
c **F**— The vastus intermedius has a wide attachment from this area.
d **T**— Along the linea aspera in the middle of the body.
e **T**— Along the proximal part of the linea aspera.

205 **The lower end of the femur:**
a   gives attachment to the adductor magnus.   (   )

b   gives attachment to the lateral ligament of the
    knee joint on the lateral epicondyle.   (   )
c   gives attachment to the plantaris muscle in a pit
    below the lateral epicondyle.   (   )
d   gives attachment to the patellar ligament.   (   )
e   has a secondary centre of ossification which
    unites with the body in the 20th year.   (   )

206 **The capsule of the hip joint:**
a   is attached along the intertrochanteric crest.   (   )

b   is attached along the intertrochanteric line.   (   )
c   carries blood vessels to the head of the femur.   (   )

d   is thickened inferiorly as the iliofemoral ligament.   (   )

e   limits flexion at the hip joint.   (   )

207 **In movements at the hip joint:**
a   abduction is produced mainly by the gluteus
    medius and minimus muscles.   (   )

b   medial rotation is produced by gluteus medius
    and minimus.   (   )
c   extension is limited by tension in the three
    capsular thickenings.   (   )
d   lateral rotation is largely performed by muscles
    supplied by the femoral nerve.   (   )

e   flexion is produced by muscles supplied by the
    femoral nerve.   (   )

a **T**— To the medial supracondylar line ending below at the adductor tubercle.

b **T**— Also the medial epicondyle gives attachment to the medial ligament.

c **F**— This is the point of attachment of the popliteus muscle.

d **F**— The tendon is attached to the tibial tuberosity.

e **T**— It appears in the 8th–9th month of intra-uterine life and is an indication of fetal maturity.

a **F**— The posterior attachment is to the neck about 1 cm proximal to the crest.

b **T**

c **T**— In the retinacular fibres of the capsule. Fractures across the neck heal poorly when these vessels are torn.

d **F**— This powerful Y-shaped ligament passes anteriorly from the anterior inferior iliac spine to the intertrochanteric line.

e **F**— The strong iliofemoral and the other capsular ligaments tighten and stabilise the joint in extension. Active flexion is limited because of the attachments of the muscles and is further limited if the knee joint is in the extended position.

a **T**— Abduction on the grounded leg is important in walking, as in it the opposite hip bone is raised, thus allowing the opposite limb to swing forwards clear of the ground.

b **T**— The iliopsoas muscle is also involved.

c **T**— These three ligaments spiral in such a way as to all limit this movement.

d **F**— This movement is performed by gluteus maximus and the short posterior articular muscles, supplied by nerves emerging through the greater sciatic notch. The femoral nerve supplies mainly the extensor muscles at the knee joint.

e **T**— Rectus femoris and sartorius are supplied by the nerve. Iliopsoas, the main flexor, is supplied by femoral and direct branches from the 12th thoracic and upper 4 lumbar nerves.

208   **The hip joint is directly related:**
  a   anteriorly to the psoas bursa.   ( )

  b   superiorly to the gluteus medius muscle.   ( )

  c   posteriorly to the sciatic nerve.   ( )

  d   inferiorly to the obturator externus muscle.   ( )

  e   to the femoral nerve.   ( )

209   **The gluteus maximus muscle:**
  a   is attached to the sacrospinous ligament.   ( )

  b   is attached to the iliotibial tract.   ( )

  c   is supplied by the superior gluteal nerve.   ( )

  d   overlies the lesser sciatic foramen.   ( )

  e   abducts the hip joint.   ( )

210   **The greater sciatic foramen transmits the nerves supplying the:**
  a   tensor fascia lata muscle.   ( )
  b   gluteal muscles.   ( )
  c   hamstring muscles.   ( )
  d   adductor muscles.   ( )

  e   perineal muscles.   ( )

a T— The bursa frequently communicates with the joint through a hole in the capsule between the iliofemoral and pubofemoral ligaments.

b F— This muscle overlaps the gluteus minimus and the reflected head of the rectus femoris muscle which separate it from the joint.

c F— The nerve is separated from the joint by the obturator internus and quadratus femoris muscles but its proximity to the joint has important surgical implications.

d T— The close proximity of all the above muscles contribute to the marked stability of the joint.

e F— The nerve lies on psoas and iliacus.

a F— Its upper attachment includes the sacrotuberous ligament, the ilium, the sacrum and the coccyx.

b T— Through which it stabilises the knee joint and produces extension at the joint.

c F— The superior nerve does not contribute. The muscle is supplied by the inferior gluteal nerve.

d T— Also the greater sciatic foramen and the vessels, nerves and muscles these foramen transmit.

e F— It is the main extensor at the hip joint.

a T— The superior gluteal nerve emerges above piriformis and

b T also supplies gluteus medius and minimus muscles.

c T— The sciatic nerve emerges below the piriformis.

d F— The adductor muscles are innervated by the obturator nerve which passes through the obturator foramen.

e T— The pudendal nerve emerges below the piriformis, hooks around the ischial spine and passes through the lesser sciatic foramen into the pudendal canal on the lateral wall of the ischiorectal fossa.

211 **The semimembranosus muscle:**
  a is attached superiorly to the ischial tuberosity. (　)
  b is attached distally to the medial aspect of the body
     of the tibia behind the attachment of the gracilis
     tendon. (　)
  c has a recurrent tendinous expansion on to the lateral
     femoral condyle. (　)
  d has a separate head attached to the linea aspera
     near the lateral lip and the upper part of the lateral
     supracondylar line of the femur. (　)
  e is supplied by the obturator nerve. (　)

212 **The sciatic nerve:**
  a is formed in the pelvis posterior to the fibres
     of the piriformis muscle. (　)
  b is directly related to the ischium. (　)
  c is directly related to the adductor magnus muscle. (　)
  d innervates part of the adductor magnus muscle. (　)
  e usually divides into its terminal branches just
     above the popliteal fossa. (　)

213 **The pectineus muscle:**
  a is attached to the upper part of the obturator
     membrane. (　)
  b is attached to the body of the femur. (　)
  c is supplied by the anterior division of the
     obturator nerve. (　)
  d lies in the same plane as the adductor longus
     muscle. (　)
  e is a medial rotator at the hip joint. (　)

214 **The adductor magnus:**
  a is attached to the anterior superior iliac spine. (　)
  b is attached to the lesser trochanter. (　)
  c is attached to the length of the linea aspera. (　)
  d is supplied by both the sciatic and obturator nerves. (　)
  e can extend the femur. (　)

a **T**— The attachment is the most medial of the hamstrings.
b **F**— The tendon is attached in a groove on the posteromedial aspect of the tibial condyle proximal to the gracilis attachment.

c **T**— This is the oblique popliteal ligament.

d **F**— This describes the attachment of the short head of the biceps muscle.

e **F**— The innervation is from the sciatic.

a **F**— It is formed on the anterior surface of this muscle from the L4, 5 and S1, 2 and 3 nerves and leaves the pelvis through the greater sciatic foramen.
b **T**— Then passing on to obturator internus and quadratus
c **T** femoris muscles which separate it from the hip joint.
d **T**— It descends between this muscle and the hamstrings and innervates the part of the adductor magnus attached to the ischial tuberosity.
e **T**— Having supplied the hamstring muscles and the hamstring part of the adductor magnus muscle.

a **F**— It is attached to the superior aspect of the pubic bone.

b **T**— Along a line joining the lesser trochanter to the linea aspera.
c **F**— The obturator nerve is a posterior relation and supplies gracilis, adductor longus and adductor brevis. Pectineus is supplied by branches of the femoral nerve.
d **T**— Obturator externus and adductor brevis muscles separate the pectineus and adductor longus in front from adductor magnus muscle behind.
e **T**— Also a weak flexor.

a **F**— Proximally it is attached to the outer surface of the ischiopubic
b **T** ramus, distally to the linea aspera, the medial supracondylar
c **T** line and the adductor tubercle.
d **T**— Branches from the sciatic nerve supply the ischial part of the muscle. The remainder is supplied by the obturator nerve.
e **T**— In addition to adducting it.

215 The obturator nerve:
a is a branch of the upper part of the lumbosacral plexus. ( )
b enters the thigh through the obturator groove. ( )

c anterior division descends between the adductor longus and the adductor magnus. ( )
d posterior division pierces the obturator internus muscle. ( )
e supplies the pectineus muscle. ( )

216 The sartorius muscle:
a is attached to the anterior inferior iliac spine. ( )
b forms the medial boundary of the femoral triangle. ( )

c is an extensor at the knee and hip joints. ( )

d roofs in the femoral vessels in the mid-thigh. ( )
e is supplied by branches of the anterior divisions of the lumbar plexus. ( )

217 The rectus femoris muscle:
a forms part of the quadriceps muscle. ( )

b gains attachment from the lateral lip of the linea aspera. ( )
c has a superior attachment to the anterior inferior iliac spine. ( )
d has lower medial fibres that run almost horizontally to the patella. ( )

e is partly supplied by the obturator nerve. ( )

a **T**— It arises from the anterior divisions of L2, L3 and L4.

b **T**— The nerve divides into anterior and posterior divisions at this point. The groove is bounded by the pubis, ischium and obturator membrane.

c **F**— It lies between the adductor longus and brevis.

d **F**— It pierces the obturator externus and lies between adductor brevis and magnus.

e **F**— This muscle is supplied by the femoral nerve.

a **F**— It is attached to the anterior superior iliac spine.

b **F**— It forms the lateral boundary. It also serves to separate the adductor muscles at the hip superomedially from the extensor muscles at the knee inferolaterally.

c **F**— It is a flexor and its actions are best demonstrated by sitting in the crossed leg position, hence its synonym, the tailor's muscle.

d **T**— They lie in the adductor canal.

e **F**— The femoral nerve (from the posterior divisions) usually supplies it.

a **T**— The quadriceps muscle mass also includes the three vastus muscles, and is a powerful extensor at the knee joint.

b **F**— The rectus has no attachment to the femur. The vastus muscles have extensive attachments to this bone.

c **T**— And a reflected head to the ilium just above the acetabulum.

d **F**— These fibres are part of the vastus medialis muscle, and prevent the patella moving too far laterally during extension.

e **F**— It is supplied by the femoral nerve.

218 The femoral triangle:
a   is bounded medially by the adductor longus muscle. (   )

b   is bounded laterally by the rectus femoris muscle. (   )
c   contains an extension of the transversalis fascia. (   )

d   contains both the femoral artery and its vein. (   )

e   has a defect in its fascial roof. (   )

219 The femoral artery:
a   is formed behind the midpoint of the inguinal
ligament. (   )

b   has the femoral nerve on its lateral side in the
femoral triangle. (   )
c   in the adductor canal has vastus medialis situated
anterolaterally to it. (   )
d   lies posterior to sartorius. (   )
e   leaves the thigh by passing inferior to the adductor
magnus tendon. (   )

220 The femoral vein:
a   passes anterior to the upper attachment of the)
pectineus muscle. (   )
b   is separated by the femoral canal from the lacunar
part of the inguinal ligament. (   )
c   lies anterior to its artery in the adductor canal. (   )

d   passes through a separate opening in the
adductor magnus from the artery. (   )

e   has the saphenous nerve lying medially in the
adductor canal. (   )

a **T**— The muscle also forms part of the floor of the triangle along with pectineus and iliopsoas muscles.
b **F**— Sartorius forms the lateral boundary.
c **T**— This fascia and the fascia of iliacus are continued beneath the inguinal ligament as the femoral sheath.
d **T**— The vein lies medially and can enlarge into the femoral canal on its medial side. These are important surgical relations.
e **T**— The saphenous opening in the deep fascia is traversed by the great saphenous vein and is an important landmark in vein surgery. The opening lies 3 cm below and 1 cm lateral to the pubic tubercle.

a **F**— The surface marking lies medial to this at the midinguinal point (midway between the anterior superior iliac spine and the symphysis pubis). The inferior epigastric artery thus forms a medial relation of the deep inguinal ring, which is situated above the midpoint of the inguinal ligament.
b **T**— The iliopsoas separates both structures from the hip joint.
c **T**— The artery lies at first on adductor longus and then adductor magnus.
d **T**— The sartorius forms the roof of the adductor canal.
e **F**— It passes through an opening in the muscle about 10 cm above the knee joint and becomes the popliteal artery.

a **T**— Then descends on adductor longus.
b **T**— The femoral canal is the space through which femoral herniae may develop.
c **F**— The vein passes from the medial to the posterior aspect of the artery.
d **F**— They are closely related in the adductor canal and pass through the single opening. The popliteal vein lies posterior to the popliteal artery.
e **T**— The nerve then passes medially to join the great saphenous vein in the lower leg.

221 The femoral nerve:

a is formed from the anterior divisions of the lumbar 2, 3 and 4 roots. ( )

b is enclosed in the lateral part of the femoral sheath. ( )

c lies in the groove between iliacus and psoas as it passes deep to the inguinal ligament. ( )

d branches are divided into superficial and deep by the medial circumflex femoral artery. ( )

e has a saphenous branch which enters the popliteal space with the femoral vessels. ( )

222 The patella:

a ossifies in mesenchyme. ( )

b has a larger lateral than medial articular facet. ( )

c receives tendinous expansions from vastus lateralis muscle on its lateral border. ( )

d receives muscular attachments from the vastus medialis along its medial border. ( )

e gives attachment to gracilis along its medial surface. ( )

223 The upper end of the tibia:

a has a prominent tibial tuberosity on its superior surface. ( )

b articulates with the lateral articular facet of the patella. ( )

c gives attachment to the ends of the cartilaginous menisci along the intercondylar ridge. ( )

d gives attachment to the semimembranosus muscle. ( )

e has a centre of ossification which fuses with the body about the 20th year. ( )

a **F**— These form the obturator nerve; the femoral arises from the posterior divisions of the same roots.
b **F**— The nerve is lateral to the artery but lies outside the sheath.
c **T**— It then divides into a number of terminal branches.

d **F**— The lateral circumflex femoral artery passes between the branches. The superficial branches are mainly cutaneous but there are branches to sartorius. The deeper branches are mainly muscular (to quadriceps femoris) but the saphenous nerve is sensory.
e **F**— The nerve leaves the adductor canal, passing under sartorius to the medial side of the knee. It accompanies the great saphenous vein in the lower leg.

a **F**— It is a sesamoid bone ossifying in cartilage, a centre appearing in the 5th year.
b **T**— Both facets are further divided transversely.
c **T**— The retinacula. Further expansions pass to the upper border of the tibia.
d **T**— These fibres stabilise the patella during knee extension when there is a tendency for the patella to dislocate laterally.
e **F**— Gracilis is attached to the upper part of the medial surface of the tibia.

a **F**— The tuberosity is on the anterior border and receives the attachment of the patellar ligament.
b **F**— The patella articulates with the lower end of the femur.

c **T**—The cruciate ligaments are also attached to this ridge.

d **T**—The muscle is attached in a groove on the posteromedial aspect of the upper end.
e **T**— The centre appears about the 9th month of intra-uterine life.

224 The body of the tibia:

a   has the interosseous membrane attached to its
    posterior border.   (   )
b   has a prominent nutrient foramen in its upper third. (   )

c   gives attachment to flexor hallucis longus below
    the soleal line.   (   )
d   gives attachment to tibialis anterior over its lateral
    surface.   (   )
e   gives attachment to peroneus brevis on its
    mid-lateral surface.   (   )

225 The lower end of the tibia:

a   extends beyond the fibula.   (   )

b   is grooved posteromedially by the tendon of tibialis
    posterior.   (   )
c   is grooved anteromedially by the tibialis anterior.   (   )

d   unites with the body before the upper end.   (   )

e   gives attachment to the deltoid ligament.   (   )

226 The fibula:

a   gives attachment to the biceps tendon at the base
    of the head of the bone.   (   )
b   is related to the tibial nerve at its neck.   (   )
c   malleolar fossa is situated posteromedially at the
    lower end of the bone.   (   )
d   gives attachment to popliteus over its upper
    posterior surface.   (   )
e   upper and lower ends unite with the body about
    the same time as those of the tibia.   (   )

a **F**—The membrane is attached to the lateral border of the body.

b **T**— On the posterior surface just below the soleal line. However, much of its blood supply is from the muscles attached and through the periosteum. Absence of muscle attachments in the lower part of the tibia is a contributory factor to the poor healing of fractures in this region.

c **F**— This muscle is attached to the fibula. The tibia gives attachment to flexor digitorum longus and tibialis posterior.

d **T**— The medial surface is subcutaneous but gives attachment to the sartorius, gracilis and semitendinosus superiorly.

e **F**— This muscle is attached to the lower two-thirds of the lateral surface of the fibula.

a **F**— The tip of the lateral (fibular) malleolus extends distal to the medial tibial (malleolus).

b **T**— Lying medial to the tendon of flexor digitorum longus.

c **F**— The anterior border is smooth and is crossed by the tendons of the muscles in the anterior compartment of the leg.

d **T**— The secondary centre appears at 1 year and unites at 18 years.

e **T**— This medial ligament of the ankle joint is triangular in shape with its apex attached to the medial malleolus.

a **T**— The fibular collateral ligament is attached in front of the apex of the head.

b **F**— The common peroneal nerve is related at this site.

c **T**— It gives attachment to the posterior tibiofibular ligament and forms a useful marker when orientating the bone.

d **F**— The soleus muscle is attached to this area.

e **T**— 20 and 18 years respectively. The primary centres for the bodies of both bones appear about the 2nd month of intra-uterine life.

227 **The knee joint:**
a is a condyloid joint. ( )
b has articular fibrocartilage covering the bony
surfaces. ( )
c patella and femoral facets are in apposition except
in full extension. ( )
d medial and lateral tibial articular surfaces are
continuous with each other anteriorly. ( )
e medial and lateral femoral articular surfaces are
continuous with each other anteriorly. ( )

228 **In the knee joint the:**
a coronary ligaments bind down the outer margins
of the medial and lateral menisci to the outer
margins of the tibial condyles. ( )
b capsule is pierced posterolaterally by the
popliteus tendon. ( )
c tendinous expansions of the vasti blend with the
capsule medially and laterally. ( )
d tibial collateral ligament is attached to the capsule. ( )

e fibular collateral ligament is attached to the apex ( )
of the fibula.

229 **The synovial membrane of the knee joint:**
a is invaginated from behind by the cruciate ligaments. ( )
b covers the inferior surface of the menisci. ( )
c is continuous with that of the infrapatellar bursa. ( )
d is continuous with that of the prepatellar bursa. ( )
e surrounds the infrapatellar fold. ( )

230 **The medial meniscus of the knee joint:**
a is formed of fibrocartilage. ( )

b is attached to the capsule as well as to the
condyles of the tibia. ( )
c embraces the ends of the lateral meniscus. ( )

d gives attachment posteriorly to the tendon of
popliteus. ( )
e gives attachment to the patellar tendon. ( )

a **T**— It is a synovial joint of the condyloid (modified hinge) variety.
b **F**— The articular cartilage is hyaline.

c **F**— They are in contact in all positions of the joint.

d **F**— The intercondylar ridge completely separates the tibial articular areas and gives attachment to the ends of the
e **T** menisci and both cruciate ligaments.

a **T**— They are capsular thickenings.

b **T**— The tendon has a synovial sheath and is attached to a fossa below the lateral epicondyle.
c **T**— Being known as the patellar retinacula.

d **T**— It has a wide inferior attachment to the medial surface of the tibia. The fibular collateral ligament is separate from the capsule and is attached to the head of the fibula.
e **F**— This is the attachment of biceps; the ligament is attached anterior to this point.

a **T**— These ligaments are intracapsular but extrasynovial.
b **F**— It lines the non-articular surfaces of the joint.
c **F**— The suprapatellar, popliteal and gastrocnemius bursae
d **F** usually communicate with the joint cavity.
e **T**— The fold fans out from the intercondylar notch on the femur to the tibia and lower patella with a 'transverse fringe', the alar fold, on each side.

a **T**— It is wedge-shaped in section and conforms to the adjacent femoral and tibial surfaces.
b **T**— This double attachment makes the medial meniscus less mobile and so more liable to injury.
c **T**— The medial is semicircular, the lateral forms three-fifths of a smaller circle.
d **F**— The tendon is attached to the lateral meniscus which is pulled backwards at the start of the flexion at the knee.
e **F**

231 **In movement at the knee joint:**

 a   flexion is limited by tension in the tibial and fibular collateral ligaments.   (   )

 b   extension is limited by tension in the cruciate, collateral and oblique popliteal ligaments.   (   )

 c   locking of the joint in full extension is by lateral rotation of the femur on the tibia.   (   )

 d   the collateral ligaments limit rotation of the femur on the tibia.   (   )

 e   unlocking of the joint is by medial rotation of the femur on the tibia by popliteus.   (   )

232 **The knee joint:**

 a   is separated posteriorly from the popliteal vein by the popliteal artery.   (   )

 b   receives an innervation from the obturator nerve.   (   )

 c   has an oblique popliteal ligament which is an extension of the semimembranosus tendon.   (   )

 d   lateral femoral condyle is more prominent anteriorly than the medial.   (   )

 e   has the line of weight passing behind the axis of rolling in the fully extended position.   (   )

233 **The superior tibiofibular joint is:**

 a   a plane synovial joint.   (   )

 b   placed on the lateral surface on the lateral tibial condyle.   (   )

 c   medially rotated during dorsiflexion of the ankle.   (   )

 d   related anteriorly to the tibialis anterior muscle.   (   )

 e   related posteriorly to the tibialis posterior muscle.   (   )

a **F**— The movement is limited by the apposition of the surfaces of the calf and thigh.

b **T**— The attachment of the anterior cruciate ligament fixes the lateral condyle, final extension being accompanied by

c **F**   medial rotation of the femur on the tibia. The direction of the fibres in the collateral and oblique posterior ligaments

d **T**   is such that it limits this rotation.

e **F**— In unlocking, popliteus laterally rotates the femur on the tibia and also draws the lateral meniscus clear of the condylar surfaces.

a **T**— The tibial nerve is superficial to both vessels.

b **T**— And from the femoral and sciatic nerves which supply the muscles acting on the joint.

c **T**— As is also the fascia over the popliteus muscle.

d **T**— This prominence helps prevent lateral dislocation of the patella during extension at the knee joint.

e **F**— The line passes in front of the axis.

a **T**— The joint cavity may rarely communicate with that of the knee joint. The inferior joint is a fibrous joint.

b **F**— It is situated on the posteroinferior surface of the lateral condyle.

c **F**— Little movement occurs between the tibia and fibula and certainly no rotation.

d **F**— The extensor digitorum longus and peroneus longus muscles are anterior relations. The popliteus tendon and synovial sheath are the main posterior relations.

e **F**— The muscle has a more distal attachment.

234   The popliteal fossa:

a   has the soleus muscle on its floor.   (   )

b   is crossed by the posterior femoral cutaneous nerve. (   )
c   is bordered laterally by the iliotibial tract.   (   )

d   is bordered medially by the gracilis muscle.   (   )

e   has the common peroneal nerve passing through it
      laterally.   (   )

235   The tibialis anterior muscle:

a   passes deep to both the superior and inferior
      extensor retinacula of the ankle joint.   (   )
b   has attachments to the fibula and the adjacent
      interosseous membrane.   (   )

c   crosses the tendon of extensor hallucis longus in
      front of the ankle joint.   (   )
d   is attached distally to the medial cuneiform bone.   (   )

e   is crossed by the anterior tibial artery in front of
      the ankle joint.   (   )

236   The peroneus brevis muscle:

a   is separated from the lateral malleolus by the
      peroneus longus as their tendons pass across the
      ankle joint.   (   )
b   is supplied by the deep peroneal nerve.   (   )

c   is bound down to the lateral malleolus by the
      superior and inferior peroneal retinacula.   (   )
d   is attached to the medial cuneiform bone.   (   )

e   has tendinous extensions to most metatarsal bones. (   )

a   F— The floor is formed by the popliteal surface of the femur, the capsule of the knee joint and the fascia over the popliteus muscle.
b   T— The roof is pierced by the small saphenous vein.
c   F— The tract lies anterolateral to the knee joint. The biceps tendon forms the lateral border of the fossa.
d   F— Semitendinosus and semimembranosus form the medial border.
e   T— The sciatic nerve usually divides into its terminal branches in the upper part of the fossa.

a   T— The tendon is surrounded by a separate synovial sheath.

b   F— It is attached to the hollowed-out upper two-thirds of the lateral surface of the tibia and the adjacent interosseous membrane.
c   F— It remains a medial relation to the extensor hallucis throughout its course.
d   T— On its medial surface and to the adjacent base of the first metatarsal bone.
e   F— The artery lies laterally.

a   F— The peroneus brevis tendon lies closer to the bone.

b   F— This nerve supplies the muscles of the anterior compartment. The superficial peroneal nerve supplies the peroneal group of muscles.
c   T— Enclosed with peroneus longus in a common synovial sheath.
d   F— The inferior surface of this bone gives attachment to peroneus longus. The peroneus brevis tendon is attached to the tubercle on the base of the 5th metatarsal.
e   F— This describes the attachment of the tibialis posterior muscle.

237   The soleus muscle:

a   is the most superficial muscle in the calf.   (   )

b   has the tibial vessels and nerve lying between it
and the gastrocnemius muscle.   (   )

c   is attached superiorly by its medial head to the
superior aspect of the medial femoral condyle.   (   )

d   is attached by the tendo calcaneus to the middle
of the posterior surface of the calcaneus.   (   )

e   is supplied by the common peroneal nerve.   (   )

238   The popliteus muscle:

a   is attached to the pit below the lateral epicondyle
of the femur.   (   )

b   passes superficial to the tibial nerve.   (   )

c   has a tendon surrounded by synovial membrane
within the knee joint.   (   )

d   assists in extension at the knee joint.   (   )

e   is closely related to the popliteal vein.   (   )

239   The flexor hallucis longus muscle:

a   is attached superiorly to the lower two-thirds of the
posterior surface of the tibia.   (   )

b   becomes tendinous in the mid-calf.   (   )

c   lies lateral to the tibial vessels and nerve,
posterior to the ankle joint.   (   )

d   is crossed by the tendon of flexor digitorum
longus in the sole of the foot.   (   )

e   is attached to the base of the middle phalanx
on the plantar aspect of the hallux and by slips
into its distal phalanx.   (   )

a **F**— The gastrocnemius muscle is more superficial for most of the calf.

b **F**— These structures lie deep to both gastrocnemius and soleus muscles.

c **F**— The soleus is attached to the upper end of the fibula, the soleal line on the tibia and a tendinous arch between. Gastrocnemius is attached to the femur.

d **T**— A bursa and a pad of fat separate the tendon from the upper part of the calcaneal surface.

e **F**— It is supplied by the tibial nerve.

a **T**— The line of attachment of the capsule of the knee joint passes between the epicondyle and the pit, which is thus intracapsular.

b **F**— It is deeply placed in the popliteal fossa and is supplied by a branch of the tibial nerve.

c **T**— The tendon pierces the posterior capsule, a slip passing to the lateral meniscus retracting it in lateral rotation of the femur at the beginning of flexion. The tendon is intracapsular but extrasynovial.

d **F**— It laterally rotates the femur on the tibia at the beginning of flexion, so 'unlocking' the knee joint.

e **F**— The popliteal artery lies between the vein and the muscle.

a **F**— It is attached to this region of the fibula and adjacent interosseous membrane. (The muscle going to the medial side of the foot (FHL) comes from the lateral bone in the leg. The muscle going to the lateral side (FDL) comes from the medial bone.)

b **F**— The tendon starts behind the lower end of the tibia.

c **T**— The tendons of flexor digitorum longus and tibialis posterior are medial to the tendon and vessels.

d **T**— It then passes forwards in the groove between the sesamoid bones in the two heads of the flexor hallucis brevis.

e **F**— It is attached to the base of the distal phalanx, plantar flexing the great toe and foot, and supporting the medial longitudinal arch.

240   The popliteal artery:

a   enters the popliteal fossa through the adductor
hiatus.   (   )

b   lies deep on the lower posterior surface of the
femur.   (   )

c   gives off the peroneal branch in the lower part of
the popliteal fossa.   (   )

d   is separated from the common peroneal nerve by
the popliteal vein.   (   )

e   gives a branch to the extensor compartment of
the leg.   (   )

241   The popliteal vein:

a   lies subcutaneous in the popliteal fossa.   (   )

b   lies between the popliteal artery and tibial nerve.   (   )

c   has a prominent branch from the superficial veins
of the calf.   (   )

d   pierces the deep fascia overlying the popliteal
fossa.   (   )

e   is closely related to the saphenous nerve.   (   )

242   The tibial nerve:

a   lies on tibialis posterior in the upper calf.   (   )

b   descends through the calf between flexor digitorum
longus medially and flexor hallucis longus laterally.   (   )

c   innervates both medial and lateral heads of
gastrocnemius.   (   )

d   innervates the skin over the back of the leg and the
lateral border of the foot through its sural branch.   (   )

e   gives rise to the medial plantar nerve.   (   )

243   The common peroneal nerve:

a   is a branch of the femoral nerve.   (   )

b   divides in the substance of peroneus longus.   (   )

c   is subcutaneous as it crosses the neck of the fibula. (   )

d   supplies the three peroneal muscles through its
superficial peroneal branch.   (   )

e   supplies the skin over the medial border of the
hallux through the medial dorsal branch of the
superficial peroneal.   (   )

a T— As a continuation of the femoral artery.

b T— Then crosses the capsule of the knee joint and the fascia over the popliteus muscle.

c F— The peroneal artery is a branch of the posterior tibial artery.

d F— This is the relation of the tibial nerve. The common peroneal nerve lies laterally in the fossa.

e T— The anterior tibial artery passes forwards above the interosseous membrane into this compartment.

a F— It is deep to the deep fascia, the nerve lying superficial to it

b T   and the artery deep.

c T— The short saphenous vein pierces the roof of the fossa.

d F— It follows the main artery through the adductor hiatus and becomes the femoral vein.

e F— The nerve lies on the medial aspect of the knee.

a T— Inferiorly the nerve is related to the capsule of the ankle

b T   joint and ends deep to the flexor retinaculum.

c T— Also plantaris, popliteus, soleus and the deep muscles of the calf.

d T— A branch of the common peroneal nerve (peroneal communicating nerve) joins the sural nerve.

e T— The medial and lateral plantar nerves are the terminal branches.

a F— It is a branch of the sciatic nerve.

b T— Into superficial and deep peroneal nerves.

c T— An important relation as it can be easily damaged in this region.

d F— The peroneus tertius is supplied by the deep peroneal nerve.

e T— Also the second, third and fourth interdigital clefts, the 1st being supplied by the deep peroneal nerve.

244 **The talus:**

a articulates with the calcaneus at facets on the under surface of its body and head. ( )

b receives a slip from the tibialis posterior tendon on the inferior part of its neck. ( )

c is grooved by the tendon of flexor hallucis longus between the lateral and medial tubercles on the posterior border. ( )

d has an articular facet for the plantar calcaneonavicular ligament on the inferior aspect of the head. ( )

e is grooved by the peroneus brevis and longus tendons. ( )

245 **The calcaneus:**

a gives attachment to the plantar calcaneonavicular ligament in the sulcus calcanei. ( )

b is grooved by the tibialis posterior tendon on the inferior surface of the sustentaculum tali. ( )

c articulates with the talus by the articular facet on the upper surface of the sustentaculum tali. ( )

d has the long plantar ligament attached to the anterior tubercle on its inferior surface. ( )

e is closely related laterally to the peroneus brevis and longus tendons. ( )

246 **The cuboid bone:**

a receives a slip from the tibialis posterior tendon on its inferior surface. ( )

b gives attachment to the peroneus brevis tendon. ( )

c is grooved by the peroneus longus tendon. ( )

d articulates superiomedially with the talus. ( )

e has a centre of ossification present at birth. ( )

a **T**— The concave posterior facet articulates with the posterior facet of the calcaneus, and the head and neck articulate with the anterior and middle calcaneal facets inferiorly.

b **F**— The bone has no muscular attachments.

c **T**— The lateral tubercle gives attachment to the posterior talofibular ligament.

d **T**— The ligament is also known as the spring ligament. The head articulates anteriorly with the navicular bone.

e **F**— These tendons groove the lower end of the fibula.

a **F**— A strong interosseous talocalcaneal ligament is attached in the groove which in the articulated skeleton is turned into a narrow tunnel, the sinus tarsi, by a corresponding groove in the talus.

b **F**— The tendon of flexor hallucis longus lies in this groove.

c **T**— The talus also articulates with the anterior and the posterior facets on the calcaneus.

d **F**— The turbercle gives attachment to the short plantar ligament. The long plantar ligament is attached to the under surface of the calcaneus in front of the medial and lateral processes.

e **T**— The tendons are separated from each other by the peroneal tubercle of the bone.

a **T**— The tendon is primarily attached with the plantar calcaneonavicular ligament to the navicular tuberosity but sends slips to all tarsal bones except the talus.

b **F**— The tendon is attached to the adjacent tubercle on the 5th metatarsal.

c **T**— The peroneus longus tendon grooves the inferior surface of the bone.

d **F**— It lies between the calcaneus and the 4th and 5th metatarsals, and articulates medially with the lateral cuneiform and sometimes the navicular bone.

e **T**— As do the talus and calcaneus. Centres appear in the other tarsal bones in the first 3 years of life.

247   The ankle joint:
a   is a synovial joint between the tibia and fibula
    superiorly and the trochlear surface of the talus
    inferiorly.   (   )
b   is more stable in plantar flexion.   (   )

c   has a medial (deltoid) ligament attached inferiorly
    to the neck of the talus.   (   )

d   has a lateral ligament attached inferiorly to the
    body of the calcaneus.   (   )
e   has the extensor hallucis longus tendon situated
    anteriorly in between the anterior tibial vessels
    laterally and the tibialis anterior tendon medially.   (   )

248   The talocalcaneonavicular joint:
a   is a synovial joint of the ball and socket variety.   (   )

b   has hyaline cartilage lining the articular surface of
    the plantar calcaneonavicular ligament.   (   )

c   is reinforced by the bifurcate ligament laterally.   (   )
d   is reinforced by the deltoid ligament medially.   (   )

e   is reinforced inferiorly by the short plantar
    ligament.   (   )

249   In movements of the foot:
a   eversion is increased in plantar flexion.   (   )
b   inversion is increased in plantar flexion.   (   )

c   eversion is produced by the tibialis posterior
    muscle.   (   )
d   inversion is produced by the tibialis anterior and
    posterior muscles.   (   )
e   eversion is limited by tension in the deltoid
    ligament.   (   )

a T— The trochlear surface is a continuous articular one formed by the superior, medial and lateral facets.

b F— The trochlear surface is wider anteriorly and the joint is thus more stable in dorsiflexion.

c T— This triangular ligament has a continuous attachment to the navicular, the neck of the talus, the plantar calcaneonavicular ligament, the sustentaculum tali and the body of the talus.

d T— It also has horizontally placed anterior and posterior talofibular parts.

e T— The deep peroneal nerve and the tendons of extensor digitorum longus and peroneus tertius are respectively placed lateral to the vessels.

a T— This joint in combination with the calcaneocuboid is known as the midtarsal joint. Together the two joints are important in inversion and eversion of the foot.

b T— The remainder of the distal articular surface is formed by the cavity of the navicular bone and the anterior and middle facets on the upper surface of the calcaneus.

c T— And the deltoid ligament medially. The bifurcate ligament

d T passes from the upper calcaneus to the adjacent cuboid and navicular bones.

e F— The ligament passes from the anterior calcaneal tubercle to the adjacent surface of the cuboid.

a F— The movement is greatest in dorsiflexion.

b T— The narrower posterior part of the talus allows movement at the ankle joint in addition to movement at the talocalcaneonavicular joint.

c F— It is produced by the peroneus brevis and longus muscles.

d T— And limited by tension in the peroneal muscles and the interosseous talocalcaneal ligament.

e T— And also by tension in the tibialis muscles. It is produced by the peroneal muscles.

250 **The arches of the foot:**
  a have the effect of concentrating the weight of the body on to a small area. ( )
  b give the foot resilience. ( )
  c are dependent largely on bony factors. ( )

  d are not present at birth. ( )
  e have more prominent plantar than dorsal ligaments. ( )

251 **The medial longitudinal arch of the foot:**
  a extends from the medial process of the calcaneus to the head of the medial three metatarsals. ( )
  b is supported by the tibialis posterior muscle. ( )
  c is supported by the tibialis anterior muscle. ( )
  d is supported by the peroneus longus tendon. ( )
  e is supported by the long plantar ligament. ( )

252 **The lateral plantar nerve:**
  a is the larger terminal branch of the tibial nerve beginning beneath the flexor retinaculum. ( )
  b supplies the flexor accessorius muscle. ( )

  c innervates the skin of the plantar aspect of the lateral three and a half toes. ( )
  d supplies flexor digitorum brevis. ( )
  e supplies abductor hallucis. ( )

253 **The deep fascia of the lower limb:**
  a is attached superiorly to the sacrotuberous ligament. ( )

  b has the saphenous opening 1 cm below and medial to the pubic tubercle. ( )
  c helps to stabilise the knee through the attachment of the lower fibres of the adductor magnus muscle. ( )

  d is thickened laterally at the ankle as the flexor retinaculum. ( )
  e forms the plantar aponeurosis. ( )

a **F**— They allow weight to be spread over a larger area.

b **T**— Which makes it well suited to absorb impacts.
c **F**— The maintenance of the arches is dependent on muscular, ligamentous and bony factors which are complementary to one another.
d **F**— They are present though masked by subcutaneous fat.
e **T**— They are stronger and more numerous.

a **T**— The talus, navicular and three cuneiform bones also take part.

b **T**— Tying together the posterior bones of the arch.
c **T**— Through its attachment near the centre of the arch.
d **F**— This supports the lateral and transverse arches.
e **F**— This passes to the base of the 4th and 5th metatarsal bones and supports the lateral longitudinal arch.

a **F**— The medial plantar nerve is the larger branch but has the smaller distribution.
b **T**— This muscle contracts when the flexor hallucis longus and flexor digitorum longus are relaxing.
c **F**— It supplies the lateral one and a half toes.

d **F**— The flexor digitorum brevis, abductor hallucis, flexor
e **F** hallucis brevis and the 1st lumbrical are supplied by the medial plantar nerve. The lateral supplies the other short muscles of the sole.

a **T**— The fascia has a continuous attachment to the pubic bone, inguinal ligament, iliac crest, back of the sacrum, the sacrotuberous ligament and the ischiopubic ramus.
b **F**— The opening is 3 cm below and 1 cm lateral to the tubercle.

c **F**— Its thickening in the thigh, the iliotibial tract, receives fibres from the gluteus maximus and tensor fasciae latae muscles and helps to stabilise and extend the knee joint.
d **F**— The flexor tendons lie medially. The deep fascia is thickened around the ankle joint as the retinacula, and over
e **T** the sole as the plantar aponeurosis.

254 **The great saphenous vein:**
  a passes behind the medial malleolus. ( )
  b passes anterior to the knee joint. ( )

  c is accompanied by the saphenous nerve in the
  lower leg. ( )
  d enters the femoral vein in the middle of the thigh. ( )

  e usually receives blood from the deep veins in the
  legs and thighs. ( )

255 **In the lymph drainage of the lower limb:**
  a the deep vessels pass with the limb arteries. ( )
  b the popliteal nodes receive afferents from the
  area drained by the small saphenous vein. ( )

  c efferent vessels from the upper superficial inguinal
  group pass to the nodes around the umbilicus. ( )
  d the deep inguinal nodes lie in the femoral canal. ( )

  e the gluteal region drains to the pararectal nodes. ( )

256 **In peripheral nerve injuries of the lower limb; section of
the:**
  a obturator nerve rarely produces loss of cutaneous
  sensation. ( )
  b tibial nerve produces loss of dorsiflexion and
  eversion of the foot. ( )
  c deep peroneal nerve gives sensory loss over the
  medial aspect of the foot. ( )

  d femoral nerve gives sensory loss over the medial
  aspect of the thigh and leg. ( )
  e femoral nerve produces loss of hip extension. ( )

a F— It is formed at the medial end of the dorsal venous arch and
b F   passes anterior to the medial malleolus and then posterior to
       the knee.
c T— The nerve can be damaged in surgery on the vein at this level.

d F— The union is in the upper thigh. The great saphenous vein
       passes through the saphenous opening in the deep fascia
       and joins the femoral vein.
e F— The valvular arrangement in the communicating veins is
       such as to direct blood from the superficial to the deep
       systems.

a T— The superficial vessels pass with the superficial veins.
b T— This is the lateral side of the foot and leg. The nodes lie
       around the termination of the vein deep to the popliteal
       fascia.
c F— There are no lymph nodes on the anterior abdominal wall.
       This area drains down to the groin and up to the axilla.
d T— They comprise one to three nodes and receive lymph from
       all superficial nodes and the deep vessels from the entire
       limb.
e F— This region drains to the superficial inguinal nodes.

a T— However, adduction is limited to the fibres of adductor
       magnus innervated by the sciatic nerve.
b F— These are the defects produced by damage of the common
       peroneal nerve.
c F— The only cutaneous loss is over the first interdigital cleft.
       There is loss of dorsiflexion and the foot becomes inverted
       by the unopposed action of tibialis posterior (foot drop).
d T— Due to damage of the medial femoral cutaneous and
       saphenous nerves.
e F— The quadriceps femoris muscle is paralysed, with loss of
       extension at the knee joint.

257 **In the normal stance the:**
a centre of gravity lies just anterior to the 2nd
lumbar vertebra.   (   )
b line of weight passes slightly behind the axis of
the hip joint.   (   )
c line of weight passes slightly behind the axis of
the knee joint.   (   )

d weight of the body tends to dorsiflex the body
over the feet.   (   )
e the digital extensors hold the toes on the ground. (   )

VIII Head and Neck

258 **On the superior aspect of the skull the:**
a sutures are all fibrous joints.   (   )

b coronal suture separates the frontal from the
parietal bones.   (   )
c bregma lies between the sagittal and lambdoid
sutures.   (   )

d anterior fontanelle is usually closed at birth.   (   )
e posterior fontanelle is usually closed by the
2nd–3rd month after birth.   (   )

259 **On the anterior aspect of the skull the:**
a inferior orbital margin is formed by the maxillary
and zygomatic bones.   (   )
b infraorbital foramen is situated at approximately
the junction of the middle and lateral thirds of the
inferior orbital margin.   (   )
c lateral wall of the orbit is formed by the frontal
and zygomatic bones and the greater wing of the
sphenoid.   (   )
d medial orbital margin is formed by the frontal,
lacrimal and maxillary bones.   (   )
e nasal aperture is produced by the frontal, nasal,
maxillary and temporal bones.   (   )

a **F**— It lies just anterior to the second piece of the sacrum.

b **T**— Hyperextension is limited by tension in the iliofemoral ligament and the contraction of the iliopsoas muscle.

c **F**— It passes just in front of the axis of the joints, hyperextension being limited by the ligaments and the contraction of the hamstrings and gastrocnemius muscles.

d **T**— This is resisted by the action of the calf muscles, especially soleus.

e **F**— This action is brought about by the long digital flexors.

a **T**— After middle age, the inner aspect of the sutures starts to ossify.

b **T**— At birth, the two halves of the frontal bone are separated by the frontal suture.

c **F**— The lambda (posterior fontanelle) is situated in this position. The bregma (anterior fontanelle) is between the sagittal, coronal and frontal sutures.

d **F**— The anterior fontanelle is diamond-shaped and usually
e **T** closed about 18 months after birth.

a **T**— This can be palpated in its whole length. Medially it ends in the lacrimal fossa.

b **F**— It lies at the junction of the middle and medial thirds in line with the supraorbital notch and mental foramen.

c **T**— The frontozygomatic suture can be palpated on the lateral orbital margin in the living.

d **F**— The lacrimal bone forms part of the medial orbital wall but not its margin.

e **F**— The frontal and zygomatic bones are not involved.

260 **On the lateral aspect of the skull the:**
a pterion is sited approximately 3.45 cm behind
and 1.5 cm above the frontozygomatic suture. ( )

b infratemporal fossa communicates with the
pterygopalatine fossa through the pterygotympanic
fissure. ( )

c zygomatic arch is formed by the zygomatic and
sphenoid bones. ( )

d external acoustic meatus is formed antero-
inferiorly by the tympanic plate of the temporal
bone. ( )

e mastoid process is partly formed by the occipital
bone. ( )

261 **On the inferior aspect of the skull the:**
a hard palate is formed by the maxillary, vomer and
palatine bones. ( )

b incisive foramen transmits the greater and lesser
palatine nerves. ( )

c incisive foramen transmits the greater palatine artery. ( )

d posterior nares (nasal apertures) are formed laterally
by the medial pterygoid plates. ( )

e pterygoid hamulus gives attachment to the tensor
veli palatini muscle. ( )

262 **On the inferior aspect of the skull the:**
a foramen ovale transmits the maxillary nerve. ( )

b spine of the sphenoid gives attachment to the
sphenomandibular ligament. ( )

c foramen spinosum transmits the middle meningeal
artery. ( )

d squamotympanic fissure is continuous medially with
the petrosquamous and petrotympanic fissures. ( )

e petrotympanic fissure transmits the chorda tympani
nerve. ( )

a **T**— This is the H-shaped union of the frontal, temporal, parietal and sphenoid bones. It overlies the anterior branches of the middle meningeal vessels.

b **F**— The communication is through the pterygomaxillary fissure.

c **F**— The arch is formed by the zygomatic process of the squamous temporal bone and the temporal process of the zygomatic bone.

d **T**— It is completed posterosuperiorly by the squamous temporal bone.

e **F**— It is a part of the temporal bone.

a **F**— The vomer separates the posterior nares but does not form part of the palate. It articulates with the upper surface of the palate.

b **F**— The greater and lesser palatine nerves have their own foramina opening on the posterolateral aspect of the palate.

c **T**— The foramina in the incisive fossa transmit the nasopalatine nerves and the terminal branches of the greater palatine arteries.

d **T**— And superiorly by the body of the sphenoid, medially by the vomer.

e **F**— The tendon of this muscle hooks around the hamulus, but the pterygomandibular raphe and the superior constrictor are attached to it.

a **F**— It transmits the mandibular nerve.

b **T**— Both structures are derived from the cartilage of the first pharyngeal arch.

c **T**— This is a branch of the maxillary artery and supplies both the dura and the skull bones. It can be damaged in skull fractures.

d **T**— A thin projection of the petrous part of the temporal bone subdivides the squamotympanic fissure into these two parts.

e **T**— This nerve carries sensory fibres (especially taste) from the anterior two-thirds of the tongue (lingual nerve) and the secretomotor fibres to the submandibular ganglion.

263 On the inferior aspect of the skull the:
a foramen lacerum is pierced by the internal carotid artery. ( )
b medial of the two grooves on the medial aspect of the mastoid process houses the occipital artery. ( )
c tip of the styloid process gives attachment to the stylomandibular ligament. ( )
d the stylomastoid foramen transmits the vestibulocochlear nerve. ( )
e hypoglossal nerve passes through the posterior condylar foramen. ( )

264 The mandible:
a gives attachment to the lateral pterygoid muscle along the coronoid process. ( )
b gives attachment to the medial pterygoid muscle along the coronoid process. ( )
c has the lingual nerve crossing the root of the 3rd molar tooth. ( )
d gives attachment to the sphenomandibular ligament at the lingula. ( )
e develops in the cartilage of the first pharyngeal arch (Meckel's cartilage). ( )

265 The maxilla:
a has a rounded tuberosity at the posterior aspect of the alveolar process. ( )
b has a large opening on its medial surface. ( )
c has the infraorbital nerve and vessels running through its superior surface. ( )
d contributes to the floor of the orbit. ( )
e develops in cartilage from a centre above the canine tooth. ( )

266 The sphenoid bone transmits the:
a mandibular branch of the trigeminal nerve. ( )
b middle meningeal artery. ( )
c internal carotid artery. ( )
d optic nerve. ( )
e ophthalmic nerve. ( )

a **F**— The foramen in life is filled with cartilage which forms the floor of the carotid canal medially.

b **T**— The lateral gives attachment to the posterior belly of the digastric muscle.

c **F**— The stylohyoid ligament is attached at this site. Both ligament and process are derived from the cartilage of the 2nd pharyngeal arch.

d **F**— It transmits the facial nerve.

e **F**— The nerve passes through the anterior (hypoglossal) foramen. The posterior transmits an emissary vein.

a **F**— The muscle is attached to the fossa on the front of the neck of the mandible. The temporalis muscle is attached to the coronoid process.

b **F**— It is attached to the medial surface of the ramus below the mandibular foramen.

c **T**— This is an important landmark in dental anaesthesia.

d **T**— Both are derived from the cartilage of 1st pharyngeal arch.

e **F**— The bone develops in the mesenchyme lateral to this cartilage which later disappears as the bone grows round it.

a **T**— One head of the medial pterygoid muscle is attached here.

b **T**— This is largely covered in the articulated skull by the bones of the lateral wall of the nose, especially the inferior concha.

c **T**— The bone in this region is thin and the nerve is usually damaged in maxillary fractures.

d **T**— The thin superior surface forms the larger part of the orbital floor.

e **F**— It develops in mesenchyme from a centre in this region.

a **T**— Via the foramen ovale in the greater wing.

b **T**— Via the foramen spinosum in the greater wing.

c **F**— The artery rests on the superior surface of the body of the sphenoid.

d **T**— Through the optic canal where it is surrounded by a sheath of the meninges and the subarachnoid space.

e **F**— Branches of the nerve pass into the orbit between the greater and lesser wings of the sphenoid.

267 **The body of the sphenoid:**
  a articulates anteriorly with the frontal bone.   (   )

  b forms the roof of the nasopharynx.   (   )

  c projects posterosuperiorly as the dorsum sellae.   (   )
  d forms the inferior relation of the cavernous sinus.   (   )
  e ossifies in cartilage.   (   )

268 **The temporal bone transmits the:**
  a trigeminal nerve.   (   )

  b facial nerve.   (   )

  c abducent nerve.   (   )

  d vestibulocochlear nerve.   (   )

  e glossopharyngeal nerve.   (   )

269 **The petrous part of the temporal bone:**
  a contains the carotid canal.   (   )

  b transmits the greater petrosal nerve.   (   )

  c transmits the lesser petrosal nerve.   (   )

  d forms the floor of the external acoustic meatus.   (   )

  e is closely related to the internal jugular vein.   (   )

a F— The lesser wings articulate with the orbital plate of the ✓
frontal bone on each side and the ethmoid medially.
b T— Small collections of lymphoid tissue in this region form the
pharyngeal tonsil (adenoids).
c T— This forms the posterior boundary of the pituitary fossa.
d T— On either side of the pituitary fossa.
e T— Only the pterygoid processes and the lateral part of the ✓
greater wings ossify in mesenchyme.

a F— The trigeminal ganglion grooves the apex of the petrous
temporal bone.
b T— This nerve enters by the internal acoustic meatus and
leaves through the stylomastoid foramen.
c F— This nerve leaves the cranial cavity through the superior
orbital fissure having crossed the apex of the petrous
temporal bone.
d T— The nerve enters the internal acoustic meatus to reach the
inner ear.
e F— It passes through the jugular foramen formed between
temporal and occipital bones.

a T— The canal transmits the internal carotid artery surrounded
with a plexus of sympathetic nerves.
b T— This nerve leaves the facial nerve at the geniculate
ganglion and becomes the nerve of pterygoid canal.
c T— This nerve comes from the tympanic plexus and passes to
the otic ganglion.
d F— It contains the internal acoustic meatus which transmits the
facial and vestibulocochlear nerves and the labyrinthine
vessels.
e T— The jugular foramen is bounded by the temporal and
occipital bones.

270 The styloid process:
  a gives attachment to the styloglossus muscle
     near its tip.   (   )
  b gives attachment to a muscle supplied by the
     glossopharyngeal nerve.   (   )
  c gives attachment to a muscle supplied by the
     facial nerve.   (   )
  d gives attachment to a muscle supplied by the
     vagus nerve.   (   )
  e ossifies in cartilage.   (   )

271 The occipital bone:
  a gives attachment to the oblique capitis inferior
     muscle.   (   )

  b is grooved by the superior sagittal sinus.   (   )

  c transmits the vestibulocochlear nerve.   (   )

  d transmits the vagus nerve.   (   )

  e develops mostly in cartilage.   (   )

272 The frontal bone:
  a transmits the zygomatic nerve.   (   )

  b articulates with the greater wing of the sphenoid. (   )
  c articulates with the zygomatic bones.   (   )
  d gives attachment to the temporalis muscle.   (   )
  e articulates only with bones formed in mesenchyme. (   )

a T— This is the lowest of its three muscle attachments. The muscle is supplied by the hypoglossal nerve.

b T— Stylopharyngeus is the only muscle supplied by this nerve.

c T— The stylohyoid muscle. It is attached between the other two styloid muscles.

d F

e T— From the cartilage of the 2nd pharyngeal arch which also gives rise to the stapes and part of the hyoid bone. The squamous and tympanic parts of the temporal bone ossify in mesenchyme. The petromastoid part of the temporal bone ossifies in cartilage (part of the chondrocranium). The malleus and incus arise from the 1st pharyngeal arch cartilage.

a F— This muscle passes from the spine of the axis to the transverse mass of the atlas. The superior oblique is attached to the occiput.

b T— This is usually in continuity with the right transverse venous sinus.

c F— This passes into the internal acoustic meatus of the petrous temporal bone. The hypoglossal nerve emerges through a foramen in front of the occipital condyle.

d F— The bone borders the jugular foramen that transmits the nerve.

e T— Only the squamous portion (above the superior nuchal line) develops in mesenchyme.

a F— The facial and temporal branches of this nerve pass through small foramina in the zygomatic bone.

b T— In the lateral wall of the orbit.

c T— Along the lateral orbital margin.

d T— In the temporal fossa.

e F— The ethmoid and the lesser wings of the sphenoid bones are the exceptions.

273   The ethmoid bone:

a   forms part of the medial wall of the orbit.   (   )

b   forms the inferior conchae.   (   )

c   articulates with the nasal bone.   (   )
d   articulates with the vomer.   (   )

e   is perforated by the olfactory nerves.   (   )

274   The palatine bone:

a   has a tubercle which separates the maxilla from the
     pterygoid process of the sphenoid bone.   (   )
b   forms part of the roof of the mouth.   (   )

c   articulates with the medial pterygoid plate.   (   )

d   meets the maxilla and forms the nasolacrimal duct.   (   )

e   forms part of the nasal septum.   (   )

275   The hyoid bone:

a   gives attachment of the superior constrictor muscles. (   )

b   is attached by a muscle to the scapula.   (   )
c   gives attachment to a muscle supplied by the
     facial nerve.   (   )
d   gives attachment to a muscle supplied by the
     hypoglossal nerve.   (   )
e   is mainly derived from the 4th pharyngeal arch
     cartilage.   (   )

276   The scalp:

a   is attached by the occipitalis muscle to the skull.   (   )
b   is attached by the frontalis muscle to the skull.   (   )
c   receives sensory innervation from the dorsal rami
     of the 2nd and 3rd cervical nerves.   (   )
d   receives part of its blood supply from the
     ophthalmic artery.   (   )
e   drains directly to the deep lymph nodes around
     the carotid sheath.   (   )

a **T**— The ethmoidal labyrinth lies between the orbit and the nasal cavity.
b **F**— This is a separate bone but the superior and middle conchae are part of the ethmoid.
c **F**— The nasal process of the frontal bone lies between them.
d **T**— By its perpendicular plate. Together they form the bony portions of the nasal septum.
e **T**— Through the cribriform plate.

a **T**

b **T**— It lies between the palatine part of the maxilla and the soft palate.
c **T**— With it forming the posterior aspect of the lateral wall of the nose.
d **F**— The bone does meet the maxilla but the greater palatine canal is formed.
e **T**— With its vertical plate.

a **F**— The middle constrictor is attached to the greater and lesser horns and the stylohyoid ligament.
b **T**— By the omohyoid muscle.
c **T**— Both the stylohyoid and the posterior belly of digastric are supplied by the facial nerve.
d **T**— Hyoglossus is attached to the body and greater horn of the hyoid bone.
e **F**— It develops from the cartilages of the 2nd and 3rd arches.

a **T**— The muscle is attached to the superior nuchal line.
b **F**— The frontalis is not attached to bone.
c **T**— Via the greater and 3rd occipital nerves behind the vertex. The trigeminal nerve supplies in front of the vertex.
d **T**— Via the supraorbital and supratrochlear branches of the ophthalmic artery.
e **F**— A superficial circle of lymph nodes around the lower parts of the skull first receives the lymph drained from the scalp.

277 The facial muscles:
  a are embedded in the deep fascia of the face.   (   )

  b are derived from the mesenchyme of the second
        pharyngeal arch.   (   )
  c share a common raphe with a constrictor muscle.   (   )

  d gain a bony attachment through the medial
        palpebral ligament.   (   )
  e have no bony attachments.   (   )

278 Buccinator:
  a is attached to both maxilla and mandible.   (   )
  b blends with orbicularis oculi.   (   )

  c has vertical muscle fibres.   (   )
  d is used during chewing.   (   )
  e is supplied by the trigeminal nerve.   (   )

279 In the development of the face the:
  a mandibular process is derived from the 2nd
        pharyngeal arch.   (   )
  b maxillary process is developed from the 1st
        pharyngeal arch.   (   )
  c greater palatine canal develops along the line of
        fusion of the frontonasal and maxillary processes.   (   )
  d part of the upper jaw bearing the incisor teeth
        develops from the frontonasal process.   (   )
  e the forehead is formed from the maxillary
        processes.   (   )

280 The superior orbital fissure:
  a is bounded by the greater wing of the sphenoid
        and the orbital plate of the frontal bone.   (   )
  b links the orbit with the pterygopalatine fossa.   (   )

  c transmits the optic nerve.   (   )

  d transmits the trochlear nerve within the common
        tendinous ring of attachment of the extraocular
        muscles.   (   )
  e transmits the lacrimal nerve within the common
        tendinous ring.   (   )

a **F**— There is no deep fascia on the face, other than that over the parotid gland.
b **T**— They are supplied by the nerve of the arch, the facial nerve.
c **T**— The pterygomandibular raphe unites the buccinator and superior constrictor muscles.
d **T**— This ligament receives fibres from the orbicularis oculi and is attached to the frontal process of the maxilla.
e **F**— Ocular muscles are attached to bone medially, and oral to the zygoma and mandible.

a **T**— It is attached to both bones and the pterygomandibular
b **F** raphe and its transverse fibres pass forwards to blend with those of orbicularis oris.
c **F**
d **T**— Its action helps to keep food between the teeth in chewing.
e **F**— It is supplied by the facial nerve.

a **F**— The mandibular process is a derivative of the 1st pharyngeal arch and the maxillary process also grows
b **T** from the mandibular process.

c **F**— The nasolacrimal duct is formed along this line of fusion.

d **T**— This premaxillary portion is formed from the median nasal process of the frontonasal process.
e **F**— It is formed from the frontonasal process.

a **F**— It lies between the greater and lesser wings of the sphenoid, linking the orbit with the middle cranial fossa.
b **F**— This fossa communicates with the orbit through the inferior orbital fissure.
c **F**— The nerve enters the orbit through the optic canal between the body and the lesser wing of sphenoid.
d **F**— The lacrimal, frontal and trochlear nerves pass through the fissure outside this attachment. The nasociliary, oculomotor and abducent nerves are within the ring.
e **F**

281 In the eyeball:
a the cornea is a derivative of the choroid layer. ( )

b the fovea centralis represents the site of entry of
the optic nerve into the eyeball. ( )

c the posterior chamber of the eye is filled with
vitreous substance. ( )

d ciliary muscle contraction produces a more convex
lens. ( )

e the medial check ligament is attached to the
maxillary bone. ( )

282 In the eyeball the:
a ciliary branches of the ophthalmic artery supply the
macular area. ( )

b long ciliary nerves come from the ciliary ganglion
and pierce the sclera posteriorly. ( )

c iris is developed from the mesenchyme. ( )

d medial check ligament is attached to the frontal
process of the maxillary bone. ( )

e suspensory ligament is an extension of the
superior oblique tendon. ( )

283 In movements of the eyeball:
a downward and medial movement is initiated
through the inferior division of the oculomotor nerve. ( )

b lateral movement is mediated through the superior
division of the oculomotor nerve. ( )

c upward and medial movement is mediated through
the abducent nerve. ( )

d downward and lateral movement is initiated through
the trochlear nerve. ( )

e medial movement is mediated through the abducent
nerve. ( )

a **F**— The cornea is derived as a condensation of the mesenchyme over the optic cup. *2un*

b **F**— The fovea and the macula lie lateral to the nerve entry and are used mainly for daylight vision.

c **F**— This chamber lies between the lens and the iris, and is filled with aqueous humor.

d **T**— The circular ciliary muscle is supplied by the parasympathetic fibres in the oculomotor nerve. The increased convexity is produced by the inherent elasticity of the lens when the suspensory ligament (zonular fibres) is relaxed.

e **F**— The medial and lateral check ligaments are respectively attached to the lacrimal and zygomatic bones. *2uy*

a **F**— The central artery of the retina, a branch of the ophthalmic artery, supplies the macula and the rest of the retina.

b **F**— These nerves are branches of the nasociliary nerve and are sensory to the cornea. The ganglion gives rise to the short ciliary nerves which contain the postganglionic parasympathetic (constrictor) fibres to the ciliary body and iris.

c **F**— Like the optic nerve and retina, it is a derivative of the primitive forebrain and hence of ectoderm. *2uy*

d **F**— It, like the lateral check and suspensory ligaments, is a thickening of the orbital fascia. It is attached to the lacrimal bone.

e **F**— It is a thickening of the orbital fascia.

a **T**— The muscle being the inferior rectus.

b **F**— The lateral rectus is supplied by the abducent nerve.

c **F**— The superior rectus muscle is supplied by the superior division of the oculomotor nerve.

d **T**— The muscle being the superior oblique.

e **F**— The medial rectus is supplied by the inferior division of the oculomotor nerve.

284   The ophthalmic artery:

a   arises from the internal carotid artery soon after it
    pierces the dura and enters the subarachnoid space. (   )

b   enters the orbit through the superior orbital fissure. (   )
c   passes from medial to lateral over the optic nerve as
    these structures pass anteriorly through the orbit. (   )

d   terminates by dividing into supraorbital and
    infratrochlear branches. (   )
e   supplies the eyeball through the central branch of the
    supratrochlear artery. (   )

285   In the eyelid the:

a   tarsal plate is formed of elastic cartilage. (   )
b   tarsal glands are modified sweat glands. (   )
c   tarsal plate is attached to the medial palpebral
    ligament. (   )
d   posterior lining is ciliated columnar epithelium. (   )

e   conjunctival fornix is lined by ciliated columnar
    epithelium. (   )

286   In the lacrimal apparatus:

a   the lacrimal gland is innervated by the
    zygomaticotemporal nerve. (   )

b   the gland is superficial to the orbicularis oculi
    muscle. (   )

c   removal of tears is entirely by evaporation from the
    exposed surface of the eyeball. (   )

d   the nasolacrimal duct descends between the
    maxillary bone and the inferior concha. (   )
e   the lacrimal canaliculi are lined by stratified
    squamous epithelium. (   )

a **T**— The internal carotid artery also gives off pituitary, trigeminal, posterior communicating and anterior choroidal branches before dividing into the anterior and the middle cerebral arteries.

b **F**— It traverses the optic canal with the optic nerve.

c **F**— The artery passes from lateral to medial over the optic nerve in company with the nasociliary nerve and near to the ciliary ganglion.

d **F**— The usual termination is into the supratrochlear and dorsal nasal arteries.

e **F**— The central artery of the retina is a direct branch of the ophthalmic.

a **F**— It is formed of firm fibrous tissue.

b **F**— These are modified sebaceous glands.

c **T**— Also to the lateral palpebral ligament.

d **F**— The conjunctiva has mainly a thin layer of stratified columnar epithelium. Over the cornea it is stratified

e **F** squamous and firmly adherent.

a **T**— From the superior salivary nucleus fibres run with the facial nerve and its greater petrosal branch to the pterygopalatine ganglion. Postganglionic fibres run in the zygomaticotemporal branch of the maxillary nerve to the lacrimal branch of the ophthalmic nerve.

b **F**— Much of the gland is surrounded by fibres of orbicularis oculi which help in the expulsion of the tears from the gland.

c **F**— Evaporation may occur under normal conditions but when excessive tears (e.g. in crying) are produced, the extra fluid passes from the lacrimal puncta into the canaliculi (about 10 mm long), under the medial palpebral ligament and into the lacrimal sac.

d **T**— It opens on to the inferior meatus of the nose.

e **T**— The lacrimal sac is lined by stratified columnar epithelium and the nasolacrimal duct by columnar epithelium that is ciliated in places.

287   The nasal cavity is:
   a   partly roofed by the cribriform plate of the ethmoid
       bone.   (   )
   b   partly floored by the inferior concha.   (   )
   c   limited medially by the ethmoid bone.   (   )

   d   limited laterally by the ethmoid and the palatine
       bones.   (   )

   e   innervated medially by the anterior ethmoidal nerve. (   )

288   On the lateral wall of the nose:
   a   the sphenoidal air sinus opens into the spheno-
       ethmoidal recess.   (   )
   b   the bulla ethmoidalis is sited under the middle
       concha.   (   )
   c   the maxillary air sinus opens in the hiatus
       semilunaris.   (   )
   d   the frontonasal duct of the frontal air sinus opens
       into the hiatus semilunaris.   (   )

   e   the inferior meatus has no openings on its lateral
       wall.   (   )

289   The lateral wall of the nose:
   a   has the lacrimal sac lying between the lacrimal and
       maxillary bones.   (   )
   b   is partly lined by pseudostratified ciliated columnar
       epithelium with goblet cells.   (   )

   c   anteriorly, drains to the parotid lymph nodes.   (   )

   d   has an upper posterior quadrant supplied by the
       nasal branches of the maxillary nerve.   (   )
   e   has a lower anterior quadrant supplied by the
       olfactory nerves.   (   )

a T— Also the body of the sphenoid, the nasal and frontal bones, and the nasal cartilages.
b F— The maxilla and palatine bones form the floor.
c T— The vertical plate of this bone together with the vomer and the septal cartilages form the medial wall.
d T— The inferior concha overlies the large defect in the medial surface of the maxilla. The medial pterygoid plate is found posteriorly.
e T— Also the nasopalatine nerve.

a T— The recess is above the superior concha.

b T— The bulla is formed by ethmoidal air cells which open on its surface.
c F— The hiatus is a groove below the bulla ethmoidalis; near its middle is the opening of the maxillary sinus.
d T— The opening is anterosuperior to that of the maxillary sinus, so that the frontal sinus tends to drain into the maxillary sinus.
e F— The nasolacrimal duct opens anteriorly. Behind the meatus, on the pharyngeal wall, is the opening of the auditory tube.

a T— The sac is thin-walled and lies near the skin at the inner angle of the orbit.
b T— This respiratory-type epithelium covers most of the wall, the upper part being lined by olfactory mucosa. The whole region is very vascular.
c F— This region drains to the submandibular nodes, and the posterior part to the retropharyngeal nodes.
d T— The anterior superior, alveolar, and greater palatine branches of the maxillary, and the anterior ethmoidal
e F branch of the ophthalmic nerves contribute to the remainder of the lateral wall. The arteries generally correspond. Olfactory mucosa is limited to the roof and upper part of the septum and lateral wall.

290   **The maxillary air sinus:**
  a   projects laterally into the zygomatic bone.   (   )
  b   is grooved by the anterior ethmoidal nerve.   (   )

  c   is related to the upper teeth except the incisors.   (   )

  d   has a small opening high on its medial wall.   (   )
  e   is partly formed medially by the sphenoid bone.   (   )

291   **In the oral cavity the:**
  a   posterior limit is at the level of the palatopharyngeus
          muscle in the posterior arch (pillar) of the fauces.   (   )
  b   parotid duct opens opposite the crowns of the
          second premolar tooth.   (   )
  c   upper incisors have a bilateral innervation from the
          anterior superior alveolar nerves.   (   )
  d   submandibular duct opens at the root of the second
          lower premolar tooth.   (   )
  e   the frenulum passes from the tongue to the base of
          the anterior arch of the fauces.   (   )

292   **In the gingivae (gums) the:**
  a   upper labial surface is partly supplied by the
          zygomatic nerve.   (   )
  b   upper lingual surface is partly supplied by the
          anterior ethmoidal nerve.   (   )
  c   lower labial surface is partly supplied by the facial
          nerve.   (   )
  d   lower lingual surface is partly supplied by the inferior
          alveolar nerve.   (   )
  e   mucous membrane is of the stratified squamous
          variety.   (   )

a F— But it does extend into the zygomatic process of the maxilla.

b F— The posterior superior alveolar nerve grooves its posterior wall. The inferior orbital nerve grooves its upper surface, passing into the infraorbital canal anteriorly.

c T— Although the premaxilla develops from the frontonasal process it is incorporated into the maxillary bone. The roots of the premolar and molar teeth, with a thin bony covering, often project into the sinus but the incisors (on the premaxilla) are not related.

d T— Drainage being, therefore, poor.

e F— The medial wall is overlapped by the inferior concha, and to a lesser extent by the lacrimal, ethmoid and palatine bones.

a F— The anterior arch (pillar) of the fauces formed by the palatoglossus muscle is the posterior limit of the cavity.

b F— It opens opposite the crown of the upper 2nd molar tooth.

c T— These branches of the infraorbital nerve are formed in the infraorbital canal.

d F— It opens on the floor of the mouth near the midline on each side of the frenulum of the tongue.

e F— It passes in the midline from the tongue to the floor of the mouth.

a F— The infraorbital and posterior superior alveolar nerves supply this region.

b F— It is innervated by the nasopalatine and greater palatine nerves.

c F— It is supplied by the buccal and mental nerves.

d F— This area is supplied by the lingual nerve.

e T— It is vascular and firmly attached to the alveolar margins.

293 **The deciduous teeth:**
  a start erupting in the 4th month after birth.   ( )

  b are 20 in number.   ( )
  c have only one upper premolar.   ( )
  d are replaced earlier in the upper jaw by permanent
    teeth.   ( )
  e derive their dentine from mesenchyme.   ( )

294 **In the hard palate:**
  a the vomer forms the posterior bony edge.   ( )

  b the incisive foramen transmits the lesser palatine
    artery.   ( )

  c the mucoperiosteum is rich in mucous glands.   ( )
  d the nasopalatine nerve innervates the muco-
    periosteum adjacent to the premolar teeth in the
    adult.   ( )
  e development is mainly by the palatine process of the
    mandibular process on each side.   ( )

295 **The soft palate:**
  a has different forms of epithelium on its upper and
    lower surfaces.   ( )

  b has an aponeurosis formed from the expanded
    tendons of the levator veli palatini muscles.   ( )
  c gives attachment to the palatoglossus muscle.   ( )
  d possesses muscles mainly innervated by nerve fibres
    arising in the nucleus ambiguus.   ( )

  e receives a sensory innervation from the mandibular
    branch of the trigeminal nerve.   ( )

a **F**— The first lower incisor erupts at about 6 months. The first permanent teeth (the first lower molars) appear at about 6 years.

b **T**— I2, C1, M2 — in each half jaw.

c **F**— There are no deciduous premolar teeth.

d **F**— The lower permanent teeth appear slightly earlier.

e **T**— The ectodermal folds growing in from the mouth cavity produce the primary dental lamina. The enamel is derived only from ectoderm. The rest of the tooth is derived from the ectodermal cup and its contained mesenchyme.

a **F**— It is formed from the palatine process of the maxilla and the horizontal plate of the palatine bones.

b **F**— The terminal branch of the greater palatine artery transverses the foramen along with the nasopalatine nerves.

c **T**— They contribute to the unevenness of the oral surface.

d **F**— The nerve traverses the incisive foramen and innervates the area behind the incisor teeth.

e **F**— The palatine process develops from the maxillary process, the palate being completed anteriorly in the midline by the premaxillary process on the frontonasal process, and posteriorly by the horizontal process of the palatine bone.

a **T**— Respiratory pseudostratified ciliated columnar epithelium covers the upper and stratified squamous epithelium the lower surface.

b **F**— The tensor veli palatini tendons from the aponeurosis.

c **T**— The muscle passes into the side of the tongue.

d **T**— The vagus innervates all muscles of the palate except tensor veli palatini through the pharyngeal plexus. The exception is supplied by the medial pterygoid branch of the mandibular nerve.

e **F**— The sensory innervation is from the palatine branches of the maxillary and the glossopharyngeal nerves.

296　The tongue:

a　has a foramen caecum situated at the base of the
　　frenulum.　　　　　　　　　　　　　　　　　　　(　)

b　is separated from the epiglottis by the valleculae on
　　each side of the midline.　　　　　　　　　　　　(　)

c　has 7–12 circumvallate papillae situated just behind
　　the sulcus terminalis.　　　　　　　　　　　　　(　)

d　is attached to the hyoid bone by the genioglossus
　　muscle.　　　　　　　　　　　　　　　　　　　(　)

e　musculature is derived from 2nd pharyngeal arch
　　mesoderm.　　　　　　　　　　　　　　　　　　(　)

297　The hyoglossus muscle:

a　lies lateral to the styloglossus.　　　　　　　　　(　)

b　has a different nerve supply from palatoglossus.　(　)

c　has the hypoglossal nerve on its lateral surface.　(　)

d　has the submandibular duct on its medial surface.　(　)

e　has the submandibular gland wrapped around its
　　posterior border.　　　　　　　　　　　　　　　(　)

298　On the tongue the:

a　circumvallate papillae are innervated by the
　　glossopharyngeal nerve.　　　　　　　　　　　　(　)

b　lymph drainage of the posterior third is to the
　　submandibular lymph nodes.　　　　　　　　　　(　)

c　lymph drainage of the anterior two-thirds is to the
　　submandibular nodes.　　　　　　　　　　　　　(　)

d　posterior third develops from two lateral lingual
　　swellings.　　　　　　　　　　　　　　　　　　(　)

e　taste impulses from the posterior third travel in the
　　glossopharyngeal nerves and are relayed in the
　　nucleus of the tractus solitarius.　　　　　　　　(　)

a **F**— The foramen caecum lies at the apex of the sulcus terminalis on the dorsum of the tongue towards the back.
b **T**— These are two shallow fossae separated by the midline glossoepiglottic fold.
c **F**— The papillae lie just in front of the sulcus.

d **F**— This muscle attaches it to the mental spine of the mandible. Hyoglossus and other muscles help anchor the tongue to the hyoid bone.
e **F**— It is from suboccipital somites migrating forward and carrying their nerve supply (hypoglossal) with them.

a **F**— The styloglossus lies laterally. The stylopharyngeus is a superolateral relation of hyoglossus muscle.
b **T**— All the intrinsic and extrinsic muscles except palatoglossus are supplied by the hypoglossal nerve. Palatoglossus is supplied by the nucleus ambiguus through the pharyngeal plexus.
c **T**— And the lingual artery on its medial surface.
d **F**— The duct is crossed twice by the lingual nerve on the lateral surface of the muscle.
e **F**— The gland lies on the lateral surface of the muscle.

a **T**— Although they lie in front of the sulcus terminalis and this approximates to the divison of the lingual and glossopharyngeal areas of innervation.
b **F**— The posterior third drains to the retropharyngeal nodes. The tip drains bilaterally to submental nodes and the sides
c **T** ipsilaterally to the submandibular nodes.

d **F**— These swellings develop into the anterior two-thirds of the tongue. The posterior third comes from the copula over the 3rd and 4th arches. The muscles are derived from occipital myotomes which migrate ventrally and carry the hypoglossal nerves with them.
e **T**— As are those of the anterior part which are carried in the lingual and chorda tympani nerves.

299 The digastric muscle:

a   receives an innervation from the hypoglossal nerve.   (   )

b   crosses the tip of the transverse process of the atlas. (   )

c   passes between the internal and external carotid
arteries.   (   )

d   has the occipital artery passing along the lower
border of its posterior belly.   (   )

e   is attached to the lateral aspect of the mastoid
process.   (   )

300 The parotid gland:

a   is separated from the submandibular gland by the
sphenomandibular ligament.   (   )

b   is related anteriorly to the lateral pterygoid muscle. (   )

c   is related posteriorly to the sternocleidomastoid
muscle.   (   )

d   has the external carotid artery running superficial to
the facial nerve within its substance.   (   )

e   receives secretomotor fibres from the facial nerve.   (   )

301 The submandibular gland:

a   like the sublingual receives its parasympathetic
innervation from the facial nerve.   (   )

b   is grooved superiorly by the loop of the lingual
artery.   (   )

c   overlies the glossopharyngeal nerve.   (   )

d   is a mixed salivary gland.   (   )

e   develops from second pharyngeal arch mesoderm.   (   )

a F— The anterior belly is supplied by the mylohyoid branch of the inferior alveolar nerve and the posterior by the facial nerve.

b T— Along with the spinal accessory nerve and other structures.

c F— It passes superficial to both arteries.

d T— And the posterior auricular artery passes along the upper border of this belly.

e F— The posterior belly is attached to a groove on the medial aspect of the mastoid process and the anterior belly to the digastric fossa on the mandible.

a F— They are separated by the stylomandibular ligament which is a thickening of the deep fascia, and forms part of the parotid capsule.

b F— The anterior surface overlaps the medial pterygoid and masseter muscles and the intervening ramus of the mandible.

c T— Also the posterior belly of the digastric muscle and the mastoid process.

d F— The nerve is superficial to the artery.

e F— The secretomotor (parasympathetic) fibres are from the glossopharyngeal nerve via the otic ganglion and auriculotemporal nerve.

a T— Fibres pass in the chorda tympani and lingual nerves, and relay in the submandibular ganglion.

b F— The loop of the lingual artery lies posterior to the gland on the middle constrictor. The facial artery passes over the superior surface of the gland.

c F— It is related to the hyoglossal nerve on the hyoglossus muscle.

d T— Like the sublingual, but not the parotid which is a serous gland.

e F— It develops as a tubular endodermal outgrowth from the floor of the mouth.

302   The submandibular duct:
  a   lies deep to mylohyoid.   (   )
  b   opens at the base of the frenulum.   (   )

  c   passes deep to the lingual nerve.   (   )
  d   passes superficial to the lingual nerve.   (   )
  e   receives all the sublingual gland secretion.   (   )

303   The temporomandibular joint:
  a   lateral ligament is taut when the jaw is elevated.   (   )

  b   is a condyloid joint.   (   )

  c   has the tendon of the medial pterygoid muscle
        attached to the fibrocartilaginous disc.   (   )

  d   has the chorda tympani nerve as a posterior relation. (   )
  e   is related to the auriculotemporal nerve posteriorly. (   )

304   The medial pterygoid muscle:
  a   is attached to the lateral pterygoid plate of the
        sphenoid bone.   (   )
  b   is attached to the maxillary tuberosity.   (   )

  c   is attached to the infratemporal surface of the
        greater wing of the sphenoid.   (   )
  d   is innervated by the buccal nerve.   (   )

  e   together with the lateral pterygoid elevates the
        mandible.   (   )

a **T**— The duct passes forward from the deep part of the gland
b **T**   between mylohyoid and hyoglossus to open in the floor of
     the mouth at the sublingual papilla at the base of the
     frenulum.
c **T**— It is crossed laterally by the lingual nerve which then turns
d **T**   medial to it.
e **F**— The sublingual gland partly secretes into the
     submandibular duct but also has 15–20 small ducts
     opening on to the sublingual fold on the floor of the
     mouth.

a **T**— This is the most stable position of the joint, the condyle
     also being housed in the articular fossa.
b **T**— It is a synovial joint of the condyloid (modified hinge)
     variety.
c **F**— The lateral pterygoid muscle is attached to the anterior
     edge of the disc, to the joint capsule and to the neck of the
     mandible.
d **T**— As the nerve passes through the petrotympanic fissure.
e **T**   The capsule of the joint is attached to the anterior edge of
     the fissure.

a **T**— The deep head of the muscle is attached to the medial
     surface of the plate.
b **T**— By the superficial head. The two heads embrace the lower
     fibres of the lateral pterygoid muscle.
c **F**— This is the attachment of the upper head of the lateral
     pterygoid muscle.
d **F**— This is a sensory branch of the mandibular nerve; the
     motor branches of the mandibular nerve supply all the
     muscles of mastication.
e **F**— The medial elevates and the lateral protrudes and
     depresses the mandible. The axis of rotation is through the
     lingula.

305   The pharynx:

a   extends from the base of the skull to the 4th
cervical vertebra.   (   )

b   is supported superiorly by the pharyngobasilar
fascia.   (   )

c   is related posteriorly to the prevertebral fascia.   (   )
d   is related anteriorly to the pretracheal fascia.   (   )

e   has a muscular attachment to the pterygomandibular
raphe.   (   )

306   The middle constrictor muscle:

a   lies medial to the superior constrictor.   (   )

b   is attached anteriorly to the stylomandibular
ligament.   (   )
c   is attached anteriorly to the stylohyoid ligament.   (   )
d   has the superior laryngeal artery between it and the
inferior constrictor.   (   )
e   is innervated by the glossopharyngeal nerve.   (   )

307   The interior of the pharynx:

a   is ridged by the salpingopharyngeus muscle.   (   )

b   receives a sensory innervation from the mandibular
nerve.   (   )

c   receives a sensory innervation from the accessory
nerve.   (   )
d   has the palatine tonsil in the lateral wall.   (   )

e   has an anterior extension on each side of the larynx
known as the vallecula.   (   )

a **F**— The latter is the level of the hyoid bone. The oesophagus and trachea commence at the level of the cricoid cartilage, opposite the 6th cervical vertebra.

b **T**— The fascia is the thickened submucosa between the upper border of the superior constrictor muscles and the base of the skull.

c **T**— This covers the prevertebral muscles.

d **F**— The pharynx is related anteriorly to the nose, mouth and larynx, these dividing it into its respective portions.

e **T**— This is the anterior attachment of the superior constrictor muscle.

a **F**— It lies medial to the inferior but lateral to the superior constrictor muscle.

b **F**— It is attached to the lesser and greater horns of the hyoid and the stylohyoid ligament.

c **T**

d **T**— The artery runs with the internal laryngeal nerve.

e **F**— This nerve supplies stylopharyngeus, but all other pharyngeal muscles are supplied by the vagus through the pharyngeal plexus and the nucleus ambiguus.

a **T**— A small diverticulum, the pharyngeal recess, is formed behind it.

b **F**— The pharyngeal branches of the maxillary, glossopharyngeal and vagus nerves provide sensory innervation.

c **F**

d **T**— This lies between the folds of mucous membrane over the palatoglossus and palatopharyngeus muscles.

e **F**— The extension is the piriform fossa.

308 **The palatine tonsil:**
  a lies on the middle constrictor muscle. ( )

  b is a posterior relation of the palatopharyngeal
    muscle. ( )
  c has its lymph drainage to the submandibular nodes. ( )

  d has a sensory innervation from the vagus. ( )

  e is a derivative of the first pharyngeal pouch. ( )

309 **The auditory tube:**
  a extends laterally into the squamous temporal bone. ( )
  b opens medially into the lateral wall of the nose. ( )

  c gives attachment to the tensor veli palatini muscle. ( )

  d sends lymph vessels to the submandibular lymph
    nodes. ( )
  e is lined by ciliated columnar epithelium. ( )

310 **In the development of the pharyngeal arches the:**
  a nerve of the 4th arch is the superior laryngeal. ( )
  b external acoustic meatus is derived from the 2nd
    pharyngeal cleft. ( )
  c sphenomandibular ligament is a remnant of the
    2nd pharyngeal arch cartilage. ( )

  d greater and lesser horns of the hyoid bone have the
    same origin. ( )
  e larynx is derived from cartilage of the 4th and
    6th arches. ( )

a **F**— The superior constrictor separates it from the facial artery and carotid sheath.

b **F**— This muscle lies in the palatopharyngeal arch and is posterior to the tonsil.

c **F**— The primary drainage is to the deep cervical lymph nodes, particularly to the jugulodigastric node.

d **F**— The sensory innervation is from the glossopharyngeal with a small contribution from the lesser palatine nerve.

e **F**— The tonsil is a derivative of the 2nd pouch, the first contributing to the auditory tube, middle ear and mastoid antrum.

a **F**— Its lateral third lies within the petrous temporal bone.

b **F**— The medial opening is in the lateral wall of the nasopharynx.

c **T**— Also the levator veli palatini and salpingopharyngeus muscles. These muscles help to open the tube in swallowing.

d **F**— It drains to the retropharyngeal nodes.

e **T**— With many mucous glands.

a **T**— The recurrent laryngeal nerve supplies the 6th arch.

b **F**— The meatus is derived from the 1st cleft.

c **F**— The 1st arch cartilage is represented by this ligament, Meckel's cartilage, the malleus and the incus. The mandibular division of the trigeminal is the nerve of the 1st arch.

d **F**— The greater horn and lower part of the body are derived from 3rd arch cartilage, the nerve of which is the

e **T** glossopharyngeal. The remainder of the hyoid bone, the stylohyoid ligament, the styloid process and the stapes are 2nd arch derivatives, their nerve being the facial.

311   The second stage (pharyngeal phase) of swallowing is:
  a voluntary.
  b initiated through the glossopharyngeal nerve.   (   )

  c partly effected through the hypoglossal nerve.   (   )
  d partly effected through the maxillary nerve.   (   )

  e partly effected through the recurrent laryngeal nerve. (   )

312   The larynx:
  a is related anteriorly to the thyroid isthmus.   (   )

  b is related laterally to the carotid sheath.   (   )
  c is formed partly of yellow elastic cartilage.   (   )

  d lies opposite the 3rd–6th cervical vertebrae.   (   )
  e gives attachment to muscles supplied by the first
      cervical nerve root.   (   )

313   The thyroid cartilage is united to the cricoid cartilage by:
  a a pair of secondary cartilaginous joints.   (   )
  b the vocal ligaments.   (   )
  c the conus elasticus.   (   )
  d muscles supplied by the external laryngeal nerve. (   )
  e muscles supplied by the internal laryngeal nerve. (   )

314   The arytenoid cartilage:
  a is united to the cricoid by a plane, synovial joint. (   )

  b gives attachment to the vocal ligament.   (   )

  c gives attachment to the vestibular ligament.   (   )

  d has a muscular process which gives attachment to
      the oblique arytenoid muscle.   (   )

  e is covered posteriorly by mucous membrane.   (   )

a   **F**— Is largely involuntary.
b   **T**— Through stimulation of the anterior arch of the fauces. It may also be initiated by stimulation of the soft palate, oropharynx and epiglottis.
c   **F**— The tongue is closely involved in the first stage of swallowing.
d   **F**— The vagus nerve, through the pharyngeal plexus, is the important innervation. The soft palate is approximated to the pharyngeal wall and closes the pharyngeal isthmus.
e   **T**— The larynx is closed off and the pharynx shortened. Respiration is also inhibited during the swallow.

a   **F**— The lateral lobes of the gland are related but the isthmus is lower and overlies the 2nd and 3rd tracheal rings.
b   **T**
c   **T**— The epiglottis and part of the arytenoid cartilage are of this form and do not calcify.
d   **T**— From the epiglottis above to the cricoid cartilage below.
e   **T**— The geniohyoid and thyrohyoid muscles are innervated by C1 fibres carried in the hypoglossal nerve. In the ansa cervicalis are nerves derived from C2–3 to other infrahyoid muscles.

a   **F**— The cricothyroid joints are plane, synovial joints.
b   **F**— These ligaments join the thyroid and arytenoid cartilages.
c   **T**— The cricothyroid ligament is the anterior edge of this structure.
d   **T**— The cricothyroid muscle is innervated by the external
e   **T**   laryngeal nerve. The other intrinsic muscles are innervated by the recurrent laryngeal nerve.

a   **T**— Because of the obliquity of their surfaces downward displacement occurs with lateral gliding.
b   **T**— This is the thickened upper border of the conus elasticus. It is covered with mucous membrane and forms the true vocal cord.
c   **T**— This thickening in the inferior edge of the aryepiglottic membrane lies within the vestibular fold.
d   **F**— This muscle passes from the apex of one arytenoid cartilage to the base of the other as a continuation of the aryepiglottic muscle.
e   **T**— Forming an anterior relation of the laryngopharynx.

315   The interior of the larynx:

a   extends into the sinus of the larynx inferior to the vocal fold.   (   )

b   is supplied by the recurrent laryngeal nerve up to the level of the vestibular fold.   (   )

c   is bounded superiorly by the aryepiglottic folds.   (   )

d   is bounded inferiorly by the rima glottidis.   (   )

e   is lined by stratified squamous epithelium down to and including the vocal fold.   (   )

316   In movements of the larynx:

a   forward rotation of the thyroid on the cricoid cartilage shortens the vocal folds.   (   )

b   the posterior cricoarytenoid muscles close the vocal folds.   (   )

c   the vocalis muscle shortens the fold.   (   )

d   the thyroarytenoid muscle adducts the vocal folds.   (   )

e   contraction of the aryepiglottic muscles approximate the vestibular folds.   (   )

317   The external acoustic meatus:

a   is approximately 1.5 cm long.   (   )

b   contains no contribution from the petrous temporal bone.   (   )

c   has its medial wall facing downwards and backwards.(   )

d   is innervated posteriorly by the vagus nerve.   (   )

e   is innervated anteriorly by the glossopharyngeal nerve.   (   )

318   The middle ear:

a   is lined with stratified squamous epithelium.   (   )

b   communicates with the mastoid antrum through the aditus.   (   )

c   is innervated by the mandibular nerve.   (   )

d   accommodates the body of the incus in the epitympanic recess.   (   )

e   communicates with the laryngopharynx through the auditory tube.   (   )

a F— The sinus lies above the vocal fold between it and the vestibular fold and extends up lateral to the vestibular fold.

b F— The internal laryngeal nerve supplies the mucosa over the vestibular fold, i.e. including the sinus of the larynx.

c T

d F— This gap between the vocal folds lies above the laryngotracheal junction at the cricoid cartilage.

e T— The covering is respiratory epithelium below this level.

a F— The movement, brought about by the cricothyroid muscles, lengthens the vocal folds.

b F— These are the only muscles which acting alone can abduct the vocal folds.

c T— And also tenses the fold.

d F— This muscle shortens the vocal folds.

e F— This approximates the epiglottis to the arytenoids, closing the opening of the larynx.

a F— This approximates only to the cartilaginous lateral third, it is about 4 cm long in total.

b T— The bony part of the canal is formed mainly of the tympanic part of the temporal bone completed posterosuperiorly by the squamous temporal bone.

c F— The lateral surface of the tympanic membrane faces downwards and forwards.

d T— The auricular branch of the vagus enters the bone from below.

e F— The anterior surface is innervated by the auriculotemporal nerve.

a F— Its lining is partly of ciliated columnar and partly of squamous epithelium.

b T— Only a thin bony roof separates both cavities from the brain.

c F— The innervation is by the glossopharyngeal nerve via the tympanic plexus.

d T— The head of the malleus is also situated in this upward extension of the cavity.

e F— The communication is with the nasopharynx.

319   In the middle ear the:
   a   facial nerve descends through the anterior wall.   (   )

   b   floor overlies the carotid canal.   (   )
   c   muscle attached to the ossicles are supplied by the
       vagus nerve.   (   )
   d   foot plate of the stapes overlies the round window
       (fenestra cochleae).   (   )
   e   the chorda tympani lies on the medial wall.   (   )

320   The cochlea of the bony labyrinth of the internal ear:
   a   opens directly into the posterior semicircular canal.   (   )

   b   has a bony medial projection partly dividing its
       cavity.   (   )
   c   contains the vestibular ganglion within the
       modiolus.   (   )
   d   contains the scala vestibuli and scala tympani which
       communicate at the apex of the coil.   (   )
   e   is spirally coiled for $1\frac{1}{2}$ turns.   (   )

321   The membranous labyrinth of the inner ear:
   a   is filled with perilymph.   (   )

   b   contains the maculae (organs of balance) within the
       utricle.   (   )
   c   receives its blood supply from the maxillary artery.   (   )

   d   contains the spiral organ (the organ of hearing)
       which consists of the hair cells and the tectorial
       membrane.   (   )
   e   receives proprioceptive fibres from the trigeminal
       nerve.   (   )

322   The anterior cranial fossa is:
   a   limited posteriorly by the squamous temporal bone.   (   )
   b   grooved anteriorly by the inferior sagittal sinus.   (   )

   c   pierced by the nasociliary nerve.   (   )

   d   pierced by the olfactory tracts.   (   )

   e   formed centrally by the body of the sphenoid bone.   (   )

a **F**— The nerve firstly runs backwards along the roof of the cavity and then descends behind the posterior wall.
b **T**— Also the jugular foramen posteriorly.
c **F**— The stapedius is supplied by the facial nerve and the tensor tympani by the mandibular nerve.
d **F**— The foot plate overlies the oval window (fenestra vestibuli).
e **F**— The nerve lies on the tympanic membrane in the lateral wall.

a **F**— The anteriorly situated cochlea opens into the vestibule which communicates posteriorly with the semicircular canals.
b **T**— This is the spiral lamina from the central bony pillar (modiolus).
c **F**— This ganglion lies in the internal acoustic meatus. The modiolus contains the cochlear ganglion.
d **T**— The communication is the small opening, the helicotrema.
e **F**— The coil has $2\frac{3}{4}$ turns around the central bony pillar.

a **F**— The cavity is filled with endolymph. Perilymph fills the space between the membranous and bony labyrinths.
b **T**— Maculae are also present within the saccule. The semicircular canals contain the cristae.
c **F**— Its main supply is from the labyrinthine branch of the basilar artery.
d **T**— The hair cells support the tectorial membrane and lie on the basilar membrane in the cochlear duct.
e **F**— The maculae and cristae are innervated by the vestibular division of the 8th cranial nerve.

a **F**— The lesser wings of the sphenoid from the posterior border.
b **F**— The vault is grooved by the superior sagittal sinus and the arachnoid granulations on each side.
c **F**— The anterior ethmoidal vessel and nerve pierce the cribriform plate.
d **F**— The olfactory tracts and bulbs rest on the floor of the fossa. The olfactory nerves surrounded by their meningeal coverings pierce the cribriform plate and enter the bulb.
e **F**— The ethmoid plate lies centrally.

323 In the middle cranial fossa the:

a   median portion is formed by the body of the
sphenoid bone.   (   )

b   the internal carotid artery enters through the
foramen lacerum.   (   )

c   the foramen rotundum transmits the oculomotor
nerve.   (   )

d   foramen ovale lies within the apex of the petrous
temporal bone.   (   )

e   foramen spinosum transmits the meningeal branch
of the mandibular nerve.   (   )

324 In the posterior cranial fossa the:

a   jugular foramen transmits the last three cranial
nerves.   (   )

b   inferior petrosal sinus grooves the dorsum sellae. (   )

c   sigmoid sinus marks the upper limit of the fossa.   (   )

d   jugular foramen lies within the occipital bone.   (   )

e   the facial nerve passes across the apex of the
petrous temporal bone.   (   )

325 In the cranial nerves:

a   special visceral efferent fibres are located in the
oculomotor nerve to the eye muscles.   (   )

b   special visceral afferent fibres are located in the
glossopharyngeal nerve.   (   )

c   general visceral afferent fibres are located in the
oculomotor nerve.   (   )

d   general somatic sensory fibres are located in the
glossopharyngeal nerve.   (   )

e   general somatic motor fibres are located in the
vagus nerve.   (   )

a **T**— The lateral portion is formed by the lesser and greater wings of the sphenoid, and the squamous and petrous parts of the temporal bone.

b **F**— The foramen floors the medial end of the carotid canal which contains the internal carotid artery.

c **F**— The foramen transmits the maxillary nerve, the oculomotor leaves the fossa through the superior orbital fissure.

d **F**— The foramen lies within the greater wing of the sphenoid and transmits the mandibular nerve.

e **T**— Also the middle meningeal vessels.

a **F**— It transmits the glossopharyngeal, vagus and accessory nerves. The hypoglossal passes through the hypoglossal canal in front of the condyle.

b **F**— The sinus descends over the medial end of the petrous temporal bone to the jugular foramen.

c **F**— The transverse sinus marks the upper limit of the fossa. The tentorium cerebelli forms the roof.

d **F**— The foramen lies between the occipital and the petrous temporal bones.

e **F**— The nerve passes into the internal acoustic meatus.

a **F**— The eye muscles, like the tongue, are derived from somatic mesenchyme whereas the special visceral muscle is that derived from the mesenchyme of the pharyngeal arches. It is supplied by the trigeminal, facial, glossopharyngeal and vagus nerves.

b **T**— These are taste fibres. Taste fibres also travel in the facial nerve.

c **T**— These are parasympathetic fibres and are also present in the facial, glossopharyngeal and vagus nerves.

d **F**— The general somatic function is subserved by the trigeminal nerve.

e **F**— These fibres are in the oculomotor, trochlear, abducent and hypoglossal nerves.

326   The olfactory nerves:

a   pierce the cribriform plate of the ethmoid.   (   )

b   lie in the wall of the frontal sinus.   (   )

c   originate in the bipolar olfactory cells of the
olfactory tract.   (   )

d   carry a meningeal sheath through the cribriform
plate.   (   )

e   supply the mucous membrane over the inferior
concha.   (   )

327   The optic nerve:

a   has its cell bodies in the internal nuclear layer of
the retina.   (   )

b   has its peripheral endings in the internal plexiform
area of the retina.   (   )

c   is surrounded by a meningeal sheath containing
cerebrospinal fluid up to the eyeball.   (   )

d   leaves the orbit through the same foramen as the
frontal nerve.   (   )

e   passes through the same foramen as the ophthalmic
artery.   (   )

328   The optic nerve:

a   has the ciliary ganglion on its lateral side.   (   )

b   is crossed from lateral to medial by the ophthalmic
artery in the orbit.   (   )

c   enters the middle cranial fossa lateral to the internal
carotid artery.   (   )

d   is separated from the pituitary gland by the
diaphragma sellae.   (   )

e   lies on the sphenoid bone.   (   )

329   The oculomotor nerve:

a   supplies the ciliary muscle with general visceral
motor fibres.   (   )

b   has its nucleus in the periacqueductal grey matter
of the midbrain.   (   )

c   supplies somatic motor fibres to the superior
oblique muscle.   (   )

d   divides into superior and inferior divisions near the
superior orbital fissure.   (   )

e   supplies the inferior oblique muscle.   (   )

a **T**— About 15–20 bundles of nerves pierce the cribriform plate on each side and enter the olfactory bulb.

b **F**

c **F**— The bipolar cells lie in the olfactory mucous membrane. ✓

d **T**— Fractures of the cribriform plate allow CSF to escape into the nasal cavity.

e **F**— The olfactory mucosa lines only the upper part of the nasal cavity.

a **F**— This layer contains retinal bipolar cells. The nerve arises in the ganglion layer.

b **T**— Where synapses occur with the bipolar cells. ✓

c **T**— Meninges are carried forward to this level.

d **F**— The optic nerve passes through the optic canal, and the frontal through the supraorbital fissure.

e **T**

a **T**

b **T**— The nasociliary nerve also crosses above the optic nerve.

c **F**— The nerve is medial to the artery and its ophthalmic branch.

d **T**— And the intercavernous sinuses. ✓

e **T**— In its short intracranial portion.

a **T**— These parasympathetic fibres synapse in the ciliary ganglion and supply the sphincter muscle in the ciliary body and the iris.

b **T**— The nucleus lies in the midline in front and in the adjacent grey matter on each side.

c **F**— This muscle is supplied by the trochlear nerve.

d **T**— And supplies all the extraocular muscles except the superior oblique (4th) and lateral rectus (6th).

e **T**— Through its inferior division. ✓

330 **The oculomotor nerve:**

a   has the longest intracranial course of the ocular nerves. ( )

b   pierces the cerebral layer of dura and passes forward in the lateral wall of the cavernous sinus. ( )

c   lies at first above and then descends medial to the trochlear nerve in the cavernous sinus. ( )

d   when injured, may be associated with dilatation of the pupil. ( )

e   passes between the posterior and inferior cerebellar arteries. ( )

331 **The trochlear nerve:**

a   has its nucleus in the lower midbrian. ( )

b   carries special visceral efferent fibres. ( )

c   passes between the posterior cerebral and superior cerebellar arteries. ( )

d   passes between the oculomotor and ophthalmic nerves. ( )

e   passes medially between levator palpebrae superioris and the roof of the orbit. ( )

332 **The trigeminal nerve:**

a   is entirely sensory. ( )

b   emerges from the brain stem at the upper border of the pons. ( )

c   leaves the brain stem as separate sensory and somatic motor roots. ( )

d   ganglion is completely surrounded by the meninges. ( )

e   ganglion lies on the body of the sphenoid bone. ( )

a **F**— The abducent nerve is longer and thinner, and is particularly susceptible to damage in raised intracranial pressure.

b **T**— It is also related to the internal carotid artery, the abducent and trochlear nerves and the ophthalmic nerve in the cavernous sinus.

c **T**

d **T**— This may occur with lateral shift of the brain in head injuries. The patient's eye is deviated and the upper eyelid droops.

e **F**— In the posterior cranial fossa the nerve passes between the posterior cerebral and superior cerebellar arteries.

a **T**— Anterior to the periaqueductal grey matter, the fibres pass posteriorly and undergo a dorsal decussation before emerging.

b **F**— The eye muscles are derived from somatic mesenchyme, so the nerve is classed as a somatic efferent nerve.

c **T**

d **T**— In the lateral wall of the cavernous sinus.

e **T**— And supplies the superior oblique muscle.

a **F**— It is also motor to the muscles of mastication.

b **F**— The nerve leaves the middle of the pons at its junction with the middle cerebellar peduncle.

c **T**— The motor root is separate and carries special visceral motor fibres. It joins the mandibular nerve.

d **F**— The dural sheath (cavum trigeminale) only partly surrounds the ganglion.

e **F**— It lies on the apex of the petrous temporal bone.

333 **The ophthalmic division of the trigeminal nerve transports parasympathetic motor fibres:**

a to the ciliary ganglion.   (   )

b from the glossopharyngeal nerve.   (   )

c from the facial nerve.   (   )

d to the submandibular ganglion.   (   )

e to the otic ganglion.   (   )

334 **The nasociliary nerve:**

a gives sensory innervation to the medial part of the forehead.   (   )

b innervates the eyeball.   (   )

c supplies sensory innervation to the dura of the anterior cranial fossa.   (   )

d innervates both anterior and posterior ethmoidal air cells.   (   )

e innervates the medial part of the upper eyelid. (   )

335 **The maxillary division of the trigeminal nerve:**

a passes through the pterygopalatine fossa.   (   )

b innervates all the teeth of the upper jaw.   (   )

c innervates the upper anterior quadrant of the lateral wall of the nose.   (   )

d innervates the upper posterior quadrant of the lateral wall of the nose.   (   )

e innervates the skin of the temple.   (   )

a **F**— These come from the oculomotor nerve through its branch to the inferior oblique muscle.
b **F**— The glossopharyngeal fibres run to the otic ganglion and then with the auriculotemporal branch of the mandibular division to the parotid gland.
c **T**— The innervation of the lacrimal gland comes from the facial nerve through the greater petrosal nerve, the pterygopalatine ganglion and the zygomaticotemporal nerve, and then through the lacrimal branch of the ophthalmic nerve.
d **F**— These come from the facial nerve through the chorda tympani and pass with the mandibular division.
e **F**— This receives parasympathetic fibres from the lesser petrosal nerve, the fibres coming from the glossopharyngeal nerve.

a **F**— The supratrochlear and supraorbital branches of the frontal nerve supply this region.
b **T**— Through the long ciliary nerves and the short ciliary nerves (via the ciliary ganglion), carrying sensory fibres from the cornea and sclera. Sympathetic fibres from the internal carotid plexus are also carried.
c **T**— The anterior ethmoidal nerve passes through the medial wall of the orbit on the cribriform plate through which it descends and supplies the nasal cavity and the skin over the nose.
d **T**— Through the anterior and posterior ethmoidal nerves. The posterior also supplies the sphenoidal air sinus.
e **T**— Through the infratrochlear nerve; it also supplies the conjunctiva and a part of the lateral wall of the nose.

a **T**— Entering it through the foramen rotundum. The pterygopalatine ganglion is suspended from the nerve.
b **T**— Through the anterior and posterior superior alveolar nerves.
c **F**— This is supplied by the anterior ethmoidal nerve.
d **T**— By the nasal nerves. The lower half is supplied by the greater palatine and superior alveolar branches of the division.
e **T**— The zygomatic nerve also carries parasympathetic fibres to the lacrimal gland.

336 The mandibular divison of the trigeminal nerve:

a lies lateral to the otic ganglion.   ( )

b supplies the levator veli palatine muscle via fibres from the medial pterygoid nerve which pass without synapsing through the otic ganglion.   ( )

c innervates the dura of the middle cranial fossa.   ( )

d innervates the posterior part of the tympanic membrane.   ( )

e supplies the buccinator muscle.   ( )

337 The lingual nerve:

a innervates the lower molar teeth.   ( )

b innervates the anterior belly of the digastric muscle.   ( )

c passes anterior to the lingula.   ( )

d carries taste fibres from the circumvalate papillae.   ( )

e carries secretomotor fibres to the parotid gland.   ( )

338 The abducent nerve:

a has its nucleus in the floor of the 4th ventricle.   ( )

b pierces the inner layer of dura over the dorsum sellae.   ( )

c lies medial to the internal carotid artery in the cavernous sinus.   ( )

d traverses the supraorbital fissure within the tendinous ring.   ( )

e is deeply placed and rarely damaged by intracranial disease.   ( )

a **T**— Between tensor veli palatini medially and the lateral pterygoid muscle laterally.

b **F**— Both the tensor tympani and tensor veli palatini muscles are innervated in this fashion. The levator is supplied by the pharyngeal branches of the vagus nerve.

c **T**— A branch passing upwards through the foramen spinosum.

d **F**— The auriculotemporal nerve supplies the anterior part of the membrane and also transports sympathetic and parasympathetic fibres to the parotid gland. The posterior part of the membrane is supplied by the auricular branch of the vagus.

e **F**— This is supplied by the facial nerve. The mandibular nerve supplies the muscles of mastication.

a **F**— All the lower teeth and the anterior belly of the digastric

b **F** and mylohyoid muscles are supplied by the inferior alveolar nerve.

c **T**— It then crosses the root of the 3rd molar tooth before passing between the mylohyoid and hyoglossus muscles.

d **F**— It carries taste and general somatic sensory fibres from the tongue in front of these papillae. Taste fibres together with parasympathetic fibres are carried in the chorda tympani nerve. The glossopharyngeal nerve supplies the circumvallate papillae and the mucous membrane behind them.

e **F**— It carries fibres from the chorda tympani for the submandibular and sublingual salivary glands.

a **T**— The facial fibres arching over it form the facial colliculus in the lower pons above the striae medullaris.

b **T**— Passing anteriorly over the apex of the petrous temporal bone.

c **F**— It is closely related to the lateral surface of the artery within the sinus.

d **T**— And supplies the lateral rectus muscle.

e **F**— Its long intracranial course makes it susceptible to increased intracranial pressure.

339   The facial nerve: true or false

a   ganglion (geniculate) contains the cell bodies of its
    parasympathetic fibres.   (   )
b   carries secretomotor fibres from the lower part of the
    salivary nucleus.   (   )
c   has its taste and secretomotor fibres as a separate
    nerve in the internal acoustic meatus.   (   )
d   leaves the skull through the mastoid foramen.   (   )

e   lies medial to the external carotid artery.   (   )

340   The facial nerve:

a   has a branch containing parasympathetic fibres
    leaving it at the facial ganglion.   (   )

b   has a branch, passing through the petrotympanic
    fissure, and then supplying the 1st pharyngeal arch
    muscle.   (   )

c   passes medial to the styloid process.   (   )

d   carries secretomotor fibres to the parotid gland.   (   )

e   innervates the temporalis muscle.   (   )

341   The vestibulocochlear nerve:

a   is formed at the base of the modiolus.   (   )

b   lies posterior to the facial nerve in the internal
    acoustic meatus.   (   )
c   enters the cerebellomedullary angle of the brain
    stem.   (   )
d   has its central nuclei in the anterior pons.   (   )

e   passes into the middle cranial fossa over the apex
    of the posterior temporal bone.   (   )

a **F**— This is a sensory ganglion mainly for taste fibres passing to the nucleus of the tractus solitarius.
b **F**— These parasympathetic fibres arise in the upper part of the salivary nucleus in the medulla.
c **T**— The nervus intermedius joins the main trunk near the facial ganglion.
d **F**— This foramen transmits an emissary vein. The nerve passes through the stylomastoid foramen.
e **F**— It lies lateral to the artery within the parotid gland.

a **T**— The greater petrosal nerve passes through the petrous temporal bone and becomes the nerve of the pterygoid canal, before reaching the pterygopalatine ganglion where its fibres synapse.
b **F**— The facial nerve supplies 2nd pharyngeal arch muscle but its chorda tympani branch, passing through the petrotympanic fissure, carries taste and parasympathetic fibres to 1st arch derivates.
c **F**— The nerve passes lateral to the styloid process on its way into the parotid gland.
d **F**— The parotid gland receives parasympathetic fibres from the glossopharyngeal nerve via the lesser petrosal nerve, the otic ganglion and the auriculotemporal nerve. The secretomotor fibres in the facial nerve pass mainly to the submandibular and sublingual glands via the submandibular ganglion.
e **F**— Its motor fibres are predominantly to the muscles of facial expression.

a **F**— The vestibular and cochlear parts unite in the internal acoustic meatus where the vestibular ganglion is situated. The cochlear ganglion is in the modiolus.
b **T**

c **T**— Lying lateral to the facial nerve.

d **F**— The vestibular nuclei lie in the floor of the 4th ventricle, and the cochlear nuclei in the floor of the lateral recess of the 4th ventricle.
e **F**— The nerve endings are situated within the petrous temporal bone and the nerve passes into the posterior cranial fossa.

342 **The glossopharyngeal nerve carries:**
a fibres from the nucleus ambiguus. ( )
b somatic motor fibres. ( )

c fibres to the nucleus of the tractus solitarius. ( )

d fibres from the lower part of the salivary nucleus. ( )

e general visceral sensory fibres. ( )

343 **The vagus nerve carries:**
a fibres from the nucleus ambiguus. ( )
b somatic motor fibres. ( )
c fibres to the nucleus of the tractus solitarius. ( )

d fibres from the upper salivary nucleus. ( )

e somatic sensory fibres. ( )

344 **The vagus nerve:**
a crosses the left subclavian artery in the root of
the neck. ( )

b carries general visceral sensory fibres. ( )

c leaves the skull between the internal jugular vein
posteriorly and the inferior petrosal sinus anteriorly. ( )
d leaves the medulla as a number of rootlets between
the olive and pyramid. ( )
e lies posterolateral to the common carotid artery. ( )

a **T—** Special visceral motor fibres supply the stylopharyngeus
b **F** muscle. These are the only fibres to voluntary muscle in the nerve.
c **T—** Special visceral sensory fibres carry taste from the posterior third of the tongue.
d **T—** General visceral motor fibres relay in the otic ganglion and pass to the parotid gland.
e **T—** From the middle ear, pharynx, palate, posterior third of tongue, carotid sinus and carotid body.

a **T—** Special visceral motor fibres supply the striated muscle of
b **F** the larynx, pharynx and palate.
c **T—** Special visceral sensory fibres carry tastes from the valleculae and the epiglottis.
d **F—** The parasympathetic (general visceral motor) fibres supply the heart, the lungs and the alimentary tract as far as the splenic flexure.
e **T—** From the posterior part of the external acoustic meatus and the tympanic membrane by its auricular branch.

a **F—** This is the relation of the right side, but on the left the nerve descends between the subclavian and common carotid arteries.
b **T—** From the mucous membrane of the palate, pharynx, larynx and also from the heart, lungs and alimentary tract.
c **T—** And between the glossopharyngeal nerve anteriorly, and the accessory nerve posteriorly in the jugular foramen.
d **F—** The rootlets lie lateral to the olive. In the jugular foramen and just below it are the two sensory ganglia of the vagus.
e **T—** With the internal jugular vein, within the carotid sheath.

345   The spinal accessory nerve:
a   carries somatic motor fibres to the sterno-
     cleidomastoid muscle.   (   )
b   carries the special visceral motor fibres to the
     trapezius muscle.   (   )

c   spinal root ascends behind the ligamenta denticulata. (   )
d   passes laterally behind the jugular vein over the
     transverse process of the atlas.   (   )
e   lies medial to the vagus nerve.   (   )

346   The hypoglossal nerve:
a   emerges, from the medulla, between the pyramid
     and the olive.   (   )
b   passes anteriorly deep to the posterior belly of the
     digastric muscle.   (   )
c   passes forwards between the internal and external
     carotid arteries.   (   )
d   carries fibres of the 1st cervical nerve to the
     geniohyoid muscle.   (   )
e   is crossed by the submandibular duct.   (   )

347   The cervical fascia splits:
a   and embraces the infrahyoid muscles.   (   )

b   and partially encloses the submandibular salivary
     gland.   (   )
c   inferiorly enclosing the jugular venous arch.   (   )
d   posteriorly around the scapula.   (   )

e   to enclose the sternocleidomastoid muscle.   (   )

348   The prevertebral fascia:
a   encloses the thyroid gland.   (   )

b   extends laterally into the upper limb as the axillary
     sheath.   (   )
c   has the cervical sympathetic chain embedded in it.   (   )
d   blends inferiorly with the anterior longitudinal
     ligament in front of the body of the 6th cervical
     vertebra.   (   )
e   splits around the hyoid bone.   (   )

a **T**— These fibres arise in the upper five cervical segments of the cord.

b **F**— The cranial root of the nerve carries special visceral fibres which join the vagus. The somatic motor fibres supply the sternocleidomastoid and trapezius muscles.

c **T**— As it represents a dorsal root nerve.

d **F**— The nerve passes in front of the vein.

e **F**— It lies lateral to the vagus as they leave the skull through the jugular foramen.

a **T**— The nucleus lies in the floor of the 4th ventricle on each side of the midline.

b **T**— Lying at first on the middle constrictor and then on the hyoglossus muscle.

c **F**— The nerve passes lateral and then anterior to both vessels and to the loop of the lingual artery.

d **T**— Also to the thyrohyoid, and to the strap muscles via the superior root of the ansa cervicalis.

e **F**— The duct has a close relationship to the lingual nerve.

a **F**— These infrahyoid muscles are embedded in its deep surface.

b **T**— It also splits and forms the covering of the parotid gland.

c **T**— In the region of the manubrial attachment of the fascia.

d **F**— It is attached to the ligamentum nuchae above and to the spine of the scapula. Below the scapula it is continuous with the thoracolumbar fascia.

e **T**— Also the trapezius.

a **F**— The pretracheal fascia encloses the gland blending inferiorly with the adventitia of the great vessels.

b **T**— The subclavian artery and the brachial plexus carry the fascia into the axilla.

c **T**— The chain lies posterior to the carotid sheath.

d **F**— It extends to the level of the 4th thoracic vertebra.

e **F**— The hyoid receives the superior attachment of the pretracheal fascia.

349   **The carotid sheath:**
- a   is attached superiorly to the base of skull.   (   )
- b   fuses with the pericardium inferiorly.   (   )
- c   lies deep to the prevertebral fascia.   (   )
- d   encloses the jugular vein and vagus nerve.   (   )
- e   encloses the external carotid artery.   (   )

350   **The posterior triangle of the neck:**
- a   is floored by the prevertebral fascia.   (   )
- b   is bordered posteriorly by the rhomboideus major muscle.   (   )
- c   has the spine of the scapula as its inferior border.   (   )
- d   is bordered anteriorly by the sternocleidomastoid muscle.   (   )
- e   is crossed by the internal jugular vein.   (   )

351   **The sternocleidomastoid muscle:**
- a   is innervated by the 2nd and 3rd cervical nerve roots.   (   )
- b   is surrounded by the cervical fascia.   (   )
- c   is attached superiorly along the lateral half of the superior nuchal line.   (   )
- d   acting with its fellow of the opposite side, retracts the face.   (   )
- e   has a single inferior attachment to the upper medial third of the clavicle.   (   )

352   **The semispinalis capitis muscle is:**
- a   attached superiorly to the mastoid process and the lateral part of the superior nuchal line.   (   )
- b   superfical to levatores costarum.   (   )
- c   mainly concerned with the maintenance of the upright position.   (   )
- d   supplied by the dorsal rami of the spinal nerves.   (   )
- e   a medial relation of the suboccipital triangle.   (   )

a **T**— It is a condensation of the fascias of the neck and below
b **T** fuses with the fibrous pericardium.
c **F**— It lies anterior to the prevertebral fascia.
d **T**
e **F**— It encloses the common and internal carotid arteries.

a **T**— Overlying the splenius capitis, levator scapulae and
scalenus medius muscles.
b **F**— The posterior border is formed by the trapezius muscle.

c **F**— The middle third of the clavicle forms the inferior border.
d **T**— The posterior border of this muscle forms the anterior limit
of the triangle.
e **F**— It is crossed by the external jugular vein, accessory nerve
and omohyoid muscle.

a **T**— Directly, but mainly through fibres carried in the spinal
accessory nerve.
b **T**— The fascia splits anteriorly and encloses this muscle and
posteriorly for trapezius.
c **T**— And to the mastoid process.

d **F**— Together they protrude the face. One muscle turns the face
towards the opposite side and also rotates the face, raising
the chin.
e **F**— A second head is attached to the anterior surface of the
manubrium sterni.

a **F**— These are the attachments of the splenius capitis deep to
sternocleidomastoid. Semispinalis is attached between the
superior and inferior nuchal lines nearer the midline.
b **T**— The latter, like the multifidus, rotatores, interspinous and
intertransversus muscles, are part of the deep short muscle
system.
c **T**— It is an antigravity muscle.

d **T**— As are most muscles in this region of the trunk and neck.
e **F**— It lies superficial to the suboccipital triangle.

353 The suboccipital triangle:

a is bounded laterally by the rectus capitis posterior major muscle. ( )

b is bounded inferiorly by the inferior oblique muscle. ( )

c is crossed superficially by the greater occipital nerve. ( )

d has the posterior atlanto-occipital membrane in its floor. ( )

e is bounded by muscles which extend and rotate the head on the cervical vertebrae. ( )

354 The scalenus anterior muscle:

a is attached superiorly to the bodies of the 3rd–6th cervical vertebrae. ( )

b is attached inferiorly to the anterior border of the 1st rib. ( )

c lies anterior to the subclavian vein on the 1st rib. ( )

d is crossed anteriorly by the phrenic nerve. ( )

e forms the posterior relation of the roots of the brachial plexus. ( )

355 The omohyoid muscle:

a is attached superiorly to the greater horn of the hyoid bone. ( )

b is attached by its intermediate tendon to the scapula. ( )

c crosses over the external jugular vein. ( )

d crosses over the scalenus anterior muscle. ( )

e crosses the accessory nerve. ( )

a **F**— This muscle passes from the spine of the axis to the occipital bone below the inferior nuchal line and forms the medial border of the triangle.

b **T**— The superior oblique forms the lateral boundary.

c **T**— And covered by the semispinalis and longissimus capitis muscles.

d **T**— The vertebral artery and 1st cervical nerve pass beneath it.

e **T**— They probably are involved in the small movements necessary in centring the visual axes, important in stereoscopic vision.

a **F**— It is attached to the anterior tubercles on the transverse processes of these vertebrae. 3 – 6th C. Vertebrae

b **F**— The scalene tubercle is on the medial border of the rib.

c **F**— The vein lies anterior; the subclavian artery and the T1 root of the brachial plexus lie posterior.

d **T**— The nerve descends along its medial border, deep to the prevertebral fascia, crosses over the muscle, and then enters the thorax.

e **F**— These nerves lie deep to the muscle.

a **F**— It is attached to the body of the bone.

b **F**— The inferior belly is attached to the superior border of the scapula. The tendon is attached to the medial end of the clavicle by a fascial sling.

c **F**— It lies anterior to the internal jugular vein.

d **T**— Separated by the contents of the carotid sheath and the phrenic nerve.

e **F**— The muscle and nerve run parallel courses as they cross the posterior triangle of the neck.

356   The thyroid gland:

a   is limited superiorly by the attachment of the
sternohyoid muscle.   (   )

b   has the recurrent laryngeal nerve ascending medial
to the lateral lobes.   (   )

c   develops from a midline ventral diverticulum between
the 2nd and 3rd pharyngeal arches.   (   )

d   is enclosed in the pretracheal fascia.   (   )

e   receives a major blood supply from the middle
thyroid artery.   (   )

357   The parathyroid glands:

a   lie between the thyroid gland and the trachea.   (   )

b   receive a rich blood supply from the superior and
inferior thyroid arteries.   (   )

c   develop eosinophil staining cells around puberty.   (   )

d   develop from a 3rd and 4th pharyngeal arch
mesenchyme.   (   )

e   are usually 6–8 mm across.

358   The trachea:

a   divides at the level of the lower border of the 4th
thoracic vertebra (the sternal angle).   (   )

b   is reinforced by 15–20 complete cartilaginous rings.   (   )

c   is a posterior relation of the jugular venous arch.   (   )

d   is a medial relation of the carotid sheath and its
contents.   (   )

e   is a posterior relation of the isthmus of the thyroid
gland.   (   )

a **F**— The upper limit is the oblique line on the thyroid cartilage to which the sternothyroid muscle is attached.

b **T**— The nerve is an important relation in surgical procedures on the gland as it accompanies the inferior thyroid vessels.

c **F**— The diverticulum starts between the 1st and 2nd arches and its position is marked by the foramen caecum on the tongue. The 4th pharyngeal pouch also contributes specialised C-cells to the gland.

d **T**— The gland has also a surface capsule within which is the venous plexus.

e **F**— This artery does not exist; the superior and inferior thyroid arteries require identification and ligation during thyroidectomy.

a **F**— They are situated on the posterior surface of the thyroid gland within its capsule.

b **T**— The presence of these vessels may help to differentiate the glands from fat lobules in surgical procedures.

c **T**— In addition to the columns of chief cells which are separated by blood spaces. The chief cells have dark staining nuclei and a chromatin network.

d **F**— The superior and inferior glands develop respectively from the 4th and 3rd pharyngeal pouch endoderm.

e **F**— They are 3–6 mm and are easily mistaken for fat globules.

a **T**— It begins below the cricoid cartilage, i.e. C6 level.

b **F**— The plates of cartilage are incomplete posteriorly where the trachea rests on the oesophagus. The gap is closed by fibroelastic tissue and smooth muscle.

c **T**— This is an important relation when a tracheotomy is being performed.

d **T**— Behind the carotid sheath is the sympathetic trunk medially with the vertebral and inferior thyroid arteries.

e **T**— This can be palpated over the 2nd and 3rd tracheal rings; it is an important relation in tracheotomy.

359 **The oesophagus:**
  a commences about 25 cm from the incisor teeth. (   )

  b receives a parasympathetic innervation from the greater splanchnic nerve. (   )

  c has smooth muscle forming its longitudinal and circular muscle coats. (   )
  d has numerous mucous glands extending into the vascular submucosa. (   )
  e has a venous drainage to both portal and systemic circulations. (   )

360 **The right subclavian artery:**
  a is formed behind the right sternoclavicular joint. (   )
  b passes laterally over the suprapleural membrane. (   )

  c terminates at the medial border of the 1st rib. (   )

  d lies posterior to the right internal jugular vein. (   )

  e is separated from its vein by the scalenus anterior muscle. (   )

361 **The left subclavian artery:**
  a is crossed posteriorly by the recurrent laryngeal nerve. (   )
  b passes anterior to the thoracic duct. (   )

  c gives rise to the costocervical trunk medial to the scalenus anterior muscle. (   )
  d crosses the left sympathetic chain. (   )

  e has the vagus on its lateral side. (   )

a **F**— The distance in the adult is about 15 cm, the organ being approximately 25 cm long.
b **F**— This nerve provides a sympathetic innervation. The vagus provides parasympathetic innervation through the recurrent laryngeal nerves to the upper part and through the oesophageal plexus to the lower part. Within the recurrent laryngeal nerve are special visceral motor fibres to the striated muscle.
c **T**— Although the upper third is composed mainly of striated muscle, there is a little smooth muscle.
d **T**— The glands are less prominent in the upper than the lower end of the oesophagus and are almost absent in the middle.
e **T**— These communications may enlarge in liver disease.

a **T**— The left artery arises directly from the arch of the aorta.
b **T**— The membrane separates the artery from the pleura and the apex of the lung.
c **F**— The subclavian artery becomes the axillary artery at the outer border of the first rib.
d **T**— The vein and the vagus nerve descend in front of the artery in the root of the neck.
e **T**— The subclavian vein lies anterior to the prevertebral fascia and its tributaries lie outside the axillary sheath.

a **F**— On the right side the nerve hooks back around the artery but on the left it passes back around the arch of the aorta.
b **F**— The duct passes in front of the artery and enters the origin of the left brachiocephalic vein.
c **T**— On the right side this usually occurs behind the muscle.

d **F**— The dome of the pleura and the apex of the lung separate the vessel from the neck of the 1st rib where the sympathetic chain is found.
e **F**— The vagus and phrenic nerves lie medially, between the subclavian and common carotid arteries.

362 The vertebral artery:
a arises from the subclavian artery medial to scalenus anterior. (   )
b is a posterior relation of the common carotid artery. (   )
c is surrounded by a sympathetic plexus derived from the inferior cervical sympathetic ganglion. (   )
d enters the foramen tranversarium of the 6th cervical vertebra. (   )
e has the dorsal ramus of the 1st cervical nerve between it and the transverse mass of the atlas. (   )

363 The thyrocervical trunk:
a gives rise to the deep cervical artery. (   )
b gives rise to the internal thoracic artery. (   )
c sends a blood supply to the thyroid gland. (   )
d divides at the level of the thyroid isthmus. (   )
e is crossed by the phrenic nerve on the right side. (   )

364 The common carotid artery:
a terminates at the level of the upper border of the thyroid cartilage. (   )
b is a posterolateral relation to the thyroid gland. (   )
c is crossed anterolaterally by the omohyoid muscle. (   )
d is crossed anterolaterally by the sternocleidomastoid muscle. (   )
e at its bifurcation, has baro- and chemoreceptors which are richly innervated by the glossopharyngeal nerve. (   )

a **T**— As do the thyrocervical trunk and internal thoracic artery. ✓

b **T**— It is also crossed by the inferior thyroid artery.

c **T**— The sympathetic nerves are distributed with the branches of the vertebral and basilar arteries.

d **T**— The artery has a very tortuous course. After passing through the foramen magnum it joins its fellow of the

e **T** opposite side and forms the basilar artery. It supplies most of the hindbrain and the medial aspect of the occipital pole of the cerebral hemisphere (visual area).

a **F**— The deep cervical and the highest intercostal arteries are ✓ branches of the costocervical trunk.

b **F**— This is a separate branch of the subclavian artery.

c **T**— Through its inferior thyroid branch.

d **F**— The short trunk soon divides into inferior thyroid, ✓ transverse cervical and suprascapular arteries.

e **F**— The transverse cervical and suprascapular branches of the ✓ trunk cross anterior to the nerve.

a **T**

b **T**— The thyroid gland may be an anterior or a medial relation to the artery.

c **T**— It is accompanied by the vagus nerve and the internal

d **T**— jugular vein. All are surrounded by the carotid sheath and crossed anterolaterally by the sternocleidomastoid muscle.

e **T**— They are also innervated from the cervical sympathetic ✓ trunk.

365 **The exterenal carotid artery:**
  a terminates by dividing into superficial temporal and
     transverse facial arteries.   (   )
  b lies lateral to the retromandibular vein.   (   )

  c has all the styloid muscles passing between it and
     the internal carotid artery.   (   )
  d is crossed medially by the lingual nerve.   (   )
  e lies deep to the hypoglossal nerve.   (   )

366 **The facial artery:**
  a is crossed laterally by the hypoglossal nerve.   (   )

  b is a branch of the maxillary artery.   (   )
  c grooves the inferior surface of the submandibular
     gland.   (   )
  d passes medially over the middle and superior
     constrictor muscles.   (   )
  e traverses the face between the superficial and deep
     muscles.   (   )

367 **The maxillary artery:**
  a lies betweeen the neck of the mandible and the
     sphenomandibular ligament.   (   )
  b passes through the infratemporal fossa.   (   )

  c traverses the sphenopalatine canal.   (   )
  d sends branches to the lateral wall of the nose.   (   )

  e sends a branch through the foramen spinosum.   (   )

368 **The middle meningeal artery:**
  a passes through the foramen ovale.   (   )
  b lies in the anterior cranial fossa.   (   )
  c lies in intimate relationship with the skull.   (   )
  d lies deep to the zygomaticofrontal suture.   (   )

  e also supplies the diploë.   (   )

a F— The superficial temporal and maxillary arteries are the terminal divisions, being formed behind the neck of the mandible.

b F— The artery lies medial to the vein and the facial nerve in the parotid gland.

c F— The stylohyoid passes lateral to both vessels. The process, styloglossus and stylopharyngeus pass between the vessels.

d F— The nerve runs in a more anterior plane than the artery.

e T Both internal and external carotids are crossed superficially by the facial nerve above and the hypoglossal nerve below.

a F— The nerve crosses the loop of the lingual artery inferior to the facial artery.

b F— It is a branch of the external carotid artery.

c F— The superior surface of the gland is grooved by the artery.

d T— Before reaching the deep surface of the submandibular gland.

e T— Supplying the upper and lower lips and facial musculature. It crosses the body of the mandible just in front of masseter muscle.

a T— The middle meningeal and inferior alveolar arteries arise from the first part of the main vessel.

b T— On the lateral surface of the lateral pterygoid muscle. It supplies all the muscles of mastication.

c F— It ends in the pterygopalatine fossa and some of its

d T terminal branches accompany the branches of the pterygopalatine ganglion.

e T— The middle meningeal artery enters the skull and divides. Its anterior branch lies medial to the pterion and is of surgical importance in skull fractures.

a F— It gains the middle cranial fossa by ascending through the

b F foramen spinosum and lies close to the skull, often

c T grooving its inner surface.

d F— Its surface marking, of importance for surgical access, is 3.5 cm behind and 1.5 cm above the zygomaticofrontal suture.

e T— The vessels are easily damaged in injuries to the skull and may cause a life-threatening haemorrhage.

369   **The internal carotid artery:**

a   enters the skull and then divides into the middle and posterior cerebral arteries.   (   )

b   is separated from the external carotid artery by the glossopharyngeal nerve.   (   )

c   is crossed laterally by the posterior belly of the digastric muscle.   (   )

d   is crossed laterally by the facial nerve.   (   )

e   within the cavernous sinus is related to the mandibular nerve.   (   )

370   **The internal carotid artery:**

a   lies in the floor of the inner ear.   (   )

b   grooves the lesser wing of the sphenoid bone.   (   )

c   lies lateral to the abducent nerve.   (   )

d   pierces the diaphragma sellae medial to the anterior clinoid process.   (   )

e   sends a branch through the optic canal.   (   )

371   **The internal jugular vein:**

a   is a continuation of the transverse cranial venous sinus.   (   )

b   receives the inferior petrosal sinus just below the base of the skull.   (   )

c   has the last four cranial nerves as medial relations at the base of the skull.   (   )

d   is crossed laterally by the hypoglossal nerve.   (   )

e   lies anterolateral to the sympathetic chain.   (   )

372   **The internal jugular vein:**

a   is crossed posteriorly by the accessory nerve.   (   )

b   lies medial to the styloid process and its muscles.   (   )

c   is crossed anteriorly from lateral to medial by the phrenic nerve in the root of the neck.   (   )

d   receives the anterior jugular vein.   (   )

e   lies posterior to the subclavian artery.   (   )

a **F**— It divides into the anterior and middle cerebral arteries. It gives off no branches in the neck. The middle cerebral artery supplies the sensorimotor areas of the cerebral cortex.

b **T**— Also the styloglossus and the stylopharyngeus muscles and the pharyngeal branches of the vagus.

c **T**— Also the stylohyoid muscle.

d **T**— Also the hypoglossal nerve.

e **F**— It is related to the ophthalmic (and maxillary) nerves and the oculomotor, trochlear and abducent nerves.

a **F**— The carotid canal is in the floor of the middle ear and the artery passes anteromedially over the foramen lacerum.

b **F**— The carotid groove is on the body of the sphenoid as the artery lies in the cavernous sinus.

c **F**— The nerve is on its lateral side.

d **T**— The optic nerve and chiasma lie medial to the artery.

e **T**— The ophthalmic artery lies lateral to the nerve in the canal and later gives off the central artery of the retina.

a **F**— It is a continuation of the sigmoid sinus through the base of the skull.

b **T**— The 9th, 10th and 11th cranial nerves lie between the two vessels in the jugular foramen.

c **T**— The hypoglossal nerve is posteromedial to the other three.

d **F**— The nerve passes forwards medial to the vein and lateral to the internal and external carotid arteries.

e **T**— Separated by the prevertebral fascia.

a **T**— The nerve then passes over the transverse process of the atlas and enters the deep surface of the sternocleidomastoid muscle.

b **T**— Below this level it lies deep to the sternocleidomastoid muscle and is crossed by the posterior belly of the digastric and then by the omohyoid muscles.

c **F**— The nerve lies posterior to the vein.

d **F**— This vein usually passes to the external jugular which enters into the subclavian vein.

e **F**— The artery passes posterior to the vein.

373   The cervical plexus:

a   gives off the greater occipital nerve from the second
     root of the plexus.   (   )

b   gives branches to the skin over the outer part of the
     shoulder.   (   )

c   supplies the inferior part of the external acoustic
     meatus.   (   )
d   lies deep to scalenus anterior muscle.   (   )

e   supplies the thyrohyoid muscle.   (   )

374   The phrenic nerve:

a   is mainly derived from the 4th cervical nerve root.   (   )
b   lies deep to the prevertebral fascia.   (   )

c   passes anterior to the subclavian artery on the left
     side.   (   )
d   crosses anterior to the internal thoracic artery, at the
     inlet of the thorax.   (   )
e   passes anterior to the subclavian vein.   (   )

375   The superior cervical ganglion:

a   lies between the prevertebral fascia and the internal
     jugular vein.   (   )

b   gives rise to the cardiac branches.   (   )

c   gives rise to the deep petrosal nerve.   (   )
d   when damaged gives rise to a Horner's syndrome.   (   )

e   gives rise to the ansa subclavia.   (   )

a **F**— This large nerve is derived from the dorsal ramus of the second cervical nerve. The cervical plexus is formed from ventral rami of cervical nerves.

b **T**— The phrenic nerve (C3, 4 & 5) supplies the diaphragm which has 'migrated down' during embryonic development. The supraclavicular nerves come from the same segments, and pain may be referred from the diaphragm to the shoulder region.

c **F**— The great auricular nerves (C2 and 3) supply the skin over the inferior auricle but not the meatus.

d **T**— On scalenus medius. The roots of the brachial plexus also lie between these two scalene muscles.

e **T**— This and the geniohyoid muscle are supplied by C1 fibres carried by the hypoglossal nerve.

a **T**— It is usually supplemented by C3 and C5 fibres.

b **T**— Passing on to the anterior surface of the scalenus anterior muscle.

c **T**— It is placed more laterally on the right side and separated from the artery by the scalenus anterior muscle.

d **T**

e **F**— The nerve lies posterior to the subclavian vein.

a **T**— It lies in the fascia on the 2nd and 3rd cervical transverse processes, deep to the angle of the mandible, and posteromedial to the vein.

b **T**— Cardiac branches arise from all three cervical sympathetic ganglia.

c **T**— From the plexus it forms around the internal carotid artery.

d **T**— With a drooping upper eyelid, small pupil and loss of sweating from that side of the face.

e **F**— The ansa subclavia passes between the middle and inferior ganglia.

376 The pterygopalatine ganglion:

a supplies the sphincter pupillae muscle through its zygomaticotemporal fibres. ( )

b supplies secretomotor fibres to the lacrimal gland. ( )
c gives passage to sympathetic fibres. ( )

d distributes secretomotor fibres to the glands of the nose, palate and nasopharynx. ( )
e receives fibres from the maxillary nerve. ( )

377 The submandibular ganglion:

a distributes secretomotor fibres to the sublingual gland. ( )
b distributes fibres from the lesser petrosal nerve to the submandibular gland. ( )

c gives passage to taste fibres from the circumvallate papillae. ( )
d is situated medial to the hyoglossus muscle. ( )

e is closely related to the mandibular nerve. ( )

378 The lymph drainage of the head and neck:

a includes a chain of lymph nodes around the nasopharynx. ( )
b includes a circular chain of lymph nodes around the base of the skull. ( )
c has a deep cervical lymph chain situated around the external and the anterior jugular veins. ( )

d on the left side passes via the carotid lymph duct into the thoracic duct. ( )
e on the right side passes into the right jugular or subclavian vein. ( )

a F— This muscle receives fibres from an oculomotor branch to the inferior oblique muscle. The postganglionic fibres arise in the ciliary ganglion.

b T— Via the zygomaticotemporal and lacrimal nerves.

c T— From the superior cervical ganglion along the plexus around the internal carotid artery, the deep petrosal nerve and the nerve of the pterygoid canal.

d T— The preganglionic fibres come in the greater petrosal nerve and the nerve of the pterygoid canal from the facial nerve.

e T— The ganglion is suspended from the maxillary nerve, sensory fibres from the nerve are distributed through branches of the ganglion to the nose, palate and nasopharynx.

a T— Also to the submandibular gland. The fibres come via the chorda tympani and lingual nerves.

b F— The lesser petrosal nerve is derived from the glossopharyngeal tympanic plexus and is distributed to the parotid gland via the otic ganglion and auriculotemporal nerve.

c F— These pass to the glossopharyngeal nerve.

d F— It is suspended from the lingual nerve on the lateral surface of the muscle.

e F

a T— Large aggregations of lymph tissue surround this region as the tubal, pharyngeal, palatine and lingual tonsils.

b T— The nodes are arranged from the submental group in front to the occipital group behind.

c F— The superficial cervical lymph chains lie around these vessels. The deep chain is situated around the internal jugular vein.

d F— On the left side, the thoracic duct receives the left jugular lymph trunk. The right jugular duct opens directly into the

e T   jugular or subclavian vein or into the right lymph duct.

IX Central Nervous System

379 **In the central nervous system the:**
a telencephalon comprises the two cerebral
hemispheres. ( )

b rhombencephalon does not include the cerebellum. ( )
c brain stem extends from the forebrain to the spinal
cord. ( )

d thalamus is part of the mesencephalon. ( )
e hypothalamus is part of the diencephalon. ( )

380 **In the attachment of the cranial nerves the:**
a olfactory bulbs represent a part of the primitive
forebrain. ( )
b oculomotor nerves emerge from the
interpeduncular fossa. ( )
c trochlear nerve emerges dorsally between the
superior and inferior colliculi. ( )
d abducent nerve emerges lateral to the facial and
vestibulocochlear nerves. ( )
e vagus emerges between the olive and the pyramids. ( )

381 **The neural crest tissue:**
a is derived from the neural plate. ( )

b contributes to the developing alar lamina. ( )
c gives rise to the autonomic ganglia. ( )
d gives rise to the cortex of the suprarenal gland. ( )

e gives rise to the marginal layer of the neural tube. ( )

a   **T**— With the diencephalon (mainly thalamus and hypothalamus) it completes the forebrain (prosencephalon).

b   **F**— It consists of the pons, medulla and cerebellum.

c   **T**— It consists of the midbrain, pons and medulla. It gives attachment to the cerebellum posteriorly but the cerebellum is excluded.

d   **F**— The thalamus and hypothalamus make up most of the

e   **T**   diencephalon. The mesencephalon is the midbrain.

a   **T**— The olfactory bulb and tract, and the optic nerve, are forebrain derivatives.

b   **T**— Just posterior to the mamillary bodies.

c   **F**— The nuclei lie ventrally in the lower midbrain, but the nerves emerge dorsally below the inferior colliculi.

d   **F**— The abducent nerve arises near the midline and medial to the other two nerves.

e   **F**— This is site of exit of the hypoglossal nerve; the vagus and cranial nerves emerge between the olive and the inferior cerebellar peduncle.

a   **F**— The neural crest tissue is derived from the junctional zone between neural plate ectoderm and embryonic ectoderm.

b   **F**— This is a derivative of neural plate ectoderm.

c   **T**— Also to the spinal and cranial nerve ganglia.

d   **F**— The medulla of the gland is derived from neural crest tissue.

e   **F**— The neural tube and its marginal layer are derivatives of neural plate ectoderm.

382   In the development of the spinal cord the:
a   ependymal layer lines the cavity in the spinal cord.   (   )
b   outer mantle layer contains mainly the nerve fibres.   (.   )

c   basal (ventral) lamina disappears.   (   )

d   autonomic neurons develop adjacent to the sulcus
limitans.   (   )

e   alar (dorsal) lamina give rise to neurons subserving
motor function.   (   )

383   In the development of the brain:
a   a ventral flexure is present at the junction with the
spinal cord.   (   )
b   the ventral flexure precedes the development of
the dorsal pontine flexure.   (   )
c   the cerebellum develops from the rostral edge of
the roof of the hindbrain vesicle.   (   )
d   a single constriction in the neural tube separates it
into the two primitive vesicles.   (   )
e   in the region of the midbrain the alar laminae come
to lie lateral to the basal laminae.   (   )

384   In the development of the forebrain:
a   the basal lamina expands on the ventral aspect of
the forebrain vesicle.   (   )
b   the hippocampus develops on the medial surface
of the hemisphere dorsal to the interventricular
foramen.   (   )
c   the piriform cortex develops on the medial surface
of the hemisphere, ventral to the interventricular
foramen.   (   )
d   commissural fibres from the piriform cortex pass
through the lamina terminalis.   (   )
e   the fornix commissure connects the two thalami.   (   )

a **T**— Although this cavity is poorly developed in the adult.
b **F**— The mantle layer is the intermediate layer containing the bodies of the neuroblasts. The outer (marginal) layer contains mainly fibres.
c **F**— The basal lamina gives rise to the neurons subserving motor function.
d **T**— The sulcus separates the ventral motor and the dorsal sensory areas. The visceral neurons adjacent to the sulcus form the lateral horn of grey matter which is prominent in the thoracic and sacral regions.
e **F**— They give rise to sensory neurons.

a **T**— This is the spinal flexure.

b **T**— As does the spinal flexure.

c **T**— At first growing into the vesicle but later becoming everted and undergoing external enlargement.
d **F**— Two constrictions occur and divide it into the three primitive vesicles of the forebrain, midbrain and hindbrain.
e **F**— This arrangement does occur in the region of the pontine flexure. Additional columns of neurons — special visceral (branchial) — are present in the brain stem, carrying taste fibres and supplying pharyngeal arch musculature.

a **F**— The basal lamina is absent. The forebrain develops from the alar lamina.
b **T**— With the enlargement of the hemisphere the hippocampus is carried backwards and then downwards and forwards on the convexity of the lateral ventricle.
c **T**— It has connections with the olfactory tracts.

d **T**— Forming the anterior commissure.

e **F**— It connects the hippocampal areas.

385   In the forebrain the:
a   falx cerebri lies within the median longitudinal
     fissure.   (   )
b   tentorium cerebelli lies in the transverse fissure.   (   )
c   corpus callosum overlies the diencephalon.   (   )

d   lobes are named after the bones that overlie them.   (   )
e   cortex has a constant pattern of sulci and gyri.   (   )

386   On the lateral surface of the cerebral hemisphere:
a   the lateral sulcus overlies the insula.   (   )

b   the central sulcus is continuous over the superior
     border on to the medial surface.   (   )

c   visual function is primarily represented on the
     lateral aspect of the occipital pole.   (   )

d   auditory sensation is represented in the inferior
     frontal gyrus.   (   )
e   speech is subserved by the inferior precentral
     gyrus of the dominant hemisphere.   (   )

387   In the cerebral isocortex:
a   layer I contains an extensive ramification of
     horizontal cells.   (   )
b   stellate neurons are mainly found in layers III
     and V.   (   )
c   the external granular layer contains numerous
     small pyramidal cells.   (   )
d   the very large pyramidal cells of the motor cortex
     are found in layer IV.   (   )
e   there is a very prominent tangently placed plexus
     in layer IV of the visual cortex.   (   )

a **T**— Partly separating the two hemispheres.

b **F**— The occipital lobe of the hemisphere rests on the tentorium
c **T** which is attached laterally to the transverse venous
sinuses. The transverse fissure lies between the corpus
callosum dorsally and the diencephalon and midbrain
ventrally.

d **T**— Namely the frontal, parietal, occipital and temporal lobes.

e **F**— It is possible usually to define the lateral, central and
calcarine sulci but many of the other surface features are
variable.

a **T**— The insula is submerged during the enlargement of the
hemisphere.

b **T**— Motor and somatosensory functions being represented on
the lateral surface are continued on to the medially placed
paracentral lobule.

c **F**— The cortex overlying the inferior margin and the posterior
half of the superior margin of the calcarine sulcus on the
medial surface of the hemisphere subserve this function.

d **F**— Auditory sensation is represented in the superior temporal
gyrus.

e **F**— The inferior frontal gyrus subserves this function.

a **T**— These cells are small and fusiform; they are prominent in
the newborn.

b **F**— These neurons are mainly in layers II and IV.

c **T**— The external and internal granular layers (II and IV) also
contain numerous stellate cells.

d **F**— These Betz cells are in layer V.

e **T**— The region is called the striate area.

388   Fibres of the corpus callosum:
  a   unite the olfactory areas of the two sides of the
       brain.   (   )
  b   pass in the internal capsule to the frontal lobe.   (   )

  c   unite adjacent and widely separated gyri in the
       same hemisphere.   (.)
  d   unite the two hippocampi.   (   )

  e   to the occipital lobe form a prominent posterior
       bundle.   (   )

389   The internal capsule:
  a   lies lateral to the caudate nucleus.   (   )

  b   carries somatosensory fibres in the posterior limb.   (   )

  c   carries fibres from the ventroanterior nucleus in
       the posterior limb.   (   )
  d   carries pyramidal tract fibres in the posterior limb.   (   )

  e   carries the visual radiation.   (   )

390   The caudate nucleus:
  a   lies on the convexity of the lateral ventricle.   (   )

  b   forms part of the corpus striatum.   (   )

  c   forms a superior relation of the anterior perforated
       substance.   (   )
  d   sends most of its efferent fibres in the stria
       terminalis.   (   )

  e   has a narrow tail.   (   )

a **F**— The olfactory (piriform) areas are linked across the midline by the anterior commissure.

b **F**— The fibres of the corpus callosum are commissural fibres. The internal capsule mostly carries projection fibres.

c **F**— This is the definition of association fibres.

d **F**— The hippocampi are joined by the fornix (hippocampal) commissure. The corpus callosum is a commissure joining other cortical areas than those in (a) and (d).

e **T**— The forceps major.

a **T**— The thalamus lies medial to the capsule and the lentiform nucleus is lateral.

b **T**— They pass from the ventroposterior nucleus of the thalamus to the somatosensory postcentral cortex.

c **F**— These and fibres from the medial nuclei pass to the frontal lobe in the anterior limb of the internal capsule.

d **T**— They pass from the precentral gyrus to the cranial nerve nuclei and spinal cells. They lie anterior to the sensory fibres in the capsule.

e **T**— Passing from the lateral geniculate body to the visual cortex.

a **F**— It lies within the concavity, the head bulging into the lateral wall and floor of the anterior horn of the ventricle.

b **T**— The name is derived from the grey matter that connects the caudate and lentiform nuclei across the anterior limb of the internal capsule.

c **T**— The expanded head lies over this area and receives blood vessels through it.

d **F**— The stria terminalis is the main efferent tract of the amygdala. It runs with the thalamostriate vein in the groove between the thalamus and the caudate nucleus. The caudate nucleus projects fibres to the globus pallidus.

e **T**— Lying in the roof of the inferior horn of the lateral ventricle.

391   The globus pallidus:
   a   forms the lateral part of the lentiform nucleus.   (   )

   b   sends efferent fibres to the ventroanterior nucleus
       of the thalamus.   (   )
   c   lies adjacent to the internal capsule.   (   )

   d   receives its main afferent fibres from the claustrum.   (   )

   e   is separated from the insula by the claustrum.   (   )

392   The hippocampus:
   a   is expanded in the roof of the inferior horn of the
       lateral ventricle.   (   )
   b   like the septal nuclei, is part of the limbic system.   (   )

   c   receives its main afferent fibres through the fornix.   (   )

   d   sends efferent fibres to the hypothalamus.   (   )

   e   is expanded inferiorly into the amygdaloid body.   (   )

393   The thalamus:
   a   is limited anteriorly by the interventricular foramen.   (   )

   b   overlies the midbrain anteriorly.   (   )

   c   lies in the floor of the body of the lateral ventricle.   (   )

   d   forms the medial relation of the anterior limb of
       the internal capsule.   (   )
   e   is related medially to the third ventricle.

a **F**— It lies medial to the putamen and they together form the lentiform nucleus.

b **T**— Also to the ventrolateral nucleus, hypothalamus, subthalamus, substantia nigra and reticular formation.

c **T**— The anterior and posterior limbs of the internal capsule are medial to the nucleus, the genu being related to the apex of the nucleus.

d **F**— Afferent fibres come from the caudate nucleus, putamen and substantia nigra. The claustrum is closely linked with the insular cortex.

e **F**— The claustrum is lateral to the putamen.

a **F**— It lies on the floor of the inferior horn.

b **T**— The system also includes the hypothalamus, fornix, cingulate and parahippocampal gyri. It is probably concerned with the emotional and visceral factors of behaviour.

c **F**— The fornix system is the main efferent pathway of the hippocampus.

d **T**— Through the fornix mainly and also to the reticular formation.

e **F**— The amygdaloid body is situated at the end of the tail of the caudate nucleus, over the tip of the inferior horn of the lateral ventricle.

a **T**— The narrower anterior end of the nucleus has a prominent anterior tubercle on its upper surface near the foramen.

b **F**— The expanded posterior (pulvinar) region of the thalamus overlies the brainstem. The hypothalamus underlies the thalamus anteriorly.

c **T**— The caudate nucleus forms the floor of the ventricle laterally and in front.

d **F**— It lies medial to the posterior limb.

e **T**— The thalami of the two sides are separated by the narrow cleft of the 3rd ventricle and joined by the interthalamic connection.

394 **In the thalamic nuclei the:**
  a anterior nucleus lies within the internal medullary lamina. ( )

  b ventroanterior nucleus receives the medial and spinal lemnisci. ( )

  c medial geniculate body sends efferent fibres to the superior temporal gyrus. ( )
  d anterior nucleus receives the mammillothalamic tract. ( )
  e dorsomedial nucleus has extensive reciprocal connections with the frontal cortex. ( )

395 **The hypothalamus:**
  a receives afferent fibres from the amygdaloid body through the fornix. ( )

  b sends efferent fibres to the anterior lobe of the pituitary in the supra-opticohypophyseal tract. ( )
  c sends efferent fibres to the cerebral cortex in the median forebrain bundle. ( )
  d is related posteroinferiorly to the posterior perforated substance. ( )

  e is linked to the pituitary stalk by the tuberoinfundibular tract. ( )

396 **The pituitary gland (hypophysis cerebri):**
  a overlies the posterior ethmoidal air cells. ( )

  b sends its venous drainage to the dural sinuses. ( )

  c is partly formed as an outgrowth of the primitive foregut. ( )

  d posterior lobe secretions affect urine production. ( )

  e is an anterior relation of the optic chiasma. ( )

a T— The lamina splits the anterior two-thirds of the thalamus, and anterosuperiorly encloses the anterior thalamic nucleus.

b F— These fibres pass with the trigeminal lemniscus to the ventroposterior nucleus. The ventroanterior nucleus receives fibres mainly from the globus pallidus.

c T— The nucleus relays the auditory impulses which travel in the lateral lemniscus.

d T— The efferent fibres pass to the cingulate gyrus.

e T— Its links with autonomic and endocrine function serve to integrate visceral and somatic activities.

a F— The fibres from the amygdaloid body pass in the stria terminalis. The fornix carries fibres from the hippocampus to the hypothalamus.

b F— The tract passes to the posterior lobe.

c F— The bundle and the dorsal longitudinal fasciculus pass from the hypothalamus to the midbrain reticular nuclei.

d F— This perforated substance is further back in the interpeduncular fossa and underlies the adjacent subthalamus and midbrain.

e T— From the tuberal and infundibular nuclei.

a F— The body of the sphenoid bone and its air sinus lie inferior to the gland.

b T— The cavernous and intercavernous sinuses form a close relation to the gland. A portal circulation also exists between the hypothalamus and the pituitary gland.

c F— The anterior and middle lobes are formed from a diverticulum of the stomadeum (Rathke's pouch). The diverticulum is of ectodermal origin, as is the posterior lobe which arises from the forebrain.

d T— Also blood pressure, and in the female, they contract the uterine muscle. The anterior lobe secretions affect most other endocrine glands.

e F— The stalk is a posterior relation to the optic chiasma.

397   In the epithalamus:
a   the habenular nuclei receive the stria medularis.   (   )

b   lesions of the habenular nuclei can influence
      metabolic regulation.   (   )
c   the posterior commissure unites the superior
      colliculi.   (   )
d   the pineal gland has reciprocal innervation with the
      hypothalamus.   (   )
e   the interpeduncular nuclei receive fibres from a
      globus pallidus.   (   )

398   The medial relations of the lateral ventricle include the:
a   head of the caudate nucleus.   (   )

b   fornix.   (   )

c   interventricular foramen.   (   )
d   amygdaloid body.   (   )
e   transverse fissure.   (   )

399   The third ventricle:
a   communicates with the 4th ventricle through
      the interventricular foramen.   (   )

b   is related superiorly to the transverse fissure.   (   )

c   is bounded anteriorly by the lamina terminalis.   (   )

d   is recessed into the mammillary body.   (   )

e   is related inferiorly to the posterior perforated
      substance.   (   )

a **T**— This narrow bundle passes over the thalamus from the septal nuclei.
b **T**— The nuclei also influence endocrine regulation.

c **T**— Also the posterior thalamic nuclei, the pretectal regions and the medial longitudinal bundles of the two sides.
d **T**— The pineal is a regulator of pituitary activity.

e **F**— These nuclei are part of the subthalamus.

a **F**— This forms the lateral and inferior relation of the anterior horn of the ventricle. The septum pellucidum lies medially.
b **T**— The fibres from the hippocampus lie in the floor of the inferior horn of the ventricle and form the fornix. The medial wall of the ventricle (mainly ependyma) is attached to the fornix and is invaginated as the choroidal fissure.
c **T**— Joining the lateral ventricle to the midline 3rd ventricle.
d **F**— This nucleus lies in front of the apex of the inferior horn.
e **T**— The choroid plexus is invaginated into the ventricle from the tela choroidea in the fissure.

a **F**— The 3rd and 4th ventricles are linked by the cerebral aqueduct. The interventricular foramina link the the 3rd and the lateral ventricles.
b **T**— The fissure lies between the corpus callosum above and the ependymal roof of the diencephalon below. The choroid plexus invaginates the 3rd ventricle from above and each lateral ventricle from the medial side.
c **T**— The anterior commissure is within it and it lies between the corpus callosum above and the optic chiasma below.
d **F**— It is recessed into the optic chiasma and infundibulum in the floor, and within the pineal stalk posterosuperiorly.
e **T**— This lies in the floor behind the mammillary bodies.

400 **In the midbrain the:**

a inferior brachium carries visual fibres from the inferior colliculus to the medial geniculate body. ( )

b trochlear nerves have a dorsal decussation around the superior colliculus. ( )

c cerebral peduncles are separated from the tegmentum by a pigmented layer. ( )

d superior cerebellar peduncles decussate in the lower tegmentum. ( )

e superior colliculus communicates with motor nuclei of the head and neck. ( )

401 **In the pons the:**

a abducent nerve emerges about the middle at the junction with the middle cerebellar peduncle. ( )

b the facial nerve emerges through the middle cerebellar peduncle in the upper pons. ( )

c basilar portion is continuous with the cerebral peduncles of the midbrain. ( )

d nucleus of the tractus solitarius lies lateral to the facial motor nucleus. ( )

e fibres from the dorsal and ventral cochlear nuclei lie in the lower pons and form the trapezoid body. ( )

402 **In the pons the:**

a vestibulospinal tract arises from the larger medial part of the vestibular nuclei. ( )

b trapezoid body sends its fibres into the medial lemniscus. ( )

c medial longitudinal fasciculus lies dorsally near the midline in the floor of the 4th ventricle. ( )

d medial lemniscus becomes more laterally and ventrally placed as it ascends. ( )

e vagus nerve emerges below the abducent. ( )

a **F**— The inferior brachium carries auditory fibres between these centres. Visual fibres pass in the less well defined ridge from the superior colliculus to the lateral geniculate body.

b **F**— The dorsal decussation lies below the inferior colliculi. The oculomotor nerves leave ventrally at the level of the superior colliculi.

c **T**— The substantia nigra. The region dorsal to the aqueduct is known as the tectum.

d **T**— Passing to the red nucleus and the thalamus. The red nucleus receives fibres from the globus pallidus and sends efferent fibres to the reticular formation of the brain stem, and to the thalamus.

e **T**— Through the medial longitudinal bundle.

a **F**— This is the site of exit of the trigeminal nerve. The abducent, facial and vestibulocochlear nerves (medial to

b **F** lateral) emerge at the lower border of the pons.

c **T**— The descending pyramidal fibres are split up by the transversely running fibres passing to the middle cerebellar peduncle.

d **T**— The facial motor fibres make a dorsal loop over the abducent nucleus before emerging. Joining the facial nerve are taste fibres (to the nucleus of the tractus solitarius) and the parasympathetic fibres from the upper part of the salivary nucleus.

e **T**— These fibres arise in the cochlear nuclei on the floor of the lateral recess of the 4th ventricle. Many pass up to the medial geniculate body in the lateral lemniscus.

a **F**— The tract arises from the larger lateral part of the nuclei and ends amongst the anterior horn cells of the same side mainly in the spinal cord.

b **F**— The fibres pass in the lateral lemniscus to the medial geniculate body and the inferior colliculus.

c **T**— The two bundles communicate through the posterior commissure. They receive fibres from the vestibular nuclei, and send fibres to the nuclei supplying the ocular muscles, and the motor nuclei of the cervical spinal cord.

d **T**— The spinal lemniscus lies on its lateral side, and the lateral lemniscus is lateral to the whole tract.

e **F**— The vagus nerve emerges in the medulla.

403 **The medulla has:**
a an anterior median fissure running uninterruptedly throughout its length.   (   )
b the hypoglossal nerve rootlets emerging between the pyramid and the olive.   (   )
c the inferior medullary velum as a dorsal relation.   (   )
d the dorsally placed gracile nucleus lying lateral to the cuneate nucleus.   (   )
e the spinal nucleus of the trigeminal nerve situated posterolaterally.   (   )

404 **In the medulla the:**
a olivary efferent fibres decussate as internal arcuate fibres.   (   )
b dorsal vagal nucleus lies medial to the hypoglossal nucleus.   (   )
c nucleus ambiguus lies deeply between the hypoglossal and dorsal vagal nuclei.   (   )
d anterior spinocerebellar tract ascends into the midbrain and enters the superior cerebellar peduncle of the same side.   (   )
e posterior spinocerebellar tract passes uncrossed in the inferior cerebellar peduncle.   (   )

405 **In the cerebellum the:**
a primary fissure divides the flocculonodular lobe from the middle lobe.   (   )
b Purkinje cells are situated in the middle of the three cortical layers.   (   )
c Purkinje fibres of the vermis project on to the dentate nucleus.   (   )
d Purkinje fibres of the paravermal zone project on to the nucleus interpositum.   (   )
e horizontal fissure divides the anterior and middle lobes.   (   )

a **F**— The fissure is crossed by the decussation of the pyramids in the lower part.
b **T**— The vagus and glossopharyngeal rootlets emerge dorsal to the olive, between it and the inferior cerebellar peduncle.
c **T**— The roof of the open medulla is completed above by the cerebellum and the superior medullary velum.
d **F**— The gracile nucleus relays impulses from the lower limb and is medial to the cuneate which is concerned with the upper limb. They form prominent elevations in the lower medulla, their fibres decussate as the internal arcuate fibres and form the medial lemniscus.
e **T**— It extends throughout the length of the medulla.

a **T**— They pass into the inferior cerebellar peduncle. Other internal arcuate fibres are the main somatosensory decussation forming the medial lemniscus.
b **F**— The hypoglossal nucleus lies near the midline in the floor of the 4th ventricle and the vagal nucleus is just lateral to it.
c **T**— Fibres from the nucleus ambiguus pass in the vagus and glossopharyngeal nerves and mainly supply muscles derived from the 4th and 6th pharyngeal arch mesenchyme.
d **T**— It passes mainly to the vermis and anterior lobe of the cerebellum.

e **T**

a **F**— The primary fissure divides the anterior and middle lobes. The posterolateral fissure separates the flocculonodular lobe.
b **T**— It has inner granular and outer molecular layers. Only about one-sixth of the markedly uniform convoluted surface is visible externally.
c **F**— The vermis projects to the fastigial nucleus. The large lateral part of the hemisphere projects to the dentate nucleus.
d **T**— This nucleus is made up of the globose and emboliform nuclei.
e **F**— The fissure divides the posterior lobe into approximately equal inferior and superior halves.

406 Cerebellar afferent fibres from the:

a cerebral cortex pass mainly to the flocculonodular lobe of the opposite side.   (   )

b vestibular nuclei pass mainly to the anterior lobe.   (   )

c olivary nuclei pass to all parts of the cerebellum.   (   )

d posterior spinocerebellar tract pass to the vermis and paravermal zone of the anterior and middle lobes.   (   )

e dorsal column of the upper spinal cord pass to the vermis and paravermal zone of the anterior and middle lobes.   (   )

407 Cerebellar efferent fibres:

a from the dentate nucleus pass to the ventrolateral nucleus of the thalamus of the opposite side.   (   )

b from the emboliform nucleus pass to the globus pallidus on the opposite side.   (   )

c from the fastigial nucleus pass to the vestibular nuclei.   (   )

d are responsible for initiating voluntary movement.   (   )

e within the middle cerebellar peduncle pass to the vestibular nuclei.   (   )

408 The 4th ventricle:

a is limited superiorly by the superior cerebellar peduncles.   (   )

b choroid plexus is formed by invagination of the superior medullary velum.   (   )

c is recessed laterally around the superior cerebellar peduncles.   (   )

d has the facial colliculus near the midline rostral to the striae medullares.   (   )

e is bounded inferiorly by the pyramids.   (   )

a **F**— They synapse in the pontine nuclei and cross to all parts of the cerebellum other than the flocculonodular lobe. The
b **F**   flocculonodular lobe receives fibres from the vestibular nuclei.
c **T**— Decussating as the upper group of internal arcuate fibres and passing through the inferior cerebellar peduncle.
d **T**— The fibres originate in the cells of the thoracic nucleus and pass uncrossed in the inferior cerebellar peduncle.

e **T**— They synapse in the accessory cuneate nucleus and pass uncrossed in the inferior cerebellar peduncle.

a **T**— The impulses are relayed to the cerebral cortex. Other impulses are relayed in the red nucleus and descend into the cord.
b **T**— Fibres from the dentate nucleus and nucleus interpositum pass through the superior cerebellar peduncle and decussate in the lower midbrain. They end in the red nucleus, ventrolateral thalamic nucleus and globus pallidus.
c **T**— Fibres pass through the superior and inferior cerebellar peduncles. Some also end in the reticular nuclei of the pons and the medulla.
d **F**— The cerebellum influences the pattern of a movement which has been initiated by the cerebrum. The effects of cerebellar disease are seen on the same side as the lesion.
e **F**— This peduncle carries predominantly pontocerebellar fibres.

a **T**— The superior medullary velum, passing between the peduncles, forms the upper roof of the ventricle.
b **F**— The invagination is of the inferior medullary velum.

c **F**— The lateral recess is around the inferior cerebellar peduncles. Each has an opening at its tip.
d **T**— The ventricle has the hypoglossal and vagal triangles and the vestibular areas overlying their respective nuclei, caudal to the striae.
e **F**— The inferior boundary is the gracile and cuneate tubercles.

409 **In the spinal cord the:**
  a grey matter of the thoracic segment is
    proportionately larger than the cervical. ( )

  b gelatinous substances overly the posterior horn
    of grey matter. ( )
  c filum terminale is formed at the lower border of
    the 4th lumbar vertebra. ( )

  d lateral horn gives rise to preganglionic autonomic
    nerve fibres. ( )
  e nucleus proprius makes up most of the dorsal horn. ( )

410 **The dorsal root ganglion contains the cell bodies of the:**
  a dorsal column of the spinal cord. ( )
  b anterior spinocerebellar tract. ( )

  c dorsolateral tract. ( )

  d lateral spinothalamic tract. ( )

  e reticulospinal tract. ( )

411 **The spinal afferent:**
  a touch fibres have their cell bodies (primary neurons)
    in the dorsal root ganglia. ( )
  b pressure fibres have their cell bodies in the dorsal
    root ganglion. ( )

  c temperature fibres comprise a thinly myelinated
    lateral division of the dorsal root. ( )
  d pain fibres pass to the ventroposterior nucleus of
    the thalamus. ( )

  e proprioceptive fibres are partly carried in the dorsal
    column. ( )

a **F**— The grey matter of the cervical and lumbar cord is increased. The enlargements correspond to the large nerve roots supplying the limbs.

b **T**— It is a region of small cells.

c **F**— The spinal cord ends at the upper border of the second lumbar vertebra in the adult. The dural sac ends at the level of the second piece of the sacrum and the vertebral canal ends at the sacral hiatus.

d **T**— It is found in the thoracic and sacral regions.

e **T**— It contains cell bodies of secondary neurons subserving touch, pain and temperature.

a **T**— The fibres ascend to the gracile and cuneate nuclei.

b **F**— The cell bodies of this tract lie in the posterior horn of the opposite side. The fibres pass to the cerebellum in the superior cerebellar peduncle.

c **T**— Some fibres in the dorsolateral tract arise in the dorsal root ganglion but most arise from neurons in the adjacent grey matter.

d **F**— The cell bodies of the tract lie in the posterior horn of the opposite side. The fibres cross in the anterior white commissure and pass to the thalamus in the spinal lemniscus.

e **F**— This contains extrapyramidal motor fibres.

a **T**— These fibres pass in the dorsal column and end in the gracile and cuneate nuclei. Fibres from these secondary

b **T** neurons cross the midline and form the medial lemniscus, passing to the ventroposterior nucleus of the thalamus. A third set of fibres pass to the postcentral gyrus.

c **T**— The medial division is heavily myelinated and conveys touch pain, vibration and proprioception.

d **T**— Many pain impulses are relayed in the posterior horn grey matter and then travel to the thalamus in the spinothalamic tracts of the opposite side of the cord. Impulses are relayed to the postcentral cortical gyrus. A further series of fibres have a diffuse representation through the reticular formation.

e **T**— These fibres mainly synapse in the accessory cuneate nucleus. Fibres from this nucleus pass uncrossed in the inferior cerebellar peduncle and take part in reflex control of movement. Some proprioceptive information reaches consciousness along with touch and pressure information.

412 **In the efferent pathways of the central nervous system the:**

a tectospinal pathways facilitate control of balance. ( )

b corticospinal tract contains approximately 100 000 fibres. ( )

c corticospinal fibres usually end directly on the anterior horn cells. ( )

d corticospinal fibres are predominantly crossed. ( )

e reticulospinal tract receives additional fibres from the cerebellum and red nucleus. ( )

413 **In the cranial nerve nuclei the:**

a general somatic efferent column innervates the muscles of the larynx. ( )

b special visceral efferent column innervates muscles derived from pharyngeal arch mesoderm. ( )

c parasympathetic fibres originate in the trigeminal nerve nucleus. ( )

d special visceral afferent column carries sensory fibres from the proximal pharynx. ( )

e general somatic afferent column carries sensory fibres in the facial nerve. ( )

414 **In the cranial dura mater the:**

a outer layer is infolded to form the falx cerebri. ( )

b tentorium cerebelli is formed from the endocranial layer. ( )

c free edge of the tentorium cerebelli passes forwards to the anterior clinoid process. ( )

d innervation is partly from the vagus nerve. ( )

e cranial nerves receive a sheath from the cerebral layer as they leave the skull. ( )

a F— They facilitate visual and auditory motor reflexes. Balance is controlled through the vestibulospinal pathways.

b F— There are approximately 1 million fibres, 60% arising from the precentral cortex.

c F— A few fibres end in this way, these being mostly to muscles performing precise movements, such as in the hand. The majority of fibres synapse through an interneuron.

d T— However, motor neurons of the upper face, tongue, pharynx and larynx receive ipsi and contralateral innervation through corticobulbar fibres.

e T— These fibres mainly innervate axial and proximal limb musculature, and are concerned with the control of muscle tone, posture and programmed limb movements, such as those used for locomotion.

a T— This column comprises the oculogyric and hypoglossal nerves.

b T— These fibres are carried in the trigeminal, facial, glossopharyngeal, vagus and accessory nerves.

c F— General visceral, afferent and efferent fibres are carried in the oculomotor, facial, glossopharyngeal and vagus nerves.

d F— This column carries taste fibres in the facial, glossopharyngeal and vagus nerves.

e F— These fibres, derived from face, scalp, nose, nasal sinuses, mouth and teeth, are carried in the trigeminal nerve.

a F— The outer (endocranial) layer is the periosteum of the bone

b F and does not leave it. It is continuous with the outer periosteum through the sutures. The dural folds are formed from the inner (cerebral) layer.

c T— The attached border passes along the apex of the petrous temporal bone to the posterior clinoid process.

d T— Also from the trigeminal, glossopharyngeal and upper three cervical nerves.

e T— That formed around the optic nerve reaches the back of the eyeball.

415   **The spinal dura mater:**
a   is continuous with the inner layer of the cranial
    dura mater.   (   )
b   has a double layer for most of its course.   (   )
c   extends downwards to the level of the 2nd
    sacral vertebra.   (   )

d   is pierced separately by the dorsal and ventral
    roots of the spinal nerves.   (   )
e   is partly stabilised within the vertebral canal by the
    dentate ligaments.   (   )

416   **The pia mater:**
a   extends into the posterior median sulcus of the
    spinal cord.   (   )

b   is invaginated into the cerebral ventricles.   (   )

c   has an opening over the inferior horn of each
    lateral ventricle.   (   )

d   extends forwards as a fold beneath the corpus
    callosum.   (   )

e   extends with the dural sac to the level of the
    2nd sacral vertebra.   (   )

417   **In the circulation of the cerebrospinal fluid:**
a   production is mainly by active secretion.   (   )

b   reabsorption is partly through spinal perineural
    lymph vessels and veins.   (   )

c   blockage within the ventricular system produces
    communicating hydrocephalus.   (   )

d   the arachnoid granulations pierce the inner layer
    of dura mater.   (   )
e   the ventricular system communicates with the
    subarachnoid space in the tela choroidea.   (   )

a **T**— The dura is separated from the bony-ligamentous vertebral canal by the fat-filled epidural space.

b **F**— There is a single layer throughout.

c **T**— The spinal cord ends opposite the second lumbar vertebra and the lower dural sheath contains the cauda equina and lumbar cistern. The filum terminale ends on the back of the coccyx.

d **T**— The dura ensheaths these and the spinal nerve as far as the intervertebral foramen.

e **F**— The ligaments are pial structures stabilising the spinal cord within the dural sac. The dural sheath is stabilised by the emerging nerves and the filum terminale.

a **F**— The pia mater extends into the anterior median fissure and the cerebral sulci. It also ensheaths the origins of the spinal and cranial nerves.

b **T**— The pia mater and the adjacent thin ependymal layer form the choroid plexus of each ventricle.

c **F**— A medial and two lateral apertures in the roof of the 4th ventricle allow cerebrospinal fluid to pass from the ventricular system into the subarachnoid space.

d **T**— This fold into the transverse fissure is known as the tela choroidea. Lateral and inferior extensions from it pass into the lateral and 3rd ventricles and form the choroid plexuses of these ventricles.

e **F**— The pia mater ends with the spinal cord, opposite the 2nd lumbar vertebra.

a **T**— The modified ependymal cells of the choroid plexus are involved in this process.

b **T**— But the main absorption is through the arachnoid granulations in the superior sagittal sinus and its lateral recesses.

c **F**— Blockage at this level causes dilatation of the ventricular system which is known as internal hydrocephalus. The communicating form is due to blockage of the arachnoid granulations.

d **T**— These then come into contact with the endothelium of the venous sinuses.

e **F**— The communications are in the roof of the 4th ventricle.

418   The internal carotid artery:
  a enters the cranium through the squamous
         temporal bone.   (   )
  b lies within the dural coverings of the cavernous
         sinus.   (   )
  c gives a branch to the choroid plexus of the 3rd
         ventricle.   (   )
  d pierces the diaphragma sella medial to the optic
         nerve.   (   )
  e has an ophthalmic branch entering the orbit through
         the superior orbital fissure.   (   )

419   The vertebral artery:
  a enters the cranial cavity through the posterior
         condylar canal.   (   )
  b unites with its fellow of the opposite side at the
         upper border of the pons to form the basilar artery. (   )
  c sends branches to the spinal cord from within the
         cranial cavity.   (   )
  d supplies the choroidal plexus of the 4th ventricle. (   )
  e supplies the cerebellar vermis through its superior
         cerebellar branch.   (   )

420   The basilar artery:
  a divides distally into two superior cerebellar arteries. (   )
  b gives branches to the lateral and 3rd ventricles. (   )
  c supplies both the motor and somatosensory cortical
         areas.   (   )
  d supplies the auditory area of cortex.   (   )
  e supplies branches to the inner ear.   (   )

a **F**— The carotid canal lies within the petrous temporal bone.

b **T**— In company with the abducent and other nerves, and covered by the venous endothelium.

c **F**— Its anterior choroidal branch supplies the inferior horn of the lateral ventricle.

d **F**— The artery lies lateral to the optic nerve.

e **F**— Its ophthalmic branch passes into the optic canal within the dural sheath of the optic nerve.

a **F**— The artery passes through the foramen magnum.

b **F**— The basilar artery is formed at the lower border of the pons.

c **T**— The anterior spinal artery comes directly from the vertebral artery and the posterior spinal artery from its posterior inferior cerebellar branch.

d **T**— The choroidal artery comes from the posterior inferior cerebellar artery.

e **F**— This is a branch of the basilar artery.

a **F**— Its terminal branches are the two posterior cerebral arteries.

b **T**— The posterior choroidal branch of the posterior cerebral artery enters the tela choroidea and supplies these ventricles.

c **F**— Most of the pre- and postcentral gyri and the superior temporal gyrus are supplied by the middle cerebral artery.

d **F**— The posterior cerebral artery supplies the occipital pole with its visual areas.

e **T**— The labyrinthine artery passes through the internal acoustic meatus.

421 **In the cerebral venous drainage the:**
  a   superior cerebral veins pass to the inferior sagittal sinus.   (   )

  b   anterior cerebral vein joins the deep middle cerebral vein.   (   )
  c   choroidal veins from the lateral and 3rd ventricles pass into the cavernous sinuses.   (   )
  d   great cerebral vein is formed from the internal cerebral vein of each side.   (   )
  e   great cerebral vein opens into the cavernous sinus.   (   )

422 **In the cranial venous sinuses the:**
  a   superior sagittal sinus passes backwards to the internal occipital protuberance.   (   )
  b   inferior sagittal sinus passes backwards to the free edge of the tentorium cerebelli.   (   )
  c   sigmoid sinus grooves the inner surface of the mastoid process.   (   )
  d   inferior petrosal sinus grooves the parieto-occipital suture.   (   )
  e   straight sinus runs posteriorly within the tentorium cerebelli.   (   )

423 **The cavernous sinus is related:**
  a   superiorly to the pituitary gland.   (   )
  b   laterally to the thalamus.   (   )

  c   posteriorly to the facial nerve.   (   )

  d   anteriorly to the superior orbital fissure.   (   )

  e   inferiorly to the ethmoidal air sinus.   (   )

a **F**— The veins pass to the superior sagittal sinus. They can be easily damaged by anteroposterior deceleration injuries of the head.

b **T**— They form the basal vein which passes over the midbrain to join the great cerebral vein.

c **F**— They join the internal cerebral vein which also receives the thalamostriate vein.

d **T**— It lies in the tela choroidea in the transverse fissure.

e **F**— It opens into the straight sinus.

a **T**— It usually joins the right transverse sinus.

b **T**— Where it joins the straight sinus.

c **T**— This relation is important in the spread of infection and in surgery of this region.

d **F**— It grooves the temporo-occipital suture and unites the cavernous sinus to the internal jugular vein.

e **T**— It usually joins the left transverse sinus.

a **F**— It is a lateral relation of the gland.

b **F**— Its lateral relation is the medial surface of the temporal lobe.

c **F**— The facial nerve lies in the posterior cranial fossa. The abducent nerve enters the sinus posteriorly.

d **T**— The ophthalmic veins and the oculomotor and trochlear nerves, and branches of the ophthalmic division of the trigeminal nerve are closely related to the sinus in this region.

e **F**— It lies on the body of the sphenoid bone.